Bob Kauser
May 2005

Reflections over the Long Haul

REFLECTIONS OVER THE LONG HAUL

A Memoir

Robert McAfee Brown

WESTMINSTER
JOHN KNOX PRESS
LOUISVILLE • KENTUCKY

Book design by Sharon Adams
Cover design by Night & Day Design
Cover photograph: © *Peter Brown*

First edition
Published by Westminster John Knox Press
Louisville, Kentucky

This book is printed on acid-free paper that meets the American National Standards Institute Z39.48 standard. ∞

PRINTED IN THE UNITED STATES OF AMERICA

05 06 07 08 09 10 11 12 13 14 — 10 9 8 7 6 5 4 3 2 1

Library of Congress Cataloging-in-Publication Data

Brown, Robert McAfee.
    Reflections over the long haul : a memoir / Robert McAfee Brown.—1st ed.
        p. cm.
    ISBN 0-664-22404-0 (alk. paper)
    1. Brown, Robert McAfee. 2. Theologians—United States—Biography.
3. Theology, Doctrinal. I. Title.

    BX9225.B7617A3 2005
    230'.51'092—dc22
    [B]   2004061168

For Sydney
Who made it all possible
My love and my *compañera*

I believe we are here to share bread with one another,
so that everyone has enough, no one has too much,
and our social order achieves this goal with maximal freedom
and minimal coercion.

Contents

Foreword

William Sloane Coffin

I have long believed in short weddings and long funerals. Properly to celebrate a life and to mourn its passing takes time. Bob Brown's first service lasted three hours, and after the closing benediction, no one wanted to leave.

Many among the mourners had read most of Bob's books, all told some thirty. He was a first-rate theologian but happily spared his readers the juiceless jargon too common in the theological trade. A faithful Bible reader, Bob knew profound things could be said in simple words. Also, his preferred audience was less professional colleagues than highly intelligent lay people. He certainly knew church doctrine and dogma but felt old positions needed to be rethought as well as reiterated. And never was he dogmatic, writing once that "the dogmatism of the undogmatic is the real sin against the truth." Bob also would be the first to admit that love of God and neighbor is an impulse equally at the heart of Islam and Judaism as well as Christianity.

A university and seminary teacher all his life, Bob was never dull, always provocative, a great synthesizer of scholarship and faith. At the funeral service, many of his former students testified to his influence on their lives.

Bob was also a refreshing oddity in academic life. Too many university and seminary professors believe analysis to be a suitable substitute for action—but not Bob, as his memoir will reveal. He believed action leads to more new ways of thinking than does thought to new ways of acting. He led by example and fortunately so, as I think university students these days need not only more information but also more commitment. "Which is worse?" rabbi Leo Baeck once asked, "the intolerance that commits outrages or the indifference that observes outrages with an undisturbed conscience?"

It is almost inevitable that people deeply engaged on many public fronts shortchange their families. To his great credit, Bob remained a caring, loving father, and in no small part because he cared so for Sydney, a devoted wife and mother and a much-admired activist in her own right. At Bob's funeral, her words and those of their children were the most touching.

Bob Brown was a remarkably humble man. He recognized that being a Christian was not so much an achieved position as a desired one. All of us at the funeral spoke both of the pleasure of being in his company and how, in his company, we tended to be our better selves. He was so quick, funny, so generous in spirit, such a believer in the good and creative potential in all human beings that I am tempted to paraphrase Ben Jonson: Not only will we not see the likes of him again, we will not even see one who puts us in mind of him.

God bless you, Bob, as you blessed us.

William Sloane Coffin

Prologue

Sydney Thomson Brown

Bob was a teacher, writer, thinker, theologian, activist for justice, husband, father, grandfather, brother, musician, storyteller, builder, comic. He was my love, my life's companion, my best friend.

He was not one to be contained. He pushed the edges. Grounded in the traditional, the traditional never contained him.

He wanted the earth to be fair and good for all. He used his many gifts to make it so. He often quoted Jon Sobrino, Salvadoran Jesuit liberation theologian, who said, "The world is not as it should be—especially for the children." Bob worked for love and justice on God's earth.

Bob was a teacher. He taught at Amherst College, Macalester College, Union Theological Seminary, Stanford University, and the Pacific School of Religion. He was committed to relate his faith to the world around, to push the boundaries of churches, seminaries, presbyteries, denominations, faiths, and nations.

He was a scholar, theologian, and writer. His passion was to make the profound accessible to the average layperson. In his writing he was translator of the incomprehensible, making it understandable—mostly English to English.

He was fed by music, his children, his students, his colleagues, friends, family—all of you who were his community. Life was an adventure.

He wanted his faith to be effective, to make the world a better place. He acted for this through his teaching, preaching, and writing—and with others, turning his ideas into action. He liked our call to "serve God with heart, mind, soul, and strength," not just one of them.

He pushed the edges, even while somehow seeming to be respectable—perhaps, I believe, because there was a shy streak in him, perhaps because he was not by nature an activist. He became an activist because his faith called him to act—his faith, his friends, his students, all of God's people.

He took risks. He was a man of courage.

He was grounded in, but not constrained by, traditional theology. He started out a respected systematic theologian; life's experience and reality shaped him into a liberation theologian—strongly influenced by and open to feminist theology, black theology, Asian theology, and contextual theology.

He decided early on not to write for the academy and libraries, but for the average intelligent layperson. He practiced on me.

When he felt institutional walls and expectations hemming him in, he moved on. After teaching happily at Union Seminary for fourteen years, he felt squeezed by traditional academic expectations. He did not want to become the world's leading expert on some small segment of Karl Barth's theology. Rather, he wanted to try out his faith and teaching in the secular world. Leaving a tenured position, he moved to undergraduate teaching at Stanford, where he taught for another fourteen wonderful years. Once again, he pushed the edges.

On returning to Palo Alto in 1982, he found new church regulations required presbyteries to reexamine the faith of returning pastors. Bob was reexamined by San Jose Presbytery. This time, in honor of his students, who were often given a hard time by conservative pastors, he decided he would state what he really believed. It was a great statement. You should look at it sometime in the first chapter of his book *Saying Yes and Saying No*.

Throughout his teaching years he acted for justice. He worked for Gene McCarthy against Joe McCarthy. Working for civil rights, he joined New York City pastors and rabbis on a Freedom Ride, ending up jailed in Tallahassee, Florida. He was cofounder of Clergy and Laity against the War in Vietnam, and he worked and schemed with many against the war. In the late 1950s, he ventured into dialogue with Catholic priests. His colleagues thought him out of his mind. Out of this he ended up as a Protestant observer at Vatican II. From teaching Elie Wiesel's novels in his religion and literature class at Stanford, he became fast friends with Wiesel, and out of that he was appointed to the U.S. Holocaust Commission. Alison, our daughter, was a high school exchange student in Chile in 1974, just after the coup d'etat; from this Bob's interest in liberation theology intensified, and he developed a deep friendship with Gustavo Gutierrez. From then on he was passionately involved in work for justice in Central America, particularly Nicaragua and El Salvador. He was a risk taker and a man of courage.

Bob was my love, my *compañero*, my friend.

Considering all this, you may wonder why I had great difficulty making the decision to marry Bob. In those days, the sequence of courtship was different from today. We met, fell in love, got married, and then lived together. Not like today's meeting, falling in love, living together, and then getting married. My searching question was: "How can one be sure that true love will endure?" After much soul searching, and on the basis, I believe, of faith, hope, love, hunch, and insufficient evidence, Bob and I were married, I at twenty-one and he at twenty-three.

We married, not knowing whether we were spenders or savers, clock watchers or laid back about time, morning people or night people, breakfast talkers or silent until noon, Republicans or Democrats (actually, we were both socialists).

We married with little evidence, mostly on the basis of hunch. My hunch told me that he would be a special friend, a good companion, a challenge to my mind, a delight to my heart, a soul mate.

My hunch and knowledge told me that we shared a common vision, were guided by the same star; that he would love our children, that he would respect me.

What I did not know was that he was a fine writer and thinker, an extraordinary teacher, a gifted musician, a man of more courage than I could imagine, a law breaker on the big things, a stickler for the law on small things, that he was a crazy, zany comic, that he would be my *compañero*, my companion on life's way.

—That he would be a wonderful father to our children, would diaper babies, read to each of our four children, book after book, night after night, would build them forts and playhouses, teach them to play baseball.

—That he would be for all of us master carpenter, builder of our Heath home, summer after summer mower of fields of hay and hardhack, weeder of blueberry fields without end, that he would wash dishes, be a better cleaner upper of the kitchen than I would ever hope to be—in spite of resolutely avoiding cooking throughout our entire marriage, except for a brief time when I was in graduate school.

—That he would be adventurer, accompanier to parts of the earth I'd never even contemplated seeing, from Central and South America to Australia and South Africa.

—That at seventy-eight he would write a magical and beautiful Hebridean-based novel, a tale of love crossing time, poignant and compelling.

I did not know that in these later years, when various faculties had been zapped—hearing, vision, back, and even memory blipped from time to time—he would carry on with such grace, hope, humor, patience, and cheer; or that he would, in his late seventies, do an inward search with an extraordinary therapist and friend.

So even though we got married on the basis of insufficient evidence, we were enormously happy. Luck, hunch, family, and friends all held us together.

Bob was my love, my best friend, my lifelong companion. Together we've been parents of four very special offspring; we've been schemers, dreamers, planners, connivers, coconspirators, strategists, *compañeros*.

Now he's gone on, leaving us larger hearted, more caring, more committed as people of faith to use our hearts, minds, souls, and strength to make this world a better place for God's children. Bob wanted us to figure out why there is suffering, hunger, rage, and despair, to dig for the root causes of misery, and then work for change. I believe today he would say: Work for justice, not revenge.

Today he would say: Pay attention. View the world with imagination, compassion, energy. See that the world is not as it was meant to be. Learn to connect your theology and your Bible to God's people and creation all around you. Be followers of Jesus—work for radical revolutions for a just and caring world. And in all this, may you be equipped with courage.

This is an unconventional autobiography of an unconventional man. In it, Bob, my husband, looks back, to reflect on "the long haul." He shares his tale of personal growth, development, and change. Though he begins his reflection on himself, solo, his story literally expands to become a story of communities of people, working together to bring about radical change for love and justice.

Bob was no solo actor, no celibate or lonely prophet. He was a husband, father, colleague, a member of a variety of communities. His actions were involved with and impacted others. With that in mind, he chose to ask us, his family, to comment on the stories as we too experienced them—me, our three sons, our daughter, and our grandchildren.

So be aware that from time to time you will find explanations or stories from another perspective—on the Freedom Rides as experienced by me, his kindergarten daughter, his school-age sons; the Vietnam War protests as seen by his high school junior and his draft-age sons, and a visit from the police deflected by our fourteen-year-old daughter. There are some thoughts on our marriage, plus a poem and a few remembrances from his grandchildren.

Bob's writing method had always been: Step 1—pour it out, get it down on paper; and then Step 2—edit, edit, edit. He loved editing almost as much as writing. Failing vision and Lewy Body Disease stood in the way of Step 2. He needed help.

About four years before he died, Bob noticed that he was having memory problems. His doctor referred him to a therapist about his concerns. After a battery of tests, he was diagnosed with Lewy Body Disease, a disease in which, in a very random way, different parts of the brain become disabled. Bob knew that he had an illness of progressive brain debility, that it might be held in check but not cured. We wanted most for him to continue in hope, and he did. Certain areas of his brain were not functioning well; others were excellent. If in the course of daily life he became confused, we simplified our activities. For the most part, we continued on as usual.

Our wonderful church community was there for him—loving him with open hearts, accepting him as Bob Brown, their cherished friend and member. When participating in discussions, he would warn people that he might lose his train of thought in midstream, and if so, would they help him out? He did, and they did. In their loving support and openness to him, they were a constant blessing.

Two God-sent, special friends stepped in to help him: Diana Gibson, highly valued colleague and our former pastor, and Pia Moriarty, onetime Stanford student of his, Roman Catholic, now a community educator and artist. Through the last three years of his life, he met weekly with each to edit the manuscript. Together the three of them whittled its six hundred typewritten and handwritten pages down to a manageable form, and entered it into a computer. Diana and Pia's biblical, theological, and activist roots, combined with their knowledge and love of Bob, equipped them for this formidable task. Without them, and without the remarkable skills of his trusted and able editor at Westminster John Knox Press, Stephanie Egnotovich, this manuscript would never have seen the light of day. The family is forever indebted to all three.

Of this experience, Pia Moriarty said, "He loved so many of the people in this book, and he wanted it to be the story of the grace that they had brought into his life. This was his reciprocal theology. Over and over again, he allowed God to move in and teach him, working through the people that hierarchies of the powerful would so mistakenly dismiss—his family, his students, his friends and colleagues from outside the Presbyterian faith tradition, outside academia, outside white, middle-class life in the United States. He let people take him to new places that were their homes, and he found them holy.

"To hear Bob tell the tale, it was all about faithfulness and a commitment to act on Christian ethics, no matter how risky those choices might appear. From my perspective, it was pastoral accompaniment all the way. Accompaniment means living with the people, going with them shoulder to shoulder. According to Christian thinking, the primal accompaniment is God's great act of incarnation. Bob worked and lived this out in his own life, and as he struggled in the end, let us walk in accompaniment with him. He went into the joyful and suffering situations of people's lives, stood by them, offered as practical a compassion as he could, and found words to honor the God that he found there. This accompaniment is a two-way street, so I give back to him the words he wrote in a handwritten letter to Eileen Purcell, his friend and former student, after he participated in a delegation she organized to accompany Salvadorans returning home from refugee camps in Honduras: 'I cannot thank you enough for including me in this venture and for your being such a wonderful, stabilizing, grace-filled presence for all of us.'"

Several days before Bob died, when it was apparent to everyone, and I think to Bob as well, that he would only have a short time left to live, Peter, our eldest son, asked him a few probing questions on life and death, really wanting to know if Bob was ready to die. He asked him, "Papa, what sounds good to you?" For a moment, Bob lay silent in his hospital bed. Then came forth his clear response: "Publish that book!"

And, finally, a word on our family.

Bob's children and grandchildren were his joy and delight. In his manuscript, Bob wrote about each of them, but in an unfinished way, so the pieces are not included here. Throughout our years together, however, Bob set aside time and space for them—each and all—our sons and our daughter, their spouses, and our six grandchildren.

We did not take this for granted: neglect of family has often been developed into a fine art in the lives of many American scholars, activists, and clergy. Not so with Bob, and though he was not perfect, he was always there.

Bob relished reading to our kids. To our older sons, Peter and Mark, he read C. S. Lewis's Narnia books—night after night; to Alison and Tom, the Tolkien trilogy. In a small booklet written this year, Mackenzie, our granddaughter, age 11, wrote, "When I was young and in the summer house, Bop would read Mary Poppins to Caitlin and me. I'd always sit on one knee, Caitlin on the other. When he read it was great; he would never say no to reading a book to anyone."

Bob had a special connection to and joy in each of our four children, who are referred to and heard from in this manuscript. Our three sons are artists and our daughter is a therapist.

Peter is a photographer, writer, and teacher; photographer of the landscape of the High Plains of our west, from Texas on up to Canada. He captures the beauty of the vast sky and the tenacity of the people as they struggle for life and livelihood in the open space, in those small towns, on that wide stretch of earth. He lives and teaches in Houston with his wife, Jill, and daughter, Caitlin. Jill, a Texan, works as a child therapist, doing intervention work with preschool children at Texas Children's Hospital. She brings newfound peace to the children and hope and understanding to their parents.

Mark is a graphic designer, digital photographer, and print maker, who on the side, when Silicon Valley employment goes into a slump, does beautiful home remodeling. He lives with his wife, Karen, and their son, Jordan, in Mountain View, California. Karen does counseling and workshops with parents of young children. We hear she is a lifesaver for parents of so-called spirited children (that is, high-energy, hard-to-contain kids). She gives wisdom, hope, and joy to harried parents.

Alison, a family therapist, is married to Paul Ehara, a third-generation Japanese American. Their home in Richmond, California, includes their sons, Colin and Aki, college aged and post-college aged. Alison works with young people, parents, and families, especially multiracial families, and teaches peer counseling to teenagers at the local high school. Paul, deeply committed to public education, is communications director of the West Contra Costa Unified School District, no easy job!

Tom and Deb moved east to Hadley, Massachusetts, with their two children, Mackenzie and Riley. Both Tom and Deb are artists and teachers. Tom's major field is metal art, but he also works in glass, ceramics, and wood, teaching at the Charlemont Academy (close to Heath, our summer home). Before her marriage, Deb was a well-known quilter (and still has quite a reputation today); she is a teacher in the elementary school system at Amherst.

All together, they make up a wonderful gathering of artists, teachers, and therapists. Paul Tillich once said to Bob (as Bob struggled over an invitation to return to New York from Macalester College): "Some day you will find that you neglect the things you *should* do for the thing you truly *love* to do. *This* that you love to do is your eros. In life's choices, you must follow your eros."

Bob went to Union. Our sons went into the arts. Our daughter is a therapist.

And he loved our grandchildren as well—their uniqueness and their diversity.

Alison and Paul's sons, Colin and Aki, adored Bob and spent many blissful years with him playing baseball, exploring the Baseball Hall of Fame, and doing wood-working projects—creating everything from swords and shields to a raft. Talented musicians, they shared Bob's love of music and his passionate commitment to activism for justice.

Mark and Karen's son, Jordan, possesses wide skills in musical instruments, a small-boy keen interest in how things work, a Jewish/Christian heritage, and present wizardry with computers.

Peter and Jill's Caitlin is an Outward Bounder, feminist, environmentalist, young cello player, singer of songs in Gaelic, avid reader, remarkable student, rock climber, and adventurer.

Tom and Deb's Mackenzie miraculously survived a rocky beginning and is now a prolific eleven-year-old writer, dancer, percussionist; and Riley is a bright rough-and-tumble kid with whom Bob had a magical connection that seems to go on over time and space.

We did not take Bob's time with us for granted, nor did he take us for granted.

Blessings on him.

Introduction

At least 98 percent of my life—the part not recorded here—has been spent in such gloriously mundane activities as grading term papers, diapering children and grandchildren, mowing the fields, washing dishes, going to the movies, reading books, writing books, carving out times with wife and children, and trying to find my glasses. It has been fun. I am prepared to argue that the activities featuring home and family constitute the *real* story of our lives and deserve infinite respect on the part of readers. Sadly, however, if an author reports too often that he or she broke a salad plate while loading the dishwasher, reader interest begins to lag.

My response to this dilemma has been to keep things a bit messy: Report more of the 98 percent than may seem appropriate, and leave out a little more of the 2 percent, so I won't become too enamored of the public events in which I have participated. This also strikes a blow for honesty. I am convinced that no other literary genre carries so many temptations for cheating as autobiography. After all, who else knows but the author what was going through his mind when the sheriff put the handcuffs on? And if there is a choice to be made between faithful reporting and self-serving reporting, who is able to avoid the temptation to report the self-serving account as the faithful account? I am very much aware of this temptation and will try not to succumb to it. Surely, among all the unrecorded commandments from Mount Sinai there must have been one that fell through the cracks: "Thou shalt not cheat on the evidence."

The photographer Robert Adams has made this point well: "The price paid for believing one's life to be whole is a tendency to suppress inconsistencies."[1] What Adams describes is a particular temptation to theologians, who, believing that life and the universe provide a consistent whole, would like to portray their lives as illustrations of that consistency. It is a temptation to be disavowed, lest the theologian's self-accounting become self-serving to a degree inconsistent with the truth.

If (to employ a theologian's vocabulary) we are all, every last one of us, made in God's image, then every last one of us is possessed of infinite *worth*. Theologians, however, go on to affirm that we have spoiled that image, and this means that no one of us is to be accorded infinite *trust*. It is a healthy oscillation between those two truths that makes possible a tolerably honest self-appraisal.

I ask the reader to bring to these pages the same approach I have tried to bring, which is that the purpose of the autobiography is not so much to learn *about* the author as to learn *through* the author about oneself. I will feel amply rewarded if the reader pauses from time to time to reflect, "Ah! Now I understand better where I was in the sixties." Or, "That is *just* like what happened to me in graduate school. I hadn't thought of it that way." Or even, "He's crazy. That's not at all what happened, and I know because I was there."

Such a process can be enhanced by recognizing that this book is not simply an autobiography. It also is intended to be a modest exercise in social history, of a volatile three score years and ten, edging up inexorably toward four score years. I participated in a number of significant events during that time, and together we accompanied one another through some hard knocks, some surprises, some challenges, a number of defeats, and a few victories.

How do I approach the totality of events that seem to defy definition or very full understanding? I offer words I wrote some years ago after the death of a much older friend: "I believe we are here to share bread with one another, so that everyone has enough, no one has too much, and our social order achieves this goal with maximal freedom and minimal coercion."

Note

1. Robert Adams, *Why People Photograph* (New York: Aperture, 1994), 116.

If I Had a Magic Wand

If I had a magic wand,
I would make everybody nicer.
I would make the poor have some money,
Make the people who are sad, happy.
Make the people who are sick, healthy.
Make the wars stop,
So there is peace in the world.
Everyone would be friends
And no one would be afraid of people who are different . . .
If I had a magic wand.

—Mackenzie Brown, age eight,
in honor of her grandfather

1

A Child of the Manse

My grandfather, Robert Leach Brown, was both the town undertaker and the proprietor of the furniture store in Harrisville, Pennsylvania, population seven hundred. The romantic woodcuts we see of men of character sitting around a hot stove in a furniture store in the dead of winter, planning public policy, seem in his case to have been accurate.

His dual vocation was carried on by my father's brother Paul, who had six daughters and one son, also named Robert, who likewise took over the family business when Paul retired. My father's other brother, Arthur, also became a mortician, this time in Montclair, New Jersey, where he was very successful. Death finally persuades. My father and mother and my elder brother, George William Brown Jr., are all buried in Harrisville, and I officiated at both of my parents' burials. But the wheel does not quite come full circle, for I will be buried in a different tiny town, Heath, Massachusetts, with an even smaller population than Harrisville.

My own father, sandwiched between morticians, felt a "call" to ministry, and after attending nearby Washington and Jefferson College, went to McCormick Seminary in Chicago, shifting his ecclesiastical loyalty from the rigors of the "United Presbyterian Church" of his youth to the "Presbyterian Church" of his mature years, forsaking the stern type of Presbyterians who would have no traffic with organs in their churches and forbade singing in their services, save for the Psalms. Of his many seminary stories, my favorite was the experience of his first evening on campus. A student in the next room was carrying on in a loud monologue in an absolutely unrecognizable language. His curiosity piqued, my father went to the doorway, in which a serious-minded student soon appeared, holding a huge book. "Excuse me," he volunteered, "but I always have my personal devotions in the Hebrew tongue." Dazzled but dismayed by this display of theological one-upmanship, my father was momentarily tempted to take the next train home.

It was a wise decision to remain at McCormick, for in addition to being properly prepared for holy orders, he met, wooed, and won Ruth McAfee, the eldest of the three daughters of the renowned Professor Cleland Boyd McAfee. It seemed foreordained that Ruth would marry a minister. Her father was one, her grandfather had been one, and at least four of her uncles and other close relations were ordained, and she was now living on a seminary campus where the ratio of eligible men to women was staggering. But she was feisty enough not to accept the conclusion of the argument with docility. Although she finally did accept it because George William Brown had arrived on the scene.

The theological burden of being a McAfee was a heavy one—almost as heavy as being a Presbyterian. Cleland Boyd McAfee rose to the highest pinnacle, being elected moderator of the General Assembly of the Presbyterian Church in 1929. He maintained a genuine pastoral rapport with his students, and as moderator, he also had a keen sense of when to lower the boom on the fundamentalist controversy. His wife was a Canadian named Harriet Brown McAfee, which got confusing when later on I had a sister named Harriet McAfee Brown. Cleland's love of family saw him through three successive defeats of his wish to have a child who could be named "Cleland." He settled with grace into a family whose children were Ruth, Catherine, and Mildred.

I remember a plaque that hung in the entrance hall of our home:

> Christ is the head of this house,
> The unseen host at every meal,
> The silent listener to every conversation.

The Sunday school side of me had no trouble with this exhibition, especially the first line, that back then seemed appropriately religious without getting too specific. Nor did I have questions about "the unseen host at every meal," since the presence of my parents at mealtime ensured observance of those Presbyterian virtues—decency and order.

It was that "silent listener to every conversation" that worried me. Jesus was overhearing my plans with Budd Welsh and Mütt Fleming to attend a movie we had been forbidden to attend? Our proposal to drive our $8 Model A Ford (without license plates) on a nearby road when the parents were all away? Our hushed conversations sharing the most recent things we had learned about girls from our up-to-date-sex-education-conscious parents? Apparently there was going to be a time of accountability.

At that point, I had not yet heard the saying, "Being a Presbyterian doesn't keep me from sinning, but it sure keeps me from enjoying it."

At age five I contracted pneumonia, and the crisis point, which usually comes in three or four days, did not arrive until day twenty-one. Two years later I had mastoiditis with complications of a sort that kept the family on ten-terhooks until a full recovery was clear. At the conclusion of this double onslaught, my grandfather confided to my parents, "God must have some-thing very important for that boy to do." When word of this prediction reached me, I initially felt proud that I was so crucial to the Almighty's plans. But I also remember a clear feeling that went: "Wait a minute! That's a heavy deal to lay on a seven-year-old."

That I was a "child of the manse" meant that religion, prayers, church, and Sunday school attendance were built into my earliest years. I remember very little of my early Sunday school years. I remember church more clearly, and sermon time most clearly of all, for when my father mounted the pulpit I knew that my mother was already surreptitiously producing what we called "a little lunch." I would sit on the floor with my back to the pulpit, the pew seat my table, and eat it. Who could feel anything but good vibes in such a situation?

My father was a good pastor. I base that judgment partly on hearsay, since exactly on my eighth birthday in 1928 he left the parish ministry in Ben Avon, Pennsylvania, to become general secretary of the American Bible Society. Near the end of my second-grade year we moved to Summit, New Jersey. He returned to the parish ministry in December 1938, having found his "execu-tive" position spiritually debilitating, and accepted a call to the West Presby-terian Church in Binghamton, New York. After several years of recurring heart trouble, the result of the flu he had contracted as an army chaplain in France in World War I, he had to take early retirement.

During our years in Summit, my father commuted to New York, just like everybody else's father, taking the 8:04 on the Delaware, Lackawanna, and Western Railroad. This exempted me from the "PK" (preacher's kid) category, rendering me more "one of the guys." Something inside me, however, caused me to accept the role of defender of the faith, rather than resident skeptic. Consequently, I was predisposed to believe that the faith "made sense," even though that sense was still hidden from me. On the other side of the ledger, there is a well-entrenched family tale that the first time I heard the story of the Israelites crossing the Red Sea dry shod, I said to my surprised parents, "I don't believe a word of it."

Most of what I experienced religiously was an inner battle. I did not wear my faith on my sleeve. I felt no calling to be a boy evangelist, and frequently got my biblical stories confused. I remember discovering (as I thought) from the story of Moses and the burning bush that not only was the entire Sinai Peninsula "holy ground," which required an approach to it barefoot, but that this condition applied to church property everywhere. Since I was not about to take off my shoes in order to cross the grass in front of the parish house, I solved the problem by sticking to the sidewalk. I was one small image of Presbyterian rectitude in a morass of infidelity.

My father's theology was "liberal," deeply influenced by the social gospel of Walter Rauschenbusch. This meant that I never had to go through a pummeling encounter with fundamentalism, as did many other "preacher's kids" of my generation. My father also became a pacifist—the result of his experience as an army chaplain—a position increasingly hard to maintain as Hitler's intentions became more strident. During World War II none of this impeded his ability to be a pastor in relationship to parishioners whose sons and husbands began to be killed in combat.

Our church in Summit, Central Presbyterian Church, was presided over by a friendly minister named Rockwell S. Brank. He was, I gradually discovered, a "fundamentalist." I wasn't quite sure what that meant, except that it was clearly what my father was *not*. When the time came for me to join the church, my father received permission from Dr. Brank to oversee my preparation, rather than enrolling me in the "communicants class." I hand it to Dr. Brank for agreeing to a request that must have seemed a vote of no confidence. There was nothing particularly new in my father's instruction, and when I had my appointed meeting with Dr. Brank, it was an amiable time.

My parents' problems with the fundamentalist tilt of Central Presbyterian Church led them to worship occasionally at the local Baptist church. They were attracted not by any crisis persuading them that baptism was necessary for salvation, but by the sermons of the new young pastor, David Barnwell, a recent Union Seminary graduate, whose theology appealed to them and to me as well. Among the additional attractions for me at the Baptist church was a carefully chaperoned group of boarding students from the Kent Place School for Girls.

In terms of my overall religious development, Camp Townsend, a Presbyterian "summer conference," outdistanced all other contributors. It was at Camp Townsend that God and nature first became intertwined for me. Each year we had a picnic supper atop Mount Baldy, with a reading of the Sermon on the Mount. On a few occasions I even got up early to watch the sun rise over our lake, and felt a part of the daily remaking of creation out of darkness. I tried very hard to "feel" things like God's presence in the wind, the sunsets, the sunrises, the other people, and most of all, the music.

I am more enamored of nature at a distance than close at hand. I detest many living things—such as flies, bugs, moths, and other insects—but from as far back as I can remember I have been enthralled with hills, lakes, stars, waterfalls, and mountains.

One summer, as a college-age counselor at Camp Pinnacle, I supervised the building of what we called "the Cathedral of the Pines," with the motto: "Through Nature to Nature's God." Later on, with perhaps too much sophistication, I decided (with help from a Swiss theologian named Karl Barth) that the order of the motto was exactly backward, and that the truth went, "Through God to God's Nature." Behind this was a dogmatic stance that God reaches to us (in Scripture, sermon, and sacrament) and that when that is squared away we can then truly see the hand of God in creation. Such matters were hardly within the purview of nine-year-olds, however, and I didn't try to do a theological number on the kids.

But the night we dedicated the new Cathedral of the Pines, I placed a windup record player behind the new altar (constructed out of a pine slab), and as people arrived they heard the Budapest String Quartet playing the first movement of Beethoven's Quartet in C Sharp Minor, op. 131, which I consider to be his most ineffable creation. Granted, it was a pretty schmaltzy gesture, and nine-year-olds don't instinctively appreciate an intricate fugue, but there was still a wonderful payoff. When the service was over and we were back in our tents for the night, one of my "boys," Dick Baldwin, quizzed me: "Hey, what was that music you played at the beginning?" And before I could offer an answer, he continued, "It sounded like God talking."

I wonder what Karl Barth would have made of that.

Shortly before World War I, my parents' first son, George William Brown Jr., died at nine months from a rare form of cancer. This made my arrival a double blessing to them—a baby, yes, but also a son, to replace the son they had lost. I imagine that my younger sisters, Het and Bet, born fourteen months apart, may have felt a tension when they intuited that being older was better, and being an older boy was best of all. Especially during my numerous childhood illnesses when priorities appeared to be skewed toward me, they always had to play quietly and in all things defer to "what was best for Bob."

I am afraid I capitalized on this "favorite child" syndrome in ways that may have been difficult for my sisters. (I've found, ironically, in later years that each of us had perceived ourselves to be the "favorite" child.) I have good memories of these years, such as the three of us playing "King and Queen" every Sunday afternoon from five to six, with thrones affixed to the top of a nursery table, while our parents listened to Harry Emerson Fosdick on the radio downstairs. A quarter of a century later I had this same Dr. Fosdick as my professor of homiletics.

Hovering over, and immersed in all our family events, was our mother. Belying her gentle demeanor as an adult, she had a rebellious streak during her upbringing, about which we children always loved to hear—from an "atheist period" to a time when she refused to come home from dates by the approved hour. The early years of her marriage were tested by our father's time in the Army (during which she heard on one occasion that he had been killed in action) and the death of her firstborn son. But the bonds were secure, and our mother, taking seriously the homemaking pattern of the time, devoted herself happily to the multiple roles of wife, mother, homemaker, and mistress of the manse. She was good at all these roles, and I never felt that she was chafing at the lack of use of the other talents she possessed. My sisters may have had more trouble with the priorities she established for herself and that she tried enthusiastically to bequeath to them.

But her time came. When our father had to resign from the pastorate in Binghamton, they moved into retirement in Princeton, New Jersey, where he could do some writing and editing, much needed, since his lifetime of paying into a Presbyterian pension yielded for life the sum of fifty dollars monthly. And she, with only one year of college behind her, was given a staff position with the Board of Christian Education of the Presbyterian Church in Philadelphia. Dad lingered on in Princeton, ultimately confined to a hospital bed set up in the living room, and one morning in March 1947, when both Sydney and I were there, he quietly died. Mother moved back to Summit, where she got a staff position at the church in which we had all grown up, and worked there until her retirement. She became progressively incapacitated with painful arthritis, which she battled with characteristic courage until—in one of those mysteries of science—a few months before her death she contracted a cancer which rapidly took her body but had the beneficial result of absorbing the pain of the arthritis, and her last months were relatively pain-free and restful.

My father was not athletically inclined, especially when it came to baseball, but we played for many years, and when it came to the time that I could beat him consistently, we moved on to golf, where we remained pretty well matched, until his heart trouble precluded further activity.

But we did a lot of construction projects together—bookcases, tables, stools, and rabbit hutches galore. As the son of Harrisville's furniture store owner, he came by this talent naturally. It was a banner Christmas when I got my own toolbox. The one thing I didn't like about our joint woodworking projects was my father's unwritten but frequently spoken law that the job wasn't finished until the work area had been cleaned. I was always of the opinion that tomorrow would be a great time to restore tidiness. This inherited love of woodworking paid big dividends in the early years of our marriage, when we possessed only what we could make or buy secondhand and fix up.

My father wasn't very musical, and thus I give him extra points for taking up the mandolin so he could play with the rest of us. And after a while, he could, by God, pluck those strings well enough to create a melody other folks could recognize. He also knew that music was important, even if it wasn't at the top of his particular list of talents. For many years I would go to New York with him on Good Friday, and at noon we would go to the Fifth Avenue Presbyterian Church and listen to the choir sing John Stainer's *The Crucifixion*. As I got to know it year after year, I used to wait with most eagerness for the vocal quartet to sing "God So Loved the World," a rendition of John 3:16–17. Even though today it seems to me lachrymose and not at all fitting the context of the words, it still takes me back to that small boy sitting in a pew with his father, who was helping him get some exposure to music that would enrich his life ever after.

I had a normal suburban kid's exposure to the joys and agonies of musical performance, alternating between the piano and the violin. My mother gave me ongoing encouragement and could create a creditable piano accompaniment for any melody I had mastered on the violin. I took the violin to college, and after an unspectacular experience in the orchestra I put it on a closet shelf forever. I continue to play the piano, although I have never progressed beyond hymns and slow movements of assorted piano pieces. I have a reasonably good ear, which means negatively that I am sensitive to music played out of tune, and positively that I can play most hymns in a number of different keys without music. If I were asked, "When do you pray?" I would be likely to respond, "When I am playing the piano" (or later in my life, the cello).

Another great musical memory was our biweekly trip to the auditorium of Brayton School, where we heard "Damrosch Concerts." Walter Damrosch was a well-known orchestra conductor who created radio programs especially designed for children. He would explain what we were about to hear, which ran the gamut from "Afternoon of a Fawn" to "The Golliwog's Cake Walk," with Mendelssohn's "Music for A Midsummer Night's Dream" thrown in for good measure. I was enchanted. Each year a prize was given for the best student notebook on the concerts. I won a book called *Violin Mastery*, and it gave me new reason to practice.

I also became intrigued with pipe organs. When our Sunday school class produced a "book" about the church, I wrote a loving description of the organ. One summer at Chautauqua, New York, my parents prevailed upon the summer organist to let me sit on the bench beside him when he practiced. Between that and baseball at the Chautauqua Boy's Club, I had a month of alternate wonders.

Over time, I became a snob about things musical, wallowing in George Frideric Handel, to whom I was especially attracted, and giving an impression of disdain for much of the jazz that was the passion of my peers.

My father also taught me something about beginning a task. It went, "Be prepared," which became for me a cardinal rule in public speaking. When my father was called upon, he always was ready, and this, by some kind of ideological osmosis, seemed to me a worthy goal. I will not make claims about the content of many speeches and sermons I have delivered over the past half century, but at least, save in dire circumstances, they were finished products, crafted as well as possible in the time available. When I lacked a full draft and had to rely on notes, I would excuse myself by remarking that I was always more spontaneous with a script. And it was true.

What I sought most was clarity, followed by charity and a determination to stay within the time structures imposed on the occasion. This use of time was important during the civil rights and Vietnam years, and the shadow of my father stood with me when I prepared texts even for open-mike rallies at Stanford.

On May 28, 1929, I turned nine years old. In October of that same year the bottom fell out of the stock market. For a little while nothing much changed. Summit, New Jersey, continued its normal routine. But before long, fathers of my friends were unaccountably at home doing tasks around the house and raking leaves instead of commuting to work, and trying to appear unconcerned. The "downswing," they assured each other, was only temporary. But it turned out to be close to permanent for a lot of them. Presumably the world was still going to need Bibles, but I could not stifle late-night concerns about possible job loss within my own family, and pretty soon I gathered from veiled comments between my parents that the American Bible Society was instituting an across-the-board pay cut of 10 percent, whatever that meant.

The next spring my father had eye trouble serious enough to need extensive care at the Mayo Brothers Clinic in Rochester, Minnesota. When he returned, his regimen included staying at home from work for a significant period of time. One afternoon after school, when we were playing baseball in Jack Proper's backyard, my father came to watch. After a few innings he left, and one of my friends asked, "Is *your* father out of work too?" I hastily denied it, my haste telegraphing, to me at least, the likelihood that the hunch was correct. That brief exchange brought the Depression home to me more than almost anything else had done.

But it did not stand alone. To heighten our awareness of what the world was like outside of a prosperous New Jersey suburb, my father took the whole family on a car ride up the west side of Manhattan, and there, somewhere in the neighborhood of 79th Street and Riverside Drive, was "Hooverville," a tattered and random collection of shanties made of cardboard, corrugated tin, and randomly sized panels of wood, in which hundreds of refugees were living—not refugees from Europe or Central America, but refugees from homelessness and bitter destruction right here. I clearly remember an unarticulated response in my mind that went, "That's unfair!"—left unarticulated, I guess, because I had no response or "explanation" that would seem plausible, and I was frightened that any space between Summit and Hooverville might be about to disappear.

I doubt if I had ever heard the word "capitalism," and if I had, living in Summit, New Jersey, it would have been on the lips of its defenders. But it had still (so I would have reasoned) produced "Hooverville."

Much of my subsequent life has been spent working through that enigma.

Depression or not, alcohol was a no-no. To a surprising degree this was true of my friends' parents as well. It was the Prohibition era, and it was illegal to buy or sell liquor, and we knew nothing of gradations within the evils of consumption. One of the biggest marks against FDR was his campaign promise to legalize 3.2 beer and other beverages as well. In a quintessential expression of our zeitgeist, my sister Bet created a poem for the 1932 presidential campaign between Roosevelt and Hoover that went, "Boo, boo, three point two," although the theme applied not only to beer but to wine and hard liquor as well. The ethical consequences were clear: One drink and you were a drunkard. We had competitions in the Central Presbyterian boys group, Knights of the King, for all who could declaim with fervor such immortal bits of poetry as "I can't, I promised mother." I was a senior in college before I stepped over the line for the first time.

Our parents once entertained the dean of London's St. Paul's Cathedral and his wife before a church gathering in Summit. We sat in the living room sharing tomato juice and crackers, and then moved across to the dining room where each place setting included a single glass, filled with water. At some point during the meal, when British and American social customs were being compared, my father remarked with considerable pride, "Our family has been teetotalers for three generations," to which Mrs. Matthews immediately replied, "Oh, I'm so sorry for you."

In 1932 in the depths of the Depression, our parents took the unprecedented step of deciding to stop renting and build a house of our own. That this was even thinkable was due to a timely inheritance from the estate of Aunt Eva in Harrisville. The actual construction took place during a period when I had been taken out of school (to be recounted later), and I spent part of each day watching the miracle of creation grow from a hole in the ground to a finished dwelling.

It was a lovely house, somewhat Colonial in style, and it cost all of ten thousand dollars. In addition to our family discussions about size, wallpaper, and whether to have two bathrooms or one, I picked up a good deal of information—the difference between girders and joists, and what "sixteen inches on center" meant, and how to reduce plumbing costs by locating the bathroom over the kitchen.

REMEMBERED FRIENDS

"Heber and I are going to run away from home," I announced to my mother one morning about eleven o'clock. The announcement of our departure struck me as a magnificent attention-getter.

My mother didn't bat an eye. "Where are you going to go?" she asked in an interested and wholly unanxious voice. This was Heber's cue: "We're going to Linvor Town," he announced with joy. Identification of our goal was of interest to me as well, since I was sure Linvor Town existed only inside Heber's head and was situated somewhere *this* side of the Ben Avon-Bellevue trolley tracks. (The Bellevue Trolley tracks identified the absolute outer limits of the world in which we could play unattended.)

"Well, that should be fun," my mother responded. "Let me fix you a picnic lunch."

This was not quite the response we had anticipated. No importunate requests to stay at home, no fearful reminders of the dangers that lay just over the horizon, no counteroffers to beguile us into a change of plans. Nothing but empathy and support. As a result, the project lost steam rapidly, and the excursion ended by our going halfway up to the trolley tracks, claiming Linvor Town as our achieved destination, and returning to eat our sandwiches on the swing in the backyard.

The creator of this ambitious scheme was my inseparable companion in my Ben Avon days, Heber Harper. We were rather unlikely companions. I was overenergetic, half sentences continually pouring out of my mouth, always trying to be first; while Heber was slow of speech, given only to utterances fully thought out. It sounds like a situation loaded with manipulative possibilities, save for the fact that Heber had an iron will. Furthermore, he possessed a marvelous nursery-sized circus with animals whose hooves had grooves so that they could perch on a ladder or trapeze and balance there with death-defying derring-do. I knew there was a commandment starting "Thou shalt not covet," but I coveted that circus beyond all things a nursery could contain, and Heber knew it. It gave him singular power in our relationship.

Heber was a Methodist. In fact, he had been named for a Methodist bishop, Reginald Heber, who wrote the words to "Holy, Holy, Holy, Lord God Almighty." My father pretended to make a big deal of the ecclesiastical split between Heber and the rest of us, and the fact that Methodists seemed to need bishops while we Presbyterians got along just fine without them. Sometimes Heber would accompany us on family outings on the Horne Camp Road on which there was a bridge with a plaque that, my father told us, prohibited Methodists from driving across it. Heber would be asked to get out of the car and walk across, to be picked up on the other side. It sounds a little cruel, but we all knew it was a game, and Heber felt very important to be singled out in such a fashion, always making the trip on foot with head held high. After the second or third repetition of this ritual, I began to wish I were a Methodist too.

I didn't really grasp the finality of the move from Ben Avon to Summit until the night before we left, when I was allowed to sleep overnight at Heber's house. I cried in the dark after Heber was asleep, and when Mrs. Harper came in to see what the trouble was, I lied barefacedly and easily that I'd had a bad dream. Just how much the friendship meant was illustrated by Heber the next morning. When we Browns piled into our blue Dodge and headed for Summit, Heber produced the donkey from his circus—and gave him to me.

One of my best friends in Summit was Milton "Mütt" Fleming. His older sister, possessing information about the umlaut, convinced us that its use would confer a dignity on his nickname that would otherwise be lacking. It was in Mütt's backyard that we built The Hut, an implausible collection of discarded boards and two-by-fours, so unaesthetically designed that the neighbor next door to the Flemings built a ten-foot fence along the property line to eclipse our jerry-built contraption. There wasn't much to do with The Hut once it was completed, so we kept adding on both horizontally and vertically, and a second-story addition went above the ten-foot line, clearly presenting a challenge to the aforesaid neighbor. An unspoken truce made it unnecessary for either neighbor to work for skyscraper status.

My interest in building was heightened in sixth grade when my teacher, Miss Vreeland, dreamed up a brilliant math project. We would learn about fractions and long division and similar mathematical mysteries by building a model house out of one-by-fours, right in the classroom. We elected to hold a circus as a fund-raiser. I wasn't into circus animals (save rabbits), but I did promote the notion of having a magician, a role I volunteered to fulfill, having gotten a magic set the previous Christmas. I billed myself as "Peter the

Great," and worked up a ten-minute show, including making a handkerchief disappear from my bare hands.

To this day, I hold magicians in awe. The fine edge of mystery is part of theology as well, and the fact that things are not always what they seem to be (the magician's stock in trade) touches a theological chord. But such thoughts were not uppermost until later. The real news was that we took in fifty-five dollars at the gate. The classroom building project, however, never materialized. By the end of the year we were still working on the blueprints. It would have been better if we had aimed to build a tennis court.

Baseball fever was in the air every spring at least from 1928 to 1938. I desperately wanted to be part of the baseball world, although I brought no skill from my heritage. I remember after school when someone said, "Let's play three o'cat," and immediately shouted, "First up!" Jack Wood shouted, "Second up!" and Mütt Fleming yelled, "Third up!" Getting into the spirit of the occasion, I shouted "Fourth up!" only to be reminded that we were playing "*three* o'cat, stupid." Unwilling to retreat to the sidelines, I asked, "Where shall I play?" The answer was a unison chorus, "Out in the guts." This explicit direction lacked only two ingredients: (1) It didn't tell me *where* "the guts" were, and (2) it didn't even tell me *what* "the guts" were.

Such rituals did not cheer my soul, but I learned one piece of useful information: When we had teams, nobody wanted to be the catcher. You had to work very hard and were bound sooner or later to get hurt. This didn't matter to me. If that was the price of being on the team, I was more than willing to pay it. I even fantasized a time when I would be hurt in a collision at home plate, in which I tagged the runner out and saved the game for us, only to writhe in agony but hear my teammates say consolingly, "Nice play, Brownie."

As the snow began to melt and the ground to firm up, we waited impatiently for that magical day when balls and bats and mitts would come to school and be taken to the playground after dismissal. To a male teenager, there is nothing quite as pleasing as the smell of a well-oiled mitt, and we oiled ours constantly throughout the winter to keep them flexible enough for this call of the diamond. The phrase "inside baseball" we made our own, and what it referred to was strategy, signals, outsmarting the other guys and keeping them off guard. The crafting of a batting order, for example, is almost the product of prayer.

Not very often did we challenge the mores of big league strategy. We were, in fact, sticklers for total imitation, save that we never got into the tobacco-chewing thing. Those men were our gods, and I cannot imagine what we would have done if we had learned of the actual off-the-field activities of any of our deities. Their interests in the bottle or the horses, or their ways with women, were parts of life that were never reported to innocent upper-middle-class suburban youth. Babe Ruth was sometimes quoted as having muttered a few "gosh darn's," as the *New York Times* decorously reported, but never more. Their pictures were on our bedroom walls, their batting averages were recomputed daily at our desks when we were supposed to be doing our math homework. Each issue of *Baseball* magazine gave us new wisdom about the players and their exemplary habits: Rogers Hornsby didn't go to the movies for fear it would affect his vision on the ball field, and three times he had batted over .400.

On opening day of the season, or the first game of the World Series, I almost always managed to come down with a cold just bad enough to keep me home from school, confined to my bedroom, where I had a small radio. By regulating the volume, depending on which part of the house my mother was in, I could get a pretty good feel for how the season or the series was going to shape up.

The side of my growing up that I feel least comfortable about reporting is my deep-seated desire to excel, dominant into my high school years and beyond. I expressed this by trying very hard to be a good boy, craving adult adulation even more than that of my peers. I wanted not only academic approval from my teachers but personal approval as well. I achieved this to some degree by being reliable, being on time, and anticipating correctly what the teachers wanted.

Along with this I had a habit, especially when tired, of displaying all manner of tics—strange movements of the eyes or neck, and frequently sniffling, in ways that must have seemed very strange to people meeting me for the first time. I do not recall being taunted by my peers for these tics, and when I became aware of them I could usually control them for a period of time.

They were, needless to say, a worry to my parents and my teachers, and when I was in fifth grade a number of people decided that the tics were due to stress, especially my zealous compunction to excel. Since I was in good shape academically, it was proposed that I drop out of school for a few months, get well rested, and enjoy a competition-free interval before returning. I do not remember having trouble accepting this proposal, even though my classmates were sure to ask embarrassing questions about why I wasn't in school. In fact, I remember rather liking the whole idea of a time of not worrying about giving reports, reading assigned books, preparing speeches in pursuit of public office, appearing in dramatic productions, or practicing the violin.

As we approached the end of this open-ended interval at home, a new idea was proposed. Instead of returning to school in the fall as a sixth-grader, where all the competitive situations were located, how about reentering as a fifth-grader?

Again, in retrospect, I am amazed that this novel idea seemed so comfortable in the face of possible comments that I had "flunked fifth grade." I think the reason for my ease in accepting this new arrangement was relief that I could continue to forego the need to excel. Furthermore, I was fortunate that the fifth-grade teacher I would have in the fall would be Mrs. Husk, whom I adored. At the end of the school year, I wrote her a letter (really a love letter) thanking her for such a wonderful year. I had never done that before, nor have I been inclined to since.

I won't pretend that the tics miraculously disappeared—anybody who knows me well can attest that they still come and go—but some of my intensity disappeared. Whenever I feel tired, I know that there will be some new manifestations of them. There has been a further related change: I don't feel so pressured to excel. That doesn't mean I don't want to do the best I can, but it does mean that I'm not so worried about getting plaudits for doing well. I hope I have internalized a very important theme in Paul's letter to the Romans that "it is a small thing to me to be judged by people; the one who judges me is the Lord." This is a passage that liberates me from all kinds of moral clutter. When we get past human judgment and have only to worry about divine judgment, that is finally a liberation, however scary at first, since the divine judgment is not how many points we get for "being good," but the fact that it isn't about points at all but about forgiveness and new beginnings, with the slate wiped clean.

The fact that my political orientation has always been with the minority suggests that if I needed human approbation to survive, I'd long since have withered away. Bill Coffin has told me that I don't know how to accept a compliment. (Bill, having had a lot of practice, is very good at accepting compliments.) I have come to the conclusion that he's right. I would probably be worried about receiving too many plaudits, convinced that I must be doing something wrong. (The Calvinist side dies slowly.)

Every now and then I get a letter from a former student thanking me for something that happened in a course we shared. That, needless to say, is always a lovely moment. But it would be a psychic disaster to count on such moments as a way to measure my professional success or failure. Two people a few years older than I have caught this point nicely. "The Christian is one who can afford to fail," is Christopher Fry's way of putting it, while Will Herberg, a Jew, says that all we can do with our lives is to offer everything to God—the failures as well as the successes—and count on God to sort them out, realizing that even the bad can be used by God to show somebody else how *not* to do it.

AMHERST

During my senior year in high school, I got good news and bad news from the admissions office at Amherst College: I was accepted, but without scholarship aid. Without being privy to the details of the family finances, I realized that since my father had taken a significant salary cut in order to return to the pastorate, the door to Amherst was probably closed. In response to my request, however, Amherst upped the ante, promising a "college job" during freshman year and a year-end reevaluation of my scholarship possibilities. My birthday came late in May, and my parents used the occasion to promise that they would at least see me through the first year. I could hardly internalize this news, which brought stability back to my universe.

When I arrived at Amherst in September 1939, the college job was working ten hours a week in the Hitchcock Memorabilia Room, filing newspaper references to Amherst alums, for forty cents an hour. I supplemented this with a one-third job as a waiter in a fraternity house, worth a hundred dollars, and a sixty-dollar-per-year job in the college choir. I worked at a boys camp each summer in Lyme, New Hampshire, which turned out to be the location of Sydney's and my honeymoon. Plus Amherst gave me an undergraduate fellowship reserved for those exploring the possibility of Christian ministry. All was well on the fiscal front.

The fall of 1939 was beautiful. There was an optimistic nip in the air that reassured us all that college life was good, and that we were privileged to be in the best of all such places. The rites of passage for entering students were administered in traditional fashion: making overtures toward roommates to whom we had been randomly assigned, sitting together as classmates at football games, not sitting on the Senior Fence (why anyone would *want* to sit on the Senior Fence was never divulged), attending pep rallies before football games, dating Smith and Holyoke girls, enduring various degrees of "hazing" before initiation into fraternities, participating in the annual rope pull across the Freshman River in a test of brawn with the sophomores, screaming our names with the prefix "Pea Green Freshman So and So" every time we entered a fraternity house, attending compulsory chapel twice a week, staying up until 3:00 a.m. to prepare for an English quiz, and (for others) quaffing more beer than was appropriate, no matter what the occasion. It was a happy, romantic, and only occasionally troubling expression of the American way of life.

There were two flaws, however, from which I distanced myself as long as I could. First, about 5 percent of my classmates got no fraternity bids at all, and thus began a four-year stint of exclusion in the midst of what should have been, as the song put it, "the joys of college days." I tucked that tension away and didn't think about it for two years. The second flaw in our perfect world was the war, which began coincidentally with our first days on campus. But the war seemed far away, which it was, and no threat to our well-being, which it would gradually become.

I was a terrible grind, always worrying that my grades would be too low for scholarship aid, always worrying that the prep school whiz kids would effortlessly surpass the academic achievements by graduates of such places as Binghamton Central High School. I was fortunate to have a roommate from Summit High, Vernon Williams, who had spent two years at Andover, and from this dual perspective could provide a reassuring reality check, reminding me from time to time that those who had not gone to prep school were not doomed to flunk out in the middle of freshman year. He also pried me away from the books now and then, pointing me in the direction of Smith College, so that I could have a fuller life than that of the solitary scholar. In this and other matters, I owe him more than he will ever know.

It was a wise decision to enroll in Professor Morgan's Music 1. When I learned about such things as "sonata form," I had a brand-new vehicle of entrance into the exciting realm of music. I had been led to believe that college dormitory life would be an unending cacophony of jazz phonographs and radios. But the longer I was around the more I began to hear the B Minor Mass or the *Jupiter* Symphony coming out of fraternity windows or one of the South College's stairwells. As a generation of musical literates began to emerge, more than just the required listening for Music 1 could be appreciated. He who was stirred by the vigorous Brahms's First moved painlessly to the pastoral Brahms's Second. To untangle the structure of Beethoven's Fifth, a relatively easy job, earned one the right to go on to his Third, a notoriously difficult job but infinitely worth the effort. To be captivated by Sibelius's Fifth (voted the favorite that year in Music 1) emboldened one to attack his Seventh, even though he had been sneaky enough to write it all in one movement.

I competed for both glee club and choir and stayed with the choir for three reasons, listed in ascending order of importance: (1) I came from a "ministerial family," and singing sacred music didn't turn me off; (2) we had to go to chapel anyhow, so why not go and sing; and (3) it paid sixty dollars a year, which was a magnificent sum in the financially uncomplicated era of the late thirties. Along the way, however, I got more than my sixty dollars' worth in the person of Henry Mishkin, a brand-new assistant professor, who directed the choir. With gentle strength he whipped us into an extraordinarily effective musical body. There weren't many religious types among us, but the sense of the holy came through at a lot of Sunday afternoon required chapels that were redeemed by the anthems if not the sermons.

"Papa Mishkin" gave us the feeling that Bach was pretty avant garde, and as a result we learned a whole treasure trove of Palestrina, Di Lassus, William Byrd, and such. I don't know what Professor Mishkin's own religious inclinations were, or whether he had any particular identification with Judaism, but he gave me a better feel for the mystery of the Christian story by the way he conducted passion music than I ever got from reading many theologians on "the doctrine of the atonement."

We could always tell whether we had come through or not; he would place the yellow pencil with which he had been conducting us back on the music rack of the organ and give us a nod, usually containing some degree of approbation. There was one luminous occasion during a Palestrina *Ave Verum* when the look on his face was as close to what a beholder of the Beatific Vision must resemble as anything else I ever expect to see. During such high moments, he got out of us a degree of musical purity that provides a musical analog to transubstantiation: As the priest by grace transforms mere bread into Christ's presence, so Professor Mishkin, by grace as well, was able to transform forty examples of rough-hewn secularity into almost pure sublimity.

Two other occasions stand out for me. One was a winter offering of William Byrd's *I Will Not Leave You Comfortless*, so purely done that I have always feared hearing it again in apprehension that it would be a letdown. The other occasion was a Christmas candlelight service when The Man with the Yellow Pencil drew from Bob McMullin an opening solo rendering of the words "Ave Maria" so effortless and soaring that it transported us to at least the third heaven—which, by his own admission, is as far as the apostle Paul ever got in this mortal life—and left us singing from there for the remainder of the service. I'm not sure I have ever gotten all the way back down.

During "Pledge Week" of freshman year, I felt some twinges of conscience about being part of a fraternity system that denied membership to those who were either Jewish or else lacked the demeanor of a "fraternity man." I shared that college job in the Hitchcock Room with Bob Webber, an "independent"—a euphemism for "unpledged"—and I recognized the injustice of the fact that I would become a member of a fraternity and he would not. I managed to stifle these concerns for well over two years and did not particularly brood on them. I am not proud of having to write that. By way of explanation, I should note that the group of friends in my delegation at Chi Psi were stellar folk, all of whom I enjoyed and even admired, and I would feel sad not to have known them. That fact probably created some moral blindness about the pluses and minuses of fraternities.

After the bombing of Pearl Harbor, another dimension of the conflict between fraternity living and human injustice emerged. Working on an editorial for the Amherst *Student* during the evening of December 7, I was struck by the fact that with the outbreak of war there were a lot of ethical issues with which I was going to have to wrestle more strenuously. One of these was the precipitous action of our government in moving Japanese Americans who lived on the West Coast (who were U.S. citizens) into "detention centers" that could in all justice be called "concentration camps." When the government decided to release some of them to go to college, I worked on a project through the Amherst *Student* to have Amherst become one of the receiving institutions. We did not succeed in this venture, but I have always cherished the fact that one of the students who joined in this project was Bill Webster, who later served as head of the FBI and the CIA. There was a strange incongruity in the fact that during the Vietnam years the FBI compiled a sizable dossier on me (which I later secured under the Freedom of Information Act). Despite that, I venture the guess that even then Bill and I had more convictions in common than separated us.

There is still more to the story. Thirty years later, our daughter Alison spent a summer in Berkeley with a group of university students, one of whom was named Paul Ehara. Paul is a *sansei*, a third-generation child of second-generation Japanese American parents, both of whom had been in the relocation camps during World War II. (When the war broke out, half of his father's family was in the United States, the other half in Japan. When his father was drafted out of the relocation camps into the military, his family was divided between two countries at war with each other.) The long and the short of it is that Paul and Alison fell in love, married, and had two sons, Colin Masashi Ehara and Akiyoshi McAfee Ehara.

I spoke at an Easter rally for peace in 1983, which Colin (age ten months) attended with his parents. I pointed out that during World War II, Colin's two sets of grandparents were designated as "enemies" and could have no dealings with one another. But something had intervened in their story that was stronger than hate, whether official or unofficial, and that was human love. Those who were "enemies" are now friends and loved ones, and that was a message Colin could exemplify even at the age of ten months. He did not have to give a speech. All he had to do was *be*.

My brief excursion into trying to arrange for Japanese Americans to come to Amherst was important also in raising to my consciousness the not unrelated issue of anti-Semitism in Amherst fraternity life. I was trying to sort out, from what was still a pacifist perspective, the moral issues that were at stake in the war. That we were putting American citizens behind barbed wire in California and Utah could not help but evoke the image of Nazis doing the same thing to Jews in Germany. (By late 1942 Hitler had the "final solution" in place, a machinery to bring about the total destruction of all Jews everywhere.)

In the light of the hysteria after Pearl Harbor, I searched for ways to differentiate our war aims from those of the enemy. It seemed to me that what Hitler was doing blatantly to the Jews in Europe was something that, in however much lower a key, we were also doing to Jews and Japanese Americans in the United States. It seemed clear to me that if we were truly opposed to the ugly treatment of Jews in Europe, one sure evidence of our sincerity would be to cease dehumanizing Jews in our own country. How could we in good conscience protest anti-Semitism six thousand miles away if we were practicing a version of it on our own campus?

The matter came to a head during the next round of campus pledging. There was an outstanding Jewish student in the incoming class, and I made a pitch for us to bid him. Whatever I said, beyond describing the merits of the individual, was a version of the kind of analysis in the preceding paragraphs. I thought the logic would be self-evident, and that we would lock arms to defy the national fraternity ban on pledging Jews.

My proposal never got off the floor. Only a few of the brothers spoke to it, and the most telling rebuttal was the argument that if we pledged one Jew he would want to bring his friends and pretty soon we would be overrun with Jews. We didn't pledge a Jew.

I didn't resign, though I now think maybe I should have. Instead, I wrote a long letter to the national headquarters of the fraternity setting forth the themes under exploration here, asked that the letter be read at the next national meeting, and that Chi Psi open its doors to all. The letter was read as requested, but according to the verbal reports I got of the meeting it was almost laughed off the agenda. Who would take seriously a comparison between Adolf Hitler and the Nordic types who made up the membership of a national fraternity? Once again I didn't resign, and I'm still torn about whether that was an act of moral cowardice or just a recognition that "you can't work to change the system from within if you're not within the system." I soon graduated, and only years later, when I was teaching at Stanford, did the local chapter of Chi Psi ask for my participation in a fraternity event. It seemed to me so out of touch with the kind of world we were experiencing on campus in the sixties that this time I *did* resign, not militantly but quietly, realizing that any chance for me to make an impact was long past.

In the spring semester of my freshman year I entered a "competition" to make the editorial board of the Amherst *Student*, and was one of the survivors. This meant that during my sophomore year there was in effect an ongoing "competition" for what would in my junior year be a significant position on the masthead, even if I failed to gain the top post of editor-in-chief. I had been a reporter on both junior high and high school newspapers, and I aspired to the editorship of my college paper as well. Furthermore, every senior post was paid, and the editor would be well into the three-digit category.

So I accepted all the assigned news stories I was offered, worked twice a week until the wee hours putting either the Monday or Thursday edition to bed, proofread at the printers on Monday or Thursday morning, and wrote as many unassigned feature articles as I had time for. As the year wore on, it became clear that Bill O'Donnell and I were the front-runners for the coveted post at the top of the masthead.

But at the very end a difficulty emerged. There was, so some argued, an unwritten rule that no fraternity house could have the editor-in-chief position two years in a row, the fear apparently being that the editor-in-chief would practice journalistic nepotism so that the position would become locked in a dynasty drawn from a single fraternity house. It so happened that the editor-in-chief whom one of us would succeed was, like myself, a member of Chi Psi, whereas O'Donnell was a member of Delta Kappa Epsilon. So when the editor, Dick Wilbur, nominated me to succeed him, the Dekes cried out "Dirty tricks!" and insisted that I was ineligible for the post due to my "fraternal" relationship with Wilbur. No allegations were made that Wilbur and I were in collusion, and, indeed, as this matter began to surface, Wilbur and I had refrained from dealings with one another that might appear questionable. However, the retiring editorial board supported Wilbur's nomination, and after several furious weeks of meetings and recriminations, I was duly elected and installed.

The event had become a mini *cause celebre* on campus, and remained such. O'Donnell continued to be deeply hurt by what he perceived as a backroom deal that had destroyed his chances, and the furor continued. Finally, at my suggestion, O'Donnell and I got together and worked out a compromise. Since U.S. involvement in World War II was already underway, Amherst for the first time in its history would have a full-time summer session, during which the paper would continue to be published. So we jointly proposed that I remain editor during the rest of the academic year and that O'Donnell assume the editorship for the summer semester, with a new editor to be chosen in the fall. This resolution was accepted by all parties.

I have often reflected on these events in later years. Did I capitulate where I should not have done so, or at least had no need to do so? Was the force of an unwritten rule properly invoked to block my appointment to the editorship? I remain certain that there was no connivance between Wilbur and me on the matter of his successor. I also have genuine sorrow that O'Donnell, a gifted journalist, felt that he had been mistreated in the process.

During the course of the controversy, I consulted various faculty whom I knew well, and talked especially with the dean of admissions, Bill Wilson, a Quaker of great integrity, about what, if anything, I should do. In typical fashion he refused to solve my problem for me, saying something like, "If you feel sure you are in the right, then you can afford to decide either way and still maintain your integrity." I am glad, in retrospect, that I chose not to stonewall my position as editor. I feel sure that I would now regret such an action and am glad there was a Bill Wilson on hand to help me make a decision freely.

At the beginning of the 1942 summer session, a new director of religious activities appeared on the scene. He was a college administrator's dream—not only did he have all the right religious credentials, but he had put himself through seminary *as a professional hockey player.* Furthermore, he was a Congregationalist, which meant that he was clearly "open" in his thinking. That he had the misfortune to have gone to Williams College could be forgiven in the light of all the pluses. His name was Bill Spurrier. Since I had been elected president of the Christian Association for senior year, our lots were cast with each other, and Bill did a lot for Amherst students, including me, before entering the Army chaplaincy two years later.

What he did for me was to help me begin to "do theology" and to reexamine the quasi-humanism with which I was about to graduate. What's more, Bill had been a student of Reinhold Niebuhr—a name we will encounter on these pages many times. He helped to ease me into the thought of a mentor and challenger with whom I would have to tangle if I ended up at Union Seminary. As I encountered difficult pages in one of Niebuhr's early works, *Moral Man and Immoral Society*, Bill was on hand to bail me out. He soon discovered that I was a pacifist, and he helped me articulate a position he did not himself share.

He was also, I must add, of immense help as I went through a tempestuous courtship with many ups and downs, moving between hope and despair until hope finally emerged triumphant (more on that later).

I had been invited to be an English major by Professor Baird, and am not sure why I declined, for he was a vigorous teacher as well as a provocative challenger of all things holy. (Perhaps that is why I declined.) He was also unconventional. On one occasion, when we were reading *The Taming of the Shrew*, he started the class by pushing us hard on why we were having such difficulty getting into the play. Finally, a little exasperated, John Conger, one of the few true intellectuals in our class, responded, "But, sir, the relationship of the sexes was different in Shakespeare's time." Baird picked up his pocket watch from the desk, glanced at it and said decisively, "Excellent! Three minutes and twenty seconds! No class has gotten to the point this quickly in a decade."

My classes and seminar hours in philosophy were divided between professors Gail Kennedy, who was wedded to British empiricism, and Sterling Lamprecht, who years before had gone to Union Seminary only to discover that he was an Aristotelian, and had subsequently equipped himself to challenge the whole religious enterprise. Both gave me a run for my money in terms of whatever faith I had brought to college, but neither one made me the object of a campaign to be enlisted in the ranks of the humanists. However, their thorough treatments of the history of philosophy began to tell me more than I really wanted to learn from what Schleiermacher called "religion's cultured despisers." But since I have spent most of the rest of my life in their company, my gratitude increases. Simply in terms of the preponderance of the people and ideas we examined, the Christian heritage emerged as a distinctly unlikely option for a contemporary student to take seriously.

To my great surprise and pleasure, when I went on to Union, escorted in my mind by a phalanx of nonbelievers, there were men on the faculty more than ready to do battle against all manner of philosophical challenges, especially Paul Tillich, Reinhold Niebuhr, David Roberts, Richard Kroner, John Bennett, and others. I remember particularly that William Temple's Gifford Lectures, published as *Nature, Man, and God,* were an ever-present help in time of trouble.

I was able to do a senior honors paper at Amherst on "Quaker Views of War" that helped me in a number of corners of my life. First, I had a forum for trying to develop a position that could stand up under scrutiny. Second, I got historical help from Quaker thinkers such as George Fox, John Woolman, and Robert Barclay, who had to be taken seriously in any treatment of the history of philosophy. Third, I could bring a Niebuhrian critique to bear on my own inquiries. Professor of religion James Cleland directed me to voices within the Christian tradition. I ended up not with a pragmatic pacifism ("This will work") but with a pacifism of witness ("Here I stand, I can do no other"). The distinction didn't last me all the way through seminary, but it at least helped me to get started there.

In retrospect, I am glad for the academic rigor of the above. I cannot say I "enjoyed" the mountains of material I had to read by Locke, Barclay, Hume, Hobbes, Spinoza, Kant, and company, but I would, again in retrospect, feel that my education had been lacking without exposure to them. They have not guided my thought in positive ways, but whenever I feel a little too secure intellectually, one or another of them will intrude from some dark corner of my memory, with such unwelcome news as "But Hume absolutely *annihilated* that position," or "You can't say that in light of Kant's critique."

Several years after all this, when I was assistant chaplain at Amherst and thus sharing responsibility for the planning of morning chapel services (half of which were "religious" and half of which were "secular"), Professor Lamprecht was asked to make the case for reason in matters religious. I chose as the hymn just before his talk, "God give us men / whose aim 'twill be / not to defend some ancient creed." He was delighted.

The days after Pearl Harbor were chaotic. Some of my friends wanted to enlist immediately. Others were just as eager to avoid the draft, at least for a while, but all such speculation had an air of unreality about it, since the *real* question in wartime was not going to be, "What shall I do?" but rather, "What will be done with me?" For the first time in our privileged lives we faced directions that were not in our power to determine. Someone else was in control of our lives.

As a pacifist, I realized that my choices might be even narrower than those of my classmates, and that all would hang on whether my conscientious objector status was upheld by my draft board. At this point, my pacifism was not going through ideological zigzags. That would come later. I attempted to touch base with reality by doing a number of editorials for the Amherst *Student*, assessing the roles all of us might be called upon to accept. A good percentage of our number anticipated that we would never even get back to college after the impending Christmas vacation, and would all end up in the Army or the Navy Reserve or a CO camp or jail. Our return to academic pursuits at Amherst might be put on hold indefinitely or even permanently.

Against this sober background, there was one collegiate rite of passage I had never sampled; neither beer nor wine nor hard liquor had ever passed my lips, part of the legacy of my upbringing, which I have already described. But that legacy ("One drink and you're a drunkard," and "Nice boys don't drink") had not been borne out in my Amherst experience. I had a lot of friends who drank, and were sterling exemplars of humanity. I felt a need to test the family mindset, and to do it with some friends, before time ran out on us all. Three other members of the Chi Psi delegation agreed that we should take the leap together before vacation. We sought and received advice from those who were veterans in the fine art of inebriation. They determined that our needs would best be met by frequent imbibing of Seabreezes, a combination of grapefruit juice and gin. Their merit, we were informed, was that they spread their effect slowly, and we could pace ourselves during the evening. We did.

If any moralists are hoping that we became violently ill, or nauseated, or lost control of our reasoning powers, I have bad news to report. None of those things happened. Instead, the Seabreezes went down so smoothly that for a while I began to wonder whether they would be effective. They induced a genial sense of increasing well-being, expressed, in my case, by a loosening of the tongue, so that (I am told) I became a raconteur, an utterly frank but not nasty commentator on the human scene, and, as the evening progressed, an increasingly happy young man. I would enter a room, discover that I knew the name of every inhabitant, and joyfully share such knowledge with those who already had ample reason to know their own names quite apart from any eleventh-hour assistance. I remember the sense of utter cosmic appropriateness

I felt when I discovered that Bill Webster came from Webster Groves, Missouri, a coincidence between person and place that struck me as terribly significant, which sentiment I felt constrained to share many times, not only with him but also with everyone else.

There were three further portions of the evening that I remember with particular affection: First, I sat down at the piano in the great hall of Chi Psi Lodge and did not surrender my seat until I had given a spontaneous rendition of at least fourteen variations on Bach's Passacaglia and Fugue in C Minor. Second, without planning to do so, I tripped on a portion of the upstairs hall carpet adjacent to the stairway, lost my balance, fell, and made the remarkable discovery upon arriving informally at the bottom of the stairway on the ground floor that I had neither spilled a single drop of my drink, nor felt any pain. Third, it occurred to someone later in the evening that we should all attend the second showing of *The Maltese Falcon*, with Humphrey Bogart and Sydney Greenstreet, which we did in boisterous but not dangerous exhilaration. Sydney Greenstreet turned out to be the approximate shape and size of Ox Eaton, one of our classmates, and I made it my task to call attention to that fact every time Ox's counterpart appeared on the screen.

Three days later, vacation having arrived, I was sitting in the living room of the Presbyterian manse in Binghamton, New York, gingerly reporting to the family my experiences on the collegiate scene. I had already decided that I must share with them my departure from the straight and narrow path of sobriety, which I had experienced only seventy-two hours earlier.

"There's something I need to tell you," I began in a voice that telegraphed a smitten conscience to my mother. She was quick to recognize that confession was in the air, and seeking to reinforce and reassure me ahead of time, she interrupted my report before it got started to say, "I don't care *what* you did, so long as you didn't get drunk."

As our January 1943 graduation approached, the names of the Bond Fifteen were announced, fifteen seniors who could compete for the Bond Oration Prize of one hundred dollars. The two finalists, T. P. Green and R. M. Brown, were to speak at the final chapel service the morning of graduation. I decided that this time I must be totally up-front about where I was coming from, and so I spoke on "The Role of the Conscientious Objector in Wartime," a matter dear to my heart, to a group of men 95 percent of whom would be in military service within a month.

I had no idea what kind of reception I would get, not only from my classmates but even more from their parents. The rapport was incredibly open and accepting, a parting gift from my alma mater that I had hardly dared hope for.

No subsequent first place has ever meant as much as that second place.

2

Expanding Boundaries:
Seminary, Marriage, and Pacifism

A huge shift in my orientation came on January 31–February 1, 1943. I graduated from Amherst on Sunday afternoon, took the night train to New York, and by 11 a.m. on Monday I was sitting in a classroom at Union Seminary being introduced, by Paul Tillich himself, to part 5 of Tillich's "theological system." Part 5 deals with "the end of history," the kind of fulfillments that are possible, and stubborn hope.

It was an appropriate way to begin seminary, for in a world at war, questions about meaning, purpose, and fulfillment are the pressing questions. I felt reassured that I was in the right place.

While at Union Seminary I also did field work at Madison Avenue Presbyterian Church, and this kept me from being too seduced by the world of books. Madison Avenue was a "fashionable" church when Henry Sloane Coffin was pastor, and remained so when George Buttrick succeeded him. The policy was that since the church was situated between Park Avenue and the East Side, it must minister to both groups at once. There were the well-to-do, and there were the poor and needy, and they were to be welcomed without distinction. This was radical stuff. My job had three components.

First, I led the class on Sunday mornings that was mainly discussion, and I could develop my own curriculum. The students were mostly in high school, which meant that we talked a lot about the war, since every eighteen-year-old male in our midst was going to get drafted. (I saw one of them off to boot camp from Pennsylvania Station very early one morning, and it was all we could do to keep from crying.) Some anti-Semitism emerged ("All Jews are draft-dodgers"), and we hung onto that one for a long time. They were convinced

25

that Jews controlled most American industries and that their impact reached down into everybody's life. I had rational arguments on hand. They were not impressed. I am fairly sure I made some impact, but you never know.

Second, on Friday nights I helped to organize fun and games in the parish house. Discipline could have been a crushing problem without the presence of several other seminarians. We offered basketball, talent shows, and a pianist who could go from Bach to boogie and back again in half a second. I don't know whether any children were conceived on our watch, but we all took turns handling "the stairway detail." Zealous seminarians from elsewhere who would view this as a type of "evangelism" would have been disappointed, for the task was really to provide exercise, games, food, and fun. Period. If students were somewhere in the gym at Madison Avenue Presbyterian Church, they were not out on the streets getting into trouble. We claimed that as a victory.

The third part of my job was pastoral calling, which was the most demanding part. On the bus going over to the East Side I would ask myself, What am I doing here? What have I possibly got to say to the parents of a senior high kid who is always on the edge of being in deep trouble? Do I pray with them? I used to hope nobody would be home so I could simply leave my card. (This counted as a "call" in the church office.) The best help I got came from a long out-of-print book by Reinhold Niebuhr, *Leaves from the Notebook of a Tamed Cynic*, a diary of his years in a Detroit pastorate. Niebuhr confessed that the hardest thing in all his ministry was calling on his parishioners, and described walking around the block twice to get up enough courage to ring the doorbell, hoping that nobody would be home. I was in good company.

I wonder: Did my calling on such families ever make a difference? Did I ever make a statement that could be recognized as "good news"? I don't know. But I did learn from calling on the East Side that if all people are made in the image of God, the image of God comes in all sizes and shapes.

Some perks accompanied working at Madison Avenue Presbyterian Church. The most valued were the chances to hear Dr. Buttrick preach every Sunday, and the evenings—about one Sunday night a month—when he and his wife welcomed us to their apartment after the evening service. The agenda on such occasions was clear: There was no agenda, save the assurance of one of Mrs. Buttrick's massive spreads when the discussion was over. One night we heard selections from an as-yet-unpublished *Screwtape Letters* by C. S. Lewis. Several times we talked about parishioners who didn't like the preacher's sermons, and in wartime the ire of many people was raised against conscientious objectors. What to do?

Dr. Buttrick didn't just talk about "being pastoral"—he *was* pastoral. I raised a question one night about dealing with conflict (never my strong suit), and in the next day's mail I got a letter from him. Dissatisfied with how he had responded the night before, he proposed lunch the following Thursday.

I would unequivocally call my years at Union the high point of my intellectual life. I believe because we were there in wartime and were exempt from military service, we realized that such time was not to be squandered. The study of theology could not help but be relevant, for it was a way of scrutinizing the world and ourselves that was demanding, liberating, and even exhilarating. The thin theology that I had brought from Amherst was reexamined, ripped apart, redrawn too quickly, ripped apart again. But it began to provide a map of the soul, or better still, of the world, and the content of the faith began to fill some of the vacuum of my mind.

During my seminary years a close college friend, Howie Murray, was killed when the destroyer on which he was serving was itself destroyed. Where does God "fit" into that? I had to discover for myself that Howie's death was not a problem I could solve (though I tried to do that in a senior sermon) but a mystery within which I simply had to live, being open to the possibility that the mystery of his death might illumine something further about the mystery of my life—a distinction I have called upon ever since.

Death was ever present in those seminary years, not only because other Howie Murrays were being killed but also because we in seminary were *not* getting killed, and why should we be exempted from death's talons that reached out so mercilessly toward those around us? On one level we were fortunate; seminary was a time to wrestle with ultimate issues at the exact moment when ultimate issues were in the very air we breathed.

Even in such an atmosphere we did our share of "normal" things. We worshiped in James Chapel, ate in the refectory, read in the library, discussed in the classroom, slept in the dormitory, went by subway to field work, pursued our romances in whatever space we could find, and even occasionally played touch football in Riverside Park.

Looking back, it is difficult to establish a chronology of theological shifts, developments, and crises. New insights sometimes came unbidden, rather than at the end of a long process that could be traced. I came from Amherst with a faith perception very much college created, worked out in large part as I wrote a thesis on Quakerism and war. I insisted, as a result of exposure to George Fox, that there is "that of God" within *everyone*. I took that to mean that I had no right to destroy "that of God" in *anyone*, so pacifism was a must. I felt that God was particularly present in the man Jesus, but I could not yet make sense out of the cross as somehow Jesus' redemptive act that saved humankind. My bottom line was "love," but without much sense of justice, and to that extent I would now acknowledge not only inadequate but irresponsible. This melange of concerns carried me to Union. There wasn't anything very distinctively Christian about it, and I was certainly open to help.

I got it.

I was at Union during the golden years of a distinguished institution, in part, President Henry Sloane Coffin argued, because it had a distinguished faculty. Credit for this went above all to Dr. Coffin himself, born wealthy but with a social conscience and the saving grace of a sense of humor. He needed both those ingredients in about equal portions to endure constant attacks from both the left and the right. It was his great genius to corral not only established scholars but also charismatic mavericks such as Reinhold Niebuhr, who had been a pastor in Detroit for twelve years and within the Union gambit emerged as one of the great theologians of our era. It was not for nothing that Dr. Coffin was also known to generations of students as Uncle Henry, and tales of his kindnesses to students and faculty are legion. There were other "greats" as well, only briefly identified here, since they frequently intrude on the overall story.

Dave Roberts, in philosophy of religion, dealt with the difficulties of belief I had encountered at Amherst and suggested ways back to affirmation. He, Pitney Van Dusen, Cyril Richardson, and Reinhold Niebuhr all proposed that Rene Descartes did not have the final word on belief, and that there were even ways to challenge the authority of David Hume. Christians did not need to wither under such philosophical challenge but could meet these philosophical worthies on their own turf.

Pitney van Dusen, professor of systematic theology (whom everyone correctly assumed was being groomed for the presidency as Uncle Henry's successor), was a dominating personality, who routinely gave sixty or seventy hours a week to "running the seminary," and expected others to do the same. I had my conflicts with Dr. Van Dusen, which will be chronicled in due course, but when occasion demanded, he was there, full of an ability to get things done. During my first year at Union, John C. Bennett, then at the Pacific School of Religion in Berkeley, was appointed to the Union faculty. He had been my mentor long before I met him, both for the clarity of his thought and the clarity of his expression. He will return later in this story. There were other giants: James Muilenburg, John T. McNeill, Daniel Day Williams, Sam Terrien. A student once said to me, "Do you know what saved me for the Christian faith? It was the back of Sam Terrien's head." When I asked for a little more information on that one, he continued, "In my most despairing times I would still go to chapel. And there he was, in about the third pew, the back of his head the only clue as to who he was. And I figured that if he not only needed whatever chapel provided but returned every day to keep it alive, then maybe I should hang in too."

Paul Tillich was magisterially on the scene. He was a systematizer to the nth degree, from whom I took many courses that were important to me, but I needed also to be surrounded by the fire of Niebuhr and by Bennett's applicability. Although austere in demeanor, partly because he was from a very different Germanic background, Tillich needed admiration and support for sheer psychic survival—which persuades me that in the long run his three books of sermons, rather than his three volumes of systematic theology, may be his most lasting contribution. He speaks with power because he preaches to himself as well.

During my years at Union I became a "convert"—no "Damascus road" experience, just a slow pilgrimage. While at seminary this was still largely an intellectual conversion (as Sydney is always the first to remind me), and much of it was wooden and often laced with the dogmatic certainty of the very young. But my conversion was not only a matter of the mind, for it related to a world at war and acknowledged the ugliness as well as the beauty that resides in the human heart. Reinhold Niebuhr was most instrumental in this gradual transformation, and he helped me, not by offering a system, but by inspiring flashes of insight in class that would burst open entirely new constellations of light, always to be examined and sometimes affirmed.

None of this, perhaps, was really new, but it was increasingly compelling. In the lingo of the day, it was called "neo-orthodoxy," a series of bruising clashes with what had come before, but with an accompanying sense of empowerment that was discernibly like the message of the Scriptures and the Reformation, with some dashes of Kierkegaard thrown in (and the biting polemics finally thrown out). A Niebuhrian throwaway lecture line, "We must take the Bible seriously but not literally," gave me both wings and an anchor, and I've been trying to fit them together ever since.

War brought few blessings, but it gave one gift to American theological education—that of the following sequence: (1) Because of the war, educational institutions had to operate around the clock, which meant (2) that "summer session" had to count as much as a regular semester, which meant (3) that Union Seminary and Yale Divinity School joined forces for the summer of 1943, which meant (4) that Yale sent its major faculty to Union in exchange for using Union's facilities, which meant (5) that Union students could take courses from the cream of Yale's faculty: H. Richard Niebuhr, Roland Bainton, Liston Pope, and a series of "open lectures" by Robert Lowly Calhoun. We got the best of both theological worlds.

Fresh from this giddy experience, I discovered that there was still a full month before the fall semester began. For reasons shortly to be amplified in splendid detail, I headed for Heath, Massachusetts, and a certain Sydney Thomson.

SYDNEY

In the spring of my freshman year at Amherst I signed up for a conference at Smith College on peace issues. I was interested in the topic, and I was also interested in meeting some Smith girls who shared such concerns. I remembered a rather tall, slender blonde, her hair braided in a crown on top of her head—an intriguing getup. Her name was Sydney—an intriguing name. I didn't see her again for two and a half years, but the name stuck, even though the braids disappeared.

As our junior year was winding down, we met again at a conference in Northampton. She had three friends with her, and in a rash moment I invited all four of them to a picnic. This was novel enough to initiate some friendships. Anna Mills was going to yet another conference in Maine, and we decided to hitchhike there together, but first I borrowed a heavy shirt from Sydney, promising that I would return it to her in New York on my way home. This is called long-range planning, and the fact that New York was not "on my way home" didn't deter me in the slightest. Her family, home from the China mission field during the war, was living in an apartment at Union.

I was eager to see Sydney again. Among other things, I wanted to check out what it meant that we encountered one another only at conferences, for despite ministerial predilections, I wasn't solely a pious, conference-going type, and I wanted to make sure she wasn't either. Our meeting at the Thomsons' Union Seminary apartment took care of all such concerns. When I got there, Sydney and her elder sister Nancy were painting their legs, for in wartime silk stockings were an unthinkable luxury, and women of modest means solved the problem as Sydney and Nancy were doing. The conference-going-China-missionary-daughter syndrome was put in a context that anticipated other things as well, all of them good.

Sydney spent the ensuing summer working for the American Friends Service Committee, and I was at Amherst summer session just as my government told me I had to be. At the end of the summer Sydney and her family vacationed briefly at Mountain Rest, a missionary summer place happily located only fifteen miles from Amherst, though most of it was uphill. So to Mountain Rest I biked one afternoon after classes. Sydney and I walked around a bit, I met her parents and brothers, and we had supper before I had to ride back to Amherst in the pitch dark, since class attendance was compulsory in wartime.

I will say this for her family: As a sizeable crew gathered on the front porch of the cottage for goodbyes, it was suddenly the case that, except for Sydney, they all quickly vanished. I like that in a family, even though all that came of it on this occasion was a hearty handshake, this being "our first date," and only a quasi-date at that. But I coasted down the hill feeling that a new chapter might have begun to unfold.

We were both seniors that fall, but I was going to graduate in January, so time was short. I did a lot of telephoning, writing, and crossing the tracks from Amherst to Smith during the fall. There were many afternoon hikes in the crisp, fall leaves and the turning weather. (This seemed a much better use of time than football practice.) On some evenings we listened to music, and I gave thanks that there was a fireplace in my fraternity house room. Things seemed to be going well. There was, however, a certain reserve on her part, which I finally attempted to overcome, mostly verbally, and I learned two things: (1) For many reasons she was not prepared to make a final commitment to anyone for a long time, and (2) as though reinforcing her keeping all options open, there was already another man, who was overseas, and nothing was going to change as long as he was in the picture. This was a blow beyond easy absorption. There was nothing to do but live with it, which meant a friendship with many constraints, unless I simply bowed out of the picture, which I had no intention of doing.

Our times together became more frequent, however. I knew by now that I wanted to marry her, and I also knew that I wanted to marry her more quickly than she wanted to marry me. And we had our own codes of honor about the realities of the case. But even with all the ambiguities there was a magic about the times together, and we had a wonderful fall.

I made one miscalculation that was not a disaster but was certainly not a plus. I left Amherst for Union, fortified by the knowledge that there would be another conference (what would we have done without them?) at Northfield, Massachusetts, in late February. Accepting the fact that I had no chance of changing my status, I nevertheless wanted to be sure she knew that I counted no future worthwhile without her. So I decided to propose to her, clearly and categorically. She could file it away for future reference if she wished, but at least my intentions would be unambiguous, whatever her response. I even picked a spot for this definitive deed, a hilltop on the Northfield campus called Round Top.

I experienced great difficulty propelling Sydney in the direction of Round Top on the appointed evening, and only years later discovered that *her* proposed agenda for the evening had been square dancing. We finally got there, albeit circuitously, and I made my declaration in stumbling fashion though the import was clear. Her response, which I anticipated, was that nothing could change. I interpreted this incorrectly, assuming that she meant, "Maybe some day," whereas what she was really saying was, "No, we simply can't make it." My miscalculation, however, was finally a plus, for I continued to hope for the future, however tenuously, rather than, as she had been trying to suggest, throwing in the towel and calling it quits. So not much was resolved except that it was clear that she would set the ground rules.

During my summers, as I have described, I was a counselor at Camp Pinnacle, in Lyme, New Hampshire, run by Mr. and Mrs. Alvin Thayer. In addition to the boys camp, the Thayers had a house by the lake, Loch Lyme Lodge, along with small cabins scattered through the woods. I thought it would be a wonderful place to spend a couple of days with Sydney before the summer. In those times, and with our respective upbringings, my invitation was about as innocent as they come. We would hike around during the days, and the Thayers would make sure we had separate bedrooms at night. Who could object to such a proposal? Remarkably enough, no one did, and we had a wonderful, carefree interlude. My camera had a self-timer, so we could photograph the two of us together. In one of them, we are sharing a copy of *Goodbye, Mr. Chips*. The discerning almost immediately notice that we are holding the book upside down. "Oh, really?" became our stock response. "We didn't notice it at the time."

That summer, Sydney was taking care of the Niebuhr children at Heath, I was at summer school in New York, and Bill Wolf, a Union friend, was the "summer pastor" at Heath. There was a month between the conclusion of summer school and the beginning of the fall semester. Could I somehow get to Heath as well? I wrote Bill, asking for help. Was there a Heath farmer who would be willing to hire, for one month, a "chore boy"—in this case a city lad who had never milked a cow, never built a mound of hay in a hay wagon, and was generally cool toward being in close proximity to horses and pigs? Bill managed to tap the latent kindness of the Heath community: Oscar Landstrom was willing to engage a chore boy, offering remuneration of board and room and a dollar a day, with Sundays off after morning chores were done. The fact that Oscar Landstrom's farm was almost three miles from Heath Center was irrelevant, the more so when Bill pointed out that slightly past the halfway mark was a splendid rendezvous, the South Cemetery. One night a week Oscar Landstrom drove to town for a meeting of the selectmen, thus providing transportation both ways. But on the other nights I either did the distance round trip on foot, or we agreed to meet either at the South Cemetery or by Whittmore Spring, on the right fork at the bottom of the hill beyond the Dickinsons. That Sydney was willing to make the trek persuaded me that I must be making some progress despite all the ambiguities remaining alive and well in Sydney's mind and heart.

The worst sounds of the day were the boots of Oscar Landstrom hitting the stairway above my first-floor bedroom, and knowing that in five or six seconds there would be a knock on my door that brooked no delay, since "chore time" was upon us and had to be completed before breakfast. No matter how drugged with sleep I might have been, depending on the time of my nocturnal return from town, I had to immediately be up and moving. Each day Oscar taught me a little more about being a chore boy: how to approach a horse in a stall by talking to it so that my arrival would not lead to getting kicked; how to strip the cows of the last drops of milk after the milking machine had done its best; how to get a huge block of ice from the icehouse into the cooler so the milk would stay fresh; how to use a scythe on those parts of the fields that the mowing machine could not negotiate. If Oscar presided in the barn, Grace Landstrom presided in the house, and by the time the morning chores were done, the cows let out, and the stable hosed clean, a hot breakfast would be ready, daughters Pearl and Ruth having been on hand to learn the further mysteries of cooking for ravenous farmers. The girls were considerably younger than I and excited about a courtship proceeding out of their house. They were persuaded that Sydney was "winnable," and kept my spirits up at times when I wasn't so sure.

At the end of the month I was at least sure that the Heath interval had been a crucial time. And with Christopher Niebuhr's help, how could I fail? Christopher (aged 8) would go to the post office every morning, describing an enigma to the town's most loquacious citizens: "If she sees him every day, why doesn't she marry him?"

Back in Princeton, where Sydney's family was now living, a few days before the fall semester was to begin, I decided to test the waters and ask whether a yes or no was forthcoming. I got a "yes." Sensation!

But it didn't last long.

I have no intention of reliving the months of our engagements (plural), for we went through the cycle of engagement, engagement broken, engagement reaffirmed, three separate times. Mrs. Niebuhr's comment, on hearing for the first time that we were finally engaged, was strangely fortifying: "You're engaged? My dears, I'm so sorry for you. Engagement is a wretched time." This had been the story of her engagement to Reinhold, and I took consolation from the fact that they had had a marvelous marriage, however many volatile moments there might have been along the way.

So my middle year at Union was a rocky road, punctuated by highs and lows of being engaged or unengaged or reengaged. I tried to go with the flow of Sydney's ups and downs. It was clear that the issue was not just another man, but that, other men or no, she felt too young and unprepared to make a commitment for a lifetime, and genuinely needed a lot more time and space than I, in my eagerness, had provided. This was a help, even if a complication. In my noblest moments, I tried to tell myself that I could at least be a comfort and stay until she could arrive at a decision that would not come unglued. But my noblest moments hardly compensated for the grim alternative of a lifetime of no Sydney. It finally came to the point that we needed more time apart from one another, to see what would happen.

Without having worked out the details for this bit of radical surgery, I began to feel that it was close to "now or never" time, and one Saturday afternoon as we were walking across the Princeton Seminary campus the fateful moment arrived unannounced. Sydney was saying something about the need for me to play "hard to get" a little more convincingly. I stopped, turned to her and said, to my complete surprise, "Okay, if that's the way you want it, I'll do just that," and turning in the direction from which we had both come, I added, "You'll have to call me. I'm not going to call you."

Big, bold Robert, putting it all on the line. But the phone didn't ring for a month. I did get one phone call from Sydney's sister Nancy, whom I perceived as being in my corner, who said that she had just talked with Sydney and that "things aren't as bad as they seem." This call was probably the lifeline that saved the courtship. When a call did come from Sydney it was on a Friday night when I was down at Madison Avenue Presbyterian Church with my youth group. A friend, Jim Bean, took the message, "Give Sydney a call," to which he appended a note, "I don't know what's going on, Brownie, but I hope it turns out well." Jim Bean, harbinger of joy. It *did* turn out well. I got through to Sydney the next morning after a nail-biting night, and the good news was that as far as she was concerned, the engagement was "on" again.

There were a couple of tense times later in the spring, but we overcame them together. I had been arranging with the Presbyterian Board of National Missions for a summer parish, either in Whitlash, Montana (for a single person), or Higgins, North Carolina (for a married couple). We agreed that the latter was decidedly the option to select, and the wedding bells actually sounded out on June 21, 1944, and our two fathers conducted the ceremony in Miller Chapel at Princeton Seminary.

We had "adapted" the text out of the Presbyterian *Book of Common Order,* an editorial decision that took a little while for my father to internalize, believing that the prose of Henry Van Dyke could scarcely be improved upon. Sydney's mother, an Episcopalian, wanted us to use the service in the Episcopal *Book of Common Prayer,* but since everybody else was Presbyterian, her proposal died for want of a second. "And besides," I said to her, citing a phrase from the Episcopal service, "I don't feel that my love for Sydney is quite the same as Christ's love for the church."

June 21, 1944, was only three weeks after D-Day in Europe, so travel to Princeton was not easy. But Sydney's brother, Ensign John Thomson, was there, along with Lieutenant William Whiteside, my roommate and best man, and a few seminary friends were present as well as members and friends of our families. We shared a pleasant reception afterward, and even though the photographer's camera broke down midstream, we salvaged a few photos. The ceremony was something of an ecumenical "first," for Princeton Seminary was not in the habit of letting outsiders use the chapel; our friendship with the president, Dr. John A. Mackay, overcame that obstacle. Years later, when I would divulge the place of my marriage to some Presbyterian gathering, there was almost always a Princeton graduate who would say, "Oh, so *you* were the one."

So, married one week, we arrived, husband and wife, in Higgins, North Carolina, a tiny town without electricity or phone, seven miles down a branch from the main road. Our manse was a substantial stone building that even had a kerosene-run refrigerator, fuel for which we could buy on our weekly shopping trip to Burnsville, the county seat. The women in the church had fixed up the house before our arrival, with lots of giggling (so a six-year-old informant named Mary Jo told us) about the preacher's move from a single to a double bed. Mary Jo spent a lot of time hanging around with us, and we didn't discover until later that she was blessed with total recall and was reporting everything we said, along with every gesture and every nuance, so that the folks in town soon knew us better than we knew them.

My task was to be responsible for three points of a seven-point parish— Higgins, Upper Jack's Creek, and Lower Jack's Creek—under the supervision of the full-time pastor, the Rev. A. H. Mutschler. Sydney, who was in the midst of a master's program at Haverford College in postwar relief and reconstruction, had persuaded Douglas Steere, who was heading the program, that living in a totally different culture for three months would be good preparation for overseas work. An elderly couple, John and "Lady" Lefever, retired in Burnsville, had done home mission work in the area for years and provided wisdom and wonderful home-cooked meals every time we got to town. There was wartime gasoline rationing, and we could not begin to cover the whole area on foot, so the task was really centered in Higgins, where we lived, and Upper Jack's Creek, which, although fifteen miles by car, was just over the mountain between one "holler" and the next.

On Sunday afternoons I preached in Upper Jack's Creek, after a morning service in Higgins, and I could use the same sermon a second time. Since they had a piano but no pianist, I had to double as director of the choir as well. Things were informal, yet my most lingering recollection of Upper Jack's Creek worship is not a happy one. On my final Sunday, I announced the closing hymn, "O Master, Let Me Walk with Thee," which, among other intrinsic virtues, was a hymn I could play on the piano without panicking. I realized soon into the first line that few folks were singing, and by the end of the first stanza nobody was singing. It was clear that the hymn was not familiar. If I had been Bill Coffin, I would have taken the opportunity to close the hymnbook, urge them to do the same, and would have led them in a rousing version of a gospel hymn. However, I was not Bill Coffin, and I didn't know any gospel hymns. I can't be held responsible for the initial shortcoming, but I should have been smart enough to acquire a repertoire of gospel hymns before arriving in Yancey County.

One of the most challenging tasks we faced was understanding some of the Appalachian phrases. The area, settled in the 1700s, had been open to the outside world for about twenty years. The dialect of the area still kept unexpected remnants of its early Scottish and English settlers. We northerners were sometimes challenged to guess what they meant. A young man, telling us that he "wouldn't much care to be in the Navy, but sure ain't ahurtin' to be in the Army" was simply saying he'd like to be in the Navy and equally surely didn't want to be called up into the Army. At the end of a call or visit, we'd rise, saying we had to go. Regularly our hosts would respond, "Don't go. Stay all night!" Our first thought was that we'd overstayed our welcome. Not at all— we were simply expected to respond with equal ease, "No, you come home with me!" Neither party was expected to take the invitation literally.

The war found its way into numerous Higgins families. One young man fought in the ground war in Sicily and became so shell-shocked that the Army sent him home and discharged him. He was alive, but he was one of the permanently walking wounded. At night, he would see Germans hiding in the barn where he was supposed to go and tie up the mule. He would encounter German advance patrols on the hillside where he had taken the low-slung sled to harvest the tobacco. His sleep was punctuated with screams as German units started climbing into the window of his bedroom to take him captive.

Many of the people in Higgins had stone houses that, while small, were substantial. They had large gardens and could grow and can almost all their food. The one cash crop was tobacco, and they were limited by law to a small acreage. But this brought in about four hundred dollars a year, which was enough to get by. During the war years there was a new home industry— punching rugs. The war created a shortage of home-crafted articles, a problem the folks in Higgins were able to help rectify. By mounting the side of a burlap bag over a frame and using an inexpensive "puncher," they could fill the frame with designs out of cloth supplied by an entrepreneur, who paid three to four dollars for each rug. An enterprising woman could do two and sometimes three rugs in a day if she let the garden grow a few more weeds. But there was one constraint. Early on, we were told, people on the way to church one Sunday had seen Maude's unfinished rug in its frame on the front porch. When they came back from church, the rug was nearly finished.

Maude had been punching a rug during the church hour. That was strictly a no-no.

There was an epidemic of polio in the area that summer, and the resulting quarantine played havoc with the vacation Bible school we were supposed to run for the whole area. It was somewhere determined that the children of Higgins could attend school in Higgins, but that no children could come from any other "hollers." We had a guidebook on running a daily vacation Bible school, and at the end of the second week we even had a "program" for the parents.

But the quarantine gave us one gift. Once a week we would load a sack with books from the children's library at the church and take them to the homes of families with children, changing the books each week. This gave us a chance to visit a bit more in their homes, and even meet people who were not part of the church, such as J. W. Wheeler, the local preacher for the Free Will Baptists, who had no dealings with Presbyterians. We thought we should at least visit him, whatever his assessment of our chances for salvation. When we got to his house he was waiting on the porch with a gun across his knees. This had a chilling effect on our desire to make his acquaintance, until he waved to us and said, "Come on up and sit awhile, and don't fret about the gun. I'm just tryin' to keep the crows away."

In our memories, Higgins is mostly a collection of wonderful people: Curt Randolph, the father of Dionysius, who knew his Bible the way one knows a friend; Max Higgins, who ran the store and sold eggs for two cents apiece, twenty-five cents a dozen, which included an attractive container; Paul Higgins, one of the "pillars," who had an inquiring mind; Dewey Higgins and his wife, both of whom had gone to Asheville Farm School; Hiram Webb, who had a courtly demeanor; Irene Higgins, who played the piano at church and didn't let the hymns drag; the Adkins family, who had us for a mammoth dinner the night we arrived and played "Life Is Like a Mountain Railroad" for us on the windup Victrola—all of them corroborating what we had already glimpsed on New York's East Side, that the image of God comes in all shapes and sizes.

PACIFISM

During my last year at Union the struggle over pacifism had to be tackled one more time. I tried once again to come to some overall conclusion that would be satisfactory and lasting.

Ever since Adolf Hitler came to power in 1933 as the legitimately elected leader of Germany, the image of "war clouds over Europe" had been a dominant one. Little by little Hitler regathered areas of the former Germany that had been taken away in the Treaty of Versailles at the end of World War I. And he did it all without firing a shot. The Kellogg-Briand Treaty, signed by signatories from over one hundred nations, renounced war as an instrument for settling international disputes, and the world was thereby defined as "safe for democracy." There were rumblings within Germany about a "Jewish threat," which were augmented by successively stricter measures against the right of Jews to live or compete within Germany's borders.

In my high school years, the viability of war was often explored and almost always rejected—at youth meetings, summer conferences, workshops, and rallies. I saw no reason to disagree. The ethos was pacifist, and—not always recognized—isolationist. World War I had been "the war to end all wars," and nobody was about to suggest otherwise. Humanity had learned its lesson: War does not pay. But "war clouds over Europe" was not only an image; it was an increasing likelihood that also served as a reality check on the depth or lack of depth of one's pacifist convictions. We confronted the possibility of war and rejected it. "The Jesus way of life," as it was sometimes called, left us no alternative, and might indeed call upon us to stand up and be counted.

At the end of the summer of 1939, just before entering college, my friends Ralph Weber, Phil Dalrymple, and I had had a glorious week exploring various trails on Maine's Mt. Katahdin. On September 1, 1939, I got up at 2 a.m. in our base camp at Chimney Pond and set out in the utter darkness to hike to the top—a foolhardy thing to do alone. But I was after spiritual deepening and was amply repaid that day by the sight of dozens of lakes becoming visible as their cloud coverlets were rolled away in the midst of the sheer beauty of a world gradually coming alive after a satisfying sleep. I shared the sunrise with a fugitive squirrel who went to great lengths to tell me how lucky we were. Indeed, we were the first creatures in the United States to see the sun that morning. Had I at that time been acquainted with Robert Browning, I would have repeated exultantly the words of Pippa: "God's in His Heaven, all's right with the world."

But two days later, when we got back to "civilization," I learned that while I had been immersed in the beauty of *nature*, Adolf Hitler had begun enacting the ugliness of *human nature*. The Polish invasion had already begun. When I entered college a few days later, my pacifism was intact, and so it remained, fitfully, during my first couple of years of college. The war was still far away.

Later on, reading Reinhold Niebuhr and working on the Amherst paper I mentioned earlier on, Quaker views of war helped me begin to distinguish between a *pragmatic pacifism*, that is, a pacifism that would "work" and bring Hitler to his knees, and a *pacifism of witness*, a position that claimed only that, especially in time of war, there needed to be those who would repudiate violence and keep the pacifist witness alive in the face of the increasing disappearance of moral constraints.

I rejected pragmatic pacifism as unrealistic and tried to embody a pacifism of witness. But increasingly, that stand too began to unravel. I felt that I was in effect saying to those of my generation, "You go and liberate the world from Hitler, possibly being killed in the process, after which I will emerge from my cocoon of safety and, with clean hands and a pure heart, do good deeds by rebuilding what you have destroyed." My position didn't feel exalted any longer.

At an interseminary conference at Union in February 1945, at just the time when the U.S. invasion of Iwo Jima was in full swing, some personal strands began to come together. Iwo Jima was a tiny Pacific island (only eight square miles), held by Japanese soldiers who made the American infantry assault both costly and bloody for all participants.

I had to offer the prayer at the interseminary conference worship service. I wish I could locate a copy of it, for into it I poured some of the personal anguish I was going through, in my realization that all of us at the conference were sitting in utter safety in James Chapel, while our counterparts, both American and Japanese, were being shot, drowned, burned to death, and bayoneted. I wish I could say that my thoughts focused on something noble like "the utter futility of war" or "there is no way to justify such madness," or that I could have genuinely felt, "even so I am in the right place after all, since nothing that is happening on the slopes of Mt. Suribachi makes any moral sense. It must be opposed."

But all that came through that day was simply the deepening recognition that I could choose where to be on that day, while those on Iwo Jima had no such choice available to them, and that to have the choice that others did not have seemed repugnant. I felt I had no right to claim it for myself.

Another factor that contributed to the challenge I was experiencing was the location of Jewish Theological Seminary diagonally across Broadway from Union. As I gradually met students at JTS, I could not ignore the fact that the war was perceived very differently by those with Jewish eyes. Some of them had escaped from the Warsaw Ghetto, and still others had friends or relations in "camps" with strange sounding names like Auschwitz, Treblinka, Dachau, Birkenau. By the tens of thousands they had simply "disappeared." We were beginning to get terrible accounts of what was going on in the camps, which appeared more and more to be nothing less than places for the mass destruction (read, "wholesale murder") of Jewish civilians. Hitler had a plan, all right. It was called the "final solution," and it sought to "free" the world from the entire Jewish race.

I found myself unable any longer to combine concern for those in such deep distress with my pacifist posture, and came to the conclusion that (in words later discovered to have been on Dietrich Bonhoeffer's lips) "only the one who cries out for the Jews has the right to sing Gregorian chant." "Crying out for the Jews" meant engaging in whatever was necessary to destroy both "the final solution" and its creator. (Translated: "Only those who cry out for the Jews have the right to sing 'Ein Feste Burg.'" It was never as exalted as that, but the shadow of a mighty fortress began to uphold me.)

The only thing "good" about the Jewish dilemma was that it presented absolutely no ambiguity.

Once I was no longer secure with my inherited conviction, I had to look at the future in a new way. I didn't feel I could hide any longer behind my seminary deferment as a way to avoid military service. A new option, the military chaplaincy, required exploration, particularly since in the past I had almost considered it a moral cop-out. I no longer felt this way, but the Army would not accept pastors into the chaplaincy until they had had at least three years of ministerial experience. The Navy, however, would accept candidates directly from seminary.

I felt that I could minister to people in uniform without having to "bless the war," and that the prohibition against chaplains bearing arms could help me keep lines of distinction clear. I discovered also that if a chaplain was issued orders he could not in conscience obey, he could appeal directly to the chief of chaplains, who had the rank of rear admiral and was therefore a considerable resource in times of trouble, since he would outrank almost anyone with whom a lowly chaplain might have to cross swords. (How easily one begins to slip into military metaphors.) But it was hard to dismiss the convictions of a lifetime, especially when my remaining pacifist friends could not help but see my defection as morally tainted, and an acceptance of the values of a murky world.

Before I could negotiate an arrangement with the Navy, however, I had to get certain ecclesiastical matters squared away within the Presbyterian Church, notably ordination. I was "under care" of the Presbytery of Binghamton, New York, but needed to transfer to the Presbytery of New York City expediently. I made an unceremonious departure from Binghamton Presbytery and an equally unceremonious arrival on the steps of New York Presbytery, pleading for acceptance. Either presbytery, I realized, could have nailed me on a dozen technicalities for such precipitous action. Fortunately, the overall mood was generous. It was surely no disadvantage that my father was a member of the Binghamton Presbytery.

The Presbytery of New York City was "liberal," which meant that I didn't have to fight certain standard battles over fundamentalism. But I still had to pass a stiff Bible examination and do a biblical exegesis, that is, take an assigned passage from the Greek New Testament and provide word studies on the main themes. This was doable, since I had taken Greek at both Amherst and Union, but it was a major chore by any reckoning. Most important, I had to prepare a "statement of faith," undergo two oral examinations on it, and satisfy the reverend fathers in the presbytery that my theology was sound. I actually relished composing a statement of faith as a chance to put down on paper the theological conclusions I had arrived at after sitting for two and a half years under Niebuhr, Tillich, Terrien, Bennett, Coffin, and others. I was in the most avid stage of my "Niebuhrian phase," and like many immature Niebuhrians I rang the changes on sin in exquisite detail. I condensed two and a half years of seminary theology into an eight-minute declaration about the state of the art. I was proud of it.

The Presbytery Committee on Candidates did not share my enthusiasm. Veterans at receiving academic-sounding treatises from seminary hotshots, the committee ripped my masterpiece to shreds. I was told, in effect, to start again from scratch, to include considerable use of the pronoun "I," followed in intimate juxtaposition by the verb "believe," and see if I could demonstrate that I personally had "good news" to share. The new statement was to be examined first by the Candidates Committee, and only when I had satisfied them could I resubmit my statement to the presbytery as a whole.

Recognizing among other things that I needed to be ordained posthaste if the Navy was to consider my candidacy, and feeling that I did, damn it all, have some "good news" to share, I tried again. Instead of presenting "An Intellectual Defense of the Faith Against All Comers," I tried to state as simply as I could what was true for me, and what I would take with me as I left the snug harbor of Union Seminary to navigate among the winds and waves of an evil world.

My response centered on where God is to be found in that evil world. My answer: God was to be found in the midst of all the evil—not apart from it. What is it like for God to be situated in the midst? We have a picture of what God is like, a picture of a man hanging on a cross, a man whom we assert by faith (no proofs here) to be the fullest representation of God that is available to us. The picture tells us that God asks of us nothing that God will not also endure. So God is in the foxhole, in the Jeep. God is in the bomber screeching down in flames. God is in the dying soldier on the beachhead. God is a vulnerable God, sharing the human predicament with us.

Every Sunday, taking the number 4 bus down to Madison Avenue Church, I went past a huge Red Cross billboard showing a wounded GI on the sand, with the legend underneath, "Whose blood will save him?" A timely question, which was used in this case to solicit blood donations. When I reflect that in such imagery "blood" is our symbol for "life," I am helped to acknowledge a sheer fact of life: that our blood, our "life," is needed by others; their "life" depends on our help. And when one human being gives blood for another and shares his or her life with another, the love of the creator of the universe is present, overseeing *and participating* in that transaction.

This is not easy to assert, let alone believe, but for me at that time it was at the center. What we believe about God, Christ, the Holy Spirit, the church, the sacraments (perhaps especially the sacraments) grows out of that kind of imagery. This is not the crude image of God sacrificing Jesus instead of taking the rap himself; it is God at the center of a sacrificial act of love that is at the very heart of the universe—an act which we are then asked to emulate.

One other symbol, at least, is needed. Along with the burdened cross must go the symbol of an empty cross, reminding us that Christ came down off the cross, and Christ came out of the tomb. Do what we must to understand this ultimate drama in the struggle between good and evil, the message that emerges is clear: Death did not have the last word. God's divine gamble, so to speak, "worked," showing us a place where brokenness would be healed and love would finally triumph.

That is heady stuff. I am aware that it makes absolutely no sense to many readers and is blasphemous to others. But in the midst of wartime, when I finally had to venture forth, it made sense to me and still does, though I must now nuance it in different and newer ways.

The ordination itself was a happy occasion. Dugald Chaffee, a seminary classmate, Jacob Siungtuk Kim, a Korean from Princeton Seminary, and I were ordained on a Sunday evening in April in Madison Avenue Presbyterian Church. Dr. Buttrick was the officiant, Reinhold Niebuhr preached the sermon, my father (who had known Dug Chaffee's father) gave the charge to the three of us, and my Sunday school class was out in full force. The issue of ordination continues to raise problems for me. But on this particular occasion, with the weight of the hands of Buttrick, Brown, and Niebuhr on my head, I could truly affirm that the power of the Holy Spirit, if not yet dazzlingly present in my life, was closer than I had realized.

In the meantime I was proceeding with the paperwork needed to get a reserve commission in the Navy Chaplains Corps when another mountain of paperwork loomed before me—my bachelor of divinity thesis on Augustine and the problems of moral choice. Under the supervision of my two mentors, John Bennett and Reinhold Niebuhr, I explored possible resolutions of my own moral dilemma—using the same approach I had used in my college thesis, examining the issue of war and morality through the eyes of George Fox and the Quakers. I had no quarrel with those who followed Fox; indeed, I envied those who could be so sure, but my mind, and gradually my heart, began to cohere in the conviction that, trite as it may sound, sometimes we have to engage in a lesser evil in the precarious hope that a greater good will emerge, and that the world we want to rebuild after the war must first be purged of Hitler's power.

By graduation I felt ready for the chaplaincy, and did not spend the short interval before I received my military orders wracked with moral indecision. I was soon sworn into the Navy and told to await orders to report to the Naval Training School for Chaplains at William and Mary College in Williamsburg, Virginia. The orders came promptly. I had to leave. It was not exactly a joyful departure. During all the thinking and rethinking about the future, consolidated in the above paragraphs, I had no trouble remembering that Sydney and I would be separated. We had not yet been married a year, and such a prospect left me bleak. Sydney claims that she felt very much out of the decision-making process about the chaplaincy, whereas I thought I was continually spilling my guts all over the floor. I attribute these conflicting recollections partly to the fact that we had been married only a short time, and were not yet attuned to how differently we made (and still make) personal decisions.

Decisions, decisions—how to make them? We each have our own ways. Sydney talks matters over with me, with family, with friends. I go off by myself and work the question through on my own. Somehow those totally different processes have worked for us. And somehow we've been able to live with the results.

I came to understand that Sydney was willing to affirm my holding a position on my own with full integrity, despite its being different from hers. Her own pacifism remained a central point of decision making for her (nonviolence as a tool for change, not simply pacifism for personal purity). It wasn't easy for her to accept my prochaplaincy decision, yet somehow she was able to affirm my hold on a position different from hers. We respected each other and moved on together.

By any standard of reckoning, however, the bleakest point in my life has remained the night we said goodbye at the Princeton railway station, and I set off for Williamsburg and active duty. My first stop was Princeton Junction, where I had to wait for the overnight train to Washington. Sydney was only four miles away, yet totally unobtainable.

I sat there thinking: My God, I've just signed away my freedom; I cannot make decisions of my own any more; my future life has been taken from my hands and put in the hands of others; I have become a tiny cog in a huge machine, subject to the commands of anyone who outranks a lieutenant (junior grade), of which, at that very moment there were thousands. The mood still gnawed away as late the next day I checked into one of the dormitories at William and Mary, stood before a desk, saluted smartly, and announced to the yeoman on duty and to the world at large, "Lt. Robert McAfee Brown, ChC, USNR, 446549, reporting for duty, sir."

3

The Navy

William and Mary College in Williamsburg, Virginia, had been assigned to the Navy Chaplains Corps during the war. The Naval Training School for Chaplains (NTS[CH]), which was located there, was run by members of the Chaplains Corps who were "career chaplains." This meant that the lieutenants and commanders and captains on the faculty were not "line officers," but chaplains acting like line officers. The principle was sound: Everyone entering the chaplaincy is either a minister, priest, or rabbi, who, like me, had probably never set foot on a naval vessel before. Unless we all learned Navy protocol "by the book," interpreted in the strictest possible manner, we were likely to fall repeatedly on our faces, thereby becoming the laughingstock of the entire U.S. Navy.

I quickly learned that my way of announcing my arrival was "non-Reg," that is, not according to a huge book entitled *Navy Regulations*. There is a right way and a wrong way to do everything. An officer does not salute an enlisted man first; it is the other way around. I should have waited for the yeoman, an enlisted man, to salute *me*. Nor is an enlisted man addressed as "sir." Only officers are addressed as "sir." It was by means of enforcing such distinctions that a discipline would be established that would help banish the scourge of Hitler.

There was plenty of time to learn such things while our class assembled from the four quarters of the nation. We were given pages of direct quotes and a copy of the hefty *Navy Regs*, and told to find the source for each quotation (Para. 62-694.13—that sort of thing). It would have been an impossible task even in a month, and everyone knew it. It was therefore okay to use an answer

45

sheet procured from someone who had finished the exercise, provided we identified the relevant portions around the quote and remembered them.

Partway through this rather unstructured week, the commanding officer of NTS(CH), Captain William Rafferty—a Southern Baptist with fire in his eye—sent for me. I was sure that something had gone askew (Too much pacifism in my background? Petty infringement of matters spelled out clearly in *Navy Regs*?). Or perhaps Rafferty had heard that I had saluted that yeoman second class and called him "sir," instead of waiting for him to salute me and call me "sir."

I knocked on Rafferty's door: "Chaplain Robert McAfee Brown, 446549, reporting, sir," I improvised. "Come in, Chaplain," was the response. I saluted the moment I was inside the door, and Chaplain Rafferty saluted back the moment I finished. A phrase from *Navy Regs* was being enacted: "Junior officers salute senior officers, and all salutes are returned." Maybe all that poring through *Navy Regs* hadn't been wasted.

Motioning me to sit down, Chaplain Rafferty was cordiality itself. He knew my aunt, Mildred McAfee Horton, who was head of the WAVES (Women Appointed for Volunteer Emergency Service) and had recently been featured on the cover of *Time* magazine. In fact, it was about Captain McAfee (my Aunt Millie) that he wanted to see me. I reflected that things weren't going too badly. I reflected too soon. "So," Chaplain Rafferty ended our informal conversation, "I just want you to know, Chaplain, that nobody here gets a free ride, no matter who they know, and that the first chance I get I'll pin your ears back. That's all, Chaplain." Clearly having been dismissed, I replied, "Thank you, sir," saluted, received a salute in return, and beat a hasty retreat.

Rafferty was no fool. He had made sure that at least one of the members of the assembling class would henceforth play it strictly by the book. In a sense, my Navy training was over before it had officially begun, though I did toward the end of the term get my ears pinned back.

From the start, Rafferty left no doubt about who was in charge. About the second or third night after we were officially assembled, a couple of the new chaplains, after a few drinks, raised a small ruckus in the officers' club at Camp Peary, just a few miles outside the town of Williamsburg. Word soon got back to Chaplain Rafferty, who at breakfast the next morning announced that because disgrace had been brought on the Chaplains Corps, *all* personnel were instructed that both Camp Peary and the town of Williamsburg were henceforth and until further notice out of bounds, and that all personnel were confined to the college campus. He kept this curfew in effect for four weeks. Thus was the honor of the Chaplains Corps redeemed.

The curriculum at NTS(CH) stressed what we in the trade call "practical theology." It was assumed that we had gained our systematic theology in seminary, although we had to learn a little about the beliefs of our compatriots since we might be on a base or a ship sharing assignments with Lutherans or Congregationalists or Dominicans. We learned about hospital visitation: If a sailor has a crucifix on a chain around his neck, don't offer him Communion; jot down the number of his bed and ward and give it to the Roman Catholic chaplain. We learned to distinguish between people legitimately asking for duty transfers ("family hardship" that could be backed up with data), and people who simply wanted easier and better duty ("Eagle Mountain Lake" was a Marine's idea of heaven on earth).

In our preaching classes, our chaplain-teachers uniformly demolished our statements about the good news for being loaded with technical jargon. One chaplain, reaching back into his seminary reading, took a phrase from William Temple's *Nature, Man, and God*, and made it a sermon topic: "The Immanence of the Transcendent and the Transcendence of the Immanent." Rafferty didn't forget that one for a long time. We also learned about various ways to distribute Communion, the value of including gospel music in our services, and how to track down a musician who could play the portable organ with which every ship and base was supplied.

In light of what lay ahead, this was time well spent; nothing could be more traumatic than being under an angry skipper. We were also advised that it was not, on the whole, a wise act to abuse the privilege of complaining directly to that rear admiral in the Chaplains Corps in Washington about perceived breaches of conduct by one's commanding officer.

During our twelve weeks of training, we spent two weeks at one of two actual military bases, either Camp Peary, six miles away by bus, or Cherry Point Marine Air Station, an hour away by plane. I was one of the lucky ones, sent to Cherry Point. The time there had a little of everything, including a few things not bargained for. I spent the first week conducting a daily vacation Bible school for the children of personnel on the base. I was not thrilled. *This* was what I had joined the Navy to do in wartime?

Preaching was a different matter. We lined up on Friday to get our assignments for Sunday morning services on the base and elsewhere. Consulting his clipboard, which obviously had us all listed in alphabetical order, the chaplain in charge called out "Brown . . . Hmm. Presbyterian . . . You Presbyterians are supposed to be good preachers. We'll assign you to the brig. Report there at 1000 and 1400 hours. Next, Carswell . . ." This was not what I had been anticipating as the location of my first sermon after ordination. It effectively killed any free time on Saturday, since I had never asked myself, "What do you preach about to men in prison?" and it brought me down to earth in a hurry. I was at least strengthened in preparation by being able to take a text from one of Paul's "imprisonment epistles."

My first celebration of Holy Communion a few weeks later at the Norfolk Navy Yard was a powerful experience. Communion means different things to different Christians, and some of the most hotly contested church battles have centered around trying to determine what it "really" means, and who can "properly" administer it. I see it among other things, as a way of dramatizing, that is, actually acting out our participation in what the human experience of sharing is meant to be.

I was assigned to lead worship on a destroyer escort, and Holy Communion was to be celebrated. Since the service was being conducted on the after gun turret (in the front of the ship with few open spaces), there was only room for three men to come forward at a time to receive the elements. The first three who came were the commanding officer of the ship, a fireman's apprentice, and a black steward's mate. In the social and professional life of the ship, as on all Navy ships at that time, there was a rigid hierarchy that went, from top to bottom: (1) white officers, (2) white enlisted men, (3) black enlisted men. At this particular Lord's Table the hierarchy disappeared. The three men knelt side by side in an absolute equality of need. For a moment there was neither bond nor free, white nor black, officer nor enlisted men. For a moment those men were precisely what God intended them to be—people who were united in Christ and therefore united in one another. And I made sure the black steward's mate was served first.

I know that when worship was over the three men went back into a world where the old barriers remained. Yet, to whatever extent they took seriously their oneness in Christ, they could never again rest comfortably with the utter incongruity of the segregation that was elsewhere imposed on them.

I was in Norfolk the day the war ended, on temporary duty at the downtown Navy "Y." The previous day we had had a full session at Fire Control School, learning what to do if we were on a ship that sustained a direct hit. With that experience in the forefront of my mind, peace seemed more desirable by the minute, and as the word came in, driblet by driblet, that the war was almost over, the citizens of Norfolk, along with several thousand Navy personnel, prepared to celebrate. By late afternoon definitive word came over the radio that Japan had surrendered unconditionally. There was also talk about a new bomb, dropped only a few days earlier on Hiroshima and Nagasaki, that had apparently speeded up negotiations, but not too much attention was focused on that. What attention was focused on was that people would no longer get killed. People would live. Navy personnel would be discharged. They would go home. They would make love and have children.

A good many of them appropriated these new agendas for the future by heavy drinking. This became a distinct problem at the Navy "Y." As the evening went on we literally stacked the bodies of inebriated sailors in the hall-way. Midway in this unpleasant activity it occurred to me that the chapel of the Navy "Y" would be a fine place to have a service of celebration and penitence, the penitence being that the celebration had to be bought with such a heavy price in human lives, both ours and the Japanese.

I announced over the PA system, and put a notice on the bulletin board, that at 2200 hours (10 p.m.), before everybody had passed out, there would be a service of thanksgiving and penitence in the small chapel, and left my body-stacking duties to others while I made some notes for a service. Save for the fact that I decided to go for broke with the dual theme, I cannot remember much about the actual content. Indeed, I have since surmised that very few people that far into the evening would even have recognized such words as "penitence" or "contrition." But whatever their state of mind or body, those who chose to attend were, indeed, celebratory, but without exception willing also to agree that there had been some gross overstepping of moral boundaries in the war, and not just by the enemy. That service persuaded me that going into uniform had been the right thing to do.

I noted earlier that I was finally cut down to size. The cutter was not Chaplain Rafferty, but the second-in-command, J. Floyd Dreith, a three-striper career chaplain who was a Missouri Synod Lutheran, all of which meant to me that J. Floyd Dreith was not an individual to tangle with on matters of discipline. Chaplain Fleming and I had been put in charge of arranging the final service of Holy Communion before our graduation. The "given" in this assignment was a carefully calibrated time within which the whole service had to be completed—0725 to 0750 as I remember it. We chose someone to read the Scripture, and he read interminably. The chaplain whom we had asked to do a "brief homily" failed to honor the adjective we had tried to stress. When we distributed bread and wine it seemed as though each communicant was reliving his whole life before deciding whether or not he was worthy to receive. To sum it all up, we went twelve minutes overtime.

I was not happy about this, but I was even less happy when I heard over the PA system that Chaplains Brown and Fleming were to report to Chaplain Dreith's office on the double. Chaplain Dreith was not so much angry as disappointed. He was very clear that what had happened was inexcusable. It might seem a small thing at NTS(CH), he went on, but suppose we had been on an aircraft carrier and a strike was due to leave at exactly 0750 hours, and they had been forced to wait until 0802 hours before taking off. The entire mission might have been jeopardized and American lives lost. Furthermore, our failure to "perform our mission successfully" (his exact words) was an unpleasant foretaste of how we might fail yet again on other presumably routine assignments.

Suppose we didn't hurry if informed over the ship's PA system that we were to report to sick bay on the double, and a sailor died without the ministrations of a chaplain?

The examples continued to pile up as Chaplain Dreith gave it to us with both barrels. In his summation, he reminded us that it was the little things that demonstrated one's true character, and the example he chose was shoe shining. Show me a man with unshined shoes, he seemed to be telling us, and I'll show you a man with a major character flaw. I was relieved by the summation. If shoe shining was the ultimate criterion, we weren't confronting the end of the world. Perhaps no expulsion from the Chaplains Corps awaited us after all. And it didn't. The interview ended with Chaplain Dreith assuring us that he never wanted to hear at any time in the future that we had been so forgetful of a Navy timetable as today. Class dismissed.

I learned something else from that experience about the Navy. Officers, at least good officers, don't hold grudges. For the remaining couple of days before our graduation ceremonies, when our wives were permitted to be present, I did my best to avoid even minimal eye contact with J. Floyd Dreith. But at the celebration, I had to introduce Sydney to him, fearing that she would be told to work on my sense of responsibility for the lives of my friends. Not a bit of it. Chaplain Dreith was cordial not only to Sydney but to me as well, and even had words for both of us about "the splendid record" I had at NTS(CH). Months later, at the district chaplain's office in San Francisco, J. Floyd Dreith came on board as the new CO, thus having jurisdiction over me. After reestablishing rapport with him, I got up my courage and asked him about the incident described above. He said he had no recollection of it. I believed him.

About a week before graduation we had to go through an interview with chaplains "from the outside," who could help determine, from talking to us individually, what our first duty station would be. I was in a delicate position here. Particularly after three months away from Sydney, the personal side of me wanted desperately to be assigned some kind of shore duty where we could be together. Another side of me (the Calvinist side) remained troubled that I had in effect "sat out the war" while others had been exposed to hardships, physical dangers, and even death. I rationalized part of what had happened to me by remembering that when I decided to go into the chaplaincy all the experts were sure that the war in the Pacific would not be over for at least two more years, and that I would surely have my share of action in the Pacific theatre before the war was over. Part of me said I should ask specifically for duty overseas or on a ship, while another part of me felt that such a posture was pretty damn phony, since there is a long distance between actually facing danger and going through the motions with none of the threat. I tried to explain the dilemma to the examining board, and had to conclude for myself that I would accept their decision—which was the only real option I had anyway.

Their response, announced two days later, was to order me to report to the district chaplain's office in San Francisco—a desk job. I don't know to this day whether it was designated as a reprieve or a reprimand. But either way, it had one big plus: Sydney would be there too. We found a one-room apartment in Berkeley, and figured that with its high ceiling, we would have had more floor space if we could have turned it on its side. But we were together, and when you are together, who needs lots of room? A routine developed. I commuted across the bay on the "F" train and then took a trolley to 895 Market Street, while Sydney got a job working in a child care center in north Berkeley. Weekends were pretty much our own, and we made friends, such as Brooke and Wendell Mordy, who have been part of our lives ever since.

It would have been a routine experience at the district chaplain's office, save for two things. The first was an often-repeated assignment that was both heartwarming and terrifying. At least thirty times I was sent out on the pilot boat, beyond the Golden Gate Bridge, to meet an incoming Navy ship bringing men back from the Pacific theatre for discharge. My task was to take Red Cross messages to men on board, or other materials that they needed and didn't have on hand, and see what could be done for the chaplain on the particular ship. I was the purveyor of good news ("Your wife will be at the pier; be sure to look for her"), but not always ("Your mother died of a stroke").

Each arrival at a pier in San Francisco was the occasion of jubilation. Some of the men had been overseas for as long as three years without leave. At every such sentimental arrival there would be a band, streamers, cheers, waves, and often tears, but in this case almost always tears of joy. Thirty times I vicariously experienced this joy and abandon. (On one occasion I was even able to go down into the engine room of the USS *Kingsbury* [APA 227] and tap Ralph Weber, one of my college roommates, on the shoulder. He didn't even know we were in the same hemisphere.) Such wonderful, healing, creative moments for all the returnees thrilled me empathetically.

But there was a price attached. As the pilot boat swung alongside battleship, carrier, or whatever, a Jacob's Ladder, as it was called, would be lowered from the quarterdeck. As the pilot boat went up and down very rapidly, I had to grasp hold of the ladder and start climbing, interminably it seemed to me, without even once daring to look up or down, hoping that I'd make it, but sure that one of these times, I wouldn't. This was always a terrifying experience. The reason: I can't stand heights. Anything above ten feet off the ground paralyzes me. There could have been no more fitting torture devised for me in any setting than to have been forced to climb the equivalent of Jacob's Ladder, swaying perilously from start to finish. That has remained, until this moment, the best-kept secret of my Navy experience.

The second redeeming feature grew out of a bit of contention I had with the head chaplain over what kind of "counseling" we were supposed to be doing, and (so I have always thought) as a kind of reprimand, he assigned me to duty in one of the areas under the jurisdiction of the district chaplain's office that was not eagerly sought after. This was to be chaplain to the naval vessel USS *North* (YBF 46). The USS *North* was an old San Francisco Bay ferry boat (I'm not making this up) that had been refurbished to provide living quarters for Navy personnel who did stevedore (deckhand) work on the San Francisco docks leased by the Navy. One day a week a chaplain was supposed to show up for a couple of hours to deal with complaints or requests, and was also to show up to conduct Sunday worship services.

These were still the days of the Jim Crow Navy, and not included in the above description is one elemental fact: All the men on board were black. There was one officer, a two-striper, who was, of course, white. It is hard to work within a structure that one feels is unjust, but I had had to deal with that problem in macrocosm by going into the Navy in the first place. There was nothing to be gained by disputing the reality of the microcosm represented by the USS *North*. It was there, it was going to remain there, and there might even be some things that could be done on it, even within a restrictive structure like the U.S. Navy.

On my first Sunday, four men showed up for the service. This, I learned, was a good turnout. Here I made a snap decision. I hadn't rehearsed it ahead of time, since I hadn't known what to expect, but I decided that from the start we needed to be very honest with each other. So at "sermon time" I spoke informally about how we were all living within a racist structure and that things within that structure were unlikely to change very much over the next few months. But all of us were going to get out of that structure within a few months when we got discharged, at which time, alas, we would be leaving a small racist structure—the U.S. Navy—for a very large racist structure—the USA. I asked a question: How could we best use the present time to prepare for this future time? What did they have to suggest?

My prayers were answered; the men started to talk. I had feared stony silence. We began to compose a list: Reinstitute the literacy program that had gotten bogged down; invite black speakers from the Bay Area to share the kinds of problems and rebuffs ex-Navy men would experience; make contacts with agencies in the Bay Area who could help with job placements, educational opportunities under the GI Bill, and so forth. I asked the four men to try to get the word out. They got the word out. Next Sunday there were fourteen in church.

We were on our way. I was very fortunate to discover a Union Seminary classmate, John Doggett, who was pastor of a black church at Hunter's Point, right by the Navy shipyard. He came to speak to our group. We had a bumper turnout, and among other things he invited us to visit his church and meet folks there.

Impressed by the musical talent on board, I got a choir going, and pretty soon we were doing things like the Black National Anthem, "Lift Every Voice and Sing," along with other examples of black choral music. We even sang at a couple of white churches, with transportation provided by Navy buses the district chaplain's office had enough clout to commandeer on Sundays.

At Christmas we had a party, including the setting up of a creche. I darkened the faces of Mary, Joseph, and Jesus to make the point in my sermon that Jesus was dark skinned and had a clearer identification with black folks than with me. (The white lieutenant didn't like that at all.) We had another source of outside help for the party, and on other occasions as well. I had made the acquaintance of a wonderful Jewish woman in San Francisco, a Mrs. Heller, who was interested in the plight of such men and the possibilities for them after discharge. She was generosity itself, giving me several hundred dollars before Christmas to provide a fund from which men with children could buy presents for them.

This time on the USS *North* was probably the best experience of being pastor to a parish that I have ever had. How it came together I don't know, but there was clearly something of the grace of God behind it all, and those two days a week down at the docks more than compensated for the routine task of sitting behind a desk at 895 Market Street. It began to look as though this would be the closest I would ever get to "sea duty," and I think it would have sufficed. But I was still excited when one day toward the end of February I received orders to the USS *Bollinger* (APA 234), a troop transport, presently anchored in San Francisco Bay, and due to leave in two or three days for Pearl Harbor as part of the "Magic Carpet," the group of ships bringing men home from overseas for discharge. It took me about thirty seconds to realize that the next time I came through the Golden Gate Bridge I wouldn't be dependent on a Jacob's Ladder, and then Sydney and I would once again be reunited.

For about six months the *Bollinger* was my home. Its assignment was to bring troops from combat areas back to the States for discharge. Three times we went to sea almost empty and returned loaded to the gills (the bunks in the forward compartment were six high). Meals for more than two thousand guest troops were being served most of the daylight hours. When the troops weren't standing in chow lines, their main task was to avoid being underfoot when the regular crew was trying to keep things shipshape. Every evening there were back-to-back showings of the same movie. In the afternoons there would frequently be a "happy hour," in which any men with discoverable talents would be invited and even cajoled into performing—invited and cajoled by the chaplain, who found out that this was one of his "collateral assignments" and who realized also that he would be held accountable by the captain for whatever was said or done on such occasions. "So it would be a great help to the chaplain," I would say, "if the humor could be kept reasonably clean." While all these things were going on, the ship itself was touching a variety of ports—two or three stops at Pearl Harbor, San Diego, Sasebo, Kwajalein, Bikini, San Francisco, and discharge.

The captain of the *Bollinger* was a kind and devout Roman Catholic, William J. Richter, a veteran of combat duty in the war, who made no secret of the fact, when I presented myself, that he was disappointed that the new chaplain was not a Roman Catholic. Fortunately, he seemed more inclined to blame the Navy rather than me for such a snafu. As far as I was concerned, we had a good relationship, though he must have felt me young and ill-equipped for the job.

On one level, my own life on board the *Bollinger* was almost perpetually unpleasant due to the presence of an officer (whose name in the spirit of undeserved charity I shall not disclose) I will refer to as "Lt. Nemesis." Since much of what I did or requested had to be approved by him, we had constant clashes. Theologically, I have been heard to describe him as a living vindication of the doctrine of original sin. I shall not document the charge in detail; there are some deeply buried memories I am not yet equipped to exorcise. I will confine myself to the final and most overt clash we had, which came shortly before my discharge. When I discovered a locker full of musical instruments on the *Bollinger*, I was able promptly to match the trumpet to one of the black members of the crew who was exceptionally talented. Lt. Nemesis hit the overhead at the thought of one of "them jigs" (his invariable term for blacks) using a mouthpiece that would be shared with white musicians. Employing a device I should have had the savvy to use months earlier, I sent a memo to the captain, which had to be routed through Lt. Nemesis and had to be forwarded by him, with any comments he wished to make. I protested the judgment that band instruments would be reserved for whites, and requested clarification from the captain about what was to be the policy concerning interracial use of the ship's instruments.

A very mollified Lt. Nemesis appeared at my cabin door about five seconds after the memo appeared on his desk. He assured me that there was no problem, and agreed with me that all sailors should have access to all instruments. Given this manifest change of heart, at least for the purposes of having a ship's band, I figured I had gotten the assurance I needed, and told him that I would withdraw the memo to the captain, provided we had a clear understanding that nobody would be denied the use of the instruments because of race.

I had a strong personal reaction the first time I sailed on the *Bollinger* past Treasure Island, under the Golden Gate Bridge, and into the Pacific Ocean on a dingy Friday morning in February 1946. I have never been able to describe it to my own satisfaction, but something may be better than nothing. With all the backlog of my flips and flops over the war, over being separated from Sydney, over the likelihood of not getting sea duty, over having virtually missed the defining event of my generation, I realized as we entered the open sea that "this can never *not* have happened. It will never be the case that I didn't have sea duty. No matter what happens on this trip, or where we get, it will always be true that I was there." This will certainly never be carved in stone, but in terms of who I am, it should perhaps be tattooed somewhere. It had become very important to me to share, as fully as I could, the experience of my generation. I was not trying to squeeze in an appearance on the pages of history; I was simply describing a reinforcement within my own psyche that I needed to articulate.

The first test for old 446549 came the same evening. Here I was, the gold on my braid still shiny instead of salt-caked with brine, fearful every time I opened my mouth that I'd say "left" or "right," instead of "port" or "starboard," making my first tour of the ship which, they had told us back in NTS(CH), was the best way to develop a "presence" on board, maybe even as time passed, to create some personal trust.

One of the first places I entered was the chiefs' wardroom. The chiefs are the heart of the Navy—not line officers like ensigns and commanders, not enlisted men like seamen third class or shipfitters first class, but "chiefs," men who have often put in twenty years. They are the real veterans, the ones who always know what the score is, not to mention the ones who can give you a really hard time if you don't know the score too.

I was greeted immediately, and asked if I would like a mug of coffee. I knew, once again from NTS(CH), that there are six or eight places on board any ship where coffee is always available and that every coffee maker thinks, nay, knows, that no coffee elsewhere surpasses his. So one always has to accept a mug of coffee, and always has to praise it for its exceptionally fine aroma and taste. Would I like a mug of coffee? Of course I would.

The mug was gargantuan, the coffee strong beyond anything that might ever previously have occurred to the mind of man. I had the feeling that if I put the spoon in the middle of the mug it would remain upright without help from an external force. I was simultaneously becoming conscious of what are called the "ground swells" off the coast of California, a part of the Pacific Ocean that is exceptionally rough. Never before having had to acquire "sea legs," I realized two things immediately: (1) It was going to be a long time before I could stand up without losing my balance, and (2) it was going to be a short time before the coffee inside me reversed direction and dishonored me. I would be forever known as the greenhorn "boy chaplain" who got seasick the first time he encountered a ground swell.

There was no way I could not finish that mug, and there was no way I could make it out of the chiefs' quarters without falling on my face. We spent a long evening together. I began to feel more at ease with the ground swells. I had no choice but to drain the mug and essay to leave without losing my balance. I made it by the grace of God, my reputation intact, or at least not yet compromised. It was a significant rite of passage. As I made my way from stern to prow the next day, I had at least five mugs of coffee before the noon hour, each, of course, better than its predecessor, though I couldn't risk such comparative judgment openly.

The days on the *Bollinger* coalesce in retrospect. When we were not carrying troops, life was idyllic, especially on beautiful sunny days ("shippin-over weather" the Navy regulars call it), the kind of days when you think about signing on for another four-year hitch. We also experienced the excitement of storms, and we had a real one between Tokyo and Sasebo, a trip that took four days, with pitching and tossing and very little sign of the land we knew was precariously near. I remember lying in my bunk at night, watching the heavy chain on my closet door swinging out from the cabinet, further and further, and realizing that if it ever got to the place where the chain was at right angles to the door, that would be a sign that we were in deep trouble.

I remember the excitement of watching the flying fish and the dolphins accompanying us for many hours, and the phosphorescent glow in the waves at night as the bow parted the waters. Toward the end of a long day with troops, when I was dead tired, I would sometimes go to the very farthest point on the prow to be alone, feeling the ship rise and fall, rise and fall (perhaps a differential of thirty to fifty feet) as it rode over one wave and plunged into another. There was occasional conversation with Phil Reilly, a Roman Catholic who had also had to wrestle with the conscientious objector question; with "Doc" Brown, the ship's doctor, who not only came to services but to Holy Communion as well; and with Bill Shambroom, a Jewish man who was one of the few people I ever met again after discharge. On the last trip, a close college friend, Otis Cary, turned up among the troops. Oat had grown up in Japan, was totally bilingual, and had been a translator in the interrogation of Japanese prisoners of war.

Every time I was summoned to the radio shack I knew that there had been a death in someone's family and I was the designated person to break the news to the sailor on board. I'm not very good at this (who is?). In one case there was a Jew whose father had died, and we read the Psalms together each afternoon in my cabin for the remainder of the trip.

These trips contained one nice light touch. Coming back from Japan we would cross the international date line and repeat the day just finished. Looking ahead, I once figured out that we would be crossing the date line almost exactly on Sydney's and my wedding anniversary. Gathering my courage, I asked the captain if the day we repeated could be June 21, and he found that he could make this determination without stretching the truth. So I got a second wedding anniversary that year and have been one ahead of Sydney ever since.

We had services on board every Sunday, whether in port or not, so I had lots of chances to preach. We got to Kwajalein on Trinity Sunday, and I tried to use our experience of getting to know Kwajalein as an analogy for getting to know the triune God. It was a dud, as Doc Brown told me: "*That* one came a cropper." But as all of us came closer to discharge, my sermonic theme, in any number of variations, became, "What will you do with a spared life, you who might have been killed and were not?"

In addition to Sunday morning services we also had an informal hymn sing on the fantail every Sunday evening. I had a wonderful chaplain's assistant named Larson who could play everything, and so we could honor all requests. The most frequently requested hymn was "The Old Rugged Cross." It had never been a favorite of mine, but it soon became positioned in my psyche right next to Larson, the portable organ, a dozen or so men singing, and on one trip Chaplain David Chambers with his trumpet. The hymn can bring a lump to my throat even today. We always closed with the Navy hymn, "Eternal Father, Strong to Save," and it also became indelibly a part of who I am as a Christian. There was a nice double entendre after the creation of the women's branch of the Navy, the WAVES (Women Appointed for Volunteer Emergency Service). The initial declaration of the hymn soon became an interrogation: "Eternal Father, strong to save, *whose* arm shall bind the restless WAVE?"

On a number of occasions there were Bible study classes. The most memorable of these occurred on the trip home from Japan, when a bunch of Marines asked if we could have a Bible study group on the Gospel of John. Never before had I heard any such request from the lips of Marines, so I quickly acquiesced. Each morning for an hour, we used a stern compartment, Blue Seven, to ponder the meaning of the incarnation. Toward the end of the trip we got to the eleventh chapter of John, which describes the raising of Lazarus from the dead—not exactly an easy passage to understand. I suggested that the event was Jesus' acting out that he was the resurrection and the life, and that more important than the reanimation of a corpse in AD 30 was whether or not Jesus' claim was true for us in 1946. I also told a story from Dostoevski's *Crime and Punishment* in which Raskolnikov, having killed an old woman and thereby destroyed himself as well, is restored to life by Sonya's reading of this gospel story to him.

There was a little discussion, but after the session in Blue Seven broke up, one Marine followed me back to my cabin. After a few false starts, the story came out. He had left his fiancée in Iowa and had spent a long time in the Pacific and later with the occupation forces in Japan. He had gotten bored and gone to a brothel, and felt that in so doing he had ruined his life; he was one of the walking dead. And every day he was getting closer to home and the woman he felt he had betrayed. Then he said something like this: "Padre, everything we read this morning pointed directly at me. I've been living in hell for the last six months. I've been dead, but after reading about Jesus and Lazarus, I know that I'm alive again. The resurrection Jesus was talking about is real right now."

When he left my cabin, he and I both knew there would be some hard times ahead, and things wouldn't automatically become easy, but we knew also that he could deal with them now. And I knew that in Blue Seven on the ship on that day in the middle of the Pacific Ocean, the miracle of resurrection had taken place. Jesus' words were true: "He that believeth in me, though he were dead, yet shall he live."

On our trip to Japan we came into Sasebo harbor in the early morning of Easter Sunday. After going through a terrible storm, we entered a harbor of unbelievable beauty, with tiny islands dotting the channel, and we tied up alongside a huge shed that had been utterly demolished by U.S. bombs. It was a macabre setting for an Easter service, which we had on the open deck in full view of the ruins. We were clearly living in a pre-Easter world in which death—or at least the marks of death—were still triumphant. This was actually not a bad location to look for pointers beyond human destruction.

We were to be in Sasebo about a week. Shore leave would be granted each day to half the crew. Looking at a map, I discovered that Nagasaki was within a couple of hours of Sasebo by train, always assuming, of course, that the rails had not been pulverized by our bombs. In ways I don't remember, I got information and tickets for any personnel who would like to visit Nagasaki, the site of the destruction by our second atomic bomb. No "tour" could be set up, but we could have three or four hours to explore the city and still make the last train back to the ship.

That day ranks as one of the most important in my life. I don't know what I was expecting to find, but the impact was beyond anything I could have foreseen. Initially, I was surprised when the train stopped out in the barren countryside, and we were told that it was the end of the line. It took me a while to realize that this had been downtown Nagasaki before the bomb. Nagasaki was in a bowl or basin surrounded by hills, so that there had not only been the original explosion, but the massive sound waves had bounced back from the surrounding hills and hit the city a second time, leveling still more buildings in their wake. *There was nothing there*, until we got into the area of the city that had been hit only by "conventional" bombs. There were damaged buildings, twisted frames, massive amounts of rubble still not cleared away, and who knows how many thousands of dead Japanese still not unearthed.

I was in uniform, and I felt sadness and embarrassment and shame.

I know the conventional wisdom: The atomic bomb ended the war. I even felt some of this on the night in Norfolk when we stacked the bodies of sailors who had passed out. But after several hours of looking at Nagasaki I began to reflect that we could have made the point about the bomb's destructive capacity by announcing that we would drop one on an isolated area and let Japanese inspection teams relay a message about its massive destructiveness. There is no excuse whatever—moral, military, psychological, or geopolitical—for dropping an atomic bomb on a city.

There was one more event of worldwide importance with which I rubbed shoulders simply by luck of the draw. After we got back from Japan and were briefly in dry dock at Hunter's Point, we got word that we would soon leave to pick up troops at Kwajalein and Bikini, atolls of eye-catching beauty. The first had been subject to invasion by U.S. forces to oust the Japanese, who had taken over shortly after the events at Pearl Harbor. As a result, Kwajalein was still littered with discarded invasion tanks, landing craft, barges, and all kinds of other equipment that figure in an amphibious attack.

Bikini, however, had not figured in our war strategy and had thus escaped unscathed. But a wartime survivor may become a peacetime casualty, and this was Bikini's fate. Shortly after we were there, the first atomic bomb exploded in peacetime was detonated nine hundred feet above a huge flotilla of deserted Navy ships so that the impact of such a blast could be measured and studied.

The USS *Bollinger* (APA 234) was the last ship with human cargo to leave before the explosion. Our job had been to gather up troops eligible for discharge and ferry them back to a West Coast port. It need hardly be remarked that we instantly became the most popular ship in the whole Pacific theatre. Everybody wanted out from Bikini before the explosion. There were some good reasons for this attitude: Nobody knew what the blast would do to the assembled ships, or to the coral reef, or to personnel located on the periphery of the blast, or to the Pacific Ocean itself. The worst-case scenario posited the creation of a monstrous tidal wave that would engulf everything within its path and swamp even the fleetest of the departees.

So everybody in that beautiful lagoon had a vested interest in leaving aboard the APA 234, in what was informally known as Operation Getting the Hell Out of Here. Somewhere, people were monitoring the requests for discharge, which would have been hard enough work back home without all the pressures of haste and the likelihood of human error. Thousands must have been disappointed not to make the first cut, but eventually everyone had to be off the island.

My exalted role in this historic endeavor was to shop around other vessels soon to leave, and trade fifteen of our movies for fifteen of theirs, thus making sure our own crew and troops got topflight entertainment on the way home. Unlike most of those on the ship, I was actually able to set foot on Bikini itself, tracking down an elusive cache of movies. There were few indigenous people still left, and those who were still there would soon be evacuated by our troops and shipped out of range, until they could be established on Rosperik, another atoll picked out for them. Needless to say, those who were still there did not have movies very high on their list of priorities, and my presence on such a mission seemed to me a kind of impertinence. I had only a couple of hours to explore briefly this tropical paradise that was soon to be rendered uninhabitable by a single boom—a paradise lost and never to be regained.

When we finally left Bikini a few days later, we had two thousand troops and fifteen movies. I watched the area slowly dipping out of sight at the horizon—a replay in reverse of our arrival. I saw dozens of vessels silhouetted against the western sky, all carefully positioned in relation to a central spot where the bomb would be exploded. These ships, of course, were now without personnel on board, all of whom were now concentrated on a few ships past the periphery of the projected destruction. After the explosion, teams with protective clothing and all manner of instruments would check the consequence of the blast and study the data for information that would provide defense in case of an atomic war in the future.

There was a lot of guesswork here. Nobody knew what the extent of the bomb's damage would be over water. But even so, the destruction was awful, as photographs showed—twisted wreckage and a mushroom cloud above the once-mighty naval vessels, now tossing like corks in a giant bathtub.

My immediate feelings about the tests at Bikini were fairly positive. Important data would be recorded, and appropriate defensive maneuvers developed, the sole object of which would be to save lives. Indeed, though the idea only flashed in the edge of my consciousness, the results might be so devastating that they would hasten a decision by all nations to make sure that there never was a situation in which the renewed use of atomic weapons would be thinkable. But as the years have passed, my subsequent reflections have turned the Bikini experiment into an event which is surrounded by so much immorality that I wish I had never been involved. This ambiguity concerns the price in human lives we are willing to pay to keep control of the world. In the case of Bikini, the "price" involved the forcible evacuation of an entire island's residents to another atoll not of their own choosing, and the Bikini atoll is still so hazardous with radioactive material that it is unsuitable for habitation and will remain so long after the death of its youngest inhabitants at the time of the blast.

What legal screen enabled our government to take such action has been hidden from me for over half a century. For when we begin to say that what is in our national interest automatically has priority over everybody else's interest—even if the "everybody else" is only a small cluster of native people, innocent of any wrongdoing against us—when we begin to think like that, we are on the brink of a moral decline that will utterly destroy us.

And there are more long-range consequences of the testing that have received very little publicity. There is so much radioactivity in the area that even on their new atoll the former residents of Bikini have been subjected to the birth of children with physical defects, such as babies born without spinal structure, who live only a few hours, and for whom there can never be measurable "recompense" or assuagement of maternal and paternal grief. We have no right to impose our will on other nations in these ways.

By the time of our return from Bikini in June 1946, even I, latecomer though I was, had enough points for discharge from the Navy. And when I landed at San Francisco this time, there was Sydney on the pier along with Brooke and Wendell Mordy. And I was now the legitimate recipient of the band, the streamers, the yells, and tears that only a few months earlier I had enjoyed vicariously with thousands of others at their homecoming. I was so eager to embrace the folks on the pier that after saluting the flag at the stern of the *Bollinger* for what I knew would be the last time, I turned and started down the gangway with such single-minded determination that I tripped and fell headlong, baggage flying in all directions, to the intense amusement and prolonged cheers of all those within eyesight. Everything exuded joy except my shinbone.

During the Korean War, I was on what was rather alarmingly called "ready reserve," meaning that I could have been called up to active duty at any time. But with the passing of the years, the choices began to get murky again. A position described as "nuclear pacifism" began to emerge among ethicists. It was argued that any use of nuclear weapons would inflict so much damage, whether used aggressively or defensively, that it could not possibly be justified either morally or geopolitically. This argument in turn reactivated appeals to the historic criteria for a "just war," and it was increasingly evident in the nuclear era that none of the historic criteria could be used to justify the use of nuclear weapons.

The implications of this conclusion could not of course be demonstrated in advance, and took a bit of a bite out of the extension of the argument. But even so, the destructive capacity of newly designed so-called conventional weapons had itself escalated to horrifying new dimensions. In the recent wars of the United States—in Vietnam, Grenada, Panama, and Iraq—nuclear weapons were not used, but the destructive power employed and the moral ambiguity of each instance of U.S. armed aggression provides a whole new set of data to suggest that war is not only passe, but intrinsically evil. One could hardly argue that there was any case—moral, military, economic, or political—for Mr. Bush's war against Panama, which resulted in massive Panamanian casualties and devastated portions of the country that are as yet unrebuilt.

Through all these arguments, and the wars that highlighted these arguments, it was becoming clearer to me that there could be no war the United States could enter in which one could any longer morally participate. That conclusion was surely well in place by the time of Vietnam and securely fixed before the war was over.

I do not call this a "pacifist" position, because I still must allow for the moral possibility of a small beleaguered country feeling that "as a last resort" it must aggressively oppose an opponent that seeks to engulf or destroy it. To be quite specific, I think that the war waged in Nicaragua by the Sandinistas to oust the Somoza government after forty years—a war that succeeded in that limited objective—was more just, or at least less unjust, than to let the Somoza regime remain in power for another forty years. And the social revolution that the Sandinistas tried to inaugurate—schools, clinics, jobs, literacy, and so on— would have worked had not our own government determined that a Sandinista victory could not be allowed to stand, a judgment that is a blot on our national record that will always remain as an incriminating symbol.

Peter: I remember asking my dad about his war experience (I must have been five and back at Macalester), about whether he had shot anyone or not—which seemed to me at the time to be the point of war. I was somewhat disappointed when he told me that he had not. I said "No one?" And he sat down and talked to me, obviously troubled by my response, about war and human life. I also remember stomping on an ant bed up at Heath at about the same age and my dad looking at me with concern and asking how I would feel if a big giant came along and stomped on my house. I never did it again.

The only story that he was able to recall that in a minor way jibed with what I thought his experience with war should have been, concerned the only time that his boat, the Bollinger, *did any shooting. After the war was over, while riding this troop transport back to Japan, someone on board noticed a mine floating in the water. The gunnery crew was brought on deck and they shot at it, and apparently missed repeatedly—and my dad was standing by as the gun was shot. This still was a very unsatisfying story to relate to my friends, but at least a gun had been fired. My friend Gerald Taylor, back at P.S. 125, had told me that his father had been eaten by a lion in Africa.*

However, our favorite war story about my dad he told much later. (And he wrote about his experiences on the Bollinger *brilliantly for the* New Yorker.*) When he was climbing down the Jacob's Ladder for shore leave in Yokohama, an activity that terrified him, his chief, a man he hated, slouched his belly over the side and yelled, "Be sure you keep out of them cathouses, Padre!" I can just imagine my dad clinging to those ropes—livid—but still, way back in his mind, appreciative of a good line.*

4

After the War:
Amherst, Union, and Macalester

After being discharged from the Navy I accepted two half-time jobs in Amherst—assistant pastor at the First Congregational Church and assistant chaplain for religious activities at Amherst College. My long-range vocational interests moved between preaching and teaching, so to work in both a church and a college was fortuitous.

At the end of the first year, Roy Pearson, the pastor at First Congregational Church, left to take a pastorate elsewhere, which meant that until a successor had been found I was "acting pastor." Roy was a tough act to follow, scoring about a 99 percent in every aspect of pastoral care and preaching, but as a result of his departure I got a more detailed look at what it would be like to preach regularly, run a church office, call on the sick, baptize the young, bury the dead, marry the living, and twenty or thirty other things that went with the territory of being a pastor.

Throughout the two years I spent at First Congregational Church, I had a chance to hone my preaching skills with the children's sermon. I created a character called "Jonathan the Bear," and frequently created theological mayhem by retelling Bible stories or making deft points in the guise of this talking bear. It so happened that there was a boy in the church named Jonathan Tuttle, for whom these sermons were an occasion of pleasure, and many years later at a peace rally in Chicago, a huge bearded demonstrator come up to me, gave me what can accurately be called a "bear hug," and said, "I'm Jonathan the Bear."

As assistant chaplain at Amherst, I worked under John Coburn, who was also rector of Grace Church Episcopal, on the village green. John went on to be the dean of a cathedral, dean of a divinity school, and (with a certain inevitability considering his talents) a bishop. John's pastoral instincts and intellectual equipment were both of the highest order, and even the most casual conversation with him would open new windows on the life of faith.

He and I came to Amherst simultaneously as naval reserve retirees, and our interests were complementary. He liked to run retreats; I liked to run study groups. Among other things, our duties involved preaching at daily chapel—daily *required* chapel, a torture device calculated to make every ordained person raise new questions about the validity of that "call" to ministry. There is nothing colder than a place of worship filled with persons who are there under duress. One day, while President Cole and I were robing before chapel, he asked me what I was going to speak about. "Drinking," I said, and saw him visibly wince, worried, I am sure, that a temperance lecture was in the offing. My theme, though, was that drinking, *excessive* drinking, that is, usually unmasks or telegraphs some deeper kind of unwillingness to face life without artificial props. (The fact that I had a great quote from Kierkegaard about anxiety may have helped.) That sermon worked, descriptively, for at least a few, and I cite it because there were so few others worth citing. Indeed, on this occasion, a much-relieved President Cole thanked me.

I learned another thing out of the mix of those two years. An elderly member of the church lost his wife, and I had the funeral service on a Thursday. I prepared a rousing sermon on race relations for the following Sunday, and that morning as I walked up to the pulpit, I saw the widower sitting in the second pew on the left, back in church to hear good news. I realized, appalled, that I had none within the sermon, and that even though there were words of comfort elsewhere in the service, I needed to take more seriously that a sermon, if it has some bad news, had better have some good news too, and vice versa.

In the meantime, I was also getting a taste of the academic side of things as an assistant to Al Martin, professor of religion, who had preceded me at Union by a few years. I taught small sections of his introductory course, read papers and exams, met with students over term paper topics, and once, when Al was away, gave the lecture to the entire class. The material under consideration was the text of Isaiah 2, surely the noblest of all the Hebrew Scriptures. I put in at least twenty hours preparing for a fifty-minute presentation, and enjoyed every minute of it. When I got home that day, Sydney took one look at my face and said with utter accuracy, "I think you've discovered what Tiggers like best." While that single lecture did not provide instant epiphany, it was a significant clearing of the air.

On one occasion, my vocational explorations received a terrific impetus when a woman in the church told me one day she was sorry I was leaving "the active ministry" to go into teaching. Periodically, I think of yet another response I wish I'd made to that devastatingly inaccurate remark. Roy and John gave me good advice and enabled me to see that I could still engage in a pastoral role through teaching. The matter for me was also the ever pressing problem of how faith and doubt are related. An attractive pair of alternatives presented themselves: In preaching you have to believe whatever you say, whereas in teaching you simply lay out the alternatives and let the students choose.

But I became surer and surer that for me, at least, this was the coward's way out. For it presupposed that there was some kind of "neutral" position from which one could teach, in which case commitment to the subject matter was not only unnecessary but unwise. On the contrary, I decided there was a faith-presupposition at work within every "neutral" or supposedly "nonbiased" conviction. One could *preach* from a stance that acknowledged all the difficulties of having faith, and one could *teach* from a stance that recognized implicit faith-commitments in every point of view, even the most skeptical. The sin in teaching was not "to believe something," the sin was to make personal adherence to that "something" a requirement for doing well. The dogmatism of the undogmatic was the real sin against the truth. It was helpful to get a preview of these concerns before starting a doctoral program, for they continued to vex me, and finally were resolved only in the doing, when, fifteen years later, I started teaching in a secular university.

Out of all this turmoil and testing, I applied for admission to the Columbia-Union PhD program, and was admitted. But something even more important was happening to Sydney and me during that second year in Amherst. After many false hopes, we were finally told definitively that Sydney was pregnant and that the baby would be born around the end of May or early June.

Now life was getting really interesting.

When Peter arrived at about 2:30 a.m. on June 5, 1948, I had something of the feeling I had experienced when the USS *Bollinger* took me under the Golden Gate Bridge: This can never *not* have happened. Here was an absolutely unique event in our lives, never before experienced and never to be repeated. We had a firstborn child. Two-thirty a.m. or not, I had to tell somebody. So when I got back to Amherst from the Northampton Hospital I started throwing small pebbles at the bedroom window of Chalmers and Pam Coe, next-door neighbors. If they thought privately that I could have waited until morning to share the good news, they were kind enough not to say so.

We spent the summer with my mother and grandmother at Jaffrey, New Hampshire, and it provided some elbow room to make the acquaintance of this long-sought and long-deferred gift named Peter. There was magic in every moment (well, *almost* every moment), when a new sound or gesture emanated from Peter. Three cheers for us, for having had the wisdom not to postpone his arrival until my dissertation was finished.

I received a year of academic credit toward a Columbia-Union doctorate from my three years of BD work and lacked only one further year of course work, plus language exams, and the writing of a doctoral dissertation. I had seen many of my friends trapped for years in the AFBTT ("all finished but the thesis") syndrome. I determined that I would complete the degree in not more than two years, rather than lugging an unfinished thesis into my first years of teaching. This played havoc with family life, parenting, and general enjoyment. It also initiated a hollow claim I was wont to trot out in moments of stress, frequently promised and seldom realized: "Things will be easier next year." Really? Ask Sydney.

The year was a perpetual round of classes, term papers, trips to Columbia, boning up for language exams, with only occasional respites to visit Sydney's sister and family in Connecticut or my mother in New Jersey, and we managed to include in this round of activities Peter's baptism by Reinhold Niebuhr.

The bane of the doctoral program at Columbia was completing four open-book written examinations for John Harman Randall's massive course on the history of philosophy. Students were known to have taken three years or more to complete them, and forty pages of single-spaced typewritten answers were not unknown. I vowed that I would not stoop to such folly, and that the exams would be done by the end of the first academic year so that I could single-mindedly deal with my dissertation.

Even though the dissertation was a project for the second year, it was imperative to carve out a topic during the first year, in order to get a jump on the summer. We got some unexpected help with this problem after making the acquaintance of Daniel and Nell Jenkins from England, who were spending a year at Union on Daniel's Commonwealth Fellowship. He had sharp and pungent comments on all things American, including American theology, which he held in rather low esteem, urging me to search for a thesis topic at least as far afield as Great Britain.

"Why not P. T. Forsyth?" he asked one day as we mulled over possible topics. Had I been totally honest, I would have responded, "Who is P. T. Forsyth?" But as he described Forsyth I felt a surge of interest. Forsyth was a product of the ultraliberal theology of nineteenth-century Great Britain. He had had a conversion that led him to a new theology that spoke both to heart and mind. I would later detect themes that resonated with Reinhold Niebuhr, but Daniel insisted that if there were a contemporary counterpart for Forsyth it was not Niebuhr but Karl Barth, and that Forsyth deserved to be described as "a Barthian before Barth." That tag seemed to fit pretty well, and my subsequent work on Forsyth gave me a free ride into Barth's concerns.

After reading several of Forsyth's recently reprinted volumes, I decided that he was my man, if the people on the Columbia side of Broadway wouldn't consider him too evangelical or, God forbid, too God-oriented. He used a lot of traditional vocabulary and wrote somewhat aphoristically, often in a subjunctive, without many footnotes. Fortunately, his statement about his intellectual development contained the phrase, "I immersed myself in the *Logic* of Hegel," which seemed to legitimate him on the far side of Broadway. There was another reason for picking Forsyth that I have never before admitted in public: He wrote in English. My struggle to get through the Columbia-Union language requirements had persuaded me that I would never attain sufficient mastery of French and German to have them as useful research tools. The thought of doing the project in my mother tongue seemed as realistic as it was preferable.

On August 15 we learned that I had been awarded a Fulbright Grant for study in the United Kingdom. Hard on the heels of it came more good news. We had had to book passage across the Atlantic on a troop transport—men in one compartment, women and children in the other—for a journey of ten days. Out of the blue, the Fulbright Office phoned us to say that Northwest Airlines would be displaying its new Boeing Stratocruiser in various European capitals, and was willing to fill up the overseas portion of the flight with free passage for students. Instead of ten days, the flight would take approximately ten hours. We decided that we could accommodate ourselves to the change of plans. In keeping with the surreal quality of this event, when the stewardess took our order for dinner somewhere over Nova Scotia, she asked, "Would the little boy like baby food or filet mignon?" We still attribute Peter's discriminating palate to the choice we made for him on that occasion.

OXFORD

In 1949 Britain was still recovering from the aftershock of war. Housing accommodations in Oxford, tight enough in ordinary times, were strained to the breaking point, particularly by the influx of "richamericans" using every trick they could to find a flat. I spent a full week pounding the pavements, contacting every "friend of a friend," running down all housing ads in the newspapers, even visiting widows of theologians with whose work I was familiar. I came close to renting a flat at 5 Folly Bridge, but was beaten out by another richamerican.

In desperation, I finally approached the pastor of the Summertown Congregational Church in north Oxford, on the grounds that my man Forsyth was also a Congregationalist. It turned out that the Rev. Mr. Moxley couldn't abide Forsyth's theology, but he commiserated with me over tea, expressing regret that their second-floor flat, presently being renovated, wouldn't be available for another six weeks. On bended knee, metaphorically at least, I assured him passionately that we would love to rent his flat and would find some place else to stay during the six-week interval. We stayed at a "private hotel" for the next three weeks, a ghastly period I consign to untapped memory. Once again Daniel Jenkins came to our aid. He saw how woebegone we were and immediately invited us to stay with his family in London until our flat was ready. This act of kindness saved our morale from utter collapse. Three weeks later we moved into a redecorated flat. It wasn't 5 Folly Bridge, but it was the bus stop for Squitchy Lane, so we were content.

We had apparently passed some cosmic rite of passage, for the rest of the year was one outpouring after another of friendship. Our landlady, Mrs. Moxley, acclimated us to shopping and banking, and when spring came she gave us a week at her seven-hundred-year-old thatched-roof cottage on the Isle of Wight (complete with a resident ghost whom we unfortunately never saw). I finished chapter 5 of the dissertation under that thatched roof. Early on in the greengrocer's shop, a woman named Marjorie Dimbleby heard Sydney having linguistic difficulties with a clerk and volunteered to help, then asked Sydney home for a cup of tea and initiated a friendship that deepened throughout the year. An American professor, Tom Mendenhall (later president of Smith College), fit his wife, three children, and we three Browns into a VW bug and showed us the Cotswolds. We gave a Thanksgiving party without ideological mishap, even after we realized that the event itself was no cause of thanksgiving in Great Britain. During Advent we went to carol services in various Oxford colleges, and found it rewarding in unexpected ways. The carols were almost entirely unfamiliar, and we learned a whole style of reflecting musically about the event in Bethlehem. *The Oxford Book of Carols* has been a staple for our home celebrations ever since.

During the fall and winter, I biked down each day to the Bodleian Library, where I made my way through fifty years of British religious periodicals. This was more complicated than it sounded. The materials could not be taken from the library, a typewriter could not be taken into the library, and the word "photocopy" had not yet been invented. I spent the second half of the year trying to decipher the mountain of handwritten notes I'd made during the first half.

I was a "fellow" at Mansfield College, the divinity school of the Free Church, habitually the Nonconformists; more bluntly, it was a "non-Anglican" residence. The principal, the Rev. Nathaniel Micklem, a venerable and wise Free Church theologian, acted as my tutor and read portions of the dissertation as they were completed. Another Mansfield don, Erik Routley, a church historian whose passion was music, was also helpful, and in later years when I taught a course on hymnody I had ample reason to rejoice in his prolific pen. The Free Church atmosphere at Mansfield was very different from the Anglican aura that hovered over most of the other colleges. I temporarily developed a love-hate relationship to Anglicans, most of whom, it seemed to me, were not quite aware that other branches of the Christian church existed, even with such luminaries as Micklem at Oxford and C. H. Dodd at Cambridge. An anonymous piece of doggerel floated about:

> Oh, nonconformist England,
> The land of Micklem and Dodd;
> Where Baptists speak only to Baptists,
> And Anglicans only to God.

For such unecumenical sentiments I was taken to task by Dr. Micklem himself. I had written (though only in a footnote) that "the Oxford University catalogue includes no course in Church History after the year 461 AD," to which I had appended the reflection, "Nothing important seems to have happened after that." Dr. Micklem admonished me: "Your statement may be true, Brown, but your comment concerning it is infelicitous." I still think that lip service at least should be paid to the Protestant Reformation, even at Oxford, and I continued to be agitated when, in any discussion of reunion, the Anglicans would say, after casting their eyes past the rest of us, that they would never consider changes to the structure of the one, holy, catholic, and apostolic church that would offend their "Roman brethren."

I mention these petty bickerings not to try to score points in retrospect, but to affirm that I nevertheless drank deeply at other Anglican wells and was refreshed.

The chief Anglican influence initiated at Oxford was Charles Williams, a lay Anglican employed by Oxford University Press, who deeply influenced such other lay Anglicans as C. S. Lewis and T. S. Eliot, not to mention Roman Catholics such as J. R. R. Tolkien, creator of hobbits and Middle-earth. Williams wrote seven novels, "supernatural thrillers" his friends called them, in which good and evil are projected out upon the universe for cosmic resolution.

C. S. Lewis was an influence on all of us in those years, whether we had been to Oxford or not. His public conversion was a mid-career fact that removed him from the "cultured despisers of religion" and made him one of its most ardent supporters. Whatever one felt about Lewis, he was never dull, and he was always provocative, two virtues I look for in vain among most professional theologians. He was at his best as a creator of imaginative fiction, especially the Narnia series for children, and a few "supernatural thrillers" of his own for adults, whereas his attempts at straight theology were less compelling. T. S. Eliot is *sui generis,* part of no "school," likewise converted to Anglicanism and displaying an ability to feel what nonbelievers feel. *Four Quartets* in particular has infinite meanings to plumb, as I know from fifty years after my first encounter with it.

My initial tutorial with Dr. Micklem almost never occurred. I discovered that a "tutorial" was a formal occasion, and that I must wear my "Oxford gown" to it. However, I possessed no Oxford gown. Indeed, I possessed no gown at all. I was caught in a catch-22: I could not see the principal without an Oxford gown, and I had no Oxford gown in which to see the principal. I tracked Dr. Micklem down in the neutral territory of a hallway and explained my dilemma. He slowed his pace long enough to reply, "No problem, Brown. Simply wear the gown of your American university." With mounting agitation, I sought the advice of my new landlord, the Rev. Charles Moxley. He was reassuring: "Don't worry, Brown. I'll loan you my Cambridge gown and nobody will know the difference." This cutting of the Gordian knot proved successful. If Dr. Micklem wondered about my strange apparel, he was kind enough not to press me for an explanation. (When a version of this episode appeared in the *New Yorker,* I felt that I should give a portion of the honorarium to Mansfield College for playing both by the letter and the spirit of the law. Dr. Micklem's reply to my small gift concluded, "So thank you again for sharing with us the moieties of your emoluments." I only had to look up two words.)

The Duke Humphrey's Library in the Bodleian is situated on the fourth floor, a beautiful room well calculated to nourish one's scholarly instincts. It is the only library in which I ever had to sign a pledge not to introduce firearms into the scholarly ambiance. No one ever had to be admonished to be quiet. Silence reigned unchallenged.

In the middle of one morning in the library, the dust of fifty years of British church periodicals began to engulf me, along with increasingly imperious calls of nature. I approached the young lady at the librarians' desk, and asked in muted terms appropriate to the surroundings, "Can you direct me to the men's lavat'ry?" giving the last word an impressive Oxonian twist only recently acquired. "What did you say?" she asked. Accelerating the importunity of my request, I asked more vigorously for "the men's lavat'ry," and could feel, if not see behind me, about fourteen scholarly heads being raised from their research either out of prurient interest or scholarly admonishment.

"Oh," she replied, "you must mean the gents room." As I responded in yet louder tones that I did indeed mean the "gents room," all seventeen faces disengaged from the life of research to make a brief foray back into the real world. Rather surprisingly, she continued our conversation with the words, "I haven't a clue where it is," surely a "proper" reaction for a lady librarian, but not one calculated to be of use to me. "Well," I responded, trying to speed up the tempo, "is there someone on the staff who would know?" At this moment, as though ordered by some divine being, a male librarian entered, and I directed my question to him.

"The men's lavat'ry?" he responded briskly. "Yes, sir. If you'll just go down the four flights of stairs by which you entered, and walk diagonally across the courtyard, you'll come to a door marked *Schola Linguarum Hebraicae et Graicae*, and if you'll just enter that door," he concluded triumphantly, "you'll find it." And, by George, I did.

While all these things were going on, Sydney had to do most of the shopping. (Why do I engage in such circumlocution? Sydney did *all* the shopping.) There was, for example, the matter of ordering the Christmas chicken. After arranging to pick one up the following week, she asked, almost in passing, "What will that come to?" Almost equally in passing, the butcher replied, "About two pounds." Sydney could visualize nothing but a scrawny neck and perhaps a couple of wings, until the butcher, reconsidering, said, "Or maybe two pounds sixpence."

We almost didn't get Peter back home. On the dock in Southampton, waiting to board the *Queen Elizabeth* (no free rides on the return trip), we were informed that there seemed to be an irregularity; there was no accommodation booked for Peter Brown. Lists were consulted, officials questioned, phone calls instigated, with no results forthcoming. Finally, remembering that using three names in Great Britain usually assumed that the last two were hyphenated, I said, "Look under the Ms." And sure enough, there he was: Master P. T. McAfee-Brown.

That night the Cunard Line served filet mignon. We had come full circle.

The boat ride home offered a chance to reflect on the thesis, finished save for retyping the first chapter. I had exceeded six hundred pages.

MACALESTER

Our last months in Oxford had been free of extreme stress, for Union offered me a one-year instructorship in theology. This was not only a chance to find out more about teaching but also to find a permanent job. Furthermore, it would help this neophyte's dossier to be able to list "Instructor in systematic theology, Union Theological Seminary" under the usually blank space headed "previous employment."

My luck continued. Early in the year Dr. Charles Turck, president of Macalester College in St. Paul, Minnesota, offered me the position of professor and head of the Department of Religion. This was a heady promontory from which to survey other possibilities, but I was content to have the matter settled. I have a hunch that Dr. Turck picked me despite the lack of a long track record because my aunt, Mildred McAfee, had been dean of students when he was president of Centre College in Kentucky, and he felt at home with the clan, especially in a Presbyterian setting. But there was a quirk to the offer: After being offered the job I was flown out to Minnesota to be looked over as a candidate. I learned later that this was not an unusual *modus operandi* for Dr. Turck, who frequently hired new faculty members on a hunch. The *ex post facto* screening process felt real, however, especially a long interview with Dr. Arnold Lowe, a formidable member of the Macalester Board of Trustees to whom I was very glad to be able to respond lightly that, yes, I had had two years of Greek.

Dr. Turck later introduced me to the dean of students: "Dean Doty, this is Mr. Brown. We are hoping Mr. Brown will be with us next year." She asked about "placement exams," which sounded a little strange since I had only recently defended my doctoral dissertation and had, so I thought, removed the word "examination" from my worry list. The conversation became more eccentric until Miss Doty herself recognized something amiss and said, "Oh, please excuse me. I thought Mr. Brown would be an entering freshman." So much for professorial dignity. I decided to consider it a compliment.

The salary for a department head in 1951 was $4,200 a year. We were eligible to live in "Macville," the GI barracks still standing after World War II, and when rental and heating oil were deducted, my take-home pay came to $202.50 a month. Fortunately for the family exchequer, I could get occasional preaching assignments on weekends, though this did not always raise my self-esteem. On a certain Sunday I arrived at a Presbyterian church north of Minneapolis, with plenty of time to go over the service of worship with the head deacon, whose chief responsibility was to arrange for the ushering and receiving of the morning offering. He pointed out to me that there was always one change in the printed program when they had a visiting preacher: The offering was moved up considerably nearer the beginning of the service. "That way," he explained shamelessly, "the deacons can count the offering while the sermon is being preached."

We settled into Macville and felt warmly received even in the chilling depths of what was a typical Minnesota winter. By this time we had two small boys—Mark had been born just shortly before our migration west, and while he was not yet able to play with Peter, his presence assured us that our family was gradually and successfully being created. Mark's birthday came two days before Peter's, which was a strain on early relationships, for Peter assumed that since he was the oldest, his birthday came first, whereas Mark, after reaching the age of reason, began claiming his birthday as the beginning of the whole cycle. To this day I am not quite sure how we worked out the impasse.

Macalester College, like other Presbyterian colleges, had required courses in religion, so we always had big enrollments and had to offer a second section whenever a course attracted more than fifty students. I am aghast when I look back on the territory I covered in just two years: the life and teachings of Jesus, the early church, the Protestant Reformation, systematic theology, Christian ethics, and church history. Whatever else it did, that course load helped me realize the extensiveness of the discipline I had presumed to claim as mine.

I was put under fire early on. When I gave my first religion examination, I tried to make it difficult enough so that "academic rigor" at Mac would be seen as the mark of the newest professor on the block. I did not monitor the exam, since I wanted to suggest that honesty went hand in hand with excellence. But a couple of students said afterward that there had been some cheating, or at least some mighty distractions during the exam itself. Here was an initial test. Would I be severe or would I crumble? I opted for severity, not the easiest virtue for me to handle. I interviewed each of the thirty-seven students individually to get a picture of what had gone on before meting out appropriate justice. I was lucky. The corporate picture that emerged was that there had clearly been some high-jinks but that no blatant cheating had been observed, so nobody had to be suspended. I got an early reputation for being serious about such matters, without having to stick a knife in some student's back. But I did decide that in the future I would join the other professors and remain in the room, "in case there should be questions about the exam."

I was at this point asked by the denomination to write a book on the Bible for high school students. Dr. Turck's benevolent Presbyterian spirit gave me permission to cut my load for the fall semester of our second year so that I could meet the deadline. That was a gift, though as I pointed out to him later, I met the spirit much more than the letter of his largesse, as we shall see.

My two years at Macalester provided an initiation into faith and politics and how they function both together and apart, in large part because we got to know Ted and Charlotte Mitau. Ted taught political science, and was also a committed participant in the political process in Minnesota. A Jewish refugee from Hitler's Germany, he wanted all students to know the wonder and responsibility of living within legitimate democratic procedures. Ted knew most of the people in the Democratic-Farmer-Labor Party and thought that Sydney and I should meet our local congressman, Eugene McCarthy, and his wife, Abigail, both committed Catholics in a time when that could be a liability in seeking public office. This was the fall of 1952, when Stevenson and Eisenhower were the presidential nominees. Gene McCarthy was in trouble, since it was also the height of the "McCarthy Era," as exemplified in Senator *Joe* McCarthy, a neofascist if there ever was one.

Ted arranged for us to meet the McCarthys at his house, and that evening, one of the defining moments of my life, provided the roots of both our subsequent political activism and Christian ecumenism. Sydney and I were immensely impressed with both Gene and Abigail, Catholics of a sort we had never seen before. Much influenced by people like Jacques Maritain, who embodied the progressive Catholicism of the 1950s, they were trying to live out their Catholic convictions in the public as well as in the private sphere. Gene had, in fact, spent a year in a Benedictine abbey testing a vocation to the monastic life. He was now struggling in his campaign for reelection because of his liberal political views, at a time when anticommunism and anti-Catholicism were the hallmark of political survival.

I was a child in such matters, but my attraction to Eugene McCarthy overcame any timidity I might have had up to that point, and the immediate result of that evening was that we became involved in working for Gene's reelection, and I engaged in a spate of activities that truly surprised me, at least in retrospect. My immersion was almost total and was accelerated by the fact that religious issues were central in the 1952 elections, especially on the district and state level.

I wasn't sure it was appropriate to bring my personal political feelings into the classroom, so I wore no button in class, but when I was walking around the campus or around town, my overcoat sported a "McCarthy for Congress" button. I made no friends for myself among the Macalester trustees, not only because I was *not* supporting the other candidate (a Protestant Republican) but because I *was* supporting Gene (a Catholic Democrat), which made me wrong on two scores. One of the trustees, the pastor of a large Presbyterian church in the Twin Cities, was so incensed by my position that when I later preached from his pulpit (on "college Sunday," organized by Macalester personnel), he refused to take part in his own service.

I spent much of that fall working downtown in Gene's office, speaking, writing, conniving, doing clerical work, saying "grace" at political banquets (an important breakthrough for a Protestant clergyman). Having ensconced myself in the downtown congressional office, I wrote news releases and wrote and distributed 250–300 letters to ministers, priests, and rabbis, not only about the qualities of my preferred candidate but about the shortcomings, moral and practical, of his opponent. (This opponent later led a useful political and public life, and I see no reason to mention to him by name. His shortcomings were more those of inexperience than of culpability, but they seemed to loom large in 1952.) I wrote a pamphlet signed by a variety of people in public life in the Twin Cities, of which 25,000 copies were distributed. I spoke on radio and at numerous public rallies. I did enough of this to get a certain amount of nasty mail and phone calls, and it was not easy to deal with.

The bad news is that there was an Eisenhower-Joe McCarthy landslide across the nation. The good news is that the other McCarthy (the "good McCarthy," as Peter called him) defied the trend and was reelected.

(All this was going on when I should have been writing *The Bible Speaks to You*, for which Dr. Turck had given me a lighter teaching load. During this period in American life, Dr. Turck was himself a target of the right wing. He had, among other things, authorized flying the United Nations flag on the campus and at the same height as the U.S. flag—a sure indicator of his communist predilections. Many of the faculty had had their own clashes with Dr. Turck, but when he was under attack in places such as *Reader's Digest*, the faculty backed him all the way. I have my own statement of gratitude to offer later.)

In addition to developing a deepened political sensitivity, I made my first ecumenical forays as a result of Ted Mitau's hospitality. Gene and Abigail McCarthy invited us to visit St. John's Abbey, where Gene had done a year's novitiate, to meet the monks and get a view of Catholicism that would be different from that displayed in my other Catholic habitat, the archdiocese of Francis J. Cardinal Spellman in New York City. It was an extraordinary visit, an embarkation into hitherto unexplored waters. I had no idea there were Catholics like the monks at St. John's, and with one of them in particular, Godfrey Diekmann, OSB, I formed a long and wonderful friendship, enhanced a few years later when we were at the Vatican Council together. Eight years later, when I coauthored the book *An American Dialogue* with Gustave Weigel, SJ, I concluded my introduction with the words, "To Gene and Abigail and Father Godfrey, that the dialogue they helped initiate may continue."

These and other activities were of a new enough sort for me that after the campaign I wrote an article for *Christianity and Crisis* entitled "Confessions of a Political Neophyte," in which I reflected on some of the lessons I had learned:

> 1. In public life developing a special kind of sensitivity is as necessary as developing a thick skin.
> 2. Your public identification ("for identification purpose only") is that and no more. Do not create the impression that you speak for everybody. Your impact will be that of a private citizen. And never fear: if you are claiming to represent your community you will be informed that you are stepping over the line.
> 3. Political choices are made in terms of a complex of issues, and a political platform always contains a variety of convictions. No candidate has everything arranged as you would prefer. I did not, nor do I now, support everything Eugene McCarthy affirms. To isolate one

issue as normative for any candidate is to journey on the road to inef-fectiveness. If you find a Catholic candidate who both your Jewish and Protestant friends can support, you had better jump on board. Keep your critical sense alive, but jump on board.

So my entrance into ecumenism—the problems of restoring a divided church—was through the door of politics. That is a reality that has been full of special meaning throughout the rest of my life, and because of the coming together of those two strands, I refuse to believe that religion and politics can be separated from one another.

Peter: Gene McCarthy was the first big name that came into our family from the outer world that I was aware of (beyond Reinhold Niebuhr, who was more a family friend). I remember my dad campaigning for McCarthy when I was five and we lived in Macville—three or four lines of Quonset huts—GI housing left over from the Sec-ond World War, at Macalester in St. Paul. Gene was the good McCarthy, distin-guished from Joe, whom my parents of course hated. I did not understand how they could have had the same name. I remember being very clear with my friends that my dad was working for the good one. And I remember Gene, who looked like the dad in all the cigarette commercials. He wore a fancy tan raincoat of some sumptuous mate-rial; he looked scrubbed down and kind of glowed. I had some mice that he was gen-uinely interested in, and he seemed to be a nice man. I was glad that my dad was working for him—and the fact that he was Catholic I thought was exotic, if a little dangerous. Even at age five, I realized that my father was taking a chance of sorts. I remember Gene visiting us in New York after we moved back to Union—and again being impressed. He was a full-fledged congressman then, and still had that aura about him. He was wearing a fancy fedora (no one I knew wore hats), and he still looked as though he came from a more perfect world.

This was also about the time when I asked my dad what he did for a living. I knew he went to his office, but I wasn't exactly sure what he did there. He said that he taught philosophy. I asked him what philosophy was. He said that it was the study of the meaning of life. I asked him what the meaning of life was, and he said that he didn't know, that no one really did. Now that left me hanging my head. What was this all about? I asked my mom later on that afternoon what the meaning of life was, and she said that it was to have fun and to make the world a better place—which still seems pretty reasonable to me. I think this would have been my father's response if he hadn't been so honest—though that fun part really had to be countered with some construc-tive work.

We were just beginning to get settled in Macalester when Dr. Van Dusen offered me the tenure-track post of assistant professor of systematic theology at Union, and urged Sydney and me to begin to build a long-term relationship with the Union community. The timing could not have been worse. I was still in my first year of teaching at Macalester and saw no way I could honorably leave, even if I had wanted to. Dr. Turck was magnanimous, assuring me that if this seemed right to me I should accept the offer; Macalester could find another department head.

Paul Tillich, a member of the Union faculty, came to Minneapolis to give some lectures on religion and art, and we had an evening with him in which his advice came down to "You must follow your eros," meaning, I think, that this was not just an intellectual issue but concerned one's whole being. It had to "feel" right; it had to wake me in the morning excited rather than morose about what lay ahead. That there would be professional excitement at being at Union for the long haul was clear, for Union was at that time an ecumenical crossroads for the whole world. When they came to the United States, international church leaders would always visit Union, the cutting edge.

Once again Sydney was caught in the middle. Broadway at 120th Street was not the place we would have chosen to raise a family. We both felt the moral problem of leaving Macalester so soon after arrival. What we finally decided, in consultation with Dr. Turck, was that we would stay at Macalester a second year, which would give time to find a replacement, and also let us pay a little more obeisance to the genuine attractiveness of Macalester as a place to live and work. I have often wondered what would have happened if we had stayed at Macalester. Two years were really not enough to judge, but they were full academically, politically, and humanly.

I left Macalester still stamped in a "Niebuhrian mold," very au courant about *sin*, which Niebuhr himself said was "the only empirically verifiable Christian doctrine," but learning a lot more about *grace*, which is much more central in Niebuhr's thought than most "Niebuhrians" ever conceded in those days. But the issues of Catholicism and ecumenism were not ones that had been central to his agenda, for historical reasons, and I felt inwardly reassured that I hadn't simply become a rubber stamp for my mentor. He was much less affirming of Karl Barth than I had become—which is interesting, because much of my own subsequent involvement on the political scene had, deep within its roots, a sense I had gotten from Barth, as well as from Niebuhr, that there is no division between theology and ethics, or between religion and politics.

Two symbols of these parallel disciplines developing together will help. During our time in Minnesota the political instincts of both Sydney and me were nurtured. By the simple expedient of attending a block meeting of the Democratic-Farmer-Labor Party, we were able to get ourselves elected to the state convention, something that would not have happened in New York City after a quarter of a century. At the same time, my theological interest in literature was coming to flower. Macalester's professor of drama, Hilding Peterson, staged T. S. Eliot's *The Family Reunion*, a serious and rather morbid play based on a Greek drama, and I was invited to do a brief article for the cover of the program, reflecting on some of the philosophical and theological issues the play raised. Ah! Interdisciplinary teaching. (Dr. Turck had an easier resolution than I for the dilemmas raised by the Fates and Furies in the play. He concluded that everything would have been all right if Harry had just "married the girl in the blue dress.")

Every once in a while the subject matter of the religion courses seemed to get hold of people. I remember vividly a series of conversations with one student, Sharon Pratt, on the matter of compromise. She thought I conceded too much (which I probably did) to have any morally distinctive position left, and I thought she was "too perfectionist" (there's a Niebuhrian theme!) to be able to make much impact on the political scene. Forty years later I got a letter from a member of the Hutterite Brethren, a "sect" movement with a noble history, from Sharon (Pratt) Melancon, and was glad to discover how steadfastly she had lived out her convictions.

During the second spring at Macalester, the single most satisfying moment in my athletic career occurred. We had a pickup team that represented the faculty in a softball league. I played first base. Picture the scene. The opposing team has men on second and third with two outs. The game, as I remember it, hangs in the balance. The batter hits a sharp ground ball to our third baseman, who fields it, turns, and uncorks a wild throw in my direction, much too high and far down the home-plate side of the base path. Two runs will score. But hold on! Brown, pulled off base by the erratic direction of the throw, leaps in the air, snares the ball with his gloved hand as the runner is rushing past him, and in one glorious motion brings mitt and ball down on the shoulder of the batter just as he is about to lunge for the initial sack. Three outs, no runs. Never since, a play like that.

5

Union Seminary and the
Freedom Rides (1953–1962)

When Union Seminary called Bob Handy to teach church history and Bob Brown to teach systematic theology in 1953, it marked a conscious change in faculty recruitment. Until then, Union's method of getting new faculty had been to pick an established scholar from another institution and bring him (seldom her) in at full professor, adding immediately and decisively to Union's already high academic profile. But now, here were Handy and Brown, the newest kids on the block and still wet behind the ears, sharing a single office in the tower, with a combined total of something like four years of classroom experience between them. The idea was to hire "promising young scholars" and let them grow to academic maturity in the presence of enabling mentors.

This "new look" also brought Bill Webber fully into the faculty orbit. Bill was a veteran of World War II, an immensely charismatic leader, who was dean of students at Union while also working at the East Harlem Protestant Parish, of which he was cofounder. It was always my hope and frequently my expectation that Bill would one day be president of Union, but he turned out to be too radical for such a post (my perception), though he demonstrated his executive and theological gifts by taking Biblical Seminary, a dying institution in New York, and reshaping it to become without doubt the most exciting venture in the Protestant theological world.

I am grateful for the trust the tenured faculty had in the three of us, along with Charlie Mathews, Bob Seaver, and others who were a little older than we, but not yet "old." Dr. Van Dusen always talked about "the senior faculty," and "the so-called junior faculty," and the distinctions were real. But there were no clearly differentiated criteria for moving from the latter to the former, and our queries about what was expected of us—did we have to write books, do out-side lecturing, publish in major periodicals, and so forth—did not receive many tangible answers. The result was that we felt encouraged to do our own thing, confident that we would be supported. To show how relaxed things were, I was offered a full professorship and tenure before my first sabbatical, and astonished everybody by asking that the offer be held in abeyance until such time as I really felt prepared to occupy such a position.

We were also encouraged to exercise considerable freedom in the courses we taught. I was asked to teach the first half of Introduction to Systematic Theology, a requirement of all entering students, which was certainly a vote of confidence, and I also agreed to teach a one-point course formidably enti-tled "The Theology of Presbyterianism," which all Presbyterians had to take to fulfill an ordination requirement in the denomination. As I will discuss later, this was a tough time in Presbyterian denominational history to teach such a course, and mine had a cryptic (though never explicit) subtitle that went, "How to Be Ordained Though Honest."

For a couple of years I taught the introduction to philosophy that was required of all entering students who failed the placement exam in philosophy, but I soon asked to be excused from teaching it, since neither my talents nor my interest lay in that field. The granting of this request also streamlined my cumbersome faculty title: Auburn Assistant Professor of Systematic Theology and the Philosophy of Religion. Systematic theology was enough to worry about, and I felt more honest, and almost cleansed, when I could leave philos-ophy to the philosophers.

In later years I was able to make a happy connection with another part of the seminary, the School of Sacred Music. Music students had to take a two-point course, designed especially for them, called "Introduction to Theology." I greatly enjoyed teaching this since it challenged me to find ways to commu-nicate without using too much technical vocabulary. The establishment of this relationship with the music school led later to a second course, designed for both music and theology students (one of the few places where this happened), entitled "The Theology of Hymnody." I mainly dealt with the theological content of the words of hymns in the Protestant tradition, though I also did some amateur musicology, in working with students on what kinds of words needed what kind of music, and vice versa. This course was another favorite of mine. As I indicated earlier, music has always been one of my primary avo-cations. (Years later I designed the format for a book on liberation theology out of an analysis of the diminished seventh chord and entitled it *Theology in a New Key.*)

Two deaths during these years had a special impact on me. One was the death of David Roberts, with whom I had hoped to work after returning to

Union from Macalester College. David was a very bright and promising teacher who was only forty-four, and his death challenged all sorts of theological securities I thought I had gotten nailed down. Whatever else his death did, it forced me to confront new depths of my own psyche, and indeed of the universe as a whole, that in the long run strengthened my faith, though his death was not a price I was prepared to pay for new and deeper assurances. (I have written about this in more detail in "Meditation on a Particular Death" in *The Pseudonyms of God*.)

The other death had a direct impact not only personally but professionally as well. While I was on sabbatical leave in Scotland in 1959–1960, I received a phone call from David Stitt, president of Austin Theological Seminary in Texas, inviting me to become dean and professor of theology. Being a dean didn't particularly appeal to me, but the thought of going to a totally different part of the country had a curious allure, and I finally agreed to fly from Scotland to Texas to examine the situation. I took the train and bus from St. Andrews to Prestwick Airport to catch a night flight, but we were informed just before boarding that due to propeller trouble we would not leave Prestwick until the next morning. I called Sydney to communicate the change of schedule, and she told me that we had just received a cable from New York that Charlie Mathews, dean of Auburn Seminary at Union, had died of a heart attack.

This was a powerful blow. Charlie, Bill Webber, Bob Handy, and I were pretty tight-knit, and the thought of pulling out from that group and going to Texas immediately began to feel like an act of disloyalty. I had all night to mull this over in the Prestwick transit lounge, reflecting also on such things as how, if at all, a doctrine of God's providence was related to a malfunctioning airplane propeller. That particular theological conundrum never became clear, but what did become very clear by morning was that I could not, in this new situation, walk out on Union Seminary. I cabled Dr. Stitt from the airport that I would not be coming after all, and telephoned Sydney that I would be returning immediately and that the Austin explorations were off. It helped my considerable trauma through these events that Dr. Stitt was gracious and understanding when I finally got him on the phone.

It was not long after Charlie's funeral that Dr. Van Dusen, who still had a seminary to run, approached by airmail his personal candidate to succeed Charlie as dean of Auburn. The candidate was a young systematic theologian on the Union faculty, who was also a Presbyterian (a significant plus) and was at the moment on sabbatical leave in Scotland, reinvigorating his Presbyterian roots. There was only one snag in his strong and (as I am sure he felt) persuasive invitation to become dean of Auburn: I did not want to be an administrator, and I had no skills to bring to such a job, and I had no intention whatever of accepting it. I am sure I was as clear as that in my letter of reply, but since it was not the reply he had been expecting, it was not a reply he was prepared to accept. I received another, even stronger, letter from Dr. Van Dusen, and then, in an action clearly orchestrated by him, I began to get letters from other faculty colleagues, and even from Charlie's widow, urging me to accept the job.

But if I have been unclear on other vocational moves, I was clear on this one. I wanted to be a teacher at Union; I did not want to be an administrator at Union-Auburn, and I would have even gone elsewhere, much as it would have grieved me to do so, to remain a teacher. This declaration was forcible enough to persuade even Dr. Van Dusen, and he finally accepted it as a true expression of my mind and heart.

In retrospect, I have always been intrigued and a little amused that this upheaval was sorted out while looking at a huge mural in the transit lounge at Prestwick Airport, singing the praises of single malt Scotch whisky. Charlie was a teetotaler his whole life, and I have always hoped that the locale of my decision making might have simultaneously opened up for him a new life in eternity in which the blessing of God's gift of malt and hops might also be enjoyed by him.

Another series of events focused on the issue of "the Presbyterian presence" at Union. The aforementioned Auburn Theological Seminary in upstate New York had to close its doors in 1939 due to a lack of sufficient regional candidates for the Presbyterian ministry. In a creative move, Auburn transferred its assets to Union, and to this day has carried on a quasi-independent existence at Union. Auburn funds built Auburn Hall in the seminary quadrangle, and Auburn funds paid my salary—though this became confusing when I left and my successor, also named Brown (Raymond Brown, a Roman Catholic priest and member of the Sulpician Order) became Auburn Professor of New Testament. Auburn's connection with Union made possible a relationship to the Presbyterian Church that satisfied the denomination's insistence that candidates for ordination attend a Presbyterian seminary and take courses on both Presbyterian polity and Presbyterian theology.

My contribution to this scheme was to give annually a course on "The Theology of Presbyterianism." This was far from a breeze. In fact, it was a perplexing and difficult course to teach during those particular years. For generations the stickiest ordination question had read, "Do you accept the Westminster Confession of Faith as containing the system of doctrine taught in Holy Scripture?" There were at least two monumental difficulties in honestly answering this question in the affirmative. First, the Westminster Confession came out of the "second generation" of the Reformers, and by comparison with earlier statements was both wooden and unyielding. I have been heard to say (though never until now for attribution) that while we believe the Holy Spirit presides over the high councils of the church, the Spirit lavished less special care on the Westminster Assembly than on any of the other occasions when Reformation confessions were created. Second, the notion that there is "a system of doctrine taught in Holy Scripture" is extremely dubious since Holy Scripture is clearly *not* a treatise on systematic theology but the unfolding story of a people—God's people—that loses its power when systematized and turns faith into the acceptance of doctrinal statements rather than the committing of one's life to serve among God's people.

The good news was that during these years a General Assembly committee was working on a *new* confession in contemporary language and content that would in effect replace the Westminster Confession, rather than simply make minor verbal changes here and there. (The latter exercise is not without merit, and in 1903 the denomination had in fact deleted portions of the confession insisting that unbaptized babies go to hell and that the pope was the antichrist, though one looks in vain for any assurance that the new dispensation was made retroactive for babies and popes who died before 1903.)

All this meant that ordinands could hardly be held accountable for every crossed "t" or dotted "i" in a document already being prepared for disposal, and the chances of an ordinand self-destructing when appearing before the presbytery to be tested were significantly diminished. In the end, the Committee for a New Confession was even more creative than anyone could have foreseen. It proposed, and the General Assembly adopted, a *group* of confessions, eight in number, from various periods in the history of the church, thereby acknowledging that every such confession is time bound and that no single statement of the faith can be fully adequate. Creeds and confessions can be *pointers* to the truth, but must never be confused *with* the truth, as the Westminster Confession had seemed for generations to be.

In all my years on the Union faculty, there are at least two events about which I feel unambiguously good: two faculty Christmas plays, directed by Betty Van Dusen, wife of the president, the texts of which I had a chance to create over various summers at Heath. The formula was almost guaranteed to succeed: Into an outrageous situation the various members of the faculty were drawn, all playing themselves and caricaturing themselves enough to demonstrate that they didn't take themselves too seriously, but could laugh at their own foibles. It was therapy of a high order.

One year the play was called *Murder in the Seminary*, produced in the style of T. S. Eliot's *Murder in the Cathedral*. Each member of the faculty came under suspicion for murdering a particularly obnoxious student. The actual perpetrator was in doubt until the final moments of act 3, when the gentle, clean-living Charlie Mathews was revealed as having committed the murder to save the seminary from what he perceived to be a forthcoming scandal—a twist worth a lot of incidental theological reflection.

The other play was entitled *The Devil Was a Junior*, featuring a student (played by Tom Driver) with information demonic enough to unveil a hidden fault in every faculty member, which, if revealed, would destroy his or her career. Thus mired in the power of evil, the seminary was saved when James Anderson, the black custodian of the general office, refused to succumb to an enticing temptation: The devil offered him the deanship of Yale Divinity School if he would only bow down and worship the devil, who was incarnate in the student.

I will be the first to acknowledge that the plotlines lose something of their verve when compressed so drastically, but there were some memorable scenes even so.

Scene: Paul Hoon, the eminently proper professor of pastoral theology, is leading a class on meditation techniques and asks for silence in which all will shut out the world outside, when suddenly the raucous tones of the Riverside Church carillon invade the scene, playing the Marine Hymn (previously taped for us) as Hoon goes absolutely bonkers.

Scene: various faculty members fuming in the basement of the administration building, waiting for the perpetually tardy elevator.

Chris Bekker (a precise New Testament scholar): "You know, I just realized there are the same number of letters in 'elevator' as in 'eschaton' (the last things)."

Dan Williams (a process theologian): "Yes, and we don't know which one will get here first."

Scene: Bob Handy (playing Paul Tillich the year Tillich was giving the Gifford Lectures in Aberdeen).

Handy: "Und now, ve vill talk about Nossingness. If you haf read my book on *Ze Being Courageous*, you vill see zat I haf established zat *nossing iss really somesing*" (followed by Tillich's beatific smile at this philosophical breakthrough).

Several times, during the intersession period between the end of the spring semester and the beginning of summer courses, I did small six-week seminars on Calvin's *Institutes*. It seemed a necessary exercise for me to work my way through the full text, and once having done so I was eager to share the degree to which much was salvageable from a text that most modern Christians ignore. This process was enhanced if one did not get too mired by the strictly polemical passages, which increased in length with each successive edition of the whole.

This is particularly true of Calvin's increasing defensiveness on treating the question of predestination. Every schoolboy knows that Calvin put much effort into this topic and finally got locked into a corner where "the horrible decree" resulted and God was charged with initiating damnation as well as salvation. Fortunately, Calvin's God was considerably larger than Calvin's mind, and there are passages in the *Institutes* that almost sing of the wonder of God's grace and love.

I found his treatment of faith to be particularly creative and liberating, and used it as the basis for a book with the title *Is Faith Obsolete?* (The short answer on which is "No.") But Calvin has penetrating things to say about ethics as well. In treating the Ten Commandments, for example, he insists that if one has more than enough money or material goods and withholds the sharing of them, such a person is breaking the commandment "Thou shalt not steal." This is strong meat, and perhaps the true reason why people want to ignore him.

Courses have a strange way of coming into being and then being subject to radical revision. During my year as an instructor at Union after our year in Oxford, I offered a course called "Contemporary British Theology," built around not only the revival of P. T. Forsyth but also on much of the work I had done as background reading for the dissertation. The course had six enrollees, as I remember, one of them being Bill Webber in the role of a faithful friend. At the end of the course I had one week on British "lay theologians," people such as Graham Greene, Charles Williams, and T. S. Eliot. I did not give the course again, but I used that final week of classes as a springboard into a course on literature and theology that I taught at Union several times, every year at Stanford to amazingly large classes, and then (in retirement) at Dartmouth, Carleton, and Santa Clara University, not to mention in various lectureships over a period of thirty years. The books we used varied from year to year, depending on what current books seemed to be raising theological issues, however guardedly. I made a point of including not only Christian authors (who were usually in the minority), but non-Christian and anti-Christian writers as well.

In later years, when I taught at Pacific School of Religion, I changed the format in such a way that I anticipated a two-volume work on *The Christian Story*, with part 1 to be on theology as narrative and part 2 to deal with theology as system. This approach never jelled into a satisfactory book format. In its stead, however, wishing to pay back a debt to a number of contemporary authors, I gathered together a variety of writings over the years on this topic, and gave them a structure in a book entitled (using a phrase from Auden)

Persuade Us to Rejoice: The Liberating Power of Fiction, including such old friends and companions as Camus, Tolkien, Wiesel, and Silone, but also some new ones such as Frederick Buechner, Alice Walker, and Ursula LeGuin.

SABBATICAL IN SCOTLAND: 1959–1960

Our address was:

> Windrush
> Lade Braes Walk
> St. Andrews
> Fife
> Scotland

One of our correspondents asked if the mail was delivered by hummingbird. By the time we went to Scotland we had two new additions to the family—our daughter, Alison, born in 1956, and a son, Tom, born in 1959. So the six of us embarked on a new adventure.

We arrived at St. Andrews for a sabbatical year the day after the closing of the Lammas Fair (what we call "Labor Day weekend"), when the town ceases to be a busy summer vacation and golf resort on the North Sea, and within twenty-four hours becomes once again a wonderful sleepy university town, dominated by students wearing scarlet gowns against all turns of the weather. St. Andrews has more than its share of ancient stories, ghosts, a crumbling cathedral, the remains of dungeons, and marvelous walks out past the long silted harbor. For a family whose address had been 606 West 122nd Street, Apt. #2E, New York 27, NY, with no hummingbirds provided, the change was sheer gift.

The biggest adaptation was for Peter and Mark, who had to relocate from P.S. 125 in Harlem to Madras College on South Street in St. Andrews. The notion of wearing a school uniform featuring short pants was abhorrent to them, but when they came home for lunch the first day, they were totally committed to shedding their American blue jeans and returning to school in the proper gray shorts. Mark learned all his times tables in Broad Scots, and long about April Peter finally "got the belt," that is, was paddled for a minor infraction of the rules. By the time we returned to New York, both boys had become well acclimated educationally. They had enjoyed wearing their MacFie and Thomson tartans to church, and took quite for granted that in the winter season one left for school in total darkness and barely got home before the last glimmer of light had fled.

Because of their ages, Alison (3) and Tom (1) did not have to engage in so much multicultural adjustment, and we were even able to leave them in the spring with Mrs. Mackie—a wonderful Scot who had raised her own family after her husband was killed in World War II—and take a more extended trip to the Hebrides than would have been possible with a retinue of six. Mrs. Mackie and Binks, her child-friendly dog, were an important part of our year.

Sydney enjoyed being in a new culture, shopping at the butcher's and the greengrocer's, and pushing Alison and Tom in an elegant pram. She organized many hikes and picnics. And together we planned The Trip to Colonsay.

Colonsay, an island in the Inner Hebrides, was the original abode of Clan MacFie, even though the clan had left the island a couple of centuries earlier. We spent several days on Colonsay that spring. Peter was off to explore every valley and ben on the island, while Mark repeatedly tested a local legend that if you stamped on the ground within a stone circle, shouting the word "Friday," the Wee Folk would spirit you off to the nether regions. Our hikes were never dull. (This and other experiences were drawn into my novel about the Hebrides, *Dark the Night, Wild the Sea*, thirty years later.)

In returning to Colonsay one day after wading across the Strand at low tide to the nearby island of Oronsay, we received our ultimate lesson in spiritual geography. Andrew McNeil, owner of the lone farm on Oronsay, drove us back in a cart hitched up to his tractor. Sydney, enthusiastic about Colonsay and all things Hebridean, lamented that Colonsay was "so far away." Andrew McNeil considered for a moment, and then asked, "From what?"

Nearer to St. Andrews were places such as the Sma' Glen, great for picnics. There were countless ruined castles to be explored, notably Kilchurn, which we approached by crossing a marsh, only to discover that we were sharing the ruins of the Great Hall with some indignant shaggy Highland cattle.

Hope Park Presbyterian Church in St. Andrews was a cultural as well as theological bridge. North Americans came to study at St. Andrews in sufficient numbers so that we were not unusual. Wilfred Hulbert, the pastor, found numerous occasions for pastoral calls, and we remember his love of "American cawfee." And how could we have managed without the ministrations of Mary Kydd and her washing machine (she was one of the angels God sometimes sends to earth in human guise) or our two doctors who made house calls to check on our children?

But it was not exclusively fun and games. I had certain well-identified projects to be completed during the year. I had a technical connection with St. Mary's College, the divinity school for the University of St. Andrews, and since it had only four students in the entering class, we could create as much or as little social life as we wished. I was free of all responsibilities save to my family and my self-appointed academic tasks—a condition that has never again been obtained in my life and is remembered with wistful longing.

My desk work consisted first of finishing *An American Dialogue*, written in conjunction with Gustave Weigel, SJ, an early attempt to have a Protestant and a Catholic stand up to one another in open debate. It would appear in the fall of 1960 during the Nixon-Kennedy campaign, when "a Catholic in the White House" was a scary thing to many Protestants. It turned out to be two separate essays bound together rather than a true "dialogue," but after Fr. Weigel read my draft and confined his critique to proposing that I move Chevtogne Monastery back to Belgium where it belonged, I figured we were off to an amiable collaboration. So it proved to be, and we spent much time together during the second session of Vatican II, where he acted as a translator for the English-speaking observers at the council. We were planning a follow-up volume after the council that his unexpected death made impossible.

While in Scotland, I got further help from another Jesuit, Bernard Leeming, SJ, at Heythrop College in the Cotswolds, to whom Wilfred Hulbert had introduced me. Father Leeming was an ecumenically minded theologian who had rather conventional views of what a reunited church would look like, but nevertheless had a wonderfully open spirit and gave me an invaluable sounding board close at hand.

As it got colder, I worked in a tiny room off the back stairs at Windrush, heated separately by a paraffin heater, the smell of which returns to me whenever I think about *An American Dialogue*. There was one unexpected spin-off from this labor. When I finished a section called "Ground Rules for the Dialogue," it occurred to me that it ought to have both a Protestant and a Catholic audience, so in a bold moment I sent copies of the text to both *Commonweal* and the *Christian Century*, proposing that they publish the "ground rules" simultaneously in each magazine. This they elected to do, and to everybody's surprise this became "an event," picked up and commented on in some detail by both the *New York Times* and *Newsweek*. All this was gratifying save that all my friends commented, after seeing a photograph of me taken for the occasion, that I was clearly consuming too much Scottish shortbread.

My second task was to finish a book long in process on *The Spirit of Protestantism*. This was a self-conscious attempt to do for my own understanding of the faith what Karl Adam's *The Spirit of Catholicism* had done for many Catholics. It was not an anti-Catholic book. Indeed, a number of subsequent reviewers chided me for being "soft on Catholicism," the way certain public figures of that time were "soft on communism." When the manuscript went back to Oxford University Press in New York, I got a negative assessment from their outside reader, which after some initial pain I decided to take seriously, with the result that for the next couple of months I rewrote more than half of the text. It was at least better than the submission I had previously made, and I feel gratitude to the honest critic. Even Fr. Leeming conceded, tongue in cheek, that it was "a very good defense of a very bad case." This unexpected but fruitful delay meant that less attention was given to my third sabbatical task than I had intended, which was to complete a reading of the volumes of Karl Barth's *Church Dogmatics*, in preparation for a course that John Bennett and I would teach later.

Two further events were part of the year. One of them, an invitation to become dean of Austin Theological Seminary, I discussed earlier. The other was an unexpected invitation to an ecumenical conference of Christians in East Germany, tendered to me by a former student, Al Currier, who was on a pulpit exchange with a German pastor. People from both East Germany and West Germany would be there. A few others were being invited, and Al made the point that if I wanted to, I could be one of them.

The "German Church struggle" between the Nazis and a small group in what was called "the Confessing Church" has always been a central visioning point in my faith. The issue was idolatry—whether to worship the true God or a false god, an idol. Those in the Confessing Church saw that a clear choice was involved. One could serve God *or* Hitler, but one could not serve God *and* Hitler. Through my whole adult life I have recognized that there are times when similar choices confront us, even if not in such spectacular terms. One cannot be a Christian and a racist. One cannot give unconditional loyalty to any state, even one's own, perhaps especially one's own. One cannot incinerate Vietnamese peasants and claim to be a follower of Jesus Christ. So the chance to meet with Christians in East Germany was irresistible.

Once again the thing I most admired was their courage, which may be the most important Christian word for our times, more important even than faith or hope or love, since it includes them all. It was relatively easy at that time for people to get out of East Germany, then under the shackles of a Stalinist form of communism. You bought a ticket in East Germany for Potsdam in East Germany and simply got off the train at the West Berlin station. Many people availed themselves of this exit. But what was impressive was how many stayed. They felt that it was somehow their destiny to remain in an oppressive country and try right there to witness to their faith. Several of them said, "I think it is easier to be a Christian in East Germany than in West Germany. Here we know exactly when we are crossing a line of activity that may get us in trouble, and we can decide what to do. But West Germans are so obsessed with reclaiming financial success that their faith gets swallowed up and lost." There was another either/or: God or mammon.

The East German government provided "secular" alternatives to all the Christian holy days, such as baptism, confirmation, and marriage. To opt for the Christian alternative under these circumstances was immediately to be in trouble. I shared in one such baptismal service and was stunned by the clarity with which the parents explained that they wanted to dedicate their child to God and not to the state. A pastor justified staying in "God's beloved East Zone" with whatever compromises might be necessary, because there was so much pastoral work to be done. He told about a functionary of the communist government who came to him and confessed that he was subverting the government from within. Pastor Johannes Hamel asked him, "Why do you tell me this, when you know I am obligated to report you to the authorities?" The troubled functionary could say clearly, looking at the Christian symbol on Hamel's lapel, "Because I trust your cross." Story after story poured out, and the tellers of the stories ministered to and nourished one another (this is what we mean by "the priesthood of all believers"), while the rest of us marveled at what we were seeing and hearing.

At the conclusion of the conference one of the participants, Beate Hein, gave me her Lutheran hymnal as a gift. On the flyleaf she had penned a prayer of Dietrich Bonhoeffer, whom she knew was very important to me. The last two lines of his prayer were "At evening and at morning God is with us, / And grants us fresh assurance each new day." Bonhoeffer had written it as a prayer for New Year's Day; Beate Hein made it a prayer for *every* day. Iron curtains make iron Christians.

So after an initial year in Oxford writing a dissertation, I spent this year, a decade later, writing in St. Andrews, and would spend a third year, another decade later, translating a book on Bonhoeffer in Geneva (more on that in chapter 6). These were all times of refreshment and excitement, even though punctuated by the occasional moments when I had to ask myself, "What am I doing, trying to understand all this stuff?" If I had those three separate years to live over, knowing what I know now, I would probably have gone to third-world countries, and instead of having only deficient French and German vocabularies at my disposal, I would have gone gung ho into the study of Spanish. But all that is based on a prescience none of us is granted.

THE FREEDOM RIDES

The battle for civil rights had to be fought on many levels—educational, moral, political, legal. The Freedom Rides, which flourished in the early 1960s, had a touch of all four, but their chief objective was legal. According to federal law, interstate bus companies had an obligation to provide integrated facilities for all travelers. Local and state ordinances in the South, however, upheld the legality of segregated facilities: segregated seating on buses, segre-

gated bus terminals, segregated restaurants or lunch counters, segregated restrooms, segregated waiting rooms, even segregated drinking fountains. There
were two of everything, one labeled "white," the other labeled "colored." It
was just like South Africa at the very same time.

Clearly there was a legal impasse. Civil rights advocates claimed that the
local and state ordinances upholding segregation were unconstitutional. If this
could be successfully argued in a court of law, the local ordinances would have
to be revised to conform to the federal laws, and not vice versa. The Freedom
Rides in 1961 and 1962 were an attempt to test the constitutionality of the
local ordinances in a court of federal law. If successful they would remove one
of the barriers to integration.

The strategy devised by the Congress on Racial Equality (CORE) was to
send integrated groups on interstate bus routes throughout the South, and
have them test the integration of all facilities along the way, from actual seating on buses to every amenity offered in a terminal. The object was not to
break the law but to comply with the law, that is, the federal law, and to ensure
its enforcement. If the integrated groups were allowed full access to all the
facilities, there was no problem. That was a successful Freedom Ride. But if
the local authorities defied the federal law, then the integrated groups, pledged
to act nonviolently, would refuse to disperse from the lunch counter or the
waiting room or whatever service was in noncompliance with federal law. Such
an impasse would finally end with the arrest of the group, justified on the basis
of the local ordinances. The arrest, however, would get the case into the
courts, and CORE made the strategic assumption (borne out by the subsequent legal rulings) that when a case was appealed beyond a local court and
made its way into a federal court, the concerns of the Freedom Riders would
be upheld. The segregated facility would either have to comply with integration standards or be found in contempt of court and forced to close. Put in the
simplest terms, by obeying a "higher" law, the groups demonstrated the ille-
gality of a "lower" law. It was one more step, however small, in overcoming
manifest injustice.

The idea of going on a Freedom Ride was not my idea. I knew that Bill Coffin (always ahead of the pack) had been on one and that another ride had ended
with the bus being burned by white supremacy advocates. But CORE members, who had been doing all the logistics, decided to organize a Freedom Ride
made up of white and black clergy, including ministers, priests, and rabbis. In
1961, Catholic priests could not yet engage in such activities outside of their
own diocese, but CORE did get two rabbis and over a dozen black and white
Protestant pastors to participate—including me. Whatever personal resistance I had initially was finally broken down, however, particularly since some
close friends and former students would be along. It wasn't easy to square the

decision with Sydney and the kids, for there was a real element of danger, and in such situations the family back home faces anxiety and fear. Sydney put much on the line.

In preparation for the trip, what most impressed me about CORE was the centrality of the pledge of nonviolence, which they insisted each member of a Freedom Ride affirm in writing. We were also amply reminded that our task was to test compliance with the federal law and to challenge noncompliance nonviolently, rather than go into a community to "make trouble." We were prepared for this by being subjected to hours of "psychodrama," in which we had to act out every conceivable situation we might encounter, especially worst-case scenarios. There was to be no violence, even to protect another rider; no smart-ass comments to police or to anyone else; no granting of private interviews along the way (each day a different member acted as leader and spokesperson for the group); no private agendas. The psychodramas were self-revealing and gave us practice in figuring out how to respond under pressure. I remember still the relish with which one of the black pastors played the part of a local judge deciding what would be the length of our jail sentences. Each of us was addressed as "BOY!" Stand over here, BOY. BOY, you say "Your Honor" when you address me. Rabbi Martin Friedman played the role of a local redneck, shouting obscenities at Chris Hartmire in an effort to provoke a bellicose response, and finally had to admit defeat, telling the rest of us, "He has a nonviolent face" (which happens to be true). The hardest thing was to find ways to interpose one's body between a violent redneck and a nonviolent Freedom Rider without the situation escalating into violence.

We were also given a "contact number" for each stop on the trip to Tallahassee in case there was trouble. This was usually a black resident who could arrange local help—but who would be in jeopardy if it were known that he or she was associated with us. So the number was to be used only in dire emergencies. There must be nothing else on the sheet of paper but the number—no name, no address. We had to memorize all that. Human lives could be at stake.

The first leg of the trip was from Washington to Raleigh, North Carolina. I had to miss this leg due to a long-standing commitment to lecture to a Presbyterian synod group at Hamilton College in upstate New York. The lectures (though it strains credulity) were on "Predestination Reconsidered." I had to give them all in one day in order to fly from Syracuse to Raleigh and catch up with the group. My advertised departure led to some of the wrong kinds of questions ("Do you think you were predestined to go on a Freedom Ride?") when I wanted to talk about how predestination (reconsidered) was not "fate," but a statement about the remarkable freedom we have to put ourselves in God's hands without worrying too much about the outcome. What I most appreciated was the drive to the Syracuse airport, during which a seminary trustee of ultraconservative viewpoint really wanted to find out why I was doing such a bizarre thing, and gave me a blessing when I got out of the car.

The next morning we assembled at the bus terminal in Raleigh for breakfast, and it too was a blessing. There were no incidents, no nasty banners, no obscene shouts. A number of the local pastors, especially Baptist William Finlator, had been working on this issue for years, and the brief time in Raleigh was a reminder (a) that one mustn't generalize about "southerners"; (b) that the process of slow but steady change does produce results, the fruits of which we were experiencing; and (c) that people who never have met before can experience instant rapport when a common vision is being shared.

Outside of Sumter, South Carolina, we had our first encounter with potential violence. As we stopped at Evans' Motor Court for a meal, a gang of twenty or thirty toughs materialized from inside their trucks. They had been waiting for us. The entrance to the restaurant was blocked by the proprietor, who said he had no contract with the bus company and wasn't about to let us in unless the "niggers" went around to the rear door and got lunch there. "We been segregated," he told us, "and that's the way we gonna stay." An emotionally charged sheriff took over the protection of the entrance, telling us, "You heard the man. Now move along. I'm ready to die before I let you cross this door." He made it very clear that if it came to dying he'd take a few of us along with him. One of the crowd raised his voice to comment that he had a rattlesnake in his pickup and couldn't wait to let it loose among us.

This was our first trial by fire and we were not clear about what to do. The fact that the proprietor did not have a contract with the bus company was a telling legal point in his favor, and it finally persuaded us that Evans' Motor Court was not the place to make our stand, since our stated concern was for interstate travel. Feeling confused and wondering if we were too timid a group for this sort of thing, we got dejectedly back on the bus, to the hoots of the crowd.

Things were clearer within Sumter, however. For the duration of our stay—noon to midnight—all the facilities were integrated, and our various "teams" tested the lunch counter, the waiting rooms, the drinking fountains, and, of course, the restrooms. I was on the restroom detail for the entire trip; a black minister and I had to integrate both white and colored men's facilities at every stop. It occurred to me that I was spending four days urinating to the glory of God.

We spent the afternoon and evening at the black Baptist church in Sumter, waiting for a midnight bus that would take us to Savannah, Georgia. We were shaken by the mores and contradictions we had experienced at Evans' Motor

Court. Did we, we wondered, lack the necessary courage? Should we have tried to go in and demand service? Or were we wise to keep to the clearly stated reason for the trip—to check on the interstate passenger facilities? We were a distraught bunch, not blaming each other, but not exuding much leadership or confidence either.

Our time in the church was an experience of sheer grace that reenergized us for the rest of the trip. Everyone had preached about grace for decades, explaining it as an undeserved gift—and here we were *receiving* it. We drifted into the sanctuary one at a time, to pray, to reflect, and (if truth be told) to rest. Pretty soon someone found the organ console, and another suggested that we sing a hymn. We did. We sang several. At first I was a little embarrassed for our three rabbis by the strong and almost exclusive christocentric emphasis of the words in the Baptist hymnal. But I finally found a hymn that had been written with our group in mind, even though it was published in 1849. The last stanza went:

> Faith of our fathers! We will love
> Both friend and foe in all our strife,
> And preach thee, too, as love knows how,
> By kindly words and virtuous life.

These words, written long ago, were our contemporary marching orders. In the reality of another era, this described exactly what we were to be about. We were to "love both friend and foe," the first demand an easy one, the second sometimes almost beyond reach. We were to do so "in all our strife"—the perfect word to describe our situation, in which "strife" was the name of the game. And we were to "preach," to exhort, not so much by words as by example, to act out our faith, making "love" both the vehicle and the content of our message. Whatever words we did use were to be "kindly words," very hard to call up in response to obscenities. We were, audaciously, to exhibit "virtuous life," which surely meant such things as nonviolence toward those with whom we disagreed. The refrain affirmed that we were once again to call up our heritage ("Faith of our fathers, holy faith") and hope that if it came down to it we could also make our own the final line of the hymn, "We will be true to thee till death." But nobody was out fishing for martyrdom.

It wasn't just a coincidence. We sang "God Moves in a Mysterious Way," and it too was radically and immediately appropriate to our situation:

> Ye fearful saints, fresh courage take,
> The clouds you so much dread
> Are full of mercy and shall break
> In blessings on your head.

There had never been words I needed to hear more than those at that partic-ular time—a recognition of the need for courage, and a belief that it was avail-able. Amen.

Cy Dreshner, one of the rabbis, prayed, and we were one with him in all of Israel's pangs and agonies over four thousand years of history. Somehow they became *our* pangs and agonies as well, and we entered into one tiny chapter in the continuing life of the people of God.

No one had suggested that we have a service, and no one had structured an order of worship. Things simply took place, and we all found ourselves instinc-tively turning to the source of our faith, the living God who visits his children in their distresses, and bolsters her sons and daughters to face whatever may lie ahead. And, of course, all of this was helped rather than hindered by our sense of rapport with the kind and brave people in the church, who provided a magnificent meal for our bodies and gave us love and courage for our souls.

About the time we were going through our ups and downs in Sumter, Syd-ney got a phone call from C. J. McNaspy, SJ, a musicologist on the staff of the Jesuit magazine *America*. Fr. McNaspy simply wanted Sydney to know that his prayers and the prayers of his fellow Jesuits were with her and with her hus-band, that he was sorry that regulations in the Catholic Church still made it impossible for people like himself to join us, and that he was totally support-ive of what we were doing. This was manna in the desert, for to a lonely and frightened spouse every word of support was welcome. And it did not stop there. Fr. McNaspy entered the scene a second time. The next week's issue of *America* reported on our eventual arrest in Tallahassee, under the headline "Our Friend in Jail." Let it also be said in extenuation that within a remark-ably short length of time the floodgates opened and Catholics of every kind and description were engaging in civil disobedience.

Back in Sumter, the bus taking us to Savannah left about midnight. A state trooper at the bus stop bade us farewell almost cordially, having been assigned to see that we made it safely out of town. Sleep is hard to come by on a Free-dom Ride. (The most I could manage were fitful moments when I would almost get to sleep and then toss and turn some more on my uncomfortable seat.) There were not only the past events of the day to drive sleep away; there was also the recognition that we would arrive at the Savannah bus terminal at 3:45 a.m. and had been told that Freedom Riders weren't exactly welcome in that part of town.

Lulled by the movement of the bus, I was almost asleep when it slowed down dramatically. The change of rhythm caused me to sit bolt upright. We were entering a town. I looked out the window and saw a long procession of hooded figures in sheets lining both sides of the street. My reaction was imme-diate: The Klan is stopping the bus. They're going to get us. I whispered my love to Sydney and tried to remember that all of us had pledged to be nonviolent even to Klan members.

It was about a second later that I came to full consciousness and realized that I was gazing at rank after rank of freshly painted parking meters.

Savannah loomed ahead with a fifteen-minute rest stop before we were to head for Jacksonville, Florida. I had worried very much about encountering Savannah in the middle of the night, because we had been told that there was "no telling" what kind of reception we might get. But the fears were groundless. Even the "white" and "colored" signs had disappeared, and we were able to complete all of our tests without trouble. At our breakfast stop in Jacksonville things were much the same, save that there were lots of people around, and it was daylight. We were able to sit together as an integrated group in the restaurant and were told that this had never happened before in Jacksonville.

Our last stop was to be Tallahassee, and we were quite buoyed up by the fact that we had had no seriously dangerous encounters since the previous morning. Maybe the walls of segregation were beginning to crumble. If so, we were the beneficiaries of all that had gone on before us, rather than the pioneers of something new for those who followed us. In this spirit, we were not prepared for the mood in Tallahassee, the end of our journey. The whites looked ugly, while the blacks were smiling. "We came down here to see history made," one of them said to me when I asked about the large black turnout.

My partner and I went to integrate the men's restrooms and for the first time found a reception committee of some of Tallahassee's less amiable citizens, very large men who bodily threw us out of the facility, an event that was captured on TV and offered as evidence at our trial. When we reported the incident to the police, they ejected the ejectors. We were seated as an integrated racial group at the lunch counter, but the white waitresses were unwilling to serve us, and the manager had to hustle in some blacks from the kitchen to take our orders. I have never seen such expressions of hatred as were on the faces of the white waitresses as they stood there observing us with contempt and disgust.

Even with the hostility, we *had* been served, and all interstate requirements had been met. So I don't think any of us expected difficulty at the airport, about six miles out of town, from which we would board an afternoon flight back to New York. We were wrong. We walked across the terminal to have our ritualistic cup of coffee in the restaurant and thereby demonstrate that interstate laws were being obeyed. We found the entrance door locked, even though there were people inside still eating. A hastily constructed sign on the door read "CLOSED." Responding to our knock, the manager was very apologetic. This was the afternoon for the monthly cleaning of the restaurant and he wouldn't be able to open again until 4:30. We did a little fast arithmetic: We were to leave at 3:25, and he was not going to open until 4:30. Perhaps we should wait until the closing sign came down, have our coffee, and take a later flight.

When 4:30 came, did the restaurant open? It did not. Nor did it reopen at supper time, nor at any time later in the evening. The fun and games were over. This time it was going to be hardball. As the hours passed, eight of our number, realizing that they had pastoral responsibilities at home, felt they had to leave before the impasse was resolved. This was only fair. But ten of us decided to wait in the terminal until we could be served. This meant no dinner, which was all right by us, though we were subjected to journalistic overkill the next morning when a newspaper reported that we were engaging in a "hunger strike."

After dark, an ugly-looking mob began to gather outside the terminal. Word had gone out that a bunch of Freedom Riders were at the airport, and members of the White Citizens' Council apparently decided to come to the airport to disperse us. The police, to their credit, did not allow them inside the building, so they simply lined up their cars outside, sat on the fenders, and gazed at us through the enormous plate glass windows, waiting for midnight when the airport would close and we would be evicted. As the mob increased in size, one of the reporters (we were almost sure) phoned the state police to come and augment the inadequate protection the city police could provide. This same reporter (we were sure) came over to us toward the end of the evening and said, "Whatever you do, *don't* go out unprotected into that mob. They are out for blood."

It was not a relaxing evening. What I marveled at most as we sat and sat and sat, and the crowd outside grew and grew and grew, was that Chris Hartmire, in the midst of all the fear, had enough trust in a benevolent scheme of things to fall asleep. I would have given a lot to have felt that secure, and in more sermons than I care to number I have cited Chris's action as a living definition of faith.

By the time the terminal closed at midnight the state police were on the scene. We were driven back to the city by black friends, in a convoy guarded by the troopers. Nobody really wanted a bloody encounter, we were pleased to realize. We slept on the floor of a black church, after the pastor's son advised us to sleep in shifts and keep all the doors locked. We learned the next morning that a state trooper had parked by the church throughout the night, so there were no further "incidents."

Determined to continue our vigil at the airport, we went back at about 7:30 a.m. The restaurant was still closed, so we had no choice but to continue our so-called hunger strike. This left us at an impasse, and the next move was clearly not to be ours. At about 12:30, a group of police crossed the lobby toward us. (I was talking to Sydney on the phone, and had to stop in mid-sentence to say, "I think we're about to be arrested"—hardly an upbeat line with which to terminate a long-distance phone call.) We were confronted by the city attorney, who told us that our presence constituted "unlawful assembly," inciting to riot, and that we had fifteen seconds to vacate the premises. Since we did not disperse but continued to assert our legal right to be there, we were placed under arrest, driven into town by a bevy of police cars, finger-printed, relieved of all personal belongings, and told to sit and wait for trans-portation to the Tallahassee jail.

Our relations with the police up to this point had had a modicum of civil-ity about them. Much as they may have hated us, they were basically "doing their job"—or so I thought. An episode took place, however, that challenged such a benign reading. It should be called "The Knife in the Police Car, or How John Collyer Saved a Human Life." Some of the police, at least, had not exhausted their bag of tricks.

We were taken to jail in groups of three per police car, with one policeman driving and a second policeman in the front seat to keep an eye on us. Once three of us were in the backseat and the door closed, I looked on the floor and there, protruding from under the driver's seat, was a large knife. "Hey, there's a knife on the floor," I called out, and in my naiveté reached over to pick it up and give it to the policeman. What else does one do with a stray knife?

John Collyer, a black pastor who was the leader of our group, was sitting next to me. He grabbed my descending wrist with fingers made of steel, totally immobilizing my arm. "DON'T TOUCH IT!" he yelled, exhibiting more street smarts in that one reaction than I had ever dreamed existed. For what John knew, out of years of experience as a black dealing with white policemen in Detroit, and what didn't even occur to me, was that the knife was a "plant" placed there by the police themselves, and that anybody who picked it up and moved with it in the direction of an officer of the law would immediately be guilty of, let us say, "threatened assault with a deadly weapon on a police offi-cer." If it suited his purposes, the officer could shoot the prisoner and argue in court that he was simply acting in self-defense.

So maybe John Collyer's quick reflexes and intuition saved a human life. At all events, the manipulation demonstrated an appalling lack of respect for human life. Whatever remaining "liberal naiveté" I still possessed was erased by the time we got to the jail.

Jail. This was my first experience of incarceration, though not my last. The same thing was probably true of most of the others in the group. Clergy fre-quently visit jails but don't usually inhabit them.

The jail was segregated, like everything else. The black pastors were there-fore in another pen not visible to us, though we could hear them. It was wonderful to discover that they were greeted as heroes, something they surely had coming to them. I didn't know how we would be received, since white prisoners might be as angry at Freedom Riders as anybody else. But I made an important sociological discovery: The inmates of a jail hate the whole judicial system so much that to them anybody challenging it, for whatever reasons, can't be all bad.

It was not a clean place, but what place built for twenty-four inmates would be clean when there were twice that number behind bars? To newcomers like us, the concrete floor was the only place we could sleep, although Marty (one of the rabbis) did manage one night on a table. After dark the first night we heard some voices talking in rather conspiratorial tones that gradually formed the words, "Let's get the Jew boy." The rest of our group began to encircle Marty, but the deciding factor was a man visibly with the "shakes" who, in the course of a stream of epithets, made clear that anybody touching that "Jew-boy" would get his head bashed in. He couldn't have put it more delicately. Help sometimes comes from unexpected quarters.

Upon arrival, every inmate is allowed to place one outside call, provided he has a dime and can get someone at the other end to accept charges. Most of us called our families, a few their lawyers. But Cy Dreshner had a friend well placed in the White House, and got him to accept a collect call. Cy described the filth, the overcrowded circumstances, the injustice of our arrest, and sundry matters, always injecting, after each devastating description, ". . . and I want you to tell *that* to the president." The prison guard who was listening in on all the calls and making notes was clearly impressed with Cy's contacts, and it is my private belief that this is why our case soon became officially entitled *Dreshner et al.*

The trial itself, held one week after we were released on ten thousand dollars bail, was a letdown. The scenario was absolutely clear before a single person had entered the courtroom. After the presentation of the city's case against us, we would be questioned separately. Our lawyer would have a chance to present our defense. The judge would then ponder his decision and then declare us guilty as charged, of "unlawful assembly with incitement to riot."

All that was locked in place. All that was not locked in place was the issue of how severe our punishment would be. Once that was determined, our lawyer would appeal the case to the Fifth Circuit Court and ask that we be released on bail until a final adjudication had been made. We had not a chance to win in the lower court, but faced a possible reversal in a higher court. We counted on it. Judge Rudd quickly filled in the missing piece of the puzzle and gave each of us the maximum sentence: a five-hundred-dollar fine and sixty days in jail, to be served whenever a final decision had been rendered.

I remember very little about the questioning and cross-questioning. Our lawyer tried to establish that I had written some books, but in Judge Rudd's court that could have been a liability as much as an asset. As a sample of the type of justice being administered in that courtroom, here is a portion of the account of the trial that appeared in the *St. Petersburg Times*:

> City witnesses testified that at no time did the Freedom Riders do any-thing to incite a riot, the basis of the law they were arrested under. In fact, City Attorney James Messer (who was also a witness) said it was the white citizens who were ready to riot. He said the Freedom Rid-ers were arrested because there were "rumors of trouble," not because they did anything but sit peacefully in the airport waiting room. None of the white group was arrested.

This was the evidence *for the prosecution.*

And there things rested for well over a year. Our case went through the Fifth Circuit Court of Appeals and then on to the Supreme Court, only to be sent back down for review on the basis of a technicality I never really under-stood. This meant that we had to return to Tallahassee and start serving our sixty-day sentence, an eventuality we had not foreseen. It was midsummer, and most of us were on vacation all over the country when telegrams from CORE arrived, informing us that we must start serving time on Monday morning in Tallahassee. Judge Rudd seemed to have ended matters in a way satisfactory to him, as we began to serve the balance of our sixty-day sentence. We made such creative contributions to the amenities of Tallahassee as sweeping the paths in one of the public parks and spending an entire day moving bricks from one pile to another.

But increasing media attention was being focused on us by church people, so much so that instead of simply being piled into a truck with other convicts in the morning, we were segregated from them during working hours and driven in a truck that met us at the rear door of the jail, hidden from the view of the press. After four days of this charade, Judge Rudd summoned us and instituted his own charade. He called attention to a racial incident that had just taken place in Buffalo, New York, which, he said, pained him deeply. In fact, he told us, things were so bad up north that he was going to release us in order that we could go back where we had come from and help solve the racial prob-lems up there, in a culture we understood, and where, as far as he was con-cerned, we could do all the civil rights protesting we wanted.

There was more dissimulation behind the scenes than even his ironic demeanor had suggested. For by commuting our sixty-day sentence into time already served, he accomplished two things that were important to him: (1) He obviated a sure reversal of his original sentence in a higher court, which had turned down our previous plea only because of a technicality; and (2) he left each of us with a permanent jail record that would cause all sorts of difficulties in the event that any of us later decided to do such revolutionary things as run for public office.

We chose to look upon his change of mind as a victory, and the rationalizations for his new action as so much window dressing to get him out of a tight spot. So we had a victory dinner in the Tallahassee Hotel, where we had booked rooms for the night—taking care that each pair in a double room included both a black and a white occupant. This was a giddy experience, since at the time of our original arrest such a thing would have been unthinkable.

As we left the dining room after dinner we were approached by a man who had obviously been waiting for us. He told us that he and some friends in Tallahassee were going to celebrate our "victory through the courts" and would be pleased if we would join them. Our flights did not leave until morning, so why not? How wonderful it would be to meet some of the "other side" of southern life. So a group of us piled into his VW van and others into accompanying cars. Our driver was not particularly voluble, we were physically and psychically exhausted, and an almost brooding atmosphere spread over us. This was increased as we were driven far beyond the city limits and began what seemed an interminable ride in the dark, through territory we did not know at all.

"Do you know who these people are?" I whispered apprehensively to John Collyer, who once again was seated next to me. "No," he replied, "I thought *you* did."

This brief exchange served only to increase my forebodings, which with remarkably little effort wove themselves into the following scenario: "These people" are either Klan members or Florida rednecks acting genteel, and they are going to dispose of us in ways known only to them, so that our bodies will never even be found. How stupid to have gotten clear to the end of our venture and walked naively into a trap as transparent as this. What could we do? The only possible response seemed to be an attempt to overpower the driver, but with those cars trailing us we'd never get away. And anyhow, wasn't "overpowering" outside the lexicon of those committed to nonviolence? And there was another thought: "If we overpower the driver, what if it turns out that the whole thing actually is legit?"

Fortunately for the cause of peace between North and South, we finally entered a long driveway in a very deserted part of northern Florida, at the end of which appeared a large mansion, well-lit, festooned with streamers and a classy jukebox, and people who turned out to be the soul of friendliness, support, and genuine charm. We were given a hero's welcome, and had a wonderful party that was not a bad approximation of what banquets will be like in the world to come.

The black people of Tallahassee were brave and kind beyond any telling. We stayed with them, of course, when we were not being entertained as guests in the Tallahassee City Jail. Meals, cars, sympathetic reporters, well-wishers were with us constantly. The black Episcopal rector, Father Brooks, made his home available to us, where we slept in borrowed sleeping bags, and put himself entirely at our disposal.

I had two visitors in jail, John Carey, a fellow Presbyterian minister who took on considerable risk by going to the local jail to visit a Freedom Rider, and Bob Spivey, one of my former students at Union, who had just moved to Tallahassee, and by visiting the jail put himself on the line. It was wonderful to see a familiar face in that alien situation. But even more wonderful was the later report of Sydney back in New York that the phone had rung one evening and a very Southern voice had not shouted epithets but had said, "Sydney, this is Bob Spivey. I've just seen Bob and he's fine." If there are rewards given in heaven, Bob Spivey and John Carey will be near the head of the line.

There were three other courageous acts that buoyed me. After I got back home, before the trial, the Rev. Harcourt Waller called from Tallahassee. Would I come down a day early and speak to his congregation about why I had participated in a Freedom Ride? This was a gift from heaven, since most contacts with Southern whites were very icy if not hostile, and I feared that many of Waller's Episcopal congregation opposed the Freedom Rides. I have little recollection of what I said, but apparently the tone was such that they could hear me and there was clearly more openness after the meeting than before. Waller may have paid a heavy price before or after, but he did a good thing.

Another gracious and courageous act was performed by the pastor of the First Presbyterian Church of Tallahassee, a congregation in the Southern counterpart of my own denomination. (The two denominations have since merged.) The Rev. Thomas was one of the few white clergymen who attended the trial, and he stayed all day, to the very end. This was an extraordinary public act of support by a man who occupied one of the "fashionable" pulpits in town and could not expect to get any local points for his deed. After we had all been found guilty of "unlawful assembly with incitement to riot," fined five hundred dollars, and sentenced to sixty days in jail and posted bail, he invited a number of us, both white and black, to spend the evening in his home—a gesture heartwarming beyond belief, particularly for me, who had come to feel that Presbyterians on the whole were not very sympathetic to Freedom Riders in general, and Presbyterian Freedom Riders in particular. Years later, speaking at a conference of Southern church musicians at Montreat Conference Grounds in North Carolina, I took occasion to refer to my earlier visit "down South," with its rather frightening byproducts, and the redeeming act of a Southern Presbyterian pastor in Tallahassee whom I had never seen since, and how important his reaching out to us had been. As I learned afterward, Rev. Thomas was in the audience. This is one of the few times in my life when I felt as though I were actually collaborating with Providence. And the church itself, later pastored by a Union Seminary student of mine, Bruce Robertson, invited Sydney and me to do a weekend retreat with its members. This time I could be billed as an ex-Freedom Rider, and it was a plus.

Finally, when the original arrests were reported in the press, I got a phone call from Dr. Charles Turck, who had been president of Macalester College when I taught there. He had also been president of Centre College in Kentucky and dean of the law school at Tulane University, a man highly respected throughout the South. Dr. Turck was a Southern gentleman to the core, and that core contained a firm ethic of love and responsibility to the neighbor. And what was the purpose of the phone call? I expected to be chastised, to be sure, in the best Southern manner, for getting involved with social forces I really knew nothing of. Instead, however, Dr. Turck told me that he was licensed to practice law in the state of Florida, and he would be honored if he could represent me at the ensuing trial.

I have seen pictures of military men being stripped of all insignia for acts deemed reprehensible to the commonweal. That would have happened, symbolically at least, to Dr. Turck had he appeared in a courtroom in 1961 to defend a Freedom Rider. CORE had already made provision for our defense as a group, so I had to tell Dr. Turck that I could not accept his wonderful offer, but that I would be forever grateful to him for it, in which he put his principles and friends above his reputation.

Peter: I was in the seventh grade at Collegiate School in New York when my dad went on the Freedom Ride. I remember Chris Komor, who sat next to me in English, being shocked when I told him this. My dad, it seemed to me, had simply gone off on another one of his trips. He did this all the time—but this spring apparently there was real risk involved. My parents at that stage of our lives still tried to shelter us (this was the end of that), and they had not completely filled us in. Plus my newspaper reading was still largely confined to the sports pages. I knew that Freedom Rides were going on, we all did, but Chris told me of people being burned, lynched, murdered. He was impressed by my father's action, if a little appalled, and so was I. I went home and talked with my mother, who tried to reassure me. But I was worried, and worried in a way that I would be again in the future.

I had gone to P.S. 125 for elementary school, a huge school right on the edge of Harlem. There were black kids, Puerto Rican kids, Chinese kids, Japanese kids, Eastern Europeans who barely spoke English, Jewish kids—the whole melting pot—and we had talked about civil rights and integration from first grade on. And here my dad was doing something directly about it. I was very proud but still nervous. Our

TV, a pathetic little green and white Philco, which we all loved, was broken, so there was no television news, and I remember my mom in tears a few times. There were phone calls from the South and lots of hugging. I spoke to friends in class about what my dad was up to, and they were wide-eyed. I knew it took great courage to do what he was doing—and when he got back, we were overjoyed. But that summer, all he could do was build a stone wall. A meticulous stone wall to be sure, but still, just a stone wall. No books. I think that experience scared him, and scared him in a way few other things ever did.

My dad didn't do too well with working-class people. He was better on paper with the oppressed and the poor. I remember him on cross-country trips trying to deal with garage mechanics who saw him coming a mile away, or his relations with a man who many years ago cut our fields up at Heath. He and his large family all spoke in boom-ing voices in close proximity to each other, as well as to my dad. He hated that kind of thing. And the thought of him in the South, dealing with rednecks, who both person-ally and politically were anathema to him, now fills me with rage and with wonder. My father knew what he was getting into, and still he went. Throughout his life he pushed himself and the world with the same drive. He was a remarkably courageous and expansive man, and he grew and changed throughout his life. He constantly ques-tioned the world and he constantly questioned his response to the world. And he acted on those responses.

We always joked that he had a martyr complex—that he put himself in harm's way hopeful of a heroic Christian death. But that was always just a joke. He loved life far too much to voluntarily give it up. He was as alive as anyone I've known, and he had a very good time for the bulk of his eighty years.

Mark: *At the end of 1959, Nixon and Kennedy were debating on tiny, grainy, black and white TVs, plotting the future of the Cold War and suggesting what you could do for your country or who in his secret heart of hearts was a Communist and should be blacklisted or jailed. I was at school at P.S. 125 in Harlem, walking on one side of a ten-foot-tall chain link fence in the playground (two acres of asphalt and no play equipment) when a skinny black kid, probably a year or two older than me, said, "Who you for, man, Nixon or Kennedy?" I said, "Kennedy." He said, "Gimme five, man!" I said, "Give you what?" He said, "Slap me some skin!" I said, "Slap you what?" He demonstrated on himself, right hand on left, and proceeded to stick his skinny hand and wrist through a single chain link diamond, up to his elbow, reaching for political consensus, across the divide of years, race, and culture. I gave him five, securing JFK's victory and putting Nixon and his vision of the dark night of the American soul into a well-deserved limbo for eight more years.*

Then came the Freedom Rides—a much more serious set of political circumstances with much higher stakes for me personally and for the nation. I remember seeing pic-tures in the New York Times *of Greyhound buses burning by the roadside somewhere in the South, ignited by bigots filled to overflowing with ignorance and hatred—buses that had been filled with good-hearted people simply hoping to integrate interstate travel and bus stop restaurants for any and all travelers. I had read stories of brave men, women, and children, some local and some from elsewhere in the country, who were being beaten, knocked down with fire hoses, attacked by police dogs, killed and blown up by vigilantes and mobs whose ideal of daily life was white supremacy. I was amazed that my father was about to become one of the people who would fight against this grave injustice. I was frightened that I might never see him again, that he could be beaten, killed, or blown up by these very same people. The image of the burning bus played over and over in my mind after he left us. He went south on a bus with a group of ministers and rabbis, and was finally arrested with his black and white clergy friends in Tallahassee, Florida, for "incitement to riot." He was jailed, released, and then suddenly sent back to jail a year later in the summer on a day's notice when we were in the midst of building a mahogany rowboat in our front yard. The skeleton of the unfinished boat was a stark reminder of how quickly things can change: of the uncertainties of the geographies of freedom and justice, of the sinking hopeless feeling I had whenever I thought of the South and my father in prison. When he was finally released, he and all of his fellow inmates for freedom and equality had permanent felonies writ large upon their personal records, made certain by the racist judge who freed them with the knowledge that none of them could ever run for political office because of the sentence he had imposed upon them.*

Both of my parents lived the courage of their convictions, regardless of the personal, political, or economic consequences. I want to thank my mother yet again for reassuring us many times that we would see my father alive in this lifetime—times when he literally laid his life on the line during the civil rights movement and was jailed and convicted as a felon in Tallahassee, Florida, for the crime of sitting next to his African American friends and asking to be served a meal in an airport; times when he was jailed during the Vietnam War for blocking the entrances to draft boards and military induction centers; times when he spent weeks on the front lines in Nicaragua during Ronald Reagan's unjust war; times when I thought he might return in a coffin or not at all.

Alison: *One of my most intense early memories of New York was when Papa was arrested in the Freedom Rides. What I remember is that there was a lot of excitement and tension. I knew something was going on. Papa went off on a trip, which wasn't anything new. But this one felt different. I remember coming home from nursery school and Mama pulling me into the kitchen to talk to me. She explained that rules could be important, but that sometimes people made up rules that were wrong and that when that happened, good people had to break those rules to make them change. She explained that there were parts of the country where it was against the law for white people and black people to eat together, to go to church together, or to ride a bus together.*

She said that Daddy had gone "south" where this was happening, on a big bus, with lots of other ministers and rabbis, both black and white, and that they were following God's rules but breaking people's laws. She said that he had been arrested and was in jail in a place called "Tallahassee" for wanting to eat in the same restaurant, at the same table, as his black minister friends. She wasn't sure how long he would be in jail, but that he was doing the right thing. She said that part of being a Christian meant that you always put God's rules before people's rules, and that if government rules were hurting people, you had to stand up to that, even if it meant going to jail.

The feeling I had at the time was intense pride in my daddy and the people he was with on the Freedom Rides, coupled with a terrible sense of a tidal wave overcoming me. It felt like all the stuff I'd seen on TV and heard in nursery school, about the policemen being there to help and the police being your friend, had all been big lies. All of a sudden, what had felt like a fairly safe and fair world looked different. There was evil that had the power of the government backing it up. There were bad, unjust people in power who made bad laws that weren't fair. And they could lock people up in jail for doing the right thing. It was a huge heartbreak to me, an outrage. Nothing would ever be the same. I know I had noticed racism before, but I hadn't realized that there was a huge institutional structure to it. I believed that there was basic fairness, that there were rules, many of which I didn't like, but that they were equally applied to all. The Freedom Rides and my father's stint in jail in Tallahassee were a turning point in my perspective on the world. I also remember hearing later that in jail they made my papa eat "grits and fatback," which he hated, and that made me really mad as well.

I also remember feeling heartbreak and outrage and not knowing what I could do about it. It was heartening to hear that grownups I loved and respected were doing something to make things better, and I always assumed that by the time I had children, the problem would be solved. I do remember picking up on the fact that what my dad was doing wasn't all that popular and that there wasn't much support in the seminary community for such radical action. I remember being teased when I got to kindergarten during recess, being told that my father was a "bad man," a "criminal," and that only bad people went to jail. I remember trying to fight back, saying that the rules were bad, not my daddy. I don't remember any of the adults around noticing or offering any help as this teasing went on. I was on my own.

The Freedom Rides were just the beginning of a long history of civil disobedience and activism in our family. The opportunities to witness against injustice and unjust laws were many and varied. Taking stands publicly was a constant, and being attacked by the media or other people was an ongoing challenge that my parents and our family faced. We were all different ages during these different events and experienced them in different ways, but I think we all ended up with a strong sense of unity as a family—a deep sense of all of us united together against evil. We always had dinner together (often with extra guests who needed a meal), and no matter what fights or disagreements were happening inside the house, on the outside we would stand up for each other against any real attack.

Sydney: *Meanwhile, back at our seminary apartment, life went on with Tom, age 2, Alison, 4, Mark, 9, and Peter, 12. I was in unexplored territory, a nice liberal who found herself married to a man who was personally defying the law in the Southern states. Up to that time, we'd been liberals who took action for our beliefs through legislation, phone calls, letters, and the courts. Of course we knew radicals, but open defiance of the law was not our way.*

My job was to keep life going at home, to explain what Bob was doing to the kids and the community. The community around us, I found, must have felt the way I myself had felt in the past with radical extremists—a bit awkward, a bit distanced, quite ill at ease. They didn't know how to deal with Bob's errant "unliberal" actions. Most were awkwardly silent. One member of the community did call, asking me, "Why's Bob done such a damn fool thing?!" The little girls of the seminary community teased Alison that her daddy was a "jailbird." John Bennett, however, was wonderful, keeping track of things, letting me know that Bobby Kennedy (then attorney general, who was watching the Freedom Rides) had said that he could go out on a limb only as far as he was pushed, so he counseled us, "Keep on pushing me." Betty Van Dusen, wife of the seminary president, broke the mold and called me, saying, "Sydney, thank God for Bob and what he is doing! At last somebody from the Union Seminary faculty is taking action on his beliefs. Thank God for Bob!" And from the outside world came a call from John McNaspy, Jesuit writer for America magazine, who said, "I wish we could be with Bob. Action outside our own dioceses is prohibited for us priests, but we are working to change that!" And they did. And when Bob returned from Tallahassee, unexpected support came from Dan and Eulalia Williams of Union, who probably did not approve of the tactics Bob was engaged in, but would never have let that point of view get in the way of an act of helpfulness. I did not drive in those days, and they volunteered to take me way out to Newark to pick Bob up from the airport.

My personal response to Bob's participation in the Freedom Rides was cold fear. Our TV chose that time to break down. I tried to keep my cool and hold our family together. I breathed deeply. I prayed. Neither breath nor prayer made the fear go away. Bob Spivey, former Union student, untenured and newly teaching at the University of Tallahassee, called to check in, telling me he would visit Bob in jail, which he did. I knew that this was a courageous act; though I've not seen him since, I will always cherish him for that.

This is what I learned from that experience: When people take "radical action," talk to them, to their families. Try to understand, ask questions, keep the connection. If you want to liberate an attorney general, keep pushing. When life for others seems filled with cold fear, offer friendship and understanding. Help your kids understand, and give them sassy answers to taunting friends.

LEAVE TAKING

My decision to leave Union, on the verge of what was described by some as a "promising career," was unremitting agony. I was firmly established at what with some justification could be called the best seminary in the English-speaking world, I had recently given the inaugural lecture that goes with tenure, we had many friends on the Union faculty, our kids were happy (especially since the calendar year provided at least two months at Heath), and New York was an ecumenical crossroads—almost everybody in the world church turned up sooner or later.

But I could not dispel a gnawing sense that professionally things weren't quite right. No matter how much others assured me that I "belonged" at Union, there remained the feeling of being something of an impostor, presuming to be doing an adequate job of teaching theology at an advanced level on the same fast track as Reinhold Niebuhr, Paul Tillich, Daniel Day Williams, John Bennett, Wilhelm Pauck, and a host of other luminaries. I faced the prospect of carving out my piece of the theological pie and specializing, specializing, specializing. Dr. Van Dusen offered me the doctrine of revelation as a centering point, needed at Union, and, so he believed, made to order for me.

One of a Union Seminary professor's main tasks was to serve on PhD dissertation committees. Nowhere was the charlatan within me more exposed. Much of my insecurity had to do with my manifest linguistic incompetence. I was a dud at languages, and I did not enjoy linguistic fakery, at which I was actually pretty good. I had had no Hebrew, no German save what I had taught myself, only two years of Greek, and no French beyond high school. I would get a thesis on, say, "Calvin's Doctrine of *Adiaphora*" and have to go home to look up the last word.

In addition to some fairly spectacular gaps in my command of two thousand years of Christian history, I had to face the question: How did I want to spend the considerable amount of time available for my own private study, course preparation, lecturing, book writing, and so on? It finally boiled down to this: I preferred to help students enter for the first time the world of Bonhoeffer's *Letters and Papers from Prison* than to supervise a doctrinal thesis on variant readings in Bonhoeffer's *Akt und Sein*. I preferred to share with students their excitement at discovering Martin Buber's *I and Thou* than do research on the philosophical influence of Schelling on the early Buber.

Ted Good, a friend from Union who was already teaching at Stanford, orchestrated a proposal by Stanford to woo me, which included a visit to our New York apartment by Philip Rhinelander, an eminent philosopher at Stanford who was also a Christian, and two trips by me to Stanford to meet with various groups of faculty and students. (One of the latter said I looked like

Barry Goldwater and almost queered the deal.) I went back and forth for months and finally sent a definitive "no" by mail, immediately after mailing which I phoned Ted to destroy it unopened. But the "no" prevailed again a few days later, and Stanford appointed a new search committee.

I had to deal with the fact that almost everybody whose judgment I valued thought I was crazy even to consider leaving Union. I had finally "arrived" professionally and I was only forty-one. Didn't I know that there were hundreds of my peers who would give everything to have such a situation within which to work? Among my colleagues on the faculty everyone but Bill Pauck urged me to stay at Union. Bill said, "I can see where the Stanford job might really attract you." Score one for him.

The hardest to deal with, of course, was Dr. Van Dusen. Having only recently crossed his will and said "no" long-distance to the deanship of Auburn Seminary, I was hardly eager to face this formidable personage on his own turf, which happened to be where I dwelt. He could not for the tiniest fraction of a second see why anybody would think of leaving Union, especially after having spent a decade there getting established. My book on *The Spirit of Protestantism* had just come out, and he insisted that I could never have written it anywhere but at Union, due to profiting from the constant faculty interchange, and he predicted that I would die a lingering theological death at a place like Stanford. This particular argument was not even moderately compelling to me, for, as I pointed out, even if I should have been doing so, I had *not* been tapping the minds of Tillich, Niebuhr, Williams, Pauck, Richardson, and so forth, in doing this particular piece of writing.

I am sure that part of Dr. Van Dusen's concern was not just for me but for the institution. By this I do not mean to imply that I was essential to Union's future, but simply that it would reflect badly on Union's reputation if a tenured full professor were to depart, suggesting that somehow all was not well at 3041 Broadway. The only full professor up to that time who had *ever* left Union was John Baillie, a Scot who could be forgiven for returning home to teach at the University of Edinburgh. The fundamental axiom was clear: People *come* to Union; they don't *leave* Union.

Even after the "final decision" to leave had been announced, Dr. Van Dusen could not accept it. There was a faculty meeting to consider search committees for two vacancies, one of which was palpably caused by my proposed departure. After the other search committee was formed and Dr. Van Dusen proposed moving to the next item on the agenda, someone asked about a second vacancy. Dr. Van Dusen replied, "Well, we're not sure about that departure yet." I should obviously have protested right then that my decision was firm, but couldn't muster the energy or nerve to do so. (I think it was at this moment that I vowed to myself never again to rethink the decision.)

I should add to this whole dreary account that while she was supportive about leaving if that was the right vocational decision for me, it was clear that Sydney would have preferred to stay at Union. Having not wanted to leave Macalester years ago and return to Union, she had at last made her peace with the city and the seminary as a place to rear young children. She had a group of friends and causes to which she was loath to say goodbye, and if the whole time was hard for me, it was doubly hard for her.

This has been the case with all our moves, and I don't feel tranquil about the number of times she had to go along with vocational decisions that were exciting to me but had no initial excitement at all for her. She was left with the unpleasant task of getting reestablished all over again in a new place, with readjustments not only for her but for the children as well—all the while that I was at the new office or in the new classroom, swimming in new currents and feeling exhilaration. We did, finally, make a later move (back to Union, as it turned out) in which we thought that finally we would be vocational partners, but that didn't work either.

Back to the Union scene with things still in balance: Weighing the final Stanford offer, I was miserable. It finally boiled down to the dilemma, if you can't survive saying no, the only alternative is to say yes, which I did in a humble and penitential call to Ted Good, realizing full well that the new search committee might already have settled on someone else. After a stern admonition from Stanford not to change my mind again, they reoffered me the job, and this time the decision to accept remained firm, with this bit of awkwardness: I had delayed so long in making up my mind that there was no honorable way I could leave Union for the upcoming academic year. So I had a final year as a lame duck. I don't recommend it.

There was at least one more significant, if bittersweet, reason to say yes to Stanford, and I have saved it till the last. A good friend of mine while we were in the Union PhD program was a New Zealander named Alexander Miller. He had been associated with the Iona Community in Scotland, a project in which I was very much interested, and we had shared together one of the greatest moments in our respective academic careers: the announcement over the phone that we had both passed the German language exam. Lex had prepared for this by a meticulous reading of a book entitled *Der Christ Sagt Ja von Karl Marx*, better known to me in English translation as *The Christian Significance of Karl Marx* by . . . Alexander Miller. Lex had found reading his own prose to be a surefire vocabulary builder.

At the end of his study at Union, Lex was headed back for New Zealand to find a job, and had arranged to teach one academic quarter at Stanford on the way. Sydney and I drove Lex and Jean and Davie down to Penn Station at the time of their departure from New York. Fourteen years later (!) Lex had increased the fledgling religion program at Stanford to sizable proportions. The Millers loved Stanford, and Stanford loved the Millers. It was a perfect match. I visited Stanford a couple of times during those years to preach, and was impressed not only with what Lex was doing but also with the fact that the university seemed to be giving him good support.

It was thus a terrific blow when, during our sabbatical year in Scotland in 1960, we got a telegram that Lex had died. Part of the attraction of moving to Stanford was the opportunity to keep building what Lex had started. "It's a fragile flower," Jean told me when I was looking the job over and being looked over. "It needs your presence."

And perhaps when all is said and done, that was the most powerful incentive of all.

6

Stanford

On the day the trustees approved my appointment to the Stanford faculty, I was in the Leon County Jail in Tallahassee, Florida. I have sometimes wondered whether, if they had known this, it would have swayed their decision, and if so, in which way.

I arrived at Stanford in the fall of 1962. The afternoon on which I delivered an initial "open lecture" as a new faculty member was the afternoon on which Nikita Khrushchev was threatening to deliver nuclear weapons to Cuba. We listened transfixed. After we could breathe again, I talked about the upcoming Vatican Council. My unlikely thesis was that in the long view of history, what was about to happen in Rome might be at least as important as what had happened just a few minutes earlier when Khrushchev backed down. I still think the prediction may turn out to have been correct, for the shakeup to which Vatican II subjected the Catholic Church had ramifications for change that are still unfolding.

The year proceeded. I had a regular teaching load. The students were splendid, immediately demolishing a prediction of my Union friends that I would find the transfer from graduate to undergraduate teaching a letdown and would miss the "stimulation" the older students provided. Actually, I discovered little difference between Union's graduate students and Stanford's undergraduates. Furthermore, there was a much wider mix of students in Stanford classes, including Jewish students and others whom Schleiermacher called "religion's cultured despisers."

The fact that I spent the fall quarter of my second Stanford year in Rome, as an official observer at the Second Vatican Council, attracted to my classes many Catholic students, who wanted to know firsthand what was going on in "their" church, and their presence immediately added impetus to the need to expand our faculty. When I arrived, we had three white Protestant males teaching religious studies, all of whom, along with my predecessor, Lex Miller, had doctoral degrees from Union Seminary. In those days, the "old boy network" was alive and well.

At Union, one could assume that the students were active investigators of religion, if not yet diligent believers, and that many of them would engage in a religious calling after graduation. Such things were not part of the Stanford undergraduate profile, and I found this a plus rather than a minus. It also meant having a pretty clear picture of the dynamics of this new situation. I decided that at the beginning of each course I would lay all my cards on the table, so the students would know where I was coming from, hoping they would reciprocate so we wouldn't have to play games with one another.

I also wanted to dispel certain stereotypes I thought were likely to be present in the minds of students and faculty. So at the first session of every course I gave over the next fourteen years, I spoke on the problems inherent in teaching religion, always speaking from the following notes:

PROBLEMS INHERENT IN A COURSE ON RELIGION

The overall problem. The study of religion involves not only the truth or falsity of the subject matter but also its impact on us personally (a freewheeling definition of "existentialism"). Our stake in the subject matter counts. Its truth or falsity makes a difference to us. There is a difference between saying, "There are tigers in the jungles of Burma," and saying, "There is a tiger loose in the hall, and I can't get the door shut."

1. *Disavowal of proselytism.* Since the truth makes a difference to us, it might be argued that I should try to bring you to the truth, by offering a propaganda course, stacking the cards in my favor, with the implicit assumption that it would be unhealthy to disagree with my point of view.

I strongly disavow this approach. We are in a classroom, not a chapel; I am giving a lecture, not a sermon; I am behind a podium, not a pulpit; I am a teacher, not a preacher. (n.b.: Sometimes I *am* a preacher, but then the ground rules are very different.)

This class is an academic exercise, demanding the same kind of preparation and attention as other classes. The object is not to convert anybody, but to inform everybody.

2. *Disavowal of "objectivity."* The material presented in class always has a "slant." Courses on the Reformation will be different, depending on whether

the one who lectures and chooses the readings is a Protestant, a Jesuit, a Marxist, or a humanist. You can take your pick, but don't assume that you are getting a "value-free" analysis.

3. *The laying bare of presuppositions.* You are entitled to have information about where I am coming from. What is my filter for interpreting the subject matter? I am a Protestant, currently learning a lot from Jews and Catholics and "third-world" Christians; a Presbyterian who believes that denominations have served their day. I was educated at a liberal arts college, an interdenominational seminary, and a secular university. I started World War II as a pacifist and ended up as a chaplain on a troop transport.

4. *The question of truth.* A personal commitment to my subject matter does not invalidate my right to teach (despite what some of my colleagues might say). It makes me more venturesome. If it *is* true, then I have nothing to fear from open discussion and challenge; if it is *not* true, the sooner I learn that the better, so that I can stop disorienting subsequent generations of undergraduates.

a. *Primacy of content.* Our first question cannot be, "Is Buber right?" It must always be, "What is Buber saying?" (This is not always easy to determine.) Only after we understand the content can we ask about its truth or falsity. There is a long history of such discussion and research (and we are in the midst of an important attempt at redefinition by the Second Vatican Council). There are creeds, confessions, true-life examples, and even some theologians who can help.

b. *The question of the truth of the content.* This is always the second question and never the first. Can we take faith assertions seriously in a scientific age? Is belief in God comparable to anything more than belief in a unicorn, that is, that both are nonexistent? At the very least we must examine accurate replicas of what faith has asserted: The "Lord's Supper" is not accurately described as "cannibalism," nor does the whole edifice of faith collapse if the whale did not really swallow Jonah. Different kinds of speech validate or invalidate religious claims.

c. *The interrelationship of truth and content.* It can be an asset to learn the content of the faith from someone who believes and practices it. We learn about Shakespeare best from a lover of Shakespeare. We learn about Hitler by reading not just Alan Bullock but *Mein Kampf.* I learned more about Roman Catholic liturgy by attending mass five days a week for ten weeks at Vatican II than I could ever have gained by reading a dozen books on the theology of the Eucharist.

Part of my task is to see that other points of view permeate the classroom. The danger is setting up stereotypical straw men and neatly demolishing them. I will frequently play the part of the devil's advocate.

5. *The responsibility of the student.* The first responsibility is to know the content and be able to reflect intelligibly upon it. Piety cannot go bail for thought. The first appeal must be to the head and not to the heart, though the heart will figure strongly later on. Prayer cannot replace exposure to the required readings. The intelligent skeptic will probably fare better than the soft-headed believer. No premium will be attached to agreeing with the professor.

Signing up for a religion course entails a certain risk. What if, after disposing of sixth-grade theology, a more mature theology begins to make sense? The student might study Paul Tillich on "ultimate concern" and discover that it was a perfect description of the new dimension of concern in the student's life.

It is not my task to force religious crises upon students, but I realize that they may come unbidden, and I am therefore available to pursue not only term paper topics but existential crises as well, keeping such discussions entirely separate from academic performance.

The big surprise that first year was that after course enrollments in the fall quarter averaged about fifteen, enrollment for my winter course on religion and contemporary literature was 250 students. Since I had not been on the scene long enough to establish a "reputation" for good or ill, I decided that the reading list posted in the bookstore was speaking to a hitherto untapped need or yearning and could give enrollees a chance to reflect on "meaning" questions without feeling trapped. The fact that I included non-Christians such as Albert Camus was probably another factor in the appeal of the course.

The course survived for over a decade, and the enrollments were of sufficient magnitude to entitle me to TAs (teaching assistants) to lead group discussions and help with the grading, which was a fearful task that first year. The TAs were mostly doctoral candidates in English, which helped build some interdisciplinary bridges, and I remember one of them, Judy Dunbar, pressing me vigorously to include Saul Bellow the next time around, which I did.

Each time around, in fact, I made some changes in the reading list, adding new books and removing old ones that didn't "connect." Interestingly enough, Holden Caulfield, the protagonist in J. D. Salinger's *The Catcher in the Rye*, who had drawn massive empathy from East Coast Ivy Leaguers at Union Seminary, turned out to be a dud on the West Coast, where students were not asking his questions.

It is my feeling that despite all the upheaval, our family settled into the new Stanford situation without major trauma, though I realize that I may be reading my hopes rather than a true discernment into the situation, since for me the adjustment was glorious. I had found my niche, and about six months later, Sydney looked out at the nearby hills and said, "I think those hills are mine now, and I can enjoy them." Peter easily adjusted to Terman Junior High, and by this time he was a veteran at coping with new surroundings, having been in four different schools in five years, counting the time at Madras College in St. Andrews. Mark fit in well at Stanford Elementary School, and didn't miss P.S. 125 one bit (where, he later confided, the main thing he had learned was "when to run fast"). Alison was in grade school on campus, to which she could walk every day with friends. Tom attended Friends Nursery and loved it.

An important help in our overall adjustment was First Presbyterian Church in Palo Alto. Each Sunday morning we had an hour of worship and an hour of study. The worship was innovative, sometimes pretty far out, but never dull, which to me is the cardinal theological sin. The pastor, George Wilson, had been a seminary student when we were at Union. He too was innovative, passionate, and committed to as much lay participation as possible.

The church was also feeling its way cautiously into the outside world, an emphasis in which Sydney soon became a moving force, as members were discovering that on the social scene, justice is as important as love. This was related to such things as the human rights struggle in the South, the boycott of grapes and Gallo wine, closer to home, and the Vietnam War, both six thousand miles away and right next door. This stress on worship and action has fed us through the years, and I indicated my gratitude in the dedication of a book called *Frontiers for the Church Today*: "To the members of the First Presbyterian Church of Palo Alto, California, who by their concern to discover new frontiers for the church have challenged all my stereotypes about upper middle-class bourgeois suburban Protestantism." But that was only the first half of the dedication. The second half went, ". . . and to the members of the Stanford University faculty, who by their concern for the whole family of man have challenged all my stereotypes about Christians having a corner on love of neighbor, this book is dedicated with gratitude and affection."

It is part of the story that later on most of those teaching religious studies would have been displeased by my accolade, even though it was not directed at them but to my "secular" faculty friends in other disciplines. But at least there were some wonderful years when my professional life and my personal life were almost at one.

As I have already noted, I arrived at Stanford just as the Second Vatican Council was getting underway, and I had done enough writing on Protestant-Catholic dialogue in the previous three or four years to be sought out for opinions on the council, much more than I was, for instance, asked to describe what it had been like to be a white Northerner living in a Southern jail, even if only for a few days. I attended the second session of the council in the fall of 1963, and upon my return was deluged with invitations to speak about it, mostly by Catholic churches and universities, many of which I accepted. This gave me a certain visibility, which was increased when I proved able to trade on friendships made in Rome and persuade Roman Catholic speakers to come and lecture at Stanford. Hans Küng, Leon Cardinal Suenens, Fr. Bernard Leeming, SJ, Msgr. Charles Moeller, Fr. Francis X. Murphy (the "Xavier Rynne" of the *New Yorker* reports on the council) were a few of those who graced our campus.

I am sure that during these early years I was perceived by the administration as an asset, and I went several times with other faculty on Stanford-sponsored weekends, reporting to alums on the state of the church, the state of the university, and even the state of the world. When I began to get publicly involved in civil rights issues and Vietnam issues, however, invitations of this sort began noticeably to taper off and finally disappeared altogether. I had become less of an asset and more of at least a potential liability, one who might be perceived as contaminating the minds of Stanford undergraduates.

I stress the point because there is another side to my relationship with the Stanford administration. No matter how much things heated up later on—and I was speaking and writing a great deal in criticism of the United States government—never once was I asked by the administration to cool it. I continued to have freedom to say whatever I felt obliged to say, and whatever outside pressures existed were never held over me as a club. Dick Lyman, provost through much of this period and later president, was especially reassuring on this point, and after Davie Napier left the post of dean of the chapel, Dick, by then president, asked me to fill in as interim dean until a replacement for Davie could be found, even though it was absolutely clear that this action would gain him no friends in high places. His act of personal trust, at a time when Dick and I often occupied different positions on campus issues, is a particularly gratifying memory of those often bitter years.

The closest there came to a showdown, as far as I know, was when *Look* magazine published an article I had submitted, entitled, "In Conscience I Must Break the Law," in which I detailed my journey from law-abiding citizen under all circumstances to practitioner of civil disobedience, "counseling, aiding, and abetting" students who felt that they too, in conscience, "must break the law." *Look* provided a more ample public forum than I had ever had before, or have ever had since, and there were some alumni pressures to do something about "that professor of religion." Not only did I have Dick Lyman's assurances of freedom, but when the FBI finally visited me in my office, Herb Packer of the law school, who was then provost of the university, got Bill Keogh of the law school to take my case in the eventuality that I was arrested and tried, as had been the case with Bill Coffin. David Levin of the English Department agreed to do fund-raising for legal costs, and from many such quarters I felt wonderfully sustained. Had I been indicted, which I was not, I would have had some of the best legal minds in the country helping me out.

Thanks to a comment from Bob Beyers of the Stanford News Bureau, that the matter of my activities might come up at the next trustees' meeting, I wrote a letter to President Wallace Sterling for use at the meeting if necessary. In it I fine-tuned some of the themes of the *Look* article, about what I would and would not do as a member of the faculty. I would not, for example, use the classroom to counsel civil disobedience, nor would I try to argue students into my position. This seemed to take some of the heat off the administrative offices in Building Ten.

My other major encounter with the trustees had been in earlier and more peaceful times, when my department colleagues and I had decided that the Department of Religious Studies needed to expand and that the direction of expansion should be to move away from white Protestant males, all of whom, as previously noted, had doctoral degrees from Union Seminary, and to seek a "Roman Catholic scholar." At the time we proposed this, such a move was rather far out for a secular university, and the trustees' initial response was to argue against the proposal, on the astonishing grounds that a Catholic (and a Jesuit at that) whom we were proposing to hire couldn't be "objective" enough in his presentation, and would have a hidden agenda of "conversion" of unsuspecting undergraduates, since a Catholic scholar would "really believe what he was teaching."

I wasn't ready for this, but I argued with considerable fervor and a little annoyance that if "really believing" one's subject matter was a sufficient reason to deny someone a teaching post at Stanford, then I too would have to be removed. I suggested that in the case of Daniel O'Hanlon, SJ, "really believing" would help him do justice to his material, and that the trustees would simply have to accept on faith that "conversion" was not an item on either of our agendas. Such a discussion seems anachronistic today, but it was very real in 1964.

On two occasions during my years at Stanford I was approached about returning to Union as its president. I can honestly say that this never tempted me as a vocational possibility, and that I was not really interested in opening the door to it. But enough friends urged me at least to consider it that I did so, thus setting myself up for one more agonizing vocational decision. During the summer when one of these offers was being propounded, I did return to Stanford from Heath to explore what the offer might mean on the Stanford scene. I pointed out that as far as my future with Stanford was concerned, we desperately needed a second full-time person to deal with issues in contemporary religious thought, the area in which I was inundated with students, papers, and exams. We had an ideal person on the scene in Jerry Irish, who had only a year-to-year appointment, and when the other members of the department concurred, we were able to get Jerry appointed to a tenure-track position. (This probably was the only time in academe that I was able to leverage something within the system. In all other situations, I have been able to say that my ablest administrative gift was the ability to avoid administrating responsibilities.)

Two people contributed specifically to my decision. Jerry's wife, Pat, knowing my lingering Calvinist propensities ("if you enjoy what you are doing there must be something wrong"), sent me a carefully constructed argument, demonstrating that the *easy* thing would be to return to Union, while the really difficult tasks would be my lot if I stayed at Stanford. The other inspired act of help was a short message from Annie Krumboltz, Alison's closest friend. It went, "Pagans in California need you more than believers in New York."

We stayed at Stanford, and the new situation was a real gift for two reasons: First, it meant being able to cope more creatively with large class enrollments, sharing the task with Jerry, and, second, it meant having Jerry as a full-time colleague in a department otherwise increasingly bereft of real "colleagues."

We knew nothing about such matters as faculty housing. At Macalester, we had lived in GI housing, converted barracks provided for veterans at fifty dollars a month including heat and light. Union also provided housing and had three sizes of faculty apartments: small, large, and massive. But the housing assignments were based on seniority rather than family needs, which led to space inequities I have no intention of dredging up again. Besides, we were one of the exceptions, landing a quasi-massive apartment (smaller living room) while our kids were still home to enjoy it. But the ratio usually went: the larger the apartment, the fewer the inhabitants.

It was from such crazy experiences with real estate that we discovered that we could buy a house at Stanford and finance a loan through the university at 4¾ percent, an unbeatable bargain even in 1962. So we did. It was a lovely house. It was a big house. We had some wonderful years there.

The house got a lot of academic use as well, not just because my study and books were there, but because all my seminars (usually 12–15 students) consistently met in our living room. Past and present came together there: Bonhoeffer deciding to join the underground; John and Diane deciding to get married; Buber and Rosenschweig working on a German translation of the Hebrew Scriptures while Rosenschweig was dying; Pia handing in her term paper in the form of a mobile; students confronting the challenge of the Holocaust and its indelible challenge to optimistic views of human nature. There was also a period when we housed students surreptitiously who were wrestling with what to do in relation to the draft, or, if already in uniform, how to handle the fact that they could no longer take part in an evil war.

SELMA

As the civil rights struggle continued to heat up in the mid-1960s, the kind of "token support" white liberals were giving to blacks, particularly in the dangerous deep South, began to seem to be too much "token" and too little "support." Blacks were being arrested, given long jail sentences, brutally treated by police and rednecks, consistently denied the right to register or to vote, and goaded almost beyond endurance. In the face of all this, that the movement for black emancipation remained consistently nonviolent is one of the miracles of God's empowerment that was handed on to others through people such as Martin Luther King Jr., Andrew Young, Jim Bevel, Jim Lawson, and William Sloane Coffin.

The biblical plea, "Come over to Macedonia and help us," which was issued by Paul at a tight spot in his ministry, was transformed into "Come down to Mississippi and help us" (or Alabama, or Florida, or Tennessee, or North Carolina). No matter that things were terrible in the North—probably almost as bad and maybe even worse for being less blatant and more subtle—there was an immediate need below the Mason-Dixon Line that required a response.

The Freedom Rides, as we have seen, came fairly early in the struggle, and they had a big impact in some quarters. But the event of Selma had an impact on everyone and became for several weeks a national event in which thousands of white and black clergy and laity descended on a tiny town in Alabama to do nothing more spectacular than help blacks establish their right to register and vote.

Before there was much white involvement, a group of blacks in Selma had started a fifty-mile march across the Pettus Bridge and on to Montgomery, where petitions and voter registration lists would be given to Governor Wallace, one of the staunchest racists of modern times. The march never even got off the ground, let alone across Pettus Bridge. Police appeared from every direction and mercilessly clubbed, kicked, and otherwise molested a group of blacks already pledged to respond nonviolently. The event was on TV that night and was seen across the nation. For millions of white Americans it was their initial exposure to what it is like for American citizens to ask for the right to vote and be denied that right simply because they had the wrong skin color.

Across the nation there was not only spontaneous revulsion but a deeply felt conviction that others should go and stand with the brothers and sisters in Selma who were seeking and being denied a patent human right. Suddenly

Selma was a magnet, drawing thousands of people committed to the civil rights struggle, determined that the march to Montgomery would be held and that they would go to Selma to assist in achieving that end.

As these things were happening, black leaders, knowing a gift when it came their way, were cranking up the logistics for a repeat of the march to the state capital, making it a national event that would be reported by every TV outfit in the nation. I was in New York at the time attending some Presbyterian meetings. We were trying to draft a new book of worship materials, and I became less and less comfortable with the fact that the *real* changes in "worship" were going to emerge not in New York but in Alabama, and that given those two locations certainly I was at the wrong one. A chartered plane of prominent East Coast clergy was to leave the next morning for Selma, and the leader of our worship committee, Eugene Carson Blake, was to be among them. When Gene voiced his dilemma about where his job responsibilities lay, I rather brashly suggested that the committee needed Gene as chair much more than it needed me as a junior functionary, and that if it pleased the Holy Spirit and pleased the group, I would be glad to take Gene's place on the charter. We didn't get a ballot from the Holy Spirit, but it apparently *did* please the group. By noon the next day I was in Selma.

There is no way to reduce Selma to a clear, consecutive story. The plotline could change on the hour, threats could be heard over the radio every half hour, instances of harassment to blacks beyond the confines of Selma were ongoing occurrences, and there were literally "teeming throngs" who arrived at Selma with very little to do but wait until the long march could be organized—a matter of days at best, considering the logistics that were involved.

At least once and often twice a day there were rallies in front of Brown Memorial Chapel in the "Negro section" of Selma, soon referred to as "the compound." Everything took place in the compound except for one afternoon march to the city hall in Selma to work out some of the kinks of marching together (e.g., Who gives the orders?), and to make a formal request to the city fathers for the right of blacks to register—a right the city fathers were emphatically not interested in discussing. One evening after dark there were reports in the compound of blacks being beaten elsewhere in Selma, and a couple of very vocal blacks argued passionately that in the light of such provocation we could not just sit where we were but must start *immediately* for the city hall and spend the night there in protest. Even I could see that in the charged atmosphere of the moment such a march would be an invitation to every white man in Wade County owning a shotgun to come to Selma under cover of the friendly mantle of a dark sky, to teach the troublemakers a lesson.

The leaders of the SCLC (Southern Christian Leadership Conference) were in a strategy session in Brown Chapel when word got back to them that

the crowd outside was in an ugly mood and threatening to take off on a spontaneous march of its own. Andy Young was deputized to join the rally, get control of the microphone, and persuade the crowd that a march at that time of
night would not only be a bad thing for people's health, but could wreak such
havoc as to jeopardize the daylight march a few days hence. I wish I could
recall the words Andy used, the arguments he propounded, the techniques by
which he turned the sentiments of the crowd in new directions. I cannot—but
I can report that however he did it, Andy Young almost surely saved the Selma
march from being torpedoed from within, not to mention saving the lives of
many people.

When it was clear that the long march was still days away from beginning,
attempts had to be made to organize activities in the compound that would tap
the expertise of the hundreds of ministers, priests, and rabbis who had arrived
on the scene. I found myself part of a group assigned to go to nearby
Greenville, Alabama, and speak at a rally in the black Baptist church that night.
A carload of us would get to the town in early afternoon, try to "talk to people," have supper at the church, hold the rally, and return to Selma. I wasn't
about to go into the local barbershop and take on a whole white establishment,
but I did go with another member of the group to talk to the local Presbyterian pastor. In a nice and polite and gentle voice he presented what to him was
an impregnable argument for the segregation of the races, just as the Bible
taught. There was no yielding on a single point. It was a good exercise for me
in the fine art of listening, and it persuaded me, among other things, that the
battle for equal rights for all of God's children was a battle that was going to
continue for a long, long time.

As we were walking back from this valiant but ineffective attempt at ecumenical dialogue, I suddenly remembered why the name of the town and the
name of the church were familiar, and the recollection had a chilling effect on
my psyche. A few days earlier the papers had been full of the murder in Selma
of a white seminarian, Jonathan Daniels, and they had mentioned, though not
nearly so prominently, that a black man named Jimmie Lee Jackson had been
shot and killed in Greenville just one week ago, coming out of the very church
in which we would be meeting. It occurred to me, not in placid fashion, that
we would be doing the same thing in a few hours ourselves, and that the mood
was such that the same greeting might be in store for us.

After we joined leaders of the black community for dinner, we had our rally
in the church, many speeches containing reference to Jimmie Lee Jackson and
the nobility of his death. Once again I marveled at the raw courage of all the
blacks present, both men and women. After the benediction we walked down
those same steps without incident and went for our car. I had figured that
should death threats not materialize, the gentlest treatment we could hope for

would be slashed tires. That one also passed us by. We had an operating vehicle to make the twenty-mile drive back to Selma on a moonless night.

I hope it sounds simply human rather than paranoid to relate that every time the headlights of a car behind us caught up and passed us, I expected that we would either be forced off the road or be the recipients of bursts of gunfire. I was quite ready to forego any theatrics or express a need to court martyrdom. If at any point we had been followed, I guess my ultimate trust was in God, but it was God being mediated through our driver, a large Catholic priest from Chicago, Father Hogan, who maneuvered that car with an ease and speed that communicated to us that even if we were uncomfortable, this sort of thing was routine procedure in Chicago any night of the week, and we could all relax. When we got back inside the compound in Selma and could consider ourselves relatively "safe," I didn't do it, but I wanted more than anything else to kneel down and kiss the ground, a gesture Pope John Paul II has since elevated into an art form.

At the end of my stay I learned one wonderful thing about the communion of saints. When working out the logistics for the big march took longer than expected, it was clear that many busy pastors would have to leave. To some who had wanted to go on the march itself, this was a big disappointment. But so many people had come that only a fraction of them would be able to march anyhow, and they would be selected by criteria not of their own choosing. I was certainly in the category of those who must leave soon. Not only had I walked out on the Presbyterians, but I was now missing my classes, without permission from on high, even though I hoped that my absence was a teaching device, since (by providential design) the ethics course was dealing that very week with what we used to call "race relations."

I was still feeling some guilt about leaving, but when I got to the Montgomery airport and my flight number was called, it turned out to be a flight that had originated in Chicago, and as the arriving passengers got off, what should I see but row upon row of clergy—hordes of clergy—most of them wearing collars so there would be no mistaking where they were headed. And I suddenly realized that my staying on for the next few days didn't matter a bit. Replacements were already on the way, and when they had to leave to go back to their churches a few days hence, another wave of clergy would replace them, as long as clergy were needed. This was not only consoling but energizing as well. So I missed the big march to Montgomery itself. But thanks to the prompting of the Spirit and the presence of the communion of saints, I was really there too.

Mark: *My parents took me to the 1963 March on Washington, where I heard Martin Luther King's "I Have a Dream" speech, a turning point in my young life.*

My father helped to create history. His attitude was: If you don't like the news, go out and make some of your own, and he did. I may be one of the few children of the sixties who was proud to have a father who was a felon.

Peter: *A good chunk of the family went to the March on Washington in 1963—and it was an eye opener of many dimensions. It was my first foray into the South and colored/white water fountains, separate entrances, and the like, and as I bathed my poison ivy–covered feet in the reflecting pool, Martin Luther King gave his speech. And I watched in wonder as a black kid about my age leaped repeatedly into the air—King's words rumbling through us. Up and up he went in joy. And I was brought to tears at this kid's release. I was just fifteen, we had spent one happy year in California, and JFK was still alive.*

FARMWORKERS/MIGRANT LABOR

It wasn't all Vietnam and civil rights even in the sixties. Two important forces converged in the early sixties on behalf of poor and belabored farmworkers in California and found power in their convergence. One was the United Farm Worker (UFW) movement, headed by Cesar Chavez, a charismatic Chicano who was the heart and soul of the union and kept the union on a clear course of nonviolence despite frequent attacks from goon squads hired by growers. The other force was the California Migrant Ministry, which had, until then, been a kind of Band-Aid activity in the Central Valley of California, helping folks in difficulty but seldom probing the reasons for their need. This changed when Chris Hartmire, a Union Seminary graduate and a fellow Freedom Rider, assumed the leadership of the Migrant Ministry and with a team of equally committed organizers began to transform it into a militant community, fighting nonviolently for contracts for workers, unionization, decent living quarters, and other minimal amenities of human survival. The two groups found one another, and things in the valley have never been the same. Chris had his own charisma, and he kept the churches in the forefront of the struggle, joining in many activities organized by the United Farm Workers. Chris and Cesar were a potent pair.

The events I shared with the Migrant Ministry particularly helped me not to vegetate on the Stanford campus as a kind of armchair theoretician. Those of us on the edge of the organization did whatever we could: supporting boycotts, picketing stores, participating in demonstrations and marches, and getting people to make the trek down to Delano, where large rallies were often held. There were often long marches—say, from San Diego to Sacramento—to present pleas to lawmakers for legislation to protect workers' rights. Along the way and among other things, Protestant participants learned about Our Lady of Guadalupe, an apparition of Mary who appeared as a pregnant indigenous woman in solidarity with the Mexican poor.

For years the groups implemented a grape boycott; it remained in place until working conditions for those who harvested grapes were brought up to minimal standards that included, for instance, protection from pesticide exposure. For years the groups and their supporters boycotted Gallo wines, and many who supported it find it hard even today to purchase Gallo products without feeling residual concern and even guilt.

The nonviolent dimension of their activity has been essential to all farmworker leaders, for it has put a stamp of moral credibility on their actions. It took tremendous courage and commitment on the part of Chicano workers to keep honoring this pledge, for the growers often brought in truckloads of goon squads to break up the picket lines and frighten others from joining them. On many occasions it must have seemed absolutely necessary to break the commitment of nonviolence in order for the union to survive, but both at the time and later, with the wisdom of hindsight, it was clear that nonviolence not only kept the image of the struggle clear but was also a means for gathering much outside support from people who were not otherwise committed to the farmworkers. On this score alone, the activities of the Chicano workers form part of the noble story of the struggle for nonviolent social change in which people like Gandhi, Chris Hartmire, Martin Luther King Jr., and Cesar Chavez were united.

I learned some important things from my activities with the farmworkers in the Delano area. I remember being there shortly before a picketing action, for which an explanatory handout needed to be prepared for distribution the next morning. I was assigned to work with those writing the text for the handout, polishing an existing draft that was to be retyped for the mimeograph machine. At some point I lost my self-control. My editorial instincts went into high gear, and almost before I knew it I was making small changes first (getting rid of split infinitives, correcting spelling, inserting paragraph breaks), and then moving into major editorial surgery. I pretty well killed off the passion in the early draft by my desire for accurate grammar.

Only gradually that day did I discover what an intolerable thing I was doing. Tomorrow's action wasn't mine, it was theirs, and they needed the words they had written, which were authentic and genuinely moving, rather than the limp prose of an outsider. I should have known that my task was not to write the text but to turn the handle of the mimeograph machine. Every gringo, I am sure, has made this kind of mistake at least once. It is almost always well meaning, but that does not make it right. Our gringo penchant for taking charge needs always to be kept on a short leash.

On one occasion we were able to fuse the domestic and the international. I was at Vatican II during the final session in 1965, when the very important council document on "The Church in the Modern World" was debated and then adopted. It had a long section on labor, on the right to organize, and on the right to strike. Chris Hartmire wisely foresaw that the document could be of considerable help to him in organizing within a basically Catholic culture. Within a few days of my return from Rome in December, Chris had set up a meeting with growers and workers in which this freshly adopted text could be read and shared as the basis for a discussion of workers' rights in the Central Valley. The meeting was not quite as newsworthy as we had hoped, for at the last minute the invited growers decided to boycott the meeting, perhaps uneasy about having 2,300 bishops lined up against them. But "newsworthy" or not, the discussion was a morale booster for the field workers, who learned through the Vatican II text that their apparently local dispute was being afforded international support by the church to which almost all of them gave their personal allegiance. Such statements as the following sounded as though they had been written with our Delano meeting in mind:

> Among the basic rights of the human person must be the right of freely founding labor unions. . . . Among such rights is that of taking part freely in the activities of these unions without risk of reprisal. . . . When, however, socio-economic disputes arise, efforts must be made to come to a peaceful settlement. Recourse must always be to engage in sincere discussion between all parties. Even in present-day circumstances, the strike can still be a necessary, though ultimate, means for defense of the workers' rights and the fulfillment of their just demands. (*Gaudium et Spes*, para. 68)

It was exciting beyond belief to watch the responses of the workers to this patent affirmation of the issues for which they had been fighting for so long.

Alison: *I would often wake up to early morning breakfast meetings with the Farmworkers. The organizers would come to the house for coffee and toast, and my parents would invite people over for breakfast to help them become involved. We went on what seemed like a very long march in Sacramento. From my parents, the Farmworker organizers at breakfast, and church, I heard about terrible injustices happening in the fields of California, and I was glad we were marching. I had good friends on farms in Heath, and I knew how hard farm labor could be. I had a picture in my mind of white, rural, New England kids when it came to farms and farmwork. When we marched on the capital, I suddenly saw that all the farmworkers had brown skin. All the farmworker kids I met were Latino, and most spoke Spanish. Most of the people marching with them were white. I had no idea until that moment that racism was* *part of the struggle of the UFW. I remember feeling outraged, shocked. It was another level of the tidal wave I had felt when I was five and my dad was arrested in Talla-hassee.*

STANFORD-IN-FRANCE

Stanford has a well-developed program of overseas campuses to which students can enroll for two quarters at a time. They have to demonstrate sufficient proficiency in the language of the area to take classes taught by local professors. Two regular Stanford professors go with each group, and lecture in English. Many students are radically changed as a result of living in a different culture for six months. I taught at Stanford-in-France in Tours, in the Loire Valley, in the fall and winter quarters of 1967–1968. Tom and Alison went along with Sydney and me, and their presence was a real asset. Students are often homesick, and ours were very glad to have our thirteen-year-old daughter and eleven-year-old son on board, since it was a little like still being at home.

Sydney and I sat in on a French class, and I was working away on a translation into English of Andre Dumas's *Une théologie de la réalité*, a book about Dietrich Bonhoeffer. But, sad to report, none of this hands-on language study brought much improvement in my linguistic skills. I count as one of my most disheartening linguistic experiences of the year the time I went into a *crêperie* with Tom and Alison, ordered, very distinctly, a *"crêpe au chocolat"* for each of us, and was rewarded with three small Coca-Colas.

The Vietnam War was at its height, and we were there during Vice President Spiro T. Agnew's instant rise to fame. Many sophomores had a hard time explaining to their French "families" how such a man could come, in so short a time, to stand within one heartbeat of the presidency. The way the dates fell, we were even able to be part of a Vietnam War protest in Paris on October 15 in front of the U.S. embassy, and repeat the performance in Madrid on November 15.

In addition to the regular academic work, the staff of Stanford-in-France very kindly arranged about one trip a week into the surrounding Loire Valley, visiting various chateaux, whose opulence always led me to ponder, "Why did it take so long for the French Revolution to start?" One visit left all others in its shadow. That was the week we visited a vintner, Rene Layeau, who had, like many others, hollowed out a huge cave, wide and deep, in the hills by the Loire riverbank. This arrangement had the merit of yielding a temperature within that never varied more than two or three degrees the year round and was thus an ideal place to let new wines mature. And what stories he had to tell.

He told us how when he was a boy he had tasted a particular wine from a certain valley far away. Years later he participated in a wine-tasting contest, the object of which was to locate as nearly as possible the area from which a given wine had come. He took one sip and felt himself transported back to that very valley of his upbringing, felt the sun on his back as it had been years ago, and even identified for the judges the side of the valley from which the wine had come—a grand moment in the life of a vintner.

But there were less grand moments as well, and he shared reminiscences with us of the wine industry during the German occupation in World War II. He told us how they had built a false front at the far end of the cave, and how they had stored the really good wines behind it. And then they constructed a *second* false front nearer the entrance and put a large supply of medium wines there. The theory was that if the Germans broke through a false wall and found wines behind it, they would be so busy congratulating themselves for having seen through the French ruse that it would never occur to them that the best wines might still be undiscovered. As for the rest of the really good wine, every night under darkness the vintner strapped six bottles of wine on his bicycle, three on each side of the rear wheel, and without a light transported them to safety elsewhere. The chords of reminiscence were deeply stored.

After his recital, the vintner was not only nostalgic but also parched, and after a moment of tense inner reflection he spoke briefly to one of the workers, who disappeared into the depths of the cave and returned shortly with a very dusty green glass bottle. The old man dusted the bottom off and held the bottle for us to see. "*Dix neuf cent quarante trois,*" he said reverently, as though in an act of consecration. "*Une mauvaise année pour la France, une bonne année pour le vin*" ("1943: a bad year for France, a good year for wine"). He unstopped the bottle and shared the wine with us, and in that shared act we were deeply bonded with him and with each other. It will not escape the reader that for me this was a beautiful secular analog—maybe even more than secular—for Holy Communion. If I brought something to the ceremony that lent it depth for me, it is also true that the holiness of the vintner's experience and the students' respectful silence gave it new breadth and relevance. Amen to all such experiences.

Back in the classroom, I tried to relate my own teaching material to the French scene—from Chartres, the pilgrim church of the Middle Ages, to the contemporary chapel designed by Le Corbusier at Ronchamp, which is a destination for modern pilgrims. One particularly French phenomenon that took place between Chartres and Ronchamp was the movement during and after World War II called *les pères ouvriers*, the worker-priests. Realizing that the people were not coming to the church, a number of priests decided to turn the process around and take the church to the people. Divesting themselves of priestly garb, they got jobs in the factories, broke bread and shared wine in fourth-floor flats with those whom they got to know on assembly lines, and took part in struggles for unionization.

It was a creative movement in French church history, but like many creative movements it was in effect destroyed by the Vatican in all but a few places. Jeanne Marie de Renusson, a member of the French faculty, told me that there was still a worker-priest in Tours, a Franciscan named Perè Antoine, who made his living as a butcher in order to give the rest of his time to work with the poor. He seemed made to order for our course, and he agreed to meet with our class, asking only that we come to his butcher shop after business hours for a free discussion. The discussion was not only free but freewheeling, raising many of the questions that contemporary, mostly secular, students raise about things ecclesiastical. Toward the end of the session, one of the students, trying hard to understand the various kinds of authority that seemed to characterize the Catholic Church, asked something like the following: "Father, you've said you believe in the rights of conscience, and so that means you believe in democracy; you are a priest, and so that means you are subject to the orders of the bishop of Tours; you are a member of the Franciscan order, and so that means you have to obey the edicts of your superior; and you are a Catholic, and so that means you are subject to the authority of the pope. So my question, Father, is: Who is your ultimate authority?"

Père Antoine didn't even pause for breath: "My ultimate authority?" he responded. "*Le bon Dieu!*"

And the students applauded.

But all was not euphoric within the walls of Stanford-in-France. A field trip to Spain went without incident, save the threat of arrest for two of our students who tried (successfully) to smuggle part of a castle in Segovia across an international boundary and back to their room at Tours. But our trip to Italy engulfed us in tragedy. Richard, one of our number, rented a motorcycle in Rome, rode out into the Italian countryside, and never came back. He was finally located in a rural area, the victim of a collision. He was in a deep coma when the police brought him to a hospital. He was still in the coma, fortunately in good medical hands, when the group had to return to France. We got word on his condition each day for over two weeks. But the inevitable report finally came: Without ever regaining consciousness, Richard had died as the result of multiple head injuries.

We had been a cohesive and caring group over the preceding months, and we had that going for us in coping with such a loss. And it worked the other way too—coping with such a loss deepened our shared roots even more. As Sydney put it: We had been a group; we were now a community. The word of

Richard's death came in mid-afternoon, and it was clear that rather than isolating ourselves from one another, we needed to deal with it as a family. Although I wasn't wearing my clergy garb in Stanford-in-France, it was known that I was an ordained minister, and so a couple of students and I were asked to work out an informal service for the evening.

I was very much aware that our "family" included all kinds of believers and nonbelievers: ex-Catholics, practicing Catholics, secular and religious Jews, varieties of Protestants ranging from conservative Baptists to high Anglicans, and that we must not impose one religious model on everybody else. I was particularly sensitive that the Jewish students might feel excluded if we summoned up too much explicit Christian terminology. We worked out some readings: Jewish and Christian to start with, and also opened the session to those who had been helped by Kahlil Gibran and Buddhist wisdom. We spent some time after this simply letting people talk about Richard; about their faith or lack thereof; about Richard's parents and their devastation so far away; and about the need for all of us to be tender to Kim, Richard's girlfriend. We then sang a few of the songs that were universally known in the sixties, such as, "Where Have All the Flowers Gone?"

I ended the service, or so I thought, with a brief, theologically inclusive benediction. But I had miscalculated. Nobody left, and the ensuing silence was not one of closure on the event, but of the expectation of more. One of the women students went upstairs and got her guitar, and upon returning started strumming chords that, to my great surprise, led into "Amazing Grace." And to my even greater surprise, they were picked up by and sung in swelling chorus by everyone—Baptists, Catholics, Jews, secularists, even the French members of the staff. I had been too timid. The students were quite mature enough to sift through the words, affirm where they could or remain silent where they needed to. We were creatively shaken up. We could cry now but we could also laugh. It brought us all closer together, and it was somehow a gift Richard gave us through his death that we could sing together throughout the remainder of the evening across all the boundaries that try so hard to divide us.

One of the things I hoped personally to accomplish during the year in France was to visit the Taizé Community, the Protestant monastic order comprised of men who enter the community under the ancient vows of poverty, chastity, and obedience. They support themselves making pottery, glassware, painting, and sculpture, and live a typically monastic life in which work and worship are so intertwined as to give beautiful continuity to the whole. Their worship includes the singing of the Psalter each month, set to new music written, appropriately, by a Roman Catholic musician, Fr. Joseph Gelineau, and a number of repeated refrains that are now used worldwide.

The Taizé Community is somewhat of an anomaly to Protestants, if truth be told, and even more so to Catholics, who might suspect that they were at a Catholic instead of a Protestant retreat center. Visitors to Taizé share in the liturgical program as they wish, and meals and lodging are provided at whatever cost the guests wish to contribute. From time to time small groups go out from Taizé into trouble spots in the world, not with a planned agenda, but simply initially to be a Christian "presence" and see what develops. I had met the prior, Roger Schutz, and the subprior, Max Thurian, when we were Protestant observers at the Second Vatican Council, and we had had several meals at the accommodations they had rented in Rome so that they could be a "presence" there as well.

Once our family was well-established in Tours, we picked a weekend to drive to Taizé in our newly purchased red VW van, and figured that we had room for four students, in case any of them wanted to spend a weekend at a Protestant monastery. I realized that that was not exactly the stuff out of which college sophomores usually construct a weekend in France. To my astonishment, forty students—about half the total group—signed up. We hired a bus.

I spoke the day we left about the situation at Taizé, pointing out that it was very accommodating to diversity and that we should, from whatever background we came, participate in the life of the community in whatever ways did not feel awkward. As I had expected, they found the music of the liturgy beautiful if strange, along with the stained glass windows created by brothers in the community expressly for their chapel.

A young brother from Scotland was assigned to lead this rather unusual group through the weekend. When he asked initially what kinds of questions we had, he must have known that questions about the strange practice of celibacy would lead all the rest. Why would anybody ever take on such a burden willingly? The brother answered in what I found a very insightful way. "Look," he said, "celibacy is not a model that we hope you will adopt in your own lives so much as it is a sign of one possible way of ordering human life as closely as possible toward God, and a reminder of a style of living that clearly works at least for a few." He went on, "Most of you, I gather, have already settled on marriage, rather than celibacy, as the sign you want to erect over your lives. So let's talk about marriage. What things should a marriage contribute in order to be a creative sign for others, whether they marry or not?" That took care of the rest of the afternoon and most of the evening, and the discussion broke new ground for everyone, perhaps even for the Scots brother. Later we talked about work, and how work might relate to all that was going on liturgically in the Taizé chapel. There was much less of a meeting of minds on the topic of why there were no women in the community, and why, if women wanted to go on a retreat, they had to go to a religious house at

Neuchâtel in Switzerland to find any counterpart to a Taizé experience. This position was pretty well rejected by both the men and women in our group on a theoretical as well as a practical level—a rejection shared by their religion professor.

We learned that the brothers do not make lifetime vows, an example of what Frere Roger calls *le dynamic provisoire*, a provisional energy which, so that it will not get itself encrusted, must be held up for new inspection every five years. This enables the community to stay rooted in the contemporary world and not suddenly find itself answering questions no one is asking any more. A few members of our group volunteered the prediction that a reassessment of the place (or lack of place) of women in the community would arise before long in somebody's five-year reevaluation.

An only slightly apocryphal tale: Taizé is persons. It is also stones, stones dug up out of fields and earlier structures and reshaped into contemporary gathering places. The new is incorporated into the old, and the old transforms in response.

Since the early sixties, young people, thousands at a time, have continued to come camping on the Taizé plains in huge army surplus tents organized by language groups. So the hospitable monks have raised their stones to build a larger chapel to accommodate the many visitors, and we are there for its mid-summer dedication at the opening of an international youth conference. But there is a problem. The new chapel is completed, but as the crowds keep arriving, it becomes clear that the worship space is still too small. Brother Roger contemplates the just-finished wall and pits the stones against the persons. The persons win. "People cannot all fit in this chapel? Then we tear the wall down."

And so it goes until there is room for all.

High above the French Riviera, as though determined not to be contaminated by the corrupt world beneath it, lies the tiny town of Vence. It is not distinguished as the site of a cathedral, a museum, or a university, but it does house a building that in itself is a work of art, the chapel of an order of women religious. The chapel is further distinguished by the fact that in every detail—from the vestments to the stations of the cross—it is the creation of a "nonbeliever," Henri Matisse, who did not create stained glass windows nearly as much as he created stained glass walls. When the sun is cooperating, these endow the bare white walls with a brilliance both turbulent and celestial.

The stations of the cross are mere numbers with minimal figures, painted when the elderly arthritic artist could function only with a large brush affixed to a long pole. In an age of belief, identifying the numbers would clearly have evoked the stages of the journey of Christ to the cross. By employing them in an age of disbelief, Matisse seems to be recognizing that the sisters, living within a mere pocket of faith in the midst of the evil world, were of sufficient piety to know, for example, that the number four was "Jesus meets his afflicted mother," and that the number seven depicted a central event, "Jesus is nailed to the cross."

Our family had made a long pilgrimage to find this holy spot, albeit as pilgrims within a red minibus rather than on foot. It was, then, with unveiled dismay and disbelief that we learned from a sister at the entrance that the chapel was open to the public only on Wednesdays. Unfortunately, it was now Thursday, and entrance was denied. I was unwilling to accept this as the final word. I laid out our case to the mother superior with more passion than I have ever been called upon to display in my own tongue, let alone in that of another people.

I identified myself as having been *un observateur protestante*, at *le deuxieme Concile Vaticane* in Rome, and thus eager to continue my pilgrimage. Even *mes enfants* were eager to visit this rich combination of art and worship, having heard much about it from the enthusiasm of *leur parents*. What is more, the chances of our family ever being together again in this part of the world were *sans doute, impossible*. Indeed, I reported, when I was at the council, many bishops and more than one cardinal had assured me that Vence was not to be missed if I wished to understand *l'esprit du Concil* and the new pulsations of faith emanating from St. Peter's to this very spot on which we were standing. I was, *en effet, un pèlerin moi-meme* and having gotten this far I must not give up. To miss seeing *la chapelle* would leave all of us *désoleé*.

The mother superior, making her way through this grammatical mayhem, decided to put grace above law on this occasion, and informed us that a sister would be provided to give us *le tour rapide*, and she hoped we would be satisfied with *un tour pendant la durée de quinze minutes*—a quarter of an hour. This was *largesse*, indeed, to be accepted with *alacrité* and *gratitude*.

We were more than recompensed. The sister guiding us seemed aware that this was a special event for us, and there was a lovely gift from her lips. She departed from the formal talk to visitors, and said, her eyes positively shining, "*Ah, Monsieur, quand le soleil brille, ah, monsieur, la chapelle, elle chante!*" Her English was about on a par with my French: "Ah, Monsieur, when the sun is shining, the chapel herself joins in our singing!"

We had overstayed our visit and it was almost dark. But whenever I remember Vence, it is a place where the sun is shining, and either birds or angels are joining in the song.

7

Vietnam

It has become popular to decry the sixties as a historical aberration. The young, obsessed with changing society for the better, succeeded only in endorsing chaos and violence. Disillusioned by their utter lack of success, they crawled back into the woodwork to emerge a few years later both wiser and more cynical, victims of a wasted decade.

I reject this analysis. In the 1960s, a campus was an exciting place to be. Yes, there was violence, there was trashing, there were drugs. But that was only what showed on the surface. There was also idealism and a belief that change was possible by peaceful means, that racism was evil, that an immoral war in Vietnam should not define their personal destinies.

To express all this by refusing induction into the armed forces was no small thing. It could mean years in jail. Going to Canada was no picnic either; there was no assurance that such "lawbreakers" could *ever* return to the United States.

I don't know whether many people in uniform were persuaded that they were on a moral crusade. If they were, it was increasingly difficult to sustain such idealism in Southeast Asia, where they found themselves under orders to kill peasants, machine-gun families, and incinerate whole villages.

The longer the war lasted, the worse things got. We were pulverizing the Vietnamese countryside with artillery shells and bombs from B-52s, and burning the inhabitants of the countryside with napalm, so diabolically effective that when it got into human flesh it continued to burn beneath the surface of the skin. There were new antipersonnel weapons designed not to harm buildings or tanks or factories, but only to harm living creatures. A single antipersonnel weapon could spray out a thousand sharp pieces of metal that penetrated so deeply into human flesh that trying to remove them surgically only made the wound more lethal. It was standard operating procedure to burn the huts of civilians, whole villages at a time, preferably with the owners still inside so that they could be incinerated too. The logic went: If the only good Vietcong is a dead Vietcong, it is an act of patriotism and even valor to destroy as many civilians as possible, since the logic of encounter was likewise clear—get them first, because otherwise they might get you first. If you happened to kill a baby at the same time, that was all right; that would mean one less revolutionary to fight in the next war. (I later heard the identical argument in the mountains of Nicaragua as a reason for U.S.-supported troops not to take Sandinistas alive.)

Some students and a few adults began to be disenchanted. Confusion, fear of painful death, outrage, and lack of any convincing rationale by our government for what was going on began to penetrate their psyches. Surely there were better ways to use the lives of young men; surely there was enough wisdom and power to bring about a truce and begin negotiations; surely there was enough residual decency to make it impossible for the war to continue. But decency failed to turn the tide, and the war continued. And many of the students found their moral choices even further tested by the "human rights struggle" in our own South. They discovered that what was happening in Alabama and what was happening in Vietnam could not be disentangled from one another. *They were part of the same struggle.*

In both cases, white leaders, white politicians, and white enforcers of "law and order" were using their power against dark-skinned peoples who were guilty of no crime save a desire to claim their full humanity, just like everybody else. It was *not* true that white-skinned and dark-skinned students were siphoned off from the "human rights" struggle into the Vietnam struggle. It *was* true that white-skinned and dark-skinned students found an issue on which they could work together.

I remember Charlie Drekmeier, one of the few political scientists at Stanford willing to get involved in the struggle, reading a description at a public rally of what had been done to a Vietnamese village by American air power, and almost breaking down before he completed the reading. Initially I believed that sentiments like this were introducing issues that should be reserved for a different time and place. We needed to be "one-issue" persons. I was wrong, and Charlie was right. We confronted not two issues but one, which tied together all the components: economics, culture, humanitarianism, geopolitics, religion.

So a lot of us had a lot of fresh homework to do. As we began to discover what our nation was really doing in Vietnam, we were confronted by the "experts" who derided our naiveté. But we soon discovered that the convictions of the "experts" depended on who had appointed them—Lyndon Johnson or William Fulbright. The important thing was that *they disagreed*, and that what the peace movement needed was not more data (of which we had plenty) but more commitment.

On one level this was encouraging; greater numbers stood for more people power to organize for freedom. But there was another less encouraging level, which was a growing unanimity about the ends to be sought, coupled with a sharp difference about the best means to realize those ends. For this reason, it was an unanticipated blessing that the early recruits to the Vietnam struggle came from the civil rights movement, as the persuasive and eloquent voice of Martin Luther King Jr. persuaded them that only nonviolence could prevail. And when he, after dozens of tense sessions with his followers, decided to link the two struggles and make them one, Martin Luther King changed the face of the protest. There was an apparatus already in place for working to end U.S. involvement in the war by nonviolent means.

It didn't stay that way for long. Many other students were wedded to doing "whatever it takes" to stop racist policies. In one area Stanford was very lucky, though not all the constituency realized it. We were blessed with the presence on campus of undergraduate David Harris, an all-American boy from Fresno High, who had a post–high school political conversion that made him a natural leader of activities for social change on the Stanford campus. David was not only a natural leader, but soon emerged as a national leader as well, who visited scores of campuses and helped hundreds of local leaders establish groups that could assist those who were working through a new relationship to moral protest that would never have been possible without his help. A fine consistency in his life is validated by the fact that he spent two years in jail for publicly propounding noncooperation with the draft.

Campuses began to resemble armed fortresses, and a lot of energy became focused on orchestrating rallies and marches and sit-ins, in which all who opposed the war could participate in good conscience. And attempts were made—sometimes successfully, sometimes not—to keep the split between violent and nonviolent means from splitting the movement itself. This was not an easy task. Although a rally might start nonviolently, there was no telling when those committed to violence might start practicing it. I frequently spoke at such rallies, and discovered how hard it was to keep a point of view alive over the course of a rally. People like myself would be invited to speak at the beginning of a rally, while a crowd was building up and the overall mood was supportive. But at some point, the heavy artillery from the other side of the ideological fence would begin to function—more high-powered rhetoric, more orchestrated cheering, more applause intruding when key phrases began to recur. And then, at the peak of emotional fervor, a specific plan would emerge, created well in advance, to turn the rally into a march, and the march into a sit-in, with a few people throwing rocks at Stanford's windows along the way. And the next morning, *The Stanford Daily* would imply that people such as the professor of religious studies who had spoken against the war were thereby sanctioning the rock throwing. To remain silent on such occasions was to appear to condone the violence in Vietnam by default, whereas to speak on such occasions was to appear to condone the violence on campus.

As the battle lines hardened and we got to know where people stood, it was still possible even for "liberals" to organize rallies, marches, teach-ins, and nonviolent civil disobedience. We knew who our friends were and were not. With the exception of one colleague, Jerry Irish, I learned not to expect much support from the folks in religious studies. This wasn't much of a loss, when compared to the intense moral support from certain Jewish faculty members in other departments, whose common bond with us was a passion for social justice, imbibed, maybe unconsciously, from the Hebrew prophets. And with amazing consistency, it would turn out that those who shared social justice concerns, while claiming to be "secular Jews," always seemed to have had at least one grandfather who was a rabbi.

As for our "secularist" allies, their query to the presumably "religious" folk, and especially the "self-avowed Christians," was a plaintive one with a sharp barb: "Why don't you follow your leader?" They knew intuitively that Jesus of Nazareth would never have been found holding an AK-47 rifle.

INTERMISSION

Here I reach a stylistic and substantive impasse. I have been describing what was happening at Stanford and elsewhere, as though one event clearly sparked another and there were logical connections between what was happening.

There weren't. There was too much chaos, too much impetuous activity, whether on the part of students, faculty, administration, and trustees, or the folks in Washington making such irresponsible use of guns. Different groups seized center stage, then lost it, then perhaps regained it by maneuvers that had little connection to other events. Furthermore, by no means did all of the "actions" take place on campus, as the report of my own activities will testify, and they too were marked by events that cannot be reported simply chronologically. So the chaos is compounded, in part at least by my own presence in the story.

I have concluded that the only way to be fair to what was going on is to let the lack of tidiness shape my reporting, and be content not to seek further for a cause-and-effect scenario. My organizing principle will be that there is no organizing principle.

So I present a collection of experiences of Stanford and elsewhere in the sixties and early seventies. Be consoled: If you do not see how it all fits together, you are probably as close to what really went on as were the participants themselves.

We were often bewildered when we were not angry, and overwhelmed when we were not despairing. But we were fortified by one another. The insecurities of the times are captured by one Stanford administrator's rule of thumb for the sixties: "Every morning when I bike to work, I count the buildings." For myself, I continue to count the friends and the lessons of those times.

Early in my time at Stanford I was invited to participate in an annual seminar, limited to fifteen students and with five faculty from different disciplines, offered throughout the year for political science credit and administered by Professor Charles Drekmeier. Although Charlie was the official convener, his wife, Margot, a teacher herself, was equally involved in the leadership. Possessed of an almost photographic memory, she would often get us back on track when the conversation had become aimless. The theme was always "social thought," and the reading and emphases varied from year to year, but there was always a strong exposure to Marx and Freud. Students gave reports and faced fairly vigorous oral examinations at the end of the year. The meetings were held off campus in the Drekmeiers' home one evening a week, and food and drink were available throughout the evening. The structure was almost entirely open-ended, even to the point that there was never an official adjournment time.

I was grateful to be included, even though Marx and Freud were hardly the thinkers in Western culture whom I knew best, and I was always a little on edge for the time when I might be asked to offer a "religious critique" of some point or other. But there was always for me a kind of academic excitement since (a) none of our various departments would let the course count as part of our teaching load, suggesting something not quite approved by those on high, and (b) the student enrollees always came from the most radical section of the student body, seeking in the seminar what they did not find in most other courses: a critique of a society that resisted social challenge and of a university, so they thought, that was unalterably dedicated to the preservation of the status quo.

The nearest thing that I can remember to an academic insurrection from this insurrection-prone group occurred at the height of "student unrest," when we professors got together before the first class to suggest some material that might initiate discussion about the direction the class would go that year, together with a proposed title and some sampling of readings we might agree to read. Bedlam ensued. Even this far-out seminar had sold out to conventional and outmoded teaching methods. Furthermore, the students had not been consulted. And the readings! Books—how bourgeois. Any book was at least a year old and therefore out of date for planning the revolution. Mimeographed materials (this was before the age of photocopying) might be okay, provided the ink was not quite dry and one didn't plan the reading list too far in advance, since "things" might change radically in the interim.

There were some "up" moments, such as when we discovered we had unexpected supporters. On one beautifully clear day in San Francisco we had an ecumenical service of worship on the steps of the federal building, culminating in the "morning offering," when eighty-seven young men placed their draft cards in the "collection plate." Phil Farnham and others working behind the scenes had done a splendid job of ensuring a large crowd, including the press looking for an event that would make it on the evening news. There were many bodies and many cameras.

Each person who put his draft card in one of the offering plates held by the participating clergy spoke his name clearly before the cameras. Each one knew that this was no inconsequential gesture, but a taking on of the possibility of up to five years in jail and a ten-thousand-dollar fine. We clergy knew that we too, by receiving the cards, made ourselves eligible for identical treatment. It wasn't a matter of braggadocio or a quest for sympathy, but simply a matter of fair play. We had no right to dump on them a risk from which we could remain exempt. As Bill Coffin put it once to a group of clergy, "We cannot educate young men to perform acts of conscience and then desert them in their hour of conscience."

We had earlier on agreed to support these young men, even if it meant our defying the government along with them. We would "aid, counsel, and abet" them in carrying out their decisions of conscience. Toward the conclusion of the service we acted out that part, especially the promise to "abet" them. We received their cards, took them inside the federal building, and mailed them back to General Hershey, the head of Selective Service in Washington. Our mutual complicity was clear, and all of it had been validated on film and could be used later on, if necessary, in a court of law.

We had—or at least thought we had—a clear understanding with all those participants that the draft cards were to be turned in, rather than burned, a device for catching attention that other groups had sometimes employed. We felt that such an action should not be part of our rally, since it seemed only to fudge the issue and the message. The issue was stopping the war, and each young man turning in his draft card embodied that message clearly and directly with a name attached. The draft card's license to kill became, in the transfer, a pledge *not* to kill.

Eighty-six of them got the word, and the cards piled up in the basket. But number eighty-seven didn't get the word, or if he did, chose to ignore it. As he approached the collection basket, he brought out a cigarette lighter and clicked it. The card caught fire, and number eighty-seven waved it in the air with evident glee.

To no one's surprise, every television camera on the scene immediately zoomed in on the action, which, whatever else it was, was certainly good theatre. But it didn't belong in the service, and at its conclusion I was, if not brokenhearted, at least disconsolate. Our attempt to communicate a clear message about the war had been negated by the action of one person, whom the evening news would surely feature centrally as another disloyal draft card burning. The real story of the eighty-six others would be lost.

We monitored the various renditions of the event on the evening news shows, prepared for the worst. And here was the place where the unexpected support emerged. We had had too little faith in those cameramen and their editors. In reporting the event, not a single channel featured the showmanship of number eighty-seven. The story was the acts of conscience of the other eighty-six.

In the spring of 1969 I began to feel the noose tightening a bit more. I had been invited to give the baccalaureate sermon at Hamilton College. I chose as a sermon topic "The Need for a New Radicalism," and tried to relate the sermon to the increasingly volatile world outside the campus—something I had never been too confident I had achieved on other less stressful visits to Hamilton in the past. However, all went according to plan, and the morning was quite sedate.

About ten days later, however, I got a phone call from the president of Hamilton, saying something like, "I don't want to alarm you unduly, Bob, but I think you ought to know that members of the FBI have just been here in my office, and they asked, among other things, whether you had preached a sermon in our chapel on commencement weekend on the topic, 'The Need for a New Radicalism.' They gave me a copy of your text, which looked to me like what I had heard you saying. They wondered . . ."

I interrupted. This wasn't quite as innocent as I had thought. "Look," I said, "I had only one copy of that sermon, and I didn't give it to anybody afterward because it was pretty messy—a typical Brown production with lots of last-minute changes and underlinings. I hadn't had time to make a clean copy before church Sunday morning."

"Well," he responded, "that's a pretty good description of the copy they showed me. You certainly didn't major in typing."

By now it was clear to both of us that the FBI had somehow gotten into my room after the sermon was preached, taken it off the desk where I had left it, made a copy, and returned my text to its original location. The episode had no conclusion. All the evidence was hearsay or circumstantial, and there was no "case" to be fought. But it did convince me that a certain amount of paranoia was becoming par for the course and that it might be a good idea to keep anything I wrote about the war under lock and key. I also learned something about the power of titles and am sure that it was that dangerous concept of "radicalism" that prompted the feds' interest.

Years later, during the Earl Lectures at Pacific School of Religion, I was invited to participate in a panel discussion at Berkeley with Archbishop Raymond Hunthausen of Seattle. He and I were to argue "no" to nuclear weapons, and the two upper-echelon physicists from the Livermore Weapons Research Laboratory were to argue "yes." Hunthausen had become an important person in the overall debate, since he was almost the only Roman Catholic bishop who was ready to push the logical argument all the way; when he said "no" he did so without qualifiers. He was asked to go first, to be followed by a scientist, to be followed by me, to be followed by the second scientist. We were each to have fifteen minutes.

The archbishop did not offer a point-by-point rebuttal to what he could have assumed the physicists would say. He did not offer statistics designed to overwhelm a debating antagonist. He spoke very simply from the heart. As someone trying to be a follower of Jesus of Nazareth, he said, he found it impossible to sanction such weapons of destruction, and offered a few quotations from the Gospels. He added that he had come to this position after watching Trident nuclear submarines being loaded with warheads in the Seattle harbor, and said that he regretted not having come to this position earlier.

End of speech. Elapsed time: about four minutes.

His approach totally unnerved the physicist who was scheduled to speak next. I guess the physicist had prepared to deal with fiery dialectic by a prince of the church, rather than a simple declaration of faith. The physicist sat there, next to me, unable to rise. I finally whispered to him that it was his turn. He fumbled with his papers and then, turning to me in utter helplessness, whispered back, "You go ahead," which I did. He recovered enough to speak fourth and last, but his heart was not in it.

I have often wondered what happened to him, who obviously for the first time in his professional life had been reduced to silence, not by brilliant oratory, but by an unassuming "believing Christian" who just happened to be wearing a black suit, a clerical collar, and a very simple pectoral cross.

One evening in our living room at a low point in war protest, when a few of us were bemoaning our lack of effectiveness, someone proposed blocking

With father, George William Brown

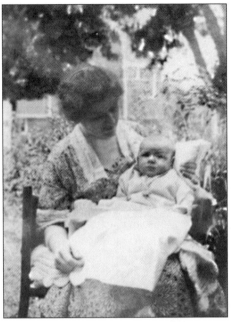

With mother, Ruth McAfee Brown

With sisters Betty and Harriet

In Summit, NJ

June 21, 1944

With son Peter in Jaffrey, NH

With son Mark in Heath

With son Tom in Heath

Sydney with Alison

With Peter Brown and Jill Brown Fryar, 1986

With Daniel Berrigan and Sydney

Blocking the San Mateo draft board office during the Vietnam War

With Pope Paul VI, 1970

With Fidel Castro

the entrance to a draft board. This wasn't exactly a new idea and had been tried in various places across the country. While the action was mainly symbolic, it had a clear message: As long as we are here, none of our youth will enter through these doors to receive a license to kill.

We expected that when we blocked a draft board, a police officer would appear and politely point out that we were in violation of some local code against blocking a sidewalk, or (more serious) impeding the entrance of people who had legitimate business with the federal government. We would reply that we felt that the Vietnam War was not only immoral but also illegal, that business with the war was never legitimate, and that in conscience we had to engage in public protest as a way of changing our government's policy. The officer would be unmoved by our logic and would give us a deadline to disperse or be arrested—ten minutes, five minutes, thirty seconds, depending on whether or not the paddy wagon had arrived.

Sometimes the police would permit us to state briefly for the assembled press and onlookers why we were breaking the law. On one such occasion, when my son Peter and I were arrested together, it was Good Friday, and I was able to use my allotted time to preach a brief sermon from the sidewalk. It wasn't always so genteel, but the police had an obligation to protect our right of free speech as far down the line as possible, and we knew it, and they knew that we knew it. Sooner or later, we would be arrested, usually handcuffed, and taken to the nearest jail, where we would be booked, fingerprinted, photographed, and given a date to appear in court. We would either be released on our own recognizance or forced to put up bail. Sometimes the charges would be dropped, or we would appear in court to be verbally spanked by the judge, fined (say, twenty-five dollars), or, occasionally, given five days in Santa Rita Prison, something Peter and I were both given the day we did it together.

Back to the Browns' living room. We pondered how to make a fresh impact. Somebody whose name is surely written in heaven but no longer inscribed on my brain dropped a bombshell: "There are five draft boards in the Bay Area," he said, ticking them off. "San Francisco, Oakland, Berkeley, San Mateo, and San Jose. What if we blocked them all on the same day?" There was a long, appreciative silence. Whatever the plan might lack in detail, it could not be charged with lacking scope. We got to work.

First item: warm bodies. It was hard enough to find seven or eight people willing to go to jail for blocking just one draft board. Could we replicate that number five times over?

Second item: hard data. When did the draft boards open? When did they close? Could we park nearby? Who would be our spokespersons? Were public restrooms available? This was routine stuff for an organizer, but big questions for a bunch of amateurs.

Third item: second thoughts. Was this off the wall? Everybody should do some individual assessment. With spouse? Very definitely with spouse. And we needed to sound out the persons we thought about under the first item.

Fourth item: no leaks ahead of time!

"Oh, and one other thing" (Brown speaking). "We are sure our phone is being tapped and has been for a long time. Corny as it sounds, we have to devise some sort of code to avoid being apprehended in advance." We finally decided to refer to ourselves as "the church committee." No cause for police alarm there. And when we referred to things we needed to do, meetings and so forth, we agreed to refer to such events as happening one day later than the actual meeting itself. "The church committee meets at seven o'clock next Tuesday" actually meant "Monday at seven," so that if the feds were on our trail they would show up twenty-four hours late.

Getting people to commit to civil disobedience turned out to be even more difficult than we had expected. Most people had good reasons why this wasn't the right time in their lives, due either to the pressure of immediate job demands or the predictable disapproval of people higher up the economic pecking order. These were not idle concerns. I am morally certain that one minister and one priest in our group had their careers altered for the worse because of their participation in our action.

A fine line had to be drawn between inviting friends to join us and unduly pressuring them. I frequently hauled out my eleventh commandment for people in times of national stress: "Thou shalt not decide that someone else should become a martyr." Despite such problems, we ended up with enough persons to issue a significant challenge at each draft board.

The scenario: On the given day our groups would go to the various draft board sites at around 8:30 a.m. and start with conventional picketing in front of the doors. However, we informed the press that at 10 a.m. a new event of some magnitude would simultaneously take place in front of all the draft boards in the Bay Area. When the hour arrived, we put down our picket signs, locked arms, and blocked the entrances, stating the reason for our action directly to the TV cameras. We intended to stand there, blocking access, until we were arrested.

At all the draft boards save San Mateo, the police moved in quickly and violently. There was a real scuffle in Oakland, and on the evening news I saw one of my graduate students, Tom Peterson, receive very rough treatment from a policeman with a billy club. In San Francisco, a potentially dangerous legal tangle developed, since the draft board was on federal property and punishment could be much more severe, and we were careful not to act on federal property after that.

But a funny thing happened on the way to San Mateo. Our group had reserved the San Mateo draft board for the "heavies" and some of their sons.

Its lineup included the president of the Academic Senate at Stanford University, a Catholic priest, a tenured math professor from UC Berkeley, two local pastors from Palo Alto, the dean of the Stanford Memorial Church, a high-level member of the Stanford administration and his draft-aged son, a respected political activist, and my son Peter and me. By any accounting, it was a fairly impressive crowd of draft board blockers, who were ready to do time for their own conviction that the Vietnam War was wrong. The San Mateo police were not ready to confront this dangerous cast of characters. The police never showed up.

So we returned the next day. Again no police appeared, and we maintained an unbroken blockade. We returned the third day. Same story. People could not stay away from their jobs indefinitely, and on the second and third days we had a few dropouts. But we also had an equal number of replacements, expanding our constituency to include women, some of whom were mothers of sons of draft age, and some in blue jeans. By the end of the third day we decided that we had made our point, so we closed off Operation San Mateo. But not before Davie Napier, dean of the Stanford chapel, had gone into the draft board office itself, through those same doors we had blocked, behind which a group of rather frightened women clerks had been in a state of siege for three days. Davie presented them with a large bouquet from us all, our own version of flower power.

We were also pleased to announce that last evening at a Stanford rally in Memorial Church that if the police were going to let white, middle-aged men in neckties block draft boards indefinitely, we figured that the war could be ended with the help of a few thousand white middle-class men in neckties.

We scored a victory at San Mateo. The forces of law and order beat a hasty retreat when confronted by unarmed people who were known and respected in their communities. The action suggested that we cannot put the burden of changing society on only a few charismatic individuals, nor on the young, who will take risks we are too timorous to take. The nonviolent movement hasn't failed; it just hasn't been sufficiently tried.

This might be a good ending to the story, save for one further event within the event that must be recorded. A young man appeared, very flustered, very angry, an ex-Green Beret who walked with a cane. He told us he *had* to get into the draft board office and even tried to smash his way through—the only such aggressive action in the entire three days—but the blockade held. Rather unwisely from his point of view, he centered his attacks on Peter and Bill Leland, the assistant dean of students at Stanford, who also helped coach the wrestling team.

All of us listened to him with understanding and even compassion, and over time his outbursts began to be more tempered. We explained what we were trying to say, and a wonderful thing happened. The anger began to drain out of the young soldier, and while he never came close to agreeing with us, he did, rather grudgingly, acknowledge that there was a point to what we were doing. As he finally left he grinned, "Too bad you guys weren't around when I was applying for military service." Then we all went home with the renewed conviction that people are always open to new points of view.

Alison: I remember the years of the draft board blockades, mostly when I was in junior high or early high school. I remember being home after school. Tom was off with friends, Peter was off participating in the civil disobedience, and Mark was living on campus in college. I was home dealing with the calls. Reporters called with questions, and angry, crazed people called, furious and threatening. I had to be very careful what I said, how I handled the calls. I remember knowing that you could never tell if it was really a reporter or someone from the FBI.

The draft board blockades happened, and the jail time happened. I remember visiting Papa at Santa Rita Prison. Almost all of the families in the visitors holding area, except a few others and us, were black and Latino. It was overwhelming to see the racism so forcefully. I remember seeing Papa in his blue jeans and work shirt prison uniform. I was glad to see what it looked like inside a prison and wondered how it was for the kids whose parents were in there for long sentences. I remember later on hearing how different my brother Peter's experience was at Santa Rita, as a young person rather than a known member of the clergy. The accounts were like night and day. From Peter's accounts I got a sense of how differently people were treated and how race was used to target people for destruction.

Peter: I went to the Santa Rita Prison with Bill Leland, then an assistant dean of students at Stanford, who also happily for me was a black belt in judo. The two of us were put in a barracks with forty or fifty African American guys from Oakland, all of whom were puzzled by our being there. When they heard our story they broke out laughing and made it clear that they thought being in jail for protesting the war was absurd. Despite this, we had some genuinely interesting talks with some very bright men: some talk about us, mostly about them and the repeated cycle from ghetto to prison to ghetto—and back—that most of them seemed to be on. The barracks were segregated (apart from the check-in place where my dad spent his five days). There were African American, Asian, Hispanic, and white barracks—and there was obvious racial tension in the prison. One of the first things I saw was a Hispanic prisoner being beaten by a white guard simply because he had asked for a cigarette.

Days were long and without much to do, but at night there was late talk about a number of things. One repeat subject that caused me more than a little alarm was very creative language about what should be done with white people—it went on and on, and it obviously was for our benefit. And it seemed strange because there wasn't a hint of it during the day. And nothing happened at night either, but it made it more than a little hard to get to sleep.

The third day we were there, a small riot broke out in the yard, which to a degree had been set off by a pacifist war protester from Stanford who foolishly had tried to break up a fight between an African American and a Chicano. These two turned on him and when they were done and he was on the ground, it was as though a fire had been lit. Fights rolled out throughout the yard. I stuck my head out the door to see what was going on, and an African American guy from another barracks clobbered me as he ran by, sending me reeling back inside. I was caught before I hit the floor and quickly tended to by a number of the men who, the night before, had been talking about beating Bill and me up. (On some level we had apparently become "barracks family.") Later that day, a homemade knife appeared ominously on my pillow. I wasn't sure if it was there for me to protect myself or if it was a plant for a guard to find. Neither was good news. I stuck it under the mattress and tried not to think about it.

Those five days were confusing, but eye-opening. When Peter Sano, a family friend who had been a prisoner of war in Siberia, picked me up, I had a huge shiner, very little respect for the American penal system, and an odd admiration for the prisoners of Barracks 26.

In order to keep war protest from being sporadic and unfocused, an interfaith group of religious leaders met in New York in April 1967 to create an ad hoc structure through which our concerns could be more effectively channeled. "Clergy and Laymen Concerned About Vietnam" later became "Clergy and *Laity* Concerned about Vietnam," to take greatest account of its gender-free agenda. It was soon known simply as CALC.

CALC's activities included the organization of rallies, marches, teach-ins, publishing a widely circulated newspaper, providing speakers and discussion leaders for local events, and generally trying to be of service to groups geographically separate and in need of a national identity. Considerable funding was made available from a generous donor, whose gift made it possible to take advantage of low airfares and many conference phone calls to plan events on a regional and national scale.

Once organized, CALC turned out to be mainly an East Coast organization as far as active personnel were concerned. There was no collusion at work, but those who had the time or energy or talents tended to be in the Boston/New York/Washington, DC, area. Living in California and being on sabbatical leave for part of the time, I was on the outer edge of the inner circle, but was frequently deputized to draft a statement or a position paper and to speak at rallies in many locales. Bill Coffin, Abraham Heschel, Dick Neuhaus, Balfour Brickner, John Bennett, and others of similar stature gave inordinately of their time and talents to keep CALC afloat. This happened often through conference calls of long duration, even when it was clear that somebody's phone line was already being tapped.

Once, when I was speaking in northern Minnesota, I was asked to participate in a conference call to help plan a rally to be held a few days later in front of the White House. A great many agendas had to be dovetailed for maximal participation, and each person had to contact further friends to enlist support. It was a complex operation. On the morning of the event, we all began to appear in Lafayette Square from various corners of the capital. A policeman, amiability itself, was also there with a can of Mace that he didn't exactly hide. The ground rules were being defined. Time went by and more of our cohorts appeared. The policeman, curious and even a little restless, asked, "When does your Philadelphia contingent get here?" This was the first time I had known that we had a "Philadelphia contingent" anywhere. It suddenly struck me with dazzling clarity that this one cop knew more about our collective agenda and timetable than all the rest of us put together. Score one for the efficiency of Ma Bell.

Credit for the many good things that were done through CALC belongs chiefly to one of the full-time staff members, Dick Fernandez. Dick possessed the analytical skills of a professional quarterback and coach rolled into one. To me, his greatest gift as an organizer was his willingness to meet each person wherever he or she was, working equally well with someone at a personally insecure point of antiwar involvement or someone who would do civil disobedience at the drop of a hat.

Dick frequently came up with new ideas one could tell he was dying to try out. But along with his zeal for action and confrontation and witness was a genuine acceptance of the fact that other people might not be there yet. He never forced his agenda if it meant leaving a lot of folks behind. Very often in "movement activities," those who didn't immediately jump on board for the next action would be pressured almost mercilessly with the implication that they were "chicken." I often found myself initially, at least, among those not yet convinced. And I never once heard him trying to cajole or pressure someone to engage in an action for which he or she did not feel sufficiently prepared. He was willing to let you be at whatever place you could be at, in good conscience, and would not try to pressure you to do something about which you weren't completely clear. This is a great gift that, I discovered, many antiwar organizers lacked.

Before one of the later national CALC assemblies in Washington, DC, I began to be importuned by another staff member by phone several times a day. He insisted that I had to get myself to Washington because a new action was going to take place and I was needed for it. What was the nature of the action and what was to be my part in it? Well, he couldn't say over the phone because that would give the plan away to the police. I wasn't ready to sign up on those terms, so he said he'd send me a special delivery letter with an outline of the plan. But when the letter came the next day, once again the nature of the action was only cryptically described, and I was left as unenlightened as before. I argued that I could not give a kind of blank check to the group, and the plan finally was dropped.

I found out later that the plan was to have me and a few other "leaders" engage in a sit-in in the office of a high official in the Pentagon with whom an appointment had been secured. The minute this began, CALC members else-where would surface and make a big deal about the government's persecution of clergy. It would work particularly well if we could manage to get arrested in the process. Maybe it would have ended the war sooner, but I'm not per-suaded. Maybe it was a good plan just to get some coverage in the media. But I resented not being trusted with any information about what I was to do with the rest of my life.

I cite this incident because it was so atypical and because Dick Fernandez would never have taken part in an attempt to muscle past someone's real mis-givings. He knew in his bones what a lot of us came to learn more slowly: that people engaged in social justice projects do not get permanently stuck at one point on an ideological spectrum; they continue to move and grow, sometimes very slowly, and sometimes with dazzling speed. Cheers, resoundingly, for Fernandez for not beginning to resemble "the enemy."

Being arrested became a commonplace in the sixties for many middle-class whites who had never before entertained the notion that it could be a signifi-cant means of social transformation. But what most middle-class whites expe-rienced in jail was frequently a far cry from the ugly experiences that were the lot of most dark-skinned peoples, or whites with long hair and beards. As both groups discovered, we have a two-track system of justice—one for a little hand-ful of the socially privileged, and another for everybody else. This phenome-non of relatively privileged people ending up in jail was a brand-new experience not only for them, but for their parents, their jailers, and even their judges.

I was arrested a number of times. My arrests happened in a Florida bus ter-minal, twice in Berkeley, once sitting in the office of our pro-war congressman, once on Good Friday preaching in front of a draft board, once while praying on my knees in clerical collar at the federal building in San Francisco, and once protesting the manufacture of nuclear weapons at Livermore Labs. Civil dis-obedience was one, but only one, part of a larger and longer-term strategy.

During the writing of these pages, Robert McNamara published *In Retro-spect: The Tragedy and Lessons of Vietnam*. The book was fiercely attacked by most of those in the peace movement; my own appraisal is somewhat different. It is a great moral achievement for a man in public life to have offered such an honest account of how people like himself, with initially good intentions, became enmeshed in structures of their own creation from which it was finally impossible to escape.

Most public servant memoirs turn out to be intensely self-serving, with their acts of political stewardship interpreted in the best possible light. Not so with Robert McNamara, who makes clear that his own activities in the public arena were activities for which he feels deep remorse and regret: "What we did was terribly, terribly wrong." His intention is not to justify his decisions but to expose them, at whatever personal cost, hoping that the lessons learned too late in the Vietnam struggle can be appropriated for use in avoiding similar struggles in the future. All honor to him for having set a pattern virtually unknown in our nation's public life.

His book relates to the present story in one particular. At the conclusion of the first Washington, DC, rally of CALC, seven of us were given an appointment with this same Robert McNamara, then secretary of defense, to present our moral concerns. As a sometime Presbyterian, McNamara was at ease with folks from church and synagogue, and began the interview by acknowledging that it was perfectly appropriate for us to be there and to be raising moral issues about our nation's use of power. This was January 1967.

Bill Coffin was our chief spokesperson, and made our case with typical cogency. Rabbi Heschel also spoke at length, with deep and throbbing passion. Before Vietnam I had admired McNamara, and as "his war" got worse and worse, he seemed to me a tragic figure rather than a villain deliberately playing God over history for evil ends. As I listened to the exchanges, I felt more and more sure that he was trying to say something to us, and it seemed pretty important. It would be unfair to put Secretary McNamara's off-the-record comments in quotation marks, but this is what I remember hearing him saying:

> We face a depth of war fever in our country that is exceedingly destructive. Before we can end the war, that attitude must change; otherwise, what any administration can do (and survive politically) will be increasingly proscribed. As the moral leaders of our nation, you clergy and laity must make it part of your task to help us create a climate of opinion in which we can de-escalate the war and bring it to a finish, without letting loose a political chaos that would tear the country apart.

That sentiment can, of course, be read in a variety of ways. Why don't the political leaders themselves take the initiative to exert moral leadership? Why does the administration ask for help and then harass and arrest those who offer help in the name of a change of policy? Would it not be more courageous to risk political defeat than to continue ordering needless deaths?

Whether rightly or wrongly, my own response was to interpret the force of McNamara's implicit request to religious leaders as genuine. I began to look for ways to accept his challenge, to create a moral climate in which de-escalation and the ultimate cessation of hostilities could be brought about. I got on the airplane back to San Francisco a couple of hours later with all this churning around in my head and my gut.

A Stanford colleague, Michael Novak, a Roman Catholic, was sitting next to me on the trip home. He nodded approval at my proposal that we accept McNamara's challenge by collaborating on a book on the war and antiwar activism written from an ecumenical perspective. There in midair, we developed an ambitious agenda. We decided that the book should be the product of Catholic, Protestant, and Jewish writers, and between the two of us we already had that problem two-thirds licked. It should be published simultaneously by Catholic, Protestant, and Jewish publishing houses to ensure maximal distribution. It should be available in paperback as well as hardcover. All royalties should go to CALC. It should be written for laypeople, and should not assume much previous acquaintance with the topic. It should be finished in less than six months. It should contain further resources, statements, pronouncements, and so forth, along with some bibliographical suggestions. Finally, it should be small. Regarding our decision to include a Jewish author, the one name that immediately occurred to us was "Abraham Heschel." By the time we were over Denver, the project was taking on a life of its own. I phoned Heschel the next morning, feeling a little presumptuous, described the project, and asked if he would contribute a Jewish reflection for us. The answer was immediate: "I am at your disposal."

The title, *Vietnam: Crisis of Conscience*, emerged over the next few weeks. We managed to meet all the specifications noted above, with even a little time to spare. I won't claim that the book changed the course of American history. But it did get a lot of use, stirred up a lot of discussion, and provided one handy place where people could get enough help so that they could no longer plead ignorance of the issues or noninvolvement in their consequences.

During these times when precarious living was the name of the game, we picked up the paper one morning and learned that Bill Coffin, along with Dr. Benjamin Spock and several others, had been indicted on federal conspiracy charges. (That story is told in detail in Coffin's autobiography, *Once to Every Man*.)

What needs to be recounted is that I, along with many others, had been doing many of the same things Bill Coffin had been doing—"aiding, counseling, and abetting" young men of conscience as they tried to work out their response to a message from Uncle Sam that began with the word "Greetings" and announced that the recipient was about to be fitted with a brand-new Army uniform. I was led to conclude that if Coffin could be indicted for such activity, so could the rest of us, and it only made sense to start planning accordingly.

I imagined, however, that the feds would try Coffin first, before proceeding with a rash of arrests, since a declaration in the courts of Coffin's "guilt" would make it easy to cite such a precedent as a basis for convicting others. I rapidly became less sanguine, however, when two men appeared at my office door one morning, flashed their FBI badges, and expressed a desire to talk with me about my antiwar activities. They played it by the book. They were courteous, even solicitous of making demands on my time, and made it perfectly clear that I was within my rights not to respond immediately and was entitled to have twenty-four hours to decide whether to respond at all. Since I had no *bon mots* on hand (as Bill Coffin would have had) to enhance the moment, I opted for the waiting period.

I will admit that I was deeply shaken. While realizing that something like this might happen, it had remained pretty theoretical. But now "the war" wasn't just something going on six thousand miles away in Southeast Asia; it now included the possibility of arrest, trial, and imprisonment, all of which were as close as the doorway to my office, 50E, Inner Quad, Stanford University 94305. At the same time, I knew that I had enviable resources. I was, after all, teaching in a university that had a first-class law school, from which help was surely available. Without wasting any time, I phoned across the quad to Herb Packer, a professor at the law school, for some initial input. He promised to talk immediately with some law school faculty who were specialists in this sort of thing and get back to me. And he counseled me not to worry.

Two or three hours later, hours that count among the longest hours I have ever endured, he rang back to say that he had already talked with Bill Keogh, who knew military law as well as civil law, having served at one time in the office of the judge-advocate general of the U.S. Army. Herb didn't say it, but I soon discovered that Bill Keogh was one tough Irishman with a heart of gold. Initially, I was a bit apprehensive about the military connection. How could someone who had worked for the JAG possibly understand alleged civil disobedience? But he opposed the Vietnam War and almost immediately offered to take my case pro bono.

Right off he gave me two pieces of advice for which I was immediately and everlastingly grateful. First, although he would take the case pro bono, there would be inevitable expenses involved in preparing for possible trial. He would need to go to the East Coast to talk with other lawyers working on the Coffin-Spock case, accumulate transcripts of other materials available only there, and so forth. But I should *not* try to raise the money for these expenses myself. He was adamant on that point. "What are friends for?" he reminded me. I should not be demeaned by having to go begging, hat in hand, and my friends should see this as a beautiful chance to be tangibly involved in a worthwhile cause. David Levin of the English Department, a specialist in the thought of Cotton Mather and thus well schooled in human depravity, was immediately willing to assume the onerous task of fund-raising, something in which he proved very adept. Soon Bill Keogh had been to New York and had the materials with which to prepare a defense, should more be needed.

Second, he left no doubt whatsoever in my mind that I should not—repeat, *not*—accept the FBI's request for a friendly talk. "They're not just collecting information about you," he said, interlacing his comments with salty Irish asides. "Their only job is to get such a good case against you that they can win in court and put you behind bars for long enough to warn other would-be draft counselors to expect no mercy."

Never having had to face an FBI interrogation before, and being sure this was a deprivation with which I could happily live, I accepted his advice, advice in which Sydney fully concurred. I phoned the FBI the next morning, telling them that "on advice of counsel" (had I ever anticipated using such a phrase?) I had decided not to cooperate with their investigation. They were urbane and polite through our entire conversation.

In the end, it never came to trial. *Coffin, Spock, et al.* lost in court, but they appealed, and in the midst of the appeals process the government quietly dropped all charges. The rest of us assumed, correctly, that there would be no further indictments.

I cannot help but reflect on how fortunate I was during this whole episode, and in many similar circumstances: first, to have Sydney, who would have paid the biggest price if things had gone askew, standing supportive on principle and still insisting that all the right questions got asked; second, to have a friend like Bill Coffin from whom over the years I have learned certain things about prophetic witness; third, to have had the resources of the Stanford Law School at my disposal. This reality made me feel guilty as hell as well as grateful, since most people protesting the war were not so amply provided for, and had to make do in court without the superior legal help I would have been able to summon; and finally, to be part of a human community like Stanford, where the Bill Keoghs and the David Levins and the Herb Packers and dozens of others suddenly appear and say yes at just the moment they are needed, willing to take on mountains of extra work with no regard but the satisfaction of helping someone in need.

None of the quarrels I later had with Stanford University could obliterate those facts.

In the midst of the ongoing and often confusing swirl of Vietnam activities, one event was both heartwarming and reassuring. It was initiated by Stansfield Turner.

Turner and I had been fraternity brothers at Amherst, until he left after two years with a commission to the U.S. Naval Academy in Annapolis. He graduated with honors, a gridiron reputation, friendship with another ensign named Jimmy Carter, and a Rhodes scholarship to Oxford University. Through it all he was a real straight arrow—decent, honest, exceptionally gifted, in whom one could invest unlimited personal trust. By the time of the Vietnam War, Stan had become a rear admiral and was the commanding officer of a Navy frigate. (Even during my brief Navy career I had never heard of a "frigate," save in adventure stories for boys, in which the pirates always maneuvered around in frigates.) I discovered that contemporary frigates were the nerve center of naval operations, jam-packed with state-of-the-art electronic devices, sophisticated computers, and other gear that demanded high intelligence on the part of those sent to serve on board.

One day I got a phone call from the Navy Yard at Hunter's Point in South San Francisco: Admiral Turner would like to speak with Professor Brown. My pulse rate increased significantly as I braced myself for what I assumed would be a friendly but probably stern lecture from my military friend about how wrong I was on Vietnam. I had it wrong. Stan's ship was to be in port for several weeks while [censored] things would be done to the frigate in dry dock, and he would love to have Sydney and me come up some night and have dinner on board. More than that, he would like me to address the officers on board about why I opposed the war.

How could I say no to such an invitation? As it turned out, I had to do so, until we could find a more mutually agreeable date. The reason, which I didn't divulge to him until later, was that there was to be a massive anti–Vietnam War rally that day in San Francisco, at which I was to speak. Fortunately we found a later date, shortly before he and the frigate would be sailing out under the Golden Gate Bridge to carry on the war. I felt as though I was living in two very separate worlds, but that Stan was somehow bringing them into earshot of one another. That in itself was a gift.

There was a second item I did not mention in the phone conversation. The invitation was to talk to "the officers on board." My question would have been, "What about the enlisted men? Do they get in on the discussion?" I decided, however, that since Stan was orchestrating this almost unprecedented event, he should retain the right to choose the guests, and so officers it was. My silence on this issue was a matter of courtesy rather than conviction.

I would give a great deal for a tape of our conversation. To me, the mood of the evening was epitomized by trust. I trusted Stan not to have set things up in such a way that I would be verbally devoured. He trusted me not to engage in cheap rhetoric or abusive arguments, and the officers treated the occasion as quite out of the ordinary (which it was) and therefore to be accorded a dignity of its own.

It was seldom fun and games on campus. The stakes were high, lofty gestures were naive, idle words had a habit of turning up on someone else's tape recorder, and telephones like ours were frequently tapped. Some of our friends on the East Coast thought we were needlessly alarmed about this.

One episode serves as a pointer to many others: Stanford already had a number of "theme houses" for students with shared interests in such things as French, music, or political science. But when students learned that U.S. troops had invaded Cambodia, they took matters into their own hands and called for a Gandhian alternative, a "nonviolence house." They helped to organize student strikes, fasted publicly on White Plaza to gather about five hundred active supporters, and negotiated with the administration. As luck would have it, one fraternity would not be able to fill its house for the coming year. Stanford's first student-run cooperative, Columbae, was born as a living/learning experiment in Gandhian activism and peacemaking. It continues to this day.

Not everyone could fit into the fifty-bed house, so students ran self-selection sessions and improvised a loose network of nonresident "house members" who could still participate in the vegetarian cooking groups, study seminars, and house meetings run by consensus (that regularly lasted well past midnight). Occasional nonstudents found sustenance and support in Columbae's communal activities as well. Columbae people were a discernible presence at rallies, marches, and demonstrations, and were always committed to creative nonviolence.

After the first few months, a nonstudent named Dan (as I shall call him) became active at Columbae, attending meetings and study groups and participating in public rallies. Like the others, Dan professed a commitment to nonviolence, but with the passage of time he began to express increasing restlessness and impatience. "We've got to find ways to end the war sooner," he would say. "Too many people are dying." "Agreed," his friends would respond. "What do you suggest?"

Dan had an agenda: more people at the rallies, stronger rhetoric, refusal to disperse when ordered to do so at demonstrations, maybe even small acts of physical destruction on campus to call stronger attention to the evils of the war. Others at Columbae expressed uneasiness about the last item, and it was always tabled. But one evening, Dan appeared with barely concealed excitement. "Listen," he said, "I've run into a guy who can get us some explosives.

We could do something really spectacular on campus and make people take us seriously about bringing the war to an end."

Craig Schindler, who had helped to found the house, was leading a fairly worn-down and searching seminar group at the time Dan made his proposal. The group listened (respectful listening was a central part of Columbae's style). Then one by one they responded that dynamite was way out of bounds for a group trying to practice nonviolence. Dan pushed the argument pretty hard, even volunteering to get the explosives himself and set up a device to detonate them, to teach the university officials that there would be more of the same if university policies in support of the war didn't change. All he needed were three or four students to help set things up. There were no takers. Over the next few days, Dan tried to recruit others at Columbae, appealing always to their sense of moral outrage and the need to stop the killing. Nobody bought on. In some exasperation, Dan brought the proposal back to the house seminar, only to be met again with the argument, "It goes against everything we stand for. No way."

It soon became apparent that Dan was no longer coming around to the house, and no more was seen or heard of him until several months later, when some "student agitators" on another campus were arrested for attempted arson. It turned out that their "leader" had mistakenly been taken into custody. He was not a member of the student body at all; he was working for the FBI. His assignment had been to infiltrate "radical" student groups. He was to persuade them to commit dangerous and illegal acts, and thus discredit the peace movement.

His name was Dan.

It is hard for people who did not live through these times to understand how all-encompassing were the years of civil rights, Vietnam, and Central America—to cite only three of the great moral crises through which we lived. There was a weekend during this period when a number of us pooled our resources to get Dick Shaull to come from the East Coast and spend a weekend helping us strategize. For many years Dick had been a missionary in Brazil and had been radicalized by observing firsthand not only the internal corruption of the Brazilian government but the way in which our own government supported and subsidized policies destructive to the poor. Dick's opening speech at the World Council of Churches conference on "Church and Society" in Geneva in 1966 had galvanized the delegates to more venturesome conclusions than had occurred to anyone before the conference.

After returning from Brazil, Dick taught ecumenics at Princeton Seminary, where he was a burr under the saddle at a conservative training ground for Presbyterian ministers. When I arrived at Princeton in the spring of 1977 to give the Warfield Lectures on liberation theology, Dick had been hung in effigy on the campus just a week earlier. We folks in the Bay Area figured there was a lot we could learn from this man.

Our informal discussion centered around the question, "Is it time for another Barmen Declaration?" The original Barmen Declaration had been issued in Germany in May 1933 as the response of the Confessing Church to the Hitler takeover, and its central ringing claim was that one could not say yes to both Jesus Christ and Adolf Hitler. It was an either/or situation, what in church history is called a *status confessionis*, in which the signatories declared that the time for equivocation was past, the debate was over, and Christians must put themselves on the line. It seemed increasingly clear to us that our own situation was analogous to that of the members of the Confessing Church.

But in one crucial way it wasn't. The Barman Declaration was unequivocally christological; that is to say, it was a rallying cry for persons who believed in Jesus Christ, but not for universities, business establishments, secular groups, leaders of culture . . . or Jews. And we who had worked so closely with Jews on civil rights issues and Vietnam issues were not about to circle the wagons in a new configuration that excluded the Jews as our ongoing comrades in the struggle. We could have adopted a nonchristological declaration, but there were plenty of those on the market, and another was not needed. Or we could have followed Barmen's example and laid out our Christian faith without reserve. But that would have destroyed many wonderful things that had been happening as Jews and Christians worked together.

So the situations were *not* parallel. And there was a further reality we had to take into account, namely, the fact that Barmen itself had not dealt with "the Jewish question," and to that degree, despite the majesty of its treatment of other issues, it was deficient.

In retrospect, I am even more grateful than I was at the time that we did not try as a result of those sessions to do an American-style Barmen. We needed to stay together—Catholics, Protestants, *Jews*—and it was a cause for thanksgiving that we did manage to work together through those fierce years.

The war went on. A few of us were occasionally arrested. A few Stanford alumni wrote the administration that they disapproved of our getting paid on what were the equivalent of "days off," that our protest of the war meant that Stanford was subsidizing the antiwar movement by all such absences with pay.

On one such occasion, I missed two scheduled classes within a week, either for being in jail or going to court or participating in a rally. We were studying existentialism as a religious commitment, with special attention that week to Albert Camus. I asked Professor Lucio Ruotolo, a tenured professor of

English and an expert on existentialism, if he would take my classes on those two days. He graciously agreed to do so, and my only complaint about the arrangement was that I could not attend the classes myself and learn from him firsthand.

I declared unequivocally that the students learned more about existentialism in two hours with him than I could have supplied them in an academic quarter. I could have given a few lectures; he drew them into the subject matter as a living, breathing existentialist himself. Thanks to the style of war protest for having suggested new styles for our teaching.

Sit-ins were a regular part of the scenario at many colleges and universities in the seventies, and Stanford was no exception. In an effort to draw attention to their concerns (e.g., to abolish ROTC and refuse to let Army recruiters on campus, to divest the university of its Honeywell stock because the company manufactured antipersonnel weapons), students would enter a campus facility and refuse to leave until their "nonnegotiable demands" were met or they were forcibly evicted by the police, whichever came first. The buildings chosen often had symbolic meaning—a place where weapons research was being done, or the office of a militantly prowar administrator or faculty member. The scenario would be played out to its inevitable conclusion: The demands were *not* met and the students were forcibly evicted by the police.

But there was a quantum leap in the nature of such confrontations in the mid-seventies when Memorial Church was occupied. University administrators, who by that time had a routine policy of calling the police, were nonetheless not enthusiastic about permitting police with billy clubs to start dragging students out the chapel door, especially when in all likelihood the next morning's *San Francisco Chronicle* would show sophomores being bashed in front of the altar or baptismal font. Students, on the other hand, were likely to see such publicity as good PR for their cause.

What to do? The post of dean of the chapel was vacant at the time, and the immediate responsibility for dealing with the situation fell to a young student assistant, Tom Goodhue (who had gone from Columbae to seminary ordination and back). His approach was novel, though not at all out of character for those who knew him. Lining up to speak at the open microphone that the students had set up in the chapel to broadcast over the student radio station, he said in substance:

"Welcome to Memorial Church! Our doors, as you know, are never locked, and people are always free to be here, day or night. You don't need to 'liberate' Mem Chu. It has always been liberated space.

"As long as you're here, we ask you to honor our schedule of regular services, choir practice, organ recitals, and other events, and we hope you will feel welcome to share in our services, singing the hymns and listening to the sermons. You need to know, however, that our facilities aren't sumptuous. We don't have a Xerox machine, and we have only one restroom. Also, when you finally go home, we ask you not to leave the place in a mess, because that is just ripping off the janitors who have a big enough job as it is. Incidentally I'm one of the janitors."

This was not the kind of treatment the campus militants had anticipated, and there was considerable confusion on their part about how to respond. After a couple of hours of discussion (all of which continued to be broadcast live across the campus), one of the students put his finger on the reason for their bafflement: "Look," he said, when he got another turn at the microphone, "there's something good about our being here, and there's something bad about our being here. The *good* thing is that they don't mind our being here; the *bad* thing is that they don't mind our being here."

About ten o'clock the next morning, the students left—voluntarily.

I don't propose this as a surefire model that would necessarily have worked in another situation, though it would have been intriguing to give it a try. But I do offer it as an example that has potential for all who refuse to remain trapped by someone else's definition of who they are.

During five and a half of the most hectic years at Stanford, Davie Napier was dean of the chapel. A masterful preacher, one of the half dozen best homileticians in the trade, he had been a professor of Old Testament at Yale Divinity School before coming to Stanford. Davie and his wife, Joy, were a team; Davie's chapel and classroom activities and the openness of their home were important realities for students being skewered by their draft boards.

When Davie moved across the bay to become president of Pacific School of Religion, he left an enormous theological and spiritual vacuum, not only in the life of Stanford University but also in my life. There was going to be a long vacancy until a search committee could come up with a successor even minimally able to stand in Davie's shoes, and for this interim, Stanford president Dick Lyman asked me to cut my teaching load in half and take on the duties of acting dean of the chapel.

I was immensely touched by this invitation because I shared all of Davie's concerns about the war, and Dick Lyman could count on gaining no points with trustees or alumni for this action. Asking me to fill the chapel post, where even my symbolic presence was sure to cause him problems, made his appointment an act of personal trust to which I felt I should respond affirmatively.

An independent alumni publication, given to such "political" causes as restoration of the name "Stanford Indians" to the football team, sent its folk to monitor the outpourings of the new acting dean. They reported as big news that in my first Sunday in the pulpit I had not said anything "very political," but (as the account continued with breathtaking prescience), "you could tell that he was laying the groundwork." Actually I preached pretty much around the theological spectrum, without trying to co-opt the pulpit for political harangue, though on Christmas Eve I had to switch gears, an episode described more fully later.

It is almost amusing to recall that the Stanford faculty members most upset by my appointment were those in the Religious Studies Department. With the exception of Jerry Irish (a qualification I have frequently to invoke when describing my colleagues), they were deeply concerned that a member of their department was being so publicly associated with Memorial Church, thereby creating the impression that perhaps some of us also believed in the truth of our subject matter. I prayed. I read the Bible out loud. I baptized children. I celebrated marriages. Such matters were not "academic," and therefore it was demeaning to have them associated with the discipline of religious studies.

One reason I survived the multiple pressures of this period was that the chapel already had an assistant chaplain, Diane Kenney, whom I promoted to associate dean as my first imperial act. She knew the Stanford scene inside and out, had worked alongside Davie for several years, and provided continuity. All the rules, however, were stretched at our Christmas Eve candlelight service in 1972.

A few days before that Christmas, President Nixon had ordered all-out bombing attacks on North Vietnam, especially Hanoi. This was his response to a temporary breakdown in negotiations. It appeared that General Curtis LeMay's prescription for ending the conflict was becoming official policy: "Bomb them back to the Stone Age."

The only way I can capture my mood at the time is to reproduce a portion of the sermon I gave in Memorial Church at that 1972 Christmas Eve service. The church itself was packed with students, faculty, and staff, augmented by at least two thousand people from Palo Alto who, at the close of a downtown candlelight service, marched to Mem Chu to share in our service as well. They poured into every nook and cranny, every available square foot of floor space in that huge ecclesiastical space, and many simply had to stand outside. I got a fearful dressing down the next day from the chief of the Stanford Fire Department for breaking every law on the books about legal seating capacity in a university facility.

That justifiable concern was relatively easy to handle; had it been a court of law I would have had no choice but to plead *nolo contendere* (I offer no excuse). What I found harder to handle was a complaint registered to me several months later by a woman whose husband was a fighter pilot in the Vietnam

War, and who had brought her young children to our service to shore up their morale since their father couldn't be home for Christmas. To her, the sermon represented an unjustifiable assault on her husband's integrity. I only hope she could finally see that the ultimate message from the pulpit that night was not darkness but light.

I discarded my up-to-date Christmas story of Joe and Mary Millstein, seeking refuge in the garage of a motel in Milpitas since she was about to have a child. I pointed out that the original Christmas Eve story was political to the core and that the story made no sense save as a challenge to the political pressures of the time, embodied in Herod and Caesar. The Christmas Eve story forced us to take sides, and we had to do so in terms of a story of both judgment and joy.

Our judgment entailed an absolute "no" to political powers raining down death from the skies on innocent civilians in Hanoi. No neutrality was possible. All of us at the service had to repudiate our government's actions. I continued: "Let me say it as plainly and as unambiguously as I can, more plainly and unambiguously than I have ever said it in my whole life, bringing all the weight I can bring of twenty-eight years as an ordained minister, who has devoted his professional and personal life to trying to understand the meaning of the Christmas heritage.

"To those of you who are *Christians*, I assert categorically that from the standpoint of the Christian faith there is no possible way to justify this insane escalation of the bombing. It is the way of Herod, not the way of Christ.

"To those of you who are Jews, I do not bring the authority of an ordination you acknowledge, but I do bring at least the authority of a lifetime of study of the Jewish and Christian Scriptures, and I assert categorically that from the standpoint of the God who commands us to do justly, to love mercy, and to walk humbly with God and humankind, there is no possible way to justify this insane escalation of the bombing. I *do* invoke the authority of my dear friend Rabbi Abraham Heschel, who died yesterday, and who said to me on the phone only three days ago, 'The new bombing is an unspeakable outrage against human dignity.'

"To those of you who call yourselves neither Christians nor Jews, but who participate in a perspective in which every one of us in this chapel participates, the perspective of a *commonly shared humanity*, I assert categorically that from that perspective, likewise, there is no possible way to justify this insane escalation of the bombing."

But that was not the whole of the sermon, for in addition to the word of judgment there was also a word of joy. My text from John's Gospel epitomized it: "The light shines on in the dark, and the darkness has not quenched it" (John 1:5). Here was the ultimate message, the message of hope, joy, peace, still real and powerful despite the immediate context that seemed to destroy it.

I continued: "What is the nature of this light? The Christian sees this light focused on the Messiah who has come. That is what we have been singing about all evening. The Jew sees the light focused on the Messiah who is still to come. For both Jew and Christian, the light has been from the beginning, it is the very foundation of all things. And for both Jew and Christian, in the end it will be all in all. For those who call themselves neither Jews nor Christians, there is still the light that is unquenchable in the human breast, the light of tenderness, hope, joy, compassion, love.

"And in tonight's context, the baby is finally more powerful than the bomber. That is either the ultimate truth or the ultimate folly."

Alison: I remember one Christmas Eve during the Vietnam War. Usually we spent Christmas Eve together, singing carols, setting up the creche, and hearing the Christmas story. But this year, Papa was leading the Christmas Eve service at Memorial Church and my mom was picking Peter up at the airport. I remember that Tom and I were sitting around the kitchen table, listening to the radio, which was broadcasting Papa's sermon. After the sermon, the radio station invited people to call in, and we listened, frozen, as a man called, enraged, saying that people like Dr. Robert Brown should be put out in a small rowboat on a stormy sea and left with no oars, to die. It wasn't a death threat, but it scared me deeply. I remember praying that Papa would get home safely and that the man wouldn't do anything to him on the way home. I knew people could be killed for their beliefs, for taking a stand. I'd learned early that you could end up in jail, but the sense that there were angry people beyond the government, who wanted people like my dad dead, hit me more strongly that night than it had ever hit me before.

They were challenging years. I remember meetings and potlucks at our house, with an array of liberals and radicals. One Maoist student often babysat us, and she and her boyfriend would take us off when we got bored at the potlucks and tell us wonderful fantasy stories. And then at the end they'd lament that it was so sad that we were such nice kids and such a nice family. It was sad, because when the revolution came, which it seemed was going to be soon, our parents would have to be killed, because they were liberals and part of the problem, not the solution. On the other hand, there were many wonderful and loving students, especially those at Columbae House who were a strong support to our family and who reached out not only to my parents but also to us kids as well, in comforting and appropriate ways.

The Christmas Eve sermon on the bombing of Hanoi, along with similar sermons from similar pulpits, had no discernible effect on U.S. foreign policy, which only became more brutal. We seemed to be at a point of no return, a *kairos* moment in which we must either act in the present or forfeit the right to act in the future. Even before the New Year, a number of groups joined forces to organize what we called a "mission of desperation." If our own government would not listen to our appeals, we must enjoin overseas governments to put even stronger pressures on our own political leaders to cease and desist the madness.

In a grace-filled gargantuan effort, Bob Bilheimer, Dick Fernandez, and others raised funds and arranged an itinerary that got seven of us to Great Britain, Holland, Germany, and the Vatican, urging the leaders with whom we met to issue the strongest possible public condemnation of U.S. international policy. The seven who made the trip were Harvey Cox, Sr. Mary Luke Tobin, Methodist bishop James Armstrong, Rabbi Leonard Beerman, Episcopal bishop Robert DaWitt, Bruno Kroker, and me. We "represented" nobody but ourselves, and whatever authority we possessed was not the authority of our office, but simply the authority of our message.

Our itinerary had the following highlights. In London, we met with the bishop of London, a representative of the archbishop of Canterbury, and officers of eight British denominations and peace groups; in Amsterdam, with representatives of five of the eight political parties; in Rotterdam, with Cardinal Alfrink, president of the international Catholic peace organization, Pax Christi; in Bonn, with delegates to the Synod of the Evangelical Church of the Rhineland, which was fortuitously meeting at the time of our visit, and with Gustav Heinemann, president of the German Republic and a signer of the famous Stuttgart Declaration of 1945, confessing Germany's guilt for the tragedies of World War II. In Stuttgart itself we met with Eberhard Eppler, a recently elected official of the Social Democratic Party, and Martin Niemoeller, who had spent seven years in one of Hitler's concentration camps. In Rome, we spoke with Msgr. Joseph Gremillion, who gathered together representatives of several Vatican agencies. I include this imposing roster only to indicate how widespread was the European openness to our message. That people of such caliber could be gathered with virtually no advance warning was an encouraging sign to us that even if we had no friends in high places at home, we were not bereft of such friends abroad. The term "communion of saints" began to take on fresh meaning.

The Christmas bombings seemed to have destroyed, worldwide, any residual faith in the appropriateness of President Nixon's actions. It was heartwarming to discover that recent White House rhetoric had made no converts. Indeed, some of the Germans (off the record) told us that the only way they could understand U.S. actions in Southeast Asia was by the German proverb "Once you have ruined your reputation, you can live without inhibitions." I think our entire delegation agreed that antiwar sentiment was strongest in

Holland. Indeed, just two days before our arrival, there had been an anti–Vietnam War rally in The Hague described to us as the largest human outpouring for such an event in all Dutch history.

The situation in Germany was more complex, as shown in one synod delegate's question: "Who are we, who did so much similar indiscriminate bombing, to tell the United States to stop doing the same thing we ourselves did?" To which we had a ready answer: "You, above all others, can bear witness to how wrong both policies have been." Rabbi Beerman was our choice to address the German synod on our behalf. He cited the powerful statement by Leo Baeck (who had been a rabbi in Berlin and for whom Rabbi Beerman's temple in Los Angeles was named): "Which is worse," Baeck asked, "the intolerance that commits outrages, or the indifference that observes outrages with an undisturbed conscience?" A query addressed to us all, German or North American.

Leonard's translator had a very familiar face that gradually moved off the dust jacket of many books into three-dimensional reality. It was Eberhard Bethge, who edited the multivolume collection of Dietrich Bonhoeffer's writings, and who himself had gone through much soul searching in World War II. I could not put out of my mind one of Bonhoeffer's statements in the 1930s, saved for us by Bethge: "Only the one who cries out for the Jews has the right to sing Gregorian chant."

The time with Niemoeller was fascinating. He was already an old man, and had been so firm in his postwar pacifist stance that he was not taken as seriously by his ecclesiastical colleagues as he once had been—their loss. He gave us an important insight for the times in which we were living: "What I have said wrong in the past," he said in his broken English, "is no excuse not to say right in the present."

In Rome we got the impression that Vatican officials had been fearing that upon our arrival we would engage in a "sit-in in the papal quarters until our demands were met." This says something about the pervasive imagery established by the peace movement when confronting power structures. For whatever reasons, we did not have a papal audience, but at the several conferences that Msgr. Gremillion arranged for us, we communicated two points that we were promised would be brought to the Holy Father's attention. The first was our gratitude for and deep endorsement of a statement about modern warfare from the Second Vatican Council's document on "The Church and the World Today." In part, it says that "the destruction . . . of extensive areas along with their populations is a crime against God and man, and merits unequivocal and unhesitating condemnation." We expressed our deep hope that the Holy Father would make use of these words as an exact description of what our bombs were doing that very day and night in Vietnam, and that the condemnations would follow. Our second action was symbolic. We gave the pope a candle made in the metal mold of an antipersonnel weapon known as a "guava bomb," which we hoped he would light as a papal beacon of peace, symbolizing the turning of swords into plowshares.

Did the trip do any good? There is no way to measure. We certainly received no immediate evidence of change. We probably alienated some people while sensitizing others. Archbishop Cramner once said of the church, "She is an anvil that has worn down many hammers." The image is less clear than it appears on an initial reading, but at best it is an exhortation not to give up the struggle.

For the record, let it be stated that Harvey Cox, who carried the metal mold from which the candle was made, took it through fourteen separate airport metal detectors without being stopped, let alone being questioned at customs.

For the record, let it also be stated that at the end of our day in Rome we had an hour and a half before the bus was to leave the Columbus Hotel for the airport. Safe on board, we compared notes on what we had done with that single respite in the four hectic days. It turned out that five of us had independently gone to a particular spot to pray for peace.

That spot was the tomb of Pope John XXIII.

Back on campus, there were faculty, students, and staff who were very visible throughout the sixties, and others who were scarcely visible at all. What is more, the degree of their visibility or nonvisibility had almost nothing to do with their effectiveness or noneffectiveness. Exhibit A in this regard was Bob Beyers.

Bob Beyers was an employee of the university. He reported on all manner of events that took place on campus and sometimes off campus as well, such as a group of students blocking a local draft board. He never sought the spotlight—indeed, he avoided it—but wherever there was a rally or a sit-in or some street theatre, Bob was there.

The students on the left were ideologically suspicious of *any* employee of the establishment. In the early sixties a group of them tried to christen him "Bob Bias," suggesting that he reported all events through a filter supportive of actions by university officials (on the right), and critical of actions by students (on the left). The pseudonym would occasionally be hoisted out, but it never took hold. The reason it never took hold was because it wasn't true. You might not personally like the way Bob Beyers reported a rally at White Plaza or the newest manifesto from *Venceremos*, a Maoist organ of the left, but you had to admit, if you were honest with yourself, that Bob had been reportorially fair and that if there was a bias at work it was not in his words, but in your perception of his words.

So, whether visible or not, Bob Beyers was always on the scene with a clipboard and usually a tape recorder as well. If it was sometimes said that ice water flowed through his veins, that was really a compliment, not only a recognition that he never lost his cool but an assurance that he would not be swayed from honest reporting by his own emotional fervor or lack thereof.

Most of the students didn't know that Bob himself, when he wasn't the professional reporter with the clipboard, was a vigorous supporter of human and civil rights, who had spent "Mississippi Summer" in 1961 in the deep South, helping to register blacks to vote, at a time in our history when you were putting your life on the line to engage in such emotionally charged activity.

I have my own reasons to be thankful to Bob Beyers. You couldn't buy his favor, needless to say, but you could always ask him a professional question and get a professional answer. It never failed. I discovered from Bob, through many moments in the heat of battle, that my chances of being correctly reported in tomorrow's press were immeasurably improved if I brought along, and distributed, copies of what I was going to say at an upcoming rally or teach-in. When we blockaded the San Mateo draft board, Bob answered our questions about the best time to hold a press conference on the site, to explain what we were trying to accomplish.

In the fall of 1967, when I got into fairly deep water with the Stanford trustees over my *Look* magazine article on the moral obligation to oppose the Vietnam War, Bob responded to a query from Sydney that a group of trustees was meeting the next day at 10 a.m. to discuss a response. Thus informed, I was able to write a letter about the article, especially for the trustees, and have it available for all of them by 10 a.m. the next day. Thus was dialogue enhanced.

Some years later, Bob helped prepare a report on the state of the university. It was deemed too critical for public consumption, and Bob resigned in protest. A man of honor, all the way.

As the stakes in the war in Vietnam got higher, "campus unrest" also escalated in intensity and, occasionally, in destructiveness. Students organized along the entire political spectrum. Alliances were quickly created and sometimes as quickly disbanded. One group that increasingly came to prominence was called *Venceremos* (Spanish for "We shall overcome"), which occupied the far left on the political spectrum and was considerably influenced by *The Sayings of Chairman Mao*. The group had some highly motivated students, along with a tenured associate professor of English, H. Bruce Franklin, who in quieter times had been known as "our Melville expert."

While teaching at Stanford-in-France a few years earlier, Bruce had gotten to know a number of Vietcong leaders in Paris and underwent an ideological conversion. (He had been a bombardier in the U.S. Air Force before his teaching career.) By the time he was well established back at Stanford, Bruce was a "self-avowed Maoist" who not only had some loyal student followers but, by exercising his oratorical skills at White Plaza rallies, was developing a campus protest group of considerable size and dedication.

As I have had occasion to note, a rally would sometimes become the staging ground for a march, and the march might or might not end as a sit-in in one of the campus buildings. When this happened, one of two things would follow. Either the students would soon leave, content to have stirred up a little excitement and perhaps attracted a few new recruits, or the students would prepare for a long occupancy. And when *this* happened, one and only one thing would follow: The administration would call the Santa Clara County Police Department, the police would soon arrive, and forced evacuation of the building would ensue. Most students responded nonviolently, which might or might not be a gesture sufficient to forego the police's use of billy clubs. Arrests would follow for those who did not manage to get away. (On one occasion, three of us from the faculty had to go into Encina Hall at 6 a.m. to warn students that the police were coming and would be in complete control, with the university unable to offer any restraints this time. Heads would be bashed, was our message. On this occasion the students left of their own will.)

Bruce Franklin's leadership was almost always in evidence at such events, but difficulty arose within the ranks when it became clear that he never got arrested himself, no matter how much he enjoined others to do so. When queried about this, he and his fellow leaders explained that this was the standard operating procedure in guerilla warfare: The leaders must not be arrested; they must be free to strategize the next moves. The principle was accepted by the true believers, but not universally appreciated by those who were instructed to await arrest and possibly get their heads bashed in. As the tension and the seriousness of this sort of combat increased, university officials became less and less willing to tolerate the presence on campus of persons who, in addition to challenging our military policies in Vietnam, challenged the right of the university to give public support to such policies. When buildings that housed delicate instruments and sophisticated machinery of possible use in the war effort were targeted for occupation, the administration began to move more aggressively.

At this time came the annual election of new members to the Faculty Advisory Board, a group of seven senior faculty members mandated to deal with such matters as faculty appointments, promotions, and tenure decisions. In addition, however, the Advisory Board had the responsibility (almost never previously noticed) to deal with any disciplinary actions that might arise within the faculty. I had been around for almost a decade, my turn to serve on the Advisory Board had apparently come, and I was elected for a three-year term. There was one fanciful theory floating around that I had been elected by a coalition of faculty members to the left of center in the hope that I would not be too much of a hard-liner in case Franklin got in deep trouble with the administration. Franklin got in deep trouble with the administration.

On March 22, 1971, Stanford president Richard Lyman filed four charges against Professor Franklin, notifying him that he intended to request the Board of Trustees to dismiss Franklin from the faculty. Exercising his right to a hearing, Professor Franklin appealed to the Advisory Board of the faculty to hold hearings in which he could defend himself against the charges.

With the exception of myself, all the members of the Advisory Board were long-seasoned Stanford veterans, and even I had been there nine years. All were men with national reputations in their fields. The chairman, Donald Kennedy, was a biologist who later became president of the university. The vice chair was David Hamburg, a psychiatrist in the School of Medicine. The other members included Lee Bach, an economist; Sanford Dornbusch, a sociologist; David Mason, a professor of chemistry; Wolfgang Panofsky, a physicist and creator and head of the Stanford Linear Accelerator (SLAC); and me, a professor in religious studies.

The hearings began formally on September 28, 1971, and (save for a tiny respite during Christmas vacation) were held five days a week from noon to 6 p.m., until the 168-page final report was finally issued on January 5, 1972. For six weeks we held public hearings, listening to over one hundred witnesses, and then spent almost two months developing our report. We had to reschedule all our classes to morning hours, so that the sessions in the afternoon would never be interrupted. Remarkably, considering the schedule of activities each member had to rearrange, no member of the board missed a single moment of the entire hearing.

I make these comments to underline the serious nature of what we were called upon to do, namely, to consider the possible firing of a tenured professor, and the acceptance of that task by all seven of the members. It was the all-absorbing fact of our lives for well over three months. The seven of us sat behind a long desk, joined only by a graduate student who took charge of all secretarial duties.

President Lyman's charges against Professor Franklin focused on four campus incidents in which he claimed that Franklin had stepped over the boundaries of "permissible speech" by urging or participating in unlawful activities on campus. Four instances of reportedly excessive speech were cited:

1. That he had contributed significantly to the disruption of a speech by Henry Cabot Lodge on campus and had made it impossible for the speaker to complete his lecture;
2. That he had spoken at a rally on White Plaza urging students to disrupt work on campus by shutting down the Computation Center;

3. That he had interfered with a police order demanding dispersal at the Computation Center, and urged students to disregard it; and

4. That in an evening rally in the Old Union Courtyard he had urged students to engage in disruptive activity on the campus during the night.

The task of the Advisory Board was to determine, in relation to each of these charges, whether or not there was "strongly persuasive" evidence to sustain the charges, and if so, whether this was of a serious enough nature to warrant dismissal. As a result of exhaustive examination of all matters pertaining to each incident, the Board ruled, on the basis of carefully established criteria, as follows:

> The Board unanimously does not sustain the charge in the Lodge incident; the Board unanimously sustains the charge in the White Plaza incident; the Board sustains the charge in the Computation Center incident, with two members (Brown and Kennedy) dissenting; the Board sustains the charge in the Old Union Courtyard incident, with two members (Brown and Kennedy) dissenting.

This report let loose an immense uproar on the campus. My guess is that most people expected some censure of Professor Franklin, but not that he would be fired. At all events, there were some vigorous rallies in defense of Professor Franklin, and a variety of activities under cover of darkness whose source could not be determined. The situation was serious enough that for several weeks the university employed guards from sundown to sunup at the homes of each faculty member on the Advisory Board, to protect him and his family from possible physical harm. That this was not an act of institutional paranoia was made clear when one of the watchmen found a firebomb at the home of Professor Dornbusch in the shrubbery by the bedroom; fortunately, it did no damage.

There is no way to reduce the intricacy of our 168-page report to a few pages of bare-boned condensation. There were parts of the report with which we could agree, and I can still pick out a few lines from my own pen, and yet the chairman, Donald Kennedy, and I, the most junior member, could not append our names to the report as it stood. We therefore wrote a joint minority decision, and since even this did not fully meet all of my own concerns, I wrote a somewhat longer addendum to the minority report for which I took full responsibility.

In our joint minority decision, Don Kennedy and I asserted that we could not accept the administration's claim that a count of guilty on any one of the four charges would have merited dismissal. We argued instead for a time of suspension rather than dismissal, after which Professor Franklin would be restored to full faculty status. We offered four reasons:

1. Suspension for a period of time is a severe penalty, involving both professional and financial hardships. We felt that it should be offered as a possible

deterrent to future actions that might otherwise "go across the line" of acceptable speech.

2. We were willing to accept at face value Professor Franklin's stated intention to be a nonparticipant in future actions that he might now recognize as "punishable."

3. We were not willing to assume that Professor Franklin's position was static, nor could we accept the proposition that dismissal was appropriate "merely because other penalties would be without effect."

4. We would argue a careful weighing of the costs of dismissal to the university relative to the risks of future violations:

(a) The university thrives on diversity and challenge. When we lose a prominent symbol of these qualities, we lose not only the substance of the challenge, but also the external perception that we can take it in stride. In some quarters, the latter effect could be damaging—for example, less well-buffered institutions may become more vulnerable to outside pressures to get rid of controversial faculty members.

(b) Because we live in a society in which there are increasingly public pressures to curb dissident speech and action, the university has a special responsibility to insulate its procedures from such influences. That need is manifested by the special significance of tenure, which historically protects the institution's faculty from social trends toward political conformity. We should therefore be scrupulous in protecting violators of university rules against excessive penalties imposed by collective judgment, especially when these violators espouse uncomfortably heterodox views.

(c) Given all these reasons, the university is obliged to tolerate a great deal of what it does not like. We see substantial costs in Professor Franklin's loss to the institution; they are measured externally in the form of corrosive effects on academic freedom, and internally in terms of lost challenge and the subtle inhibition of dissent.

In my addendum to the minority I made one final point: a recognition that *many aspects of the university needed to be changed*. Those of us within the university shared responsibility for many of the evils of our society, sometimes by our neglect of means for bringing about change, and sometimes by our tacit if not overt approval of the involvement of the university and university personnel in ongoing social structures of human oppression.

> Albeit in a harsh and strident manner, Professor Franklin has helped to call attention to many of these realities. He has not been alone, of course, in doing this, and others may have joined the issues more effectively and creatively than he has done. But his has been an important voice, however uncomfortable it makes the rest of us. Dismissal would deprive us of that voice, whereas a penalty short of dismissal

would not do so, unless Professor Franklin chose in the future to disregard its warning.

I believe very strongly that, however much I and many of my colleagues may disagree with what Professor Franklin says or how he says it, Stanford University will be less of a true university without him, and more of a true university with him. I fear that we may do untold harm to ourselves and to the cause of higher education unless, by imposing a penalty short of dismissal, we seek to keep him as a very uncomfortable but very important part of what this University, or any university, is meant to be.

In preparing this chapter, I reread the minority report for the first time in at least twenty years. I still affirm it as strongly as I did when it was first written—on reflection, even more so.

Professor Franklin was granted full pay until August 31, 1972, but was no longer permitted to teach at Stanford. He received no new academic appointment for over two years, and appeared to have been blacklisted by the academic community, since at no point in the hearings was his competence as a teacher or researcher called into question. He was finally appointed to teach at the Newark campus of Rutgers University, where he has ever since been a productive scholar. He filed a countersuit against the university in civil court that was under legal consideration for several years but now appears to be dormant.

This whole episode was a difficult and trying time for me. We had agreed not to discuss the case with outsiders while the hearing was in process, and the lonely burden of silence became increasingly heavy as we approached a verdict and realized that it would create repercussions not only for Professor Franklin and Stanford but for the whole field of higher education as well. When the report was first released, Franklin called a press conference at which, among other things, he was particularly scathing in his attitude toward me, presumably because I was the one closest to exonerating him and had failed to do so. Later he acknowledged that at least Don Kennedy and I had the facts straight.

There is a postscript to this story. It begins not on the campus of Stanford University but at First Presbyterian Church in Palo Alto. Our church was just emerging from a year-long debate over whether or not we would provide sanctuary for young men who could no longer in good conscience fight in Vietnam and who needed a place to sort out what to do about it. This was serious stuff. For the man in uniform, it involved at least being AWOL and might involve being thrown into the brig and charged with desertion or even treason. Our church agreed that our church would be a place where men in uniform could seek counsel in deciding if and when to "surface," and use our church building as the place to do it.

A young Navy enlisted man, Rick Larsen, sought us out. His aircraft carrier had been launching round-the-clock air strikes up and down the Vietnamese coast, and the thought of doing this incessantly to defenseless villagers and peasants was more than he could justify. He wanted a discharge from the Navy but had no idea whether the Navy would grant it or not. We offered to let him stay in our home until he could decide on his own whether or not to seek sanctuary.

So here we were, housing—not for the first time—a person who in a technical sense was a fugitive from the law. Just at this time, in response to threats from the far left, Stanford University decided to provide sundown to sunup protection for the homes and families of the Faculty Advisory Board members during the Franklin trial.

It was in the midst of all this that our daughter Alison, then 14, opened the door to find uniformed members of the Stanford Police Force. They requested entrance to the house, and told her that they wanted to examine our backyard, our fence, and all other possible modes of entrance and exit in the house.

Because of our history of civil disobedience and FBI investigations, we already had a family understanding that our children were to be very careful about what they told any of their friends. If police or FBI ever came to the door, our children were to answer no questions about us, our family, or anybody staying with us. Alison, to whom at the age of four during the Freedom Rides it became clear that the police were not generally our friends or to be trusted, refused to let the officers enter the house. She knew that Rick was upstairs and that we were protecting him from the police. The Stanford police officers continued to try to persuade her to let them in, and that this was all part of a plan to protect her and her family.

But Alison was not deterred or confused. She was clear where she and her family stood, and who they stood by. She would not let the police enter the house, and instructed them to contact her parents for any further information or access.

And so we entered a period where we had a security guard outside our house all evening and night, while harboring a fugitive in our home. We spent hours in our living room, helping Rick sort out his plan to seek sanctuary, while at the same time being protected just outside in front, from Maoist groups on campus. It was a strange and interesting set of contradictions for our children to sort through, but I guess it's being able to sort out such things that preserves the democratic way of life and keeps the struggle for justice alive and well.

Larsen stayed with us for several days, talking with us and many sympathetic listeners about the pros and cons of the dangerous thing he was proposing—to surrender to the naval authorities and ask for a discharge on the grounds of conscientious objection. Seeking CO status was a risky road at that time, even for preinduction draftees. Things were improving a little with the increasing presence of the churches on the scene, but getting CO status *after* going into the service was doubly difficult.

Three churches in Palo Alto—First Presbyterian Church, St. Anne's Catholic Church, and the Friends Meeting—were joining efforts to secure fair chances for conscientious objectors. After talking with a variety of others as well, Rick concluded, through communication from a Jesuit at the parish house of St. Anne's, that he wanted to go for it. The moral cost of not doing so was too high.

In the meantime, First Presbyterian continued to debate the issue. The ruling body (the session) had voted to give public support to persons who felt their consciences moved in the same direction as Larsen's. There were only a couple of abstentions from members not yet fully clear on all the ramifications, since the action might well make the church liable for multiple fines and other punishment. A later series of votes finally sealed a decision to give sanctuary to people—whether in the service or not—who asked for help.

First Presbyterian Church was chosen from among the three churches as the place for Rick to be publicly available if and when the Navy chose to arrest him. He stayed in our sanctuary day and night. The Navy did nothing for over a week, which made possible a tremendous buildup of public support. Even Rick's parents came from Michigan, his father a truck driver, his mother an ex-marine.

It was a gala time that week. People came with food, clothing, and sundry other items helpful to one likely to go to the brig. Rick became good at interviews, and firmed up his reasoning and his diction, as well as his courage and commitment. The Communion table in the sanctuary became a "real" table, on which real meals were placed and eaten. Joan Baez even appeared one night. (Rick said sometime later it would almost have all been worth it just to get a kiss from Joan Baez.) After more than a week of this, the locus of the witness was moved down the street to St. Anne's. It was there that, in a few days, the inevitable arrest took place, and the Navy carried Rick off in handcuffs.

At that point our "responsibility" was over. Rick had the best help we could give him, and his backbone was strengthened by the ongoing support. Even an ordinary discharge would have been a winner. But there was an even happier ending to this particular story. He asked the naval court martial for an honorable discharge, and a little bit later, to our surprise and joy, it was forthcoming. He walked out of the hearing with his conscience intact, and a lot of pluses for standing firm.

Every once in a while you win one.

Sydney: *In the midst of a service at First Presbyterian Church one Sunday morning, Tony Meyer, a young Jesuit from St. Anne's Catholic Church, walked down the aisle, interrupting our service, to ask us to join with other congregations (St. Anne's, the Friends Meeting, and the First Baptist Church), members of the Bay Area Interfaith Coalition to End the Vietnam War, in offering our church as a place of sanctuary for servicemen who could no longer in good conscience participate in the military. George Wilson, our pastor, responded, proposing that we hold an open session meeting before the whole congregation, immediately after the service. We met as a session, sitting in a row, facing the congregation, and voted eleven to two to join in this effort, and offer First Presbyterian Church of Palo Alto as a place of sanctuary.*

At this time, there was a young, nineteen-year-old Navy fireman, first class, on an aircraft carrier off the coast of Vietnam. He was from Detroit, his mother an ex-marine and his father a truck driver for the Detroit Free Press. *One night, on the flight deck of the aircraft carrier, he watched plane after plane take off on bombing missions. He asked the officer in charge, "When do they quit taking off?" "Never," came the reply. "We never quit. We bomb Vietnam twenty-four hours a day."*

Rick Larsen, the nineteen-year-old from Michigan, decided he could no longer participate in this inhuman venture. He had heard on the radio that some West Coast churches were offering "sanctuary" to disaffected servicemen, and he decided to seek one out. On leave, he flew into the San Francisco airport. He caught a cab and asked the driver if he knew of those Bay Area churches, and would he take him to one? The driver swung around, looked at him and said, "Yeah, I've heard of them. I'll take you to one."

He took him to University Lutheran Church in Berkeley, a part of the Bay Area Network, to Gus Schultz, chaplain at the church. Rick talked at length with Gus, then told him that he didn't want to take sanctuary in a hokey place like Berkeley but rather in a "real American town." So Gus put him in touch with the Palo Alto Network, and he came to us. When he arrived, he needed three or four days to think things over, work things out, in a quieter place, so he moved in with us. (It's a felony to aid and abet a military deserter.)

After taking time to talk things through, he moved to take sanctuary in our church. He came to our congregation, and was there in our sanctuary, accompanied twenty-four hours a day by members of the church network—Quakers, Roman Catholics, Baptists, Presbyterians, and other supporters. If and when he was arrested by the military, it would be a public and publicized action.

Through those days, we were with him in the sanctuary. Potluck meals were served from the Communion table. People slept in the church. Evening celebrations, services, and gatherings were held, day after day. Joan Baez came and sang with us. We all sang. My daughter Alison said that it was then that she felt the church become a true church, a living reality of what our faith is all about. And I remember Rick saying that it was worth it all just to be hugged by Joan Baez. After several days, he moved over to St. Anne's Chapel, and from there he was arrested by MPs and taken to the Navy brig in Oakland. He applied for conscientious objector status and was finally discharged as a CO.

Our church, our congregation, had moved to be the people we aspired to be. But the experience was not without a downside. Some families and members responded by leaving our church and moving their membership to the Menlo Park Presbyterian Church. People at that church noticed this and looked to see where these people were coming from, and why, and that began a steady stream of new people in our direction—wonderful members who have been with us ever since—the Webers, the Cuthbertsons, Peter Milward, Mildred Martin, and many others. This was a trend that had already started before, but the sanctuary experience led to an influx of wonderful new members of our community.

As all this was going on, our son Mark, then a senior at Gunn High School, asked me to approve his request to do an independent study course on the Theater of the Absurd. I said okay, but it seemed a bit sick to me. At the very same time that we were harboring, aiding, and abetting an AWOL member of the military in our home, we were also being given overnight security protection from "radical Stanford students" by security guards hired by Stanford. Bob was on a Stanford judicial committee, deciding on the tenure of Bruce Franklin, a radical Stanford professor who was seen by the university to have incited students to violence. A Molotov cocktail had been thrown at one of the committee member's homes. It had exploded but had done no damage.

So as the security guard was there to guard us overnight, AWOL Rick Larsen was upstairs in the house, gathering his thoughts and courage to face prosecution from the military. And on the side, the security guard had asked me if it would be okay for him to work on his Rolls-Royce car engine in our driveway while he was on duty during the night. Theater of the Absurd, sick? No way. Theater of the Absurd was simply reality.

Mark: *Unlike most people in the academic world, my father taught by moral, physical, and political example. He always knew that the act of exposing evil and hypocrisy by itself does not make you a moral person. You have to do something about it. He staked his liberty and often his life on his beliefs, and the world is now a better place because of him, though he would be the first to caution us, especially now, that the struggle is never over. I am blessed and privileged to be his son.*

Peter: *I was not going to go to war. I knew that, and had applied for conscientious objector status on turning eighteen. We talked of bringing the war home. And on the Stanford campus, genteel as it appeared, it was done with more than a little vengeance. (For starters, new students had been assigned a book called* Beyond Berkeley, *required reading on the free speech movement before we even set foot on campus—depending on your point of view, one of the best or worst decisions an admissions office ever made.)*

David Harris was student body president and the charismatic leader of the Resistance, and things were happening both on campus and off that were exciting and not a little unsettling. It was not easy. We were eighteen to twenty years old and really not that well informed. The war changed much of this, and many friends have nostalgia for the time. It was one of ferment, unrest, freedom, change, joy—all those things and more. But my gut feelings as I waded and wandered through those political waters and those moral swamps were often of confusion, fear, and a somewhat justified paranoia— all of this with the added irony that our nation, in one of its darkest times, seemed to be looking to its young for guidance and moral reckoning. It helped to have parents who had prepared us for some of these questions—but the bottom line still was that dangerous territory had spread everywhere. There was an Oz-like landscape at home and a napalmed one abroad.

Still, we knew absolutely that the war was wrong and that we had to do what we could to end it. And although the routes to the end were not always apparent, we had purpose, and when we were not overwhelmed, we had a tremendous amount of fun. We went to Yosemite often and hiked in the Sierras on a regular basis. We hitchhiked and drove up and down the coast, and a good group of friends developed out of Stanford, many of whom have continued in academia and have continued to be politically and socially active.

But I have to say, in relationship to my father, it was also in many ways a bad time for me to be so close to home. Had I known that Vietnam was going to explode in the way it did, I would have gone elsewhere. Stanford in normal times would have been big enough for me to have lived a separate existence from my family. But these were anything but normal times, and my dad had a national focus on him. And I, a young guy who still didn't know what he wanted to do with himself beyond exploring the world, found himself agreeing with most of what the old man had to say. And at that age, all rationality aside, the need to rebel is strong. At minimum there is the urge for some social separation.

The only real political options for me in this odd psychological box seemed self-defeating: a completely apolitical stance (something that given my birthright I could no more do than change into a dog); a right-wing swing (join the Young Americans for Freedom or enlist—I don't think so); a leftist end run that would have put me in with the Maoists and SDS (people with whom I seemed to have little in common beyond an opposition to the war); or I could do what I did, which was to come down at the end patch of the liberal/radical left, the place I came out intellectually on my own, with some footnoting questions about my parents' politics, but not too many.

So there I was, in school with my famous dad, finding to my frustration that I was unable to disagree with him, simply because what he had to say was so right, so impassioned, and so reasonable. From a distance this seems both precious and comical, but at the time it did not. Despite these internal rumblings, my dad and I did many things together. We were at rallies, sit-ins, and demonstrations and eventually committed civil disobedience a number of times and went to jail—all of which I'm proud of still.

But to complain about all this lack of distance is paradoxical, for the war also took my dad away from the family in new ways—which none of us liked. (The guy just couldn't win!) If he was on the road speaking before, he was all the more so now. And— as it was during the times he went to Rome for the Vatican Council for months—we were confronted with the conflicting needs of the church in relationship to our own needs for a father, and had to agree that the needs of the wider church should come first. In the same way, it was difficult to disagree with his repeated trips to preach the word against the war, if through these trips actual lives might be saved.

The dilemma was a constant over the years—and was always hard to resolve. I know that my father genuinely struggled with it, particularly in the latter part of his life, feeling that he had overplayed his hand in regard to the world and had given the family short shrift. We tried to reassure him, and Heath was a big help in this regard, but parts of us certainly would have agreed with him from time to time. His later apologies (we finally ended up shouting at him that it was okay—it really was!) and the increasing closeness that we all had with him for the last thirty years of his life did all that was needed to put this stuff to bed.

The political work was of obvious importance, and we did a lot of it together.

Alison: *I loved listening to dinner table conversations: worker-priests, AWOL sol-diers, people from South Africa or El Salvador seeking asylum, Chilean journalists, activists, refugees, ex-nuns, priests, all members of what my parents called "God's underground." I loved lying in bed at night, either in California or Heath, listening to political discussions, talks about people's lives, personal struggles, faith. From my bedroom, I overheard conversations between my mom and brothers about drugs, alco-hol, civil disobedience, and other topics. I liked overhearing struggles between my mother and father over how much we should be told about illegal activities they were planning. Papa always argued that we would be safer and happier being protected from knowing what was going on until absolutely necessary. Mama always argued that we'd be better off knowing everything and being well informed. Mama won out, and we were told in advance of upcoming illegal actions, controversial stands, media attention, and the like. We were told very clearly that we could not talk to any of our friends about what was going on, and were reassured that only one parent would ever be arrested at a time, leaving the other to raise us, should the arrested parent get a long prison sentence. This was not really that reassuring.*

The first clearly organized and aggressive act of protest on the Stanford campus had taken place on April 3, 1969. Abbreviated for easy identification as the A3M (April Movement), it involved a takeover of several days' duration of buildings in which faculty members conducted weapons research. There were numerous arrests before the action was terminated.

As the twenty-fifth anniversary of the event approached, veterans of the initial action decided to hold a reunion of all who had been involved. The Stanford Alumni Association cooperated in the venture, supplying addresses, stationery, office space, and postage, to get the word out to as many graduates as possible. This was an astute move, not only positive in its own right but as a means for the Alumni Association to make fresh contact with a generation of students whose subsequent giving to the university had been noticeable by its absence.

The reunion spread over two and a half days and provided times for informal reminiscing but also for some structured talks and panel discussions to assess the ongoing impact of the events a quarter of a century ago. Almost without exception, participants said that they would do it again, but they were very upfront in acknowledging that there had been a great many stupid and even harmful things done in the course of messing up a lot of weapons research. The notion of "weapons research" was still a plainly immoral concept.

A great many of the participants had subsequently finished their degrees, married, had children, and were raising them in ways very different from their own upbringing, building on many of the communal emphases of respect and sharing that had marked their time of "movement activity" at Stanford. As they described what they were doing now, many reported that they were still working, albeit more quietly, for social change, and that rather than climbing the corporate ladder to fiscal rewards, they were employing whatever entrepreneurial skills they had to teaching and other vocations they still believed were full of long-run revolutionary import. Affluence was not a central part of their collective goal, and they seemed on the whole content with that. One woman reported rather uncomfortably that she had gone on from Stanford into a high position with Wells Fargo Bank—an admission greeted with relaxed laughter rather than the stern censoriousness that would have accompanied such an admission a quarter of a century earlier. She finished her report with an invitation: "If you ever need a loan, come and see me." The response was not a laugh of derision but laughter that leads to hope, and it was rather wonderful to see that some of the students had gotten that far. I had been asked to reflect on how things looked to me twenty-five years later. I was appreciative of the invitation, and as I reflected on what to say, I realized that I had probably become more radicalized in the last twenty-five years than many of them had. As I have kept in touch with students who were at Stanford in the sixties, it has not been my experience that cynicism or disillusionment took over their lives. On the contrary, they have gone on to lead creative and productive lives, their values solidified out of what was good in the sixties, and they themselves possessed of a maturity that makes me hopeful for the future of the human family.

And to reassure the Stanford administrators who also made it through the sixties: Nobody is counting the buildings any more.

Why did the Vietnam War emerge as a vehicle for widespread protest, especially by the young, when such degrees of involvement were lacking in previous wars and seem likely to be lacking in future wars?

1. The Vietnam War confronted us with relatively clear moral demands. A major world power was pulverizing a minor power, and we were the guilty party. The "collateral damage" (the Army's euphemism for civilian casualties) was appalling. No moral justification by the war's proponents was ever persuasive.
2. There was an increasing feeling that in this particular struggle, the peace movement might actually make a difference in the outcome.
3. Those in the corridors of American power found themselves on the defensive—a new posture in which they did not know how to behave.
4. Personal fear of being drafted or imprisoned undoubtedly played a part—especially not to be underestimated in the case of the young—but it was subordinate for those of my generation.
5. Many Americans were reasonably well-treated by the police at rallies, sit-ins, and arrests.
6. Much of the protest was located on college and university campuses, where there was a wider tolerance for dissent than at "ordinary" citizen rallies on the village green.
7. There was no villain or group of villains to oppose, at least not in the same sense as there had been in World War II. If there were villains, they were embodied in the American abuse of power, not in the moral outrages of an "enemy."
8. The war came so close to our living rooms (through the nightly TV news) and was rendered so vividly that it could not be held at arm's length or "put on hold" until a more convenient time for protest had been established.
9. The apparatus and the attitudes for nonviolent political protest were already in place, thanks to several years of domestic experience in the civil rights movement. The two causes became one, each strengthening the other.

8

West to East and Back Again: Dealing with Failure

Maybe I was going through a mid-life crisis and didn't know it, but in the mid-seventies I found myself more and more restless at Stanford. The departure of Jerry Irish after the university refused to grant him tenure told me more than I wanted to know about Stanford's criteria for advancement. That was one moment of clarification. Another was the day, in the midst of a department meeting about finding a replacement for Jerry, when I suddenly realized that if I were applying for the job, there probably wouldn't be a single colleague who could be counted on to vote for me. This helped me recognize that I wasn't cut out to be a loner, that I needed some colleagues, of which I now had precisely none. That was a great moment of clarification.

At the same time, I think the department felt that at least one theological oddball could be accommodated and that, if I were to resign, I had become enough of a fixture on the Stanford scene that my departure would not go unnoticed and might, for some folks, even have reflected unfavorably on the department. Pacific School of Religion, knowing of my dissatisfaction at Stanford, had been making signals in my direction, and I worked out a one-year compromise with both schools: The next year I would divide my teaching responsibilities—half-time at Stanford and half-time at Pacific School of Religion. We would see what happened.

In the midst of this trial separation, out of the blue came an invitation to return to the faculty of Union Seminary in New York. This offer was matched by PSR. After months of anguish and the loss of a lot of sleep, I accepted Union's offer.

Leaving Palo Alto after fourteen years was not easy. The fact that our decision to return to Union had been clouded with so many queries and quandaries didn't help.

When I returned to Union in 1976 after fourteen years at Stanford, I thought I had a few good symbolic things going for me. In earlier times I had been a professor of systematic theology, and this time around I would be a professor of practical theology, a shift which very accurately described what had happened to me in the fourteen-year interval. Theological system-building no longer attracted me, while a theology dealing with "the practical" attracted me very much, since it admitted such disciplines as sociology, economic analysis, people's experiences, and something I was beginning to discover called "a preferential option for the poor." Within the field of practical theology I also liked my particular slot as "professor of ecumenics and world Christianity." While somewhat brazenly unlimited in its scope, it too described where I was at. I looked on all my teaching as ecumenical, both confessionally and etymological (*oikoumene* meaning "the inhabited world"). My theological interests now encompassed "world Christianity," which no longer assumed that all good theology originated in Germany and gradually caught on elsewhere, but I believed that much of the *real* theology was being done in the third world, in places like Latin America, Asia, and Africa (especially South Africa). This didn't go over too well with my new colleagues in the practical field. The first comment addressed to me at the first area meeting I attended was a suggestion that I would probably be happier in the theological, rather than the practical, field.

I had also declined to accept a tenured appointment. I had seen the tenure question destroy so many young teachers at Stanford that I wanted no part of its continuation and figured that at a place like Union it would be possible to find some kindred souls on the faculty who would be interested in working out another system of periodically assessing one's worth to the institution and perhaps breaking some new ground. In this expectation I was totally naive. No member of the faculty even wanted to raise the issue, and colleagues accused me of declining tenure to avoid committee work.

As I have said frequently, Union thought it was getting good old Bob Brown back, and good old Bob Brown thought he was returning to the Union he had known so well fourteen years earlier. And both Union and good old Bob Brown were wrong. Neither of us asked enough questions, or even the right questions. I was coming back in a kind of crusading spirit, to a place where I thought there was lots of room for experimentation and new ways of doing things. What I found was an institution rather cautiously beginning to rebuild after the sixties and eager to become a "good seminary" again. My feeling was that the church didn't need another "good seminary." There were plenty around, maybe even some excellent ones. What the church did need was a brand-new approach to theological education, a willingness to experiment with new forms and new vision, and with faculty and trustees open to new ideas—the sort of seminary Union had been in almost all of its history, and which I thought it could become once more.

Even so, there were pluses. Sydney and I were able to do a few things, thanks to a gift of $25,000 for each of the first two years, provided by friends who had helped us out under similar circumstances elsewhere. One of the things we did was take an extended trip (described below) to Latin America to sound out possibilities for collaboration between Union and third-world seminaries, both Protestant and Catholic. This led to the establishment of some lines of communication that could be picked up by others after we left.

We also tried to make our apartment—711 McGiffert Hall, one of the big ones—available for student meetings, discussion, entertaining of visiting third-world Christians, and so on. Having had a home at Stanford where we could do this, we were pleased that adequate space was available at Union. We had groups in at least twice a week and sometimes more often, which also enabled Sydney to develop rapport with a cross section of the Union community she might otherwise have missed. When we got an ecumenical student committee formed, called *Oikoumene*—which became a household word at Union—we had a structure for beginning to correlate everybody's concerns and hopes and fears, and we were buoyed by wonderful students from a variety of backgrounds, races, and cultures who kept the time from being ill-spent.

Our own "family" was an important part of the mix. It started with Hugo, a sheepdog of gigantic proportion, who always wanted to be taken for a walk. I attribute the fact that I physically survived at Union to the necessity of walking Hugo several times a day, even though it would be truer to say that he took me walking. Without that compulsory exercise, I would have been a great target for a heart attack. In addition to Hugo, there were Sydney and Tom, our youngest son, who helped redeem the time for Sydney by continually reminding her that this episode in our family history was an *adventure*. Then there was Karen Parker, Tom's friend, who was in the ballet. We also had Teruo Kurobayshi living with us, a Japanese graduate student who did things like translating Tillich into Japanese, and Carlos Rojas, a Chilean refugee whose escape from prison and torture was made possible because our daughter, living in Chile that year, laid the groundwork for us to sponsor his release to become and remain a close part of the family. And there was Jennifer, niece of one of my earlier students at Union and also a ballet dancer. For several months we had Merdat, from Iran, who arrived needing a place for a couple of nights and slept on the floor behind the sofa for four months, along with two South African students who had had to flee the country because they refused to serve in the South African military forces. And there was Janet

Walton, a musician, and a member of the religious order of the Sisters of the Sacred Names of Jesus and Mary, who often had evening meals with us while getting a doctorate in education. (Janet is now a tenured member of the Union faculty—a Roman Catholic sister who teaches liturgy and the arts and is in charge of the worship at a Protestant seminary.)

There was nothing planned in all of this. We had the space, and the rest of it just "happened" as long as we could fit people in. It was, not by conscious design, an informal showcase of lived-out ecumenism, made up of all sorts and kinds of persons, and it was one of the big pluses for us of our three years back at Union.

Various faculty were supportive, but none could make the establishment of an ecumenical program a priority in their personal or professional lives. Our closest friends and allies the first year were four visiting professors on the scene only temporarily. They included Henri Mottu, a radical New Testament scholar, preacher, and teacher from Switzerland; Eberhard and Renate Bethge, to whom many of the letters in Bonhoeffer's *Letters and Papers from Prison* were written; Dorothee Soelle, a radical German theologian too controversial to get a full-time position in Germany; and Gustavo Gutierrez, one of the chief creators of Latin American liberation theology, whom I already knew through his writings and whom Sydney and I got to know very well in the two semesters he taught at Union. With a lineup like that, one can hardly imagine being anything but overjoyed. We were. And then, the next fall, they had all gone home.

LATIN AMERICA

One of the hopes in returning to Union was that Sydney and I could give serious attention to the study of liberation theology. Our exposure was still mainly from its reading, with occasional contacts as Latin Americans appeared on the scene. Since an ecumenical presence was to be part of Union's future, Sydney and I were able, thanks to help from our friends the Montgomerys, to take a month-long trip to Latin America soon after our arrival at Union. Our main task was to explore possible locations for student exchanges. We visited five, each of which had attractive possibilities for welcoming North Americans— and for sending students of theirs to Union. In each situation, contacts and experiences reinforced the desirability of a more ecumenical mix in theological education.

A particular attraction of Lima, Peru, was our friendship with Gustavo Gutierrez, who had just been at Union for a semester, along with the work he was doing at the Bartolomé de Las Casas Center he had helped to establish.

There were also possible connections within the university in Lima, where Gustavo taught one day a week.

We happened to be in Lima during the famous "summer course," in which Gustavo and others taught thousands of laypersons every year, who then returned to their "base communities" with new material to share. The courses became so popular that a question was raised each year: Would the government permit the course, since public officials with dim theological vision realized that powerful stuff was being shared and appropriated?

The most impressive expression of this tension occurred at the last day each year, when the enrollees poured out of the church singing the Magnificat, the song Luke reports Mary singing after the angel has informed her that she will bear a son to be called Jesus (Luke 1:46–55). This suggests a lullaby scene to most North Americans, but we and they hear very different sounds from the same script. To the poor, Mary's song is a rousing affirmation of a new kind of future. First of all, the decks are cleared: "God has put down the mighty from their thrones," and then, to complete the reversal, "God has exalted those of low degree." Another contrast is offered: "God has filled the hungry with good things, and the rich God has sent away empty."

Those who were singing and marching were virtually invulnerable, despite revolutionary rhetoric, for these were the words of Jesus' own mother, the "Blessed Virgin," and the one whom all those on duty acknowledged as "Queen of Heaven." To open fire on marchers singing such words would be like an attack on Mary herself, an unthinkable action. So the nurturing words of Mary's song resounded in the plaza, and the singers reinforced one another for the long haul when they got back home.

Jesus' advice of long ago was not going unheeded that day in Lima: "Be wise as serpents and harmless as doves."

Arriving at Santiago and Viña del Mar, Chile, was like a homecoming to people who had never been there, for our daughter Alison *had* been there before, on an American Field Service high school student exchange, and had created an atmosphere of impregnable trust, which was very necessary to us since this was still the time of Pinochet, the ruthless general who had taken control during a bloody coup four years before. Our guide and helper was Pepo, Alison's friend, a priest who had suffered much during the hostile regime and was putting himself on the line for us, knowing (as he told us) that the DINA (the secret police) would already know from which plane we had disembarked and would undoubtedly follow us during our stay. But people were willing to take the risk even so, and in company with Pepo we met priests of the underground, courageous women running the soup kitchens for the children, and leaders of the Vicaria de Solidaridad, the church agency that intervened on behalf of victims of injustice and the place where we first met

Carlos Rojas. We had been working on his scholarship for many months so that he could get out of the country and live with us at Union. Carlos had been a young leader in the barrio where he had grown up and was active in the resistance after the coup d'etat. He had been arrested and tortured and had escaped, and then we sponsored him as a political refugee. The Vicaria made the final arrangements so expeditiously that Carlos actually got to the United States before we did. He learned English, got a GED, became a highly skilled machinist, and has been living near us in the Bay Area for years.

What stands out, in retrospect, is the courage of these and many other people who need not have risked themselves on our behalf and did so anyway. Our deepest memory was an evening Pepo arranged with a group of priests working in a depressed barrio. They told us about one of their liturgies, again drawn from the Magnificat. In a dialogue between priests and people, certain contrasts were established between the Mary of the Magnificat and the Mary of the "holy pictures" for sale in the churches. In the latter, Mary is standing on a crescent moon. She is wearing a crown. She has rings on her fingers. She has a blue robe embroidered with gold.

In a spirited response, the worshipers insisted that such a description was not faithful to the Mary of the song. Various ones picked up on this theme:

"The Mary of the song would not be standing on the moon. She would be standing in the dirt and dust where we stand."

"The Mary of the song would not be wearing a crown. She would have on an old hat just like the rest of us, to keep the sun from causing her to faint."

"The Mary of the song would not be wearing jeweled rings on her fingers. She would have rough hands like ours."

"The Mary of the song would not be wearing a silk robe, embroidered with gold. She would be wearing old clothes like the rest of us."

And then the breakthrough: "Father, it may be awful to say this, but it seems as though Mary would look just like me. My feet are dirty, my hat is old, my hands are rough, and my clothes are torn."

The priest assured her that she was not wrong; she was deeply right. Only such a Mary can speak to, and act for, the poor, the neglected, the victims, those at the bottom of the heap. It is indeed true, as Scripture reports, that "God exalts those of low degree and fills the hungry with good things." The priests ended the liturgy with the question, "How could we begin to help God bring those things to pass?" Formally, it was a question; in reality, it was a set of marching orders.

Over the Andes from Santiago, Chile, is Buenos Aires, Argentina. Located in Buenos Aires is ISEDET, a well-established Protestant seminary giving good academic preparation to students from many parts of South America, and where I thought a "formal" relationship might indeed be established. In a meeting with the faculty to discuss plans for the future, there was a potential snafu that actually became an asset to the discussion. I was asked *either* (a) "What do you think you can do for us?" *or* (b) "What do you think we can do for you?" In my answer I apparently tried to respond to both questions at once, without distinguishing between them. But out of the confusion we were able to establish that we could not in fact separate the questions, and that an answer to either one had to be an answer to both. (In addition to all this the faculty was in quiet anxiety, as one of their group had "disappeared" and there was no word of him.)

At the Buenos Aires airport, while waiting for a midnight departure to San José, Costa Rica, a moment of truth came to Sydney and me in ways neither of us would care to repeat. I had with me letters to various liberation theologians in Latin America that Sergio Torres, head of the Theology in the Americas project, had asked me to mail for him in Costa Rica. The reason for this was that if the envelopes had U.S. stamps they would create suspicion, and if they were stamped in Latin American countries other than Costa Rica, they would almost routinely be opened. In either case, the consequences for the writers *and recipients* would be catastrophic. I had placed them in my briefcase in a brown folder, to keep track of them in any cursory inspection.

But the inspection in Buenos Aires was far from cursory. Suitcases, boxes, and finally briefcases had to be opened and inspected. Sydney had gone first and passed inspection. I was still in possession of my briefcase, waiting for inspection and feeling more naked and exposed every moment. Members of the army were watching the proceedings. The books came out. No problem. Also some magazines. No problem. Finally the brown folder containing the letters was taken out, and its contents briefly examined as I desperately tried to remember how to say that I had simply run out of stamps. And then the customs official made the infinitely beautiful human gesture—an upraised thumb—meaning, "Okay. No problem." He had been looking for drugs.

I rejoined Sydney, whose pounding heart during this brief episode had been reverberating in perfect timing with mine, audible we were sure, to the farthest reaches of the airport complex. "Jesus Christ!" I breathed to her as I sat down. She asked, "Was that a prayer or a curse?" I replied, "I don't know. Probably both!" But I am sure that for that interminable twenty-four seconds, close to midnight, we both experienced the terror with which our sisters and brothers in Latin America have lived for years, during the twenty-four hours of every day and every night, when a knock on the door, or an examination of one's belongings, can mean death.

We could relax in Costa Rica, at least in comparison to Argentina, chiefly because Costa Rica has no army. To be sure, its police force is of awesome size, but I felt safe enough the very morning we arrived to ask a policeman the way to the post office. I wanted to get those letters out of my hands as soon as possible.

The situation at the Protestant Seminario Bíblico in San José was different from anywhere else we visited. It had been founded by Protestant missionaries to train students to express the Christian faith of an ultraconservative sort. Put most explicitly, the decisions were not made by indigenous faculty in San José, but by Anglo-Saxon trustees in Paramus, New Jersey. Tensions between faculty and trustees were strong in 1977 during our visit, and later on there was a parting of the ways. Happily, a very creative indigenous justice-centered biblical faith has been established that is making Seminario Bíblico an exciting place for North Americans as well as Central Americans to study. There is also DEI (Departamento Ecuménico de Investigaciones) at the secular University of Costa Rica, which was doing extensive research and analysis from a theological-political-economic point of view. Over the years there have been a number of student and faculty exchanges between that school and Union.

Our last port of call was Mexico City. Here we were taken in tow by a Baptist seminarian, Moisés Mendez, and his wife, both of whom Alison had met in a class on liberation theology at Harvard, taught by Craig Schindler, a former student and leader at Columbae House. There is a splendid complex of buildings in Mexico City housing several Protestant seminaries that suggest that long-range planning for interaction could be beneficial to all. In addition to Moisés and his wife, we had interesting visits with two leaders of theological thought in Mexico, who had taken very different roads but clearly shared some basic concerns.

José Porfirio Miranda, an ex-Jesuit, was teaching mathematics, philosophy, and law, but his heart was in biblical studies. A huge bear of a man, whose hugs of welcome threaten to crush ribs, he put similar energy into approaching any given text. He would employ all the instruments of textual criticism, taking on the biblical scholars on their own turf, and emerging with a radical reading not only unexpected but fortified by sound scholarship. He described leaving the Jesuits poignantly: "I had to choose between Jesus Christ and the church," making clear what an agony it was to have had to face such alternatives.

His particular concern had been the relationship of Christianity and Marxism, and the titles of several of his books reveal his direction: *Marx and the Bible, Communism in the Bible,* and *Marx against the Marxists.* He felt that the Marxists had betrayed Marx (just as he felt the Christians had betrayed Christ) and that everybody missed the point that the New Testament teaches a consistently communistic ethic. When we met him, he was just finishing *Marx against the Marxists.* "I have read all thirty-seven volumes of Marx's *Collected Works,*" he told us. "You will be surprised at what I have found." What a colossal misfortune that he could not teach in the areas of his greatest love.

Another meeting Moisés arranged for us was with Mendez Arcéo, the large and kindly bishop of Cuernavaca, about an hour south of Mexico City. He was one of the most creative and dedicated leaders of the church, and therefore (one must add sadly) had been in constant trouble with Rome. Mendez was a socialist. Mendez believed that psychoanalysis was a useful tool in pastoral work. Mendez was an important presence at Vatican II. Mendez had taken leadership in getting the church engaged in the plight of the poor. Obviously, he was a troublemaker.

A beautiful symbol of Mendez's relationship to the church is his cathedral in Cuernavaca. Shortly before Vatican II, he cleaned house, removing all the clutter and bric-a-brac of several centuries. He whitewashed the walls and created a wonderful space for the community and for individuals as members of the community. The atmosphere is both serene and electric—a wonderful statement about continuity and change, the old and the new, the innovative and the lasting.

When the bishop would process into the cathedral for mass, his crozier (the symbol of episcopal authority) was not a gold-plated staff, but a young sapling, suggesting life-giving power. When it was time for the homily, rather than mounting a pulpit, he sat in a chair near the altar, his robe a simple pale green cotton cloth, crossed his legs, and read the lectionary passage for the day, commenting on it with the congregation verse by verse.

To meet such people as are described here is reward enough for many grueling trips by plane, bus, and auto. That in the future more seminarians might meet such people is reward enough to do whatever is necessary to bring that to pass.

A final comment: We made the trip early in 1977, shortly after Jimmy Carter had been sworn in as president. Without once raising the issue ourselves, we heard the same question at every stop along the way: Do you think Mr. Carter will *really* do anything about worldwide human rights abuses? The question was not academic. It came from people whose families and friends had been subjected to torture unimaginable in its intensity, many of the techniques having been taught to Latin American military leaders at the U.S.-sponsored School of the Americas in Georgia. The question came also out of the sheer ignoring of the issue during the Nixon-Kissinger era, epitomized by Mr. Kissinger's bald statement of hemispheric policy: "We can't let Chile go communist just because the Chileans don't know any better." Translation: anything goes, including torture.

All we could answer to the question was a statement of our hope that things *would* change, and the Carter administration certainly made a valiant beginning. But as the administration's power diminished, the vigorous start was increasingly bypassed or neglected, and the twelve years of Reagan/Bush policy put concern for human rights on a far, far back burner.

This is an inescapable issue for Christians, and no respite is in sight.

There came a time when it was clear that I wanted to resign from Union. Before the end of the first year I knew that I was in the wrong place. I resigned formally in November of the second year, but Union prevailed on me to stay a third year to give Union more time to find a successor. Happily, our concerns didn't go down the drain with our departure. Janet Walton took over the task of developing the ecumenical program for the next year and got some things put in place that still survive, so that when Kosuke Koyama appeared on the scene as my successor, the way had been paved for him.

Union came out of this period well; it got Koyama, an outstanding Japanese scholar and teacher, who was much better for the long haul than I could ever have been. And at the end of the day I came out of this period well also. I was hired to finish my teaching years as a member of the Pacific School of Religion in Berkeley, California.

Sydney: In going back to Union, we were naive in assuming we were going back to the Union we once knew. And they were naive in thinking they were getting the old Bob Brown back, with me as an appendage.

We should have known that Union had gone through the sixties and had changed, even as we'd gone through the sixties and had also changed. We came to know that the old Union had been under an onslaught of pressure—structurally and financially— and that money was tight. Departments had lost staff; overall retrenchment was the modus operandi. Faculty goals were to restore and reinvigorate the traditional ways and areas of study even as, at the same time, unheard of new theologies were springing up, demanding room and money: black theology, feminist theology, black feminist theology, Asian theology; there were even murmurings of environmental theology and a theology that accepted gays and lesbians. Into the midst of that we came with our visions and hopes based more on liberation theology. It was not surprising we found less interest in and support for our proposed program than we'd naively hoped for.

Bob and I came to Union with a rather ill-defined understanding that we would do our work at the seminary in a collaborative way in positions where we were defined as co-equals. That was not realistic. Bob came as academic professor. The seminary probably assumed that as "co-equal" I would do the office work for the ecumenical program. That was not where my interests or skills lay. In spite of this, we two did work together in our own way. We gathered some interested faculty, a wonderful collection of students, and gradually created the program.

The move to Union was initially hard for me—leaving my home, friends, work, and community. And I'll always be grateful to our Tom for challenging me with, "Come on, Ma, this is an adventure!"

The move to Union was also a blessing to me; it opened new doors and put me in a much wider world than I'd been in before. I connected with people and organizations involved in work and economic justice issues, ecumenical organizations, church and trade union groups working against plant closures and job loss, women's organizations working for economic justice for women. I taught a course at Union called Work and Vocation and found I really liked teaching. I formed a group with friends, Project Work, that explored alternative workplaces in New York City—co-ops, worker-owned businesses, and the like. I also put together an investigatory trip by jeep (with Union students, a Hispanic Baptist seminary graduate, a Puerto Rican agronomist/marine biologist) to explore ways we at Union might connect with progressive groups in Puerto Rican churches and seminaries in the future. We talked with the people of Vieques (the island and bay, long used by the U.S. military as a bombing range), were told by fishing communities of the deadly pollution to their rich fisheries from toxic run-off from U.S. pharmaceutical companies, and met many other groups and individuals. This was done as a part of our future ecumenical program. Pulling up my old roots had been wrenching; venturing in a much wider world fed my soul.

I was upset, if not outraged, that the Union administration told the wider world through press and media that because I couldn't find a place for myself at Union and in New York, Bob had decided to leave. This was certainly not true.

The return to California was not easy for me. Once again, I had to start from scratch. But I found allies and colleagues: John Moyer, who had returned from working for the World Council of Churches in Geneva; Donna Ambrogi, a recent Stanford law graduate; and John Lind of California/Nevada Interfaith Center for Corporate Responsibility. We came together and formed the Northern California Interfaith Council on Economic and Environmental Justice, for which I worked with excitement and pleasure for nearly twenty years. And Bob moved happily back to teach at Pacific School of Religion.

RETURN TO PSR

So here I was, fifty-nine years old and looking for a job in an overcrowded field. Pacific School of Religion president Davie Napier had just retired, but the acting president, John von Rohr, was willing to listen when I raised the question of whether or not there might still be a role for me at PSR. John was wonderful. As acting president, he had every right to terminate the conversation with the patent truth that a new president should choose a new faculty member. But he gave it a try—sounding out his colleagues, talking with trustees, working on the financial problems entailed. He was hopeful.

In the meantime, I had come to another decision point. I had only one more slot of time before retirement. How did I really want to spend it? I most wanted to have more time for writing. It occurred to me, in an unusual moment of clarity: Why wait until I am sixty-five? Why not claim some of that time now? Emboldened but apprehensive, I proposed to John that we establish a half-time appointment, which was good news for John von Rohr money-wise, good news for Bob Brown writing-wise, maybe even (for a change) good news for Sydney family-wise and job-wise. We might even have more time together.

We established that for five years I would be a fully available faculty member in the spring semester, and the rest of the time I could write. Every part of the arrangement was a plus save for one appropriate but inexorable law of life: One who teaches half-time receives half a salary. I had no moral or fiscal leverage with which to challenge this law, and I accepted it as a fair price to pay for the otherwise euphoric set of conditions. Sydney's work made up the difference.

I had left Stanford in 1976 pretty angry. I had left Union in 1979 disappointed and sad. I realized I was really not comfortable in my position at Union as professor of ecumenics and world Christianity. I felt far more comfortable in my position at PSR in theology and ethics. The years were unambiguously good. I admired and worked well with my new colleagues, I relished the ecumenical contacts, especially with the Jesuits, and I could be fully present at Berkeley, my office door open all the time, since the writing and the students were not in competition anymore. And it is written down somewhere that I even enjoyed the faculty meetings, which is about as euphoric as an academic can get.

There was a symmetrical symbolism in my arrival and departure from PSR. Shortly after my arrival, an "action" was planned to protest UC Berkeley's ongoing support of the Livermore Weapons Laboratory, which was dedicated to making more advanced atomic weapons. People like Dan Berrigan, Louis Vitale, and Dan Ellsberg were suddenly on hand, along with a group of students who would sit in on the eleventh floor of the administration building, urging the university to sever its connection with Livermore. I joined the group as a support for the students. We took possession of a portion of the eleventh floor shortly after lunch. Following some initial hesitancy, the university officials adopted a policy of studiously ignoring us. Not until after eleven o'clock that night did the police arrive to arrest us, an hour chosen by them to preclude the possibility that the event would make the morning newspapers. We were cited and released on our own recognizance to the cheers of several hundred seminarians. I felt that I was once more among friends.

Six years later, just as I was leaving PSR, there was another "action," this time at the federal building in San Francisco, a very familiar location where many of us had been involved in demonstrations during the Vietnam years. This time the issue was covert U.S. support for the contra war in Nicaragua. When Senator Pete Wilson refused to let us visit his office, we protested by kneeling in prayer on the steps of the federal building until handcuffed and hauled off by the police. This time there was a slightly escalated legal response. We were not only cited, but we were assigned trial dates. My date was in mid-September (it was now June) and since I was to be teaching at Dartmouth College that fall, as an emeritus professor, I asked for my court appearance to be earlier. Not a chance. I should have thought of that before I broke the law. So I had to fly back from New Hampshire to San Francisco and stand trial. The judge let each of us speak to the court about our motives. We were then sentenced to "eighteen hours of community service," which was no more than a slap on the wrist, but I had to make special arrangements to do my "community service" in New Hampshire. It had a nice twist: A former Union student, Jim Breeden, now on the Dartmouth staff, was assigned to be my parole officer and to see that his former professor didn't step out of line.

Thus, both my arrival and departure from PSR were enfolded by arrests. I am content with the symbolism.

MY TEACHING AND SPEAKING METHOD

Whatever personal putdowns I have engaged in while reexamining my life, there is one virtue I will claim: Whenever I do any public speaking—lecture, sermon, seminar, prayer, speech at a rally, homily at a baptism or wedding—I try to be prepared, which means having a full text I have gone over enough times to be familiar with, so that I won't stumble around, split infinitives, leave dangling participles, or just generally commit verbal mayhem. I'm not good at just "winging it." When caught in a situation where such preparation isn't possible, I remark, hoping for laughs, "I can be much more spontaneous with a script."

Until these later years at PSR, my classes had consisted of well-prepared lectures, with occasional time for questions. I always put an outline on the board, and referred to it whenever I could drag myself away from all those typewritten assurances on the podium. My break with this tried and true method came in the early seventies, after I had started teaching about liberation theology, and read in Paulo Freire's *Pedagogy of the Oppressed* about the "banking method." In banking education, the professor "deposits" material in the student's brain, and the student "withdraws" portions of it to pay the "debt" in an examination.

Whatever else this was, Freire persuaded me that the banking method was not real education. This new emphasis also came to the fore when students were beginning to rebel against the stern teacher/pupil models and to demand more participation themselves. I began to be extremely self-conscious about professorial imperialism when I went to PSR, knowing that I would be confronting very verbal graduate students.

I removed any podium within sight (with its symbolic message of magisterial authority), and instead of standing in a privileged place, I sat down, usually behind a table. I would ask for comments about what was going on in the world and in their lives as the class was assembling, and from that went into a brief statement (not a lecture) on the theme for the day. I asked questions and asked *for* questions, and frequently broke the larger class into smaller discussion groups, among which I would circulate, listening, and from which new questions could be focused. I invariably had difficulty getting them to disband and form a larger group again. They would be thoroughly into an issue and wanted to keep pursuing it. So when they wouldn't reassemble quickly, I counted that not a defeat but a triumph.

This whole approach was more threatening to me than giving a lecture (an ancient art form I didn't totally disavow), but it meant that almost everybody was involved, and almost nobody was simply a passive recipient of information. And this meant, of course, that things weren't nearly as tidy at the end of the hour as they might otherwise have been. It wasn't as idyllic and successful a time as it may seem in retrospect. I don't think I was terribly effective in this new style, which broke the mold of a lifetime of experience, not to mention the models earlier mentors had bequeathed to me. But I continued giving it a try at the places I taught briefly after retirement—Dartmouth College, Carleton College, and Santa Clara University—and I had the feeling that at least I was on the right track.

It was still a fairly recent discovery to realize that one's point of ethnic origin, one's skin color, one's cultural situation, and one's economic status have a tremendous impact not only on how one does theology but on the substantive content as well. It seemed to me important for students, particularly white North American students, to read theology created by people fresh from different backgrounds, since our tendency is always to think of *our* position as normative and other positions as interesting cultural variants. So we read such books as Kosuke Koyama's *Waterbuffalo Theology* (Japanese); James Cone's *A Black Theology of Liberation* (African American); Rosemary Ruether's *Sexism and God-Talk* (feminism); *The Dutch Catechism*, a liberated "Catholic" approach; Gustavo Gutiérrez's *A Theology of Liberation* (Latin American); and so on. I felt that the approach was beginning to work when one student, reporting on *The Dutch Catechism*, said, "This work is by a group of white, Dutch, Roman Catholic males, and may be of some use if you happen to be a white, Dutch, Roman Catholic male yourself."

In the "required" course there were two main writing assignments. One went pretty well, though we had a near catastrophe for which I was responsible; the second went very well, and I remain happy about it. The first assignment was for small groups to develop a theological position they could affirm as their own (with space for minority reports when necessary), and then to discover a way to share it with the rest of the class. One resourceful group ended its presentation, and the course itself, with a foot-washing service.

But I made a serious miscalculation in forming the groups for this initial assignment, out of which I learned some deeper lessons. I had proposed a variety of social and cultural backgrounds in each group, so that each student could challenge and learn from other students' perspectives. I assigned at least one black student to each group, assuming that these students would welcome a chance to describe their perspectives as well as to challenge the racism that might exist among their white brothers and sisters. It seemed to me that there was a great deal other students could learn from their unique perspective. However, I failed to fully understand the depth of the experience of racism of the black students in the seminary. I learned something new as I watched the black students firmly resist my approach. They quite expressly wanted their own group. They wanted to work together on their issues and have each other's support in order to express their views as a unified group to this predominantly white class of students. This was a profound learning moment for me. Providently, the student TA for the class, Thee Smith, a wonderful black student whom I knew well, was able to mediate things between the black students and me in a way that helped us all learn together.

Meanwhile, various faculty groups, across the theological spectrum, spent time working out new courses with such titles as "Peace and Justice" and even "Spirituality and Justice." For the former, we created a course in which students were required to be involved in some kind of peace and justice project in Berkeley (not too hard to find), and to arrange for members of such special interest groups to make their pitch in the classroom. In the second instance, Bernard Adeney and I developed a course on spirituality and justice. Bernie stood in a tradition far to the right of mine, and we took special care that he did not get labeled as the "devotional" partner, while I assumed the role of "activist" partner. I think some stereotypes were broken down with this arrangement, and a large enrollment of students from many backgrounds helped to make it increasingly possible for students at New College, the more evangelical seminary where Bernie taught, to cross-register at the Graduate Theological Union, or GTU, a consortium of theological schools and other religious institutions in the Berkeley and San Francisco Bay areas.

But all of this was small beer when compared to the establishment of the Network Ministry, initially proposed by a Presbyterian pastor in San Francisco, Glenda Hope, who managed to make the Network Ministry "work" for a number of years until pressures, mainly financial, forced it to be put on hold, from which it escaped several years later.

All second-year students at participating GTU seminaries could apply to be among a dozen students who would comprise the group for a year's commitment to urban ministry. They would all get field work jobs in San Francisco, meet with spiritual directors from time to time to check how the year was going, take identical classes for an entire year and—here was a point of amazing novelty—have the classes meet on the work sites of the students, whether in a church parish house, the city jail, or an on-the-street mission. This may have provoked some problems for the students, but the faculty members were the ones who were really stretched. Professors accustomed to the quiet, sedate atmosphere of "Holy Hill" had no consistent place for blackboards, no control over street noise, and constant challenges over how the profound words we spoke actually related to the homeless persons who would burst into the classroom looking for food, shelter, or work, confronting a group of demonstrably incompetent human beings. My own initial reaction to teaching in such places came at about 11:15 on the first morning, when a din began under our windows and got persistently louder. One part of me wanted to open a window and demand quiet. I am glad this part did not win the inner battle, for the din was created by the practical logistical matters being negotiated at a site where a free meal was about to be provided at noon. I would not want to have pitted my feeble words against their powerful deeds. Such experiences are worth a dozen lectures about how food and fellowship must be related to one another theologically. I had never quite realized how much the locale influences what we think, what we believe, what we pray about, how we understand sin and corruption, and perhaps most of all, how we maintain hope.

I wrote above that the Network Ministry was plagued by financial problems. That is true, but it is not the whole truth. It became increasingly difficult to get seminaries to "loan" one faculty person full-time for a whole semester to teach only a dozen students. But at least as important, the whole concept was still pretty far-out, and there were never more than three seminaries simultaneously involved in the creation and survival of the Network Ministry. I believe that the problems, partly financial, were also, in even larger part, theological. However, without the Network Ministry and similar experiments elsewhere, the institutional church as we have known it will atrophy and die on the vine. Even when the Network Ministry closed for a while, I had to believe that it was not dead; resurrection time is always just around the corner.

During these years I became acutely aware of the plight of gay and lesbian students who experience a call to ministry. They can come to seminaries like PSR and feel themselves in an almost totally supportive community. But let them raise the question of ordination, and with an infinitesimal number of exceptions, the church doors are unceremoniously slammed in their faces.

I know of nothing in the life of the church today more cruel and un-Christian than the ways developed for excluding homosexuals from holy orders. The bottom line is that the denominations define gays and lesbians as second-class citizens. They may join our churches, but they may not hold office. The most generous attitude is expressed when a church body may say, in effect, and never quite out loud, "Don't tell us you are lesbian or gay. Deny that part of who you are, and maybe we can get you through." What this says in ordinary English, of course, is summarized by the admonition: Cheat. Don't tell the truth. Base your ministry on a lie. Sometimes an offer will be made: "If you will repudiate your lifestyle and live as a celibate, we might be able to welcome you." This again necessitates a lifetime of deception and denial, and fails to acknowledge the true personhood of the candidates.

Someday, of course, the structures forbidding this will be removed, but even that hope does not compensate for the destructiveness of present policies and the needless irrevocable hurt they daily impose. My own denomination's stand on this issue fills me with shame.

But I must end this chapter on a more hopeful note. The episode I recall has a Jew and a Catholic as its main participants. I have been instructed by them both. My most poignant memory out of all the years of teaching and writing about Elie Wiesel came in a course given at PSR, and it involved the importance of something Elie wrote and its impact on one of my students, Molly Fumia, a Roman Catholic and mother of seven children. Those do not seem as though they would share much in common. But Molly found a place in Wiesel's writings that spoke directly to her after she had struggled over many years with the death of her firstborn child, Jeremy, at the age of seven days. Elie's writing about the death of his sister, Ziporah, at Auschwitz, touched powerful chords in Molly's life, which her term paper helped to lift out of the morass in which they had been lodged for years. Molly's paper was too creative to be consigned to a file, and at my suggestion she filled out her story into an almost lyrical account of how the death of Elie's sister became redemptive for her as she finally came to terms with the death of her own son. And in her book, *A Child at Dawn*, two apparently unrelated stories joined forces to provide a healing for Molly because Elie was willing to share his pain, and new doors for the future opened up.

That's a good place to stop.

9

Ecumenism: Vatican II
and the Holocaust Commission

Will Herberg, a Jew, and I were, early in the ecumenical movement, invited to share the platform at a meeting in St. Peter's College in Jersey City. We arrived together at the entrance to an imposing building. I felt a bit like Dorothy in *The Wizard of Oz* entering the land of the Munchkins, for this was my initial venture into the mysterious land of the Jesuits.

Herberg and I walked in at the front entrance, and the door was firmly closed behind us, sealing off all access to the free world outside. We proceeded through another door, likewise closed behind us, and as we walked down an interminably long and dimly lighted corridor, black-robed Jesuits seemed to converge on us, silently, from all directions. Thus heavily, if not indeed oppressively, escorted, we were ushered into the office of the father rector. After his door had been firmly closed, we heard a voice say, "I think we'll just line you up against the wall and shoot you right here."

The voice, I am happy to report, was that of a photographer.

THE SECOND VATICAN COUNCIL

If I had predicted in the fifties what was descriptively true of the shift in Catholic-Protestant attitudes even in the seventies, I would have been dismissed as exhibit A of wishful thinking. Three things account for the shift. The most obvious was the brief but irreversible reign of John XXIII—"Good Pope John" as the world called him; he enfolded the entire human family within his capacious arms. But John was not operating in a vacuum. There were, on both sides of the divide, "the ecumenical pioneers," who were reaching out toward one another before it was popular or even safe to do so. There was a foundation on which Pope John could build.

The second reason was the lasting fruit of his endeavors, the bringing into being of the Second Vatican Council (1962–1965), even though he died after the first of its four sessions in 1963. He opened the doors of the church so that much-needed fresh air could blow in. The task was Herculean. His advisors opposed the very notion of a council and fought it every inch of the way. They lost. Let a Protestant say it: There are occasional advantages in having papal power. The planning proceeded apace.

The third reason is less tangible, though just as palpably "real," partly fed by, and partly feeding on, the spirit of the times: an increasing recognition that (a) Christians should not be divided, and (b) that even though divided they should not be fighting one another, and (c) an admission that both sides have lived sinfully self-enclosed lives and that they must engage in dialogue—the big word of the times. A less complicated description would be to attribute the council to the renewed activity of the Holy Spirit. Even to my most secular friends, I claim that this ingredient was the most important of all.

My own engagement in the Catholic dialogue came about without any initiative on my part. I grew up with all the conventional anti-Catholic stereotypes: Catholics believe that all Protestants are going to hell along with everybody else save Catholics, since "outside the church there is no salvation"; Catholics do not believe in religious liberty for anybody but Catholics, since "error does not have the same rights as truth"; everything the pope says is infallible and therefore irreformable; as soon as Catholics become 51 percent of the voting public in the United States, they will "take over"; all parochial schools are run in totalitarian fashion; Catholics believe whatever the priest tells them; the only hope for us, "the sheep outside the fold," is to convert, and given the above set of convictions, that alternative was not attractive.

The fact that I went to Union Seminary in the heart of New York City, the archdiocese of Francis Cardinal Spellman, did nothing to dispel my anti-Catholic sentiments, but rather fed them with reinforcing evidence. On one occasion, Cardinal Spellman crossed a picket line created by the grave-diggers local and was photographed shoveling two scoops of dirt on a grave to symbolize the wrongheadedness of the union's demands. My Protestant hackles were sufficiently aroused by this episode to inspire a blistering editorial written for *Christianity and Crisis*, in which I argued that in facing the two great menaces of our time—communism and Catholicism—the choice was easy: Catholicism was more dangerous because it not only had a set of beliefs but also had the arrogance to claim divine authority for every item in the set. At least in combating communism we were not dealing with divine truth but only with human error. Fortunately, wiser heads prevailed, and the blistering editorial was never published.

To offset this mind-set, which at some level of my being I had to concede was crazy, I began to read a little more widely in Catholic writings. Karl Adam's *The Spirit of Catholicism* made a deep impression on me, and I wrote a favorable review about it that *was* published in *Christianity and Crisis*. It was the inspiration for my own attempt at a Protestant counterpart some years later, called *The Spirit of Protestantism*. I began to subscribe to *Commonweal*, a "liberal" lay-edited Catholic journal. I wrote a not-too-polemical letter to the editor, in response to an ironic article by John Cogley, who was urging Protestants not to be so nervous about "Catholic power."

This opened a few doors. We were living in St. Paul, Minnesota, a stronghold of "Commonweal Catholics," and Sydney and I, as I mentioned earlier, began to meet living, breathing, three-dimensional Catholics, including our local congressman, Gene McCarthy, in whose reelection campaign I became involved, and Godfrey Diekmann, OSB. They were Catholics of a sort we had never even seen before—open, gracious, ironic, and eager to pursue common concerns despite apparently insurmountable obstacles farther down the line

As a result of my ecumenical activity and friendships, I was invited by James McCord, president of Princeton Seminary, to represent the World Alliance of Reformed and Presbyterian Churches as a Protestant "observer" at the forthcoming opening of the Second Vatican Council in 1963.

Since all the liturgy and speeches would be in Latin, I decided that a linguistic brushing up was in order, and that I must try to recapture the urgency of Miss Rosenberg's Latin II class at Binghamton Central High School. I tracked down a copy of *The Vocabulary of the Mass in Twenty Lessons, for Priests Making a Late Vocation*, edited by Scanlon and Scanlon, and by fall I was ready to share in the responses and have some idea of what they meant. My other mode of preparation was to steep myself again in the Reformed-Calvinist heritage, which I would be representing at the council.

In addition to rereading a lot of Reformed theology, mostly Karl Barth, I counted on a trip to the Isle of Iona, en route to Rome, to help me recover the existential reality of my own religious roots. But this small island deserves more credit than that.

Iona is a tiny island in the Hebrides off northwest Scotland, a jewel beyond compare, three and a half miles long and less than a mile wide. It has one mountain, Dun I, that reaches toward the heavens with all of its altitude of 311 feet. The beaches are pure white, the water lapping on them is many-hued, depending on the tide, and there can be few shades of blue not represented. Most of the isle is open pasture, with a few crofts, a post office, a shop, and two small hotels.

But also there is an abbey, Benedictine in origin, that after the Reformation was gradually reduced by Protestant zeal to the status of a noble ruin. There are wild tales about the Celts and Vikings, who were there before St. Columba and the Christians and who frequently tried to repossess the isle at great loss of human life on all sides. One beach is called Martyrs' Bay to commemorate a bloody history.

But Iona had been basically a place of peace and not of bloodshed, and in the late thirties a group from the Church of Scotland under the leadership of the Rev. George McCleod, pastor of the prestigious Guvan parish in Glasgow, got permission to rebuild the structures surrounding the abbey and make Iona once more a place of prayer and pilgrimage. Members of the Iona Church Community worked on the rebuilding in the summer months and, to save the whole concept from romanticism, worked in the Gorbels, a notorious Glasgow slum, during the winter, trying to embody the truth that beauty and squalor have to engage in the care of one another. So craftsmen and pastors, islanders and mainlanders, even in the midst of World War II, gradually reclaimed habitable space, and Iona has indeed become a modern place of pilgrimage.

I visited Iona in early September on my way to Rome, after the summer crowds were gone, and shared both in the worship and the ongoing construction. It was important for me to go there and actually put in place a few stones in the west wall and become, in however token a fashion, one of the rebuilders.

High on the nether wall of the chapel at Iona, carved in bas relief, there is a face that the preacher sees every time he ascends the pulpit. The face is contorted by hopelessness and pain, clearly the face of a human being in the throes of eternal damnation. It goes back many centuries and is there to inspire the preacher to reach even to this soul with his words. This is well and good, but I see more faces on that pulpit wall; this suffering soul needs the company of another face, covered with joy. There could even be a sculptured host of rejoicing people from the whole human family who have heard and responded to the Word. That way, no preacher would be able to pass the tribunal without also confronting the testimony of salvation, which is a message of hope that somehow the world in which grace exists is still more potent.

Knowing that Vatican II would be reworking its documents on liturgy, I wanted also an experience of the Iona community's work to recover the Reformed liturgy. Influenced by early Benedictine disciplines, the inseparability of work and worship was liturgically symbolized—no, actualized—each day. The handful of us in attendance would gather together after breakfast to share a call to worship for the beginning of the day, followed by the appointed Scripture lesson, some prayers, and perhaps a hymn or a psalm to close, but no closing benediction. At the end of the day we would gather again, and have, once more, Scripture readings, prayers, a hymn or psalm, and this time a closing benediction. This pattern, in a remarkable way, engaged us in one single activity from morning to night, which was the undifferentiated praise of God through craftsmanship and prayer. The worship was our work, and our work was our worship, all of a piece from morning till night.

Evenings ended with a cup of tea at 9 p.m., and not being used to this, I frequently had to get up during the night. On one such excursion, I noted out of a hall window that there was a glow outside, emanating as nearly as I could discern from the burial place of St. Columba, who had founded the Christian settlement 1,500 years earlier. I had an impulse to go downstairs and switch off the light—my arrival on Scottish soil having reactivated a sense of thrift bequeathed to me by my forebears—but the inclination was too half-hearted to be transformed into a deed.

In the morning, however, I prowled around the area of Columba's tomb, and made what I interpreted as an awesome discovery: There was no electricity anywhere near the tomb. The glowing light, whatever it was, appeared not to have been the product of any human technology. Although my life before and since has been singularly devoid of voices or visions, in this case I remain sure that St. Columba was in some sense "there," and was welcoming me and lighting the way for the rest of my pilgrimage.

I have been back to Iona on numerous occasions since then, and each time I try, rather surreptitiously, to corroborate my distinct impression that the glow was not of human origin, without success. I never saw the glowing again. To me, it still represents a tie with life on Iona 1,500 years ago, and reminds me that my religious roots go back even further than I had thought. If there are further reflections, let them come from the wee folk.

There were no visions surrounding my departure from the island two days later. A wild storm whipped up during the night, making it impossible for the ferry to make the five-minute run from Iona to Fionnphort and thus connect me with a scheduled bus departure. I was in a dither, as I usually am about such things, and made it known to many people that I had a plane to catch in Glasgow the next day and would accept any sort of passage across the tiny strip of water. Toward noon the storm had abated sufficiently for the ferry to operate. I made a bus connection and got to the far side of Mull, where I had to catch the Macbrayne steamer for Oban on the mainland. I missed the connection.

But a curious vessel appeared at the pier, which I can only describe as a "sheep barge." It was mostly deck, with a tiny cabin amidships. Having agreed to this form of travel, I was ushered into the cabin only moments before hundreds of sheep followed me on board and filled the deck so completely that had I wished to do so, I could have walked along their backs with never a worry about slipping down beneath them. When we got to Oban, the sheep disembarked on cue and were herded down the main street, amid buses and people galore, to a pen somewhere beyond my line of vision. Sheep and lambs are important biblical symbols, and a central part of the Mass, the *Agnus Dei*, celebrates the "Lamb of God, who takes away the sins of the world." But for me, that night in Oban, their message was more immediate. The sheep had ushered me toward the next stop on my pilgrimage: Rome.

The English priest beside whom I sat on the bus ride into Rome from Fiumicino Airport could not have been more gracious. He too would be at the council, and he pointed out various sights as we lurched into the Eternal City. "If you'll just look ahead when we go around the next corner," he advised me, "you'll get your first glimpse of St. Peter's." I did as I was bidden, but any sight of St. Peter's eluded me. Only a bit nonplussed, my self-appointed host accepted defeat graciously. "Ah, well," he mused, remembering that I was a Protestant, "perhaps they've torn it down as an ecumenical gesture."

The Vatican's Secretariat for Christian Unity, part of whose job was to look out for us, had rented most of a *pensione* within walking distance of St. Peter's, and I had a room with a spectacular view of Hadrian's tomb. There were a lot of "fussy" things to attend to immediately upon arrival, such as finding a photographer, getting a photo, securing a "passport" to the Vatican, getting the photo affixed therein, and developing some orientation to Rome itself. Armed with a map and no Italian, I found on the first afternoon what became my favorite spot in Rome, the Piazza Navona, a beautiful collection of buildings in the classical style surrounding a square that, on our last night in Rome, was decked out as a Christmas fair. We gradually assembled at the *pensione* and all kinds of old friends emerged, veterans of meetings and assemblies of the World Council of Churches. We were a community from the start.

For many of us, the newness of the experience, surrounded by the ever-so-thoughtful priests assigned to help us, induced a gentle defensiveness on our part: Don't give way too easily to Rome's blandishments. I report this because the mood didn't correspond to the reality. The genuineness of the welcome to us opened many doors, some of which we didn't even know existed.

Indeed, the best "times" at the council (putting on hold the actual sessions themselves) were evening get-togethers with any of the myriad of priests and even bishops who would invite us out to dinner—usually quite lavish dinners—and with whom, by the second or third round of toasts, a human camaraderie was established in which all topics were fair game. There was a self-critique of things Roman by these hosts of ours that staggered us by its honesty. They seemed to know that this was the chance of a lifetime for change in the church, and after they listened to our genial polemics they would offer us some stern ones of their own. Out of a mélange of such evenings, I refined a new axiom for ecumenical dialogue that went: "Elbow bending is better than arm twisting." And so it was, from the very start.

A similar openness and repentance for past injuries was expressed in high places as well. In his opening allocution for the second council session a few days later, the pope made a real breakthrough that would have been unthinkable for a pope even half a decade earlier. Commenting on the divisions of the past, Paul VI said, "If we are in any way to blame for that separation, we humbly beg God's forgiveness and ask pardon, too, of our brethren who feel themselves to have been injured by us. For our part, we willingly forgive the injuries which the Catholic Church has suffered, and forget the grief endured during the long series of dissentions and separations." In such an atmosphere, our Protestant reserve and wariness were gradually overcome. We realized that the Catholics almost desperately wanted the council to "work," and we ourselves became more interested in that goal than we could have imagined ahead of time. While we all came as formal observers, many of us remained as informal participants. It was clear that the success of the council would have favorable consequences for *all* Christians, and that became for us as well a consummation devoutly to be wished.

The Secretariat for Christian Unity, charged with all things ecumenical, made its task *our* task as well. Every Tuesday afternoon the observers would meet with a variety of Catholic theologians and bishops and be urged to speak in all candor about how we felt things were going. The high point of this particular exercise came during the third session, when a number of us commented that the section in the text describing "Protestantism" was one in which we could not identify ourselves. "Very well," responded one of the bishops, "give us a statement with which you *can* identify, and we'll see if we can get it in the final draft." This is why, if you look at a certain section of the text of *Lumen Gentium*, you will discover melodic Latin phrases created by that great Methodist Latinist, Albert Outler, in which we found a true representation.

A further example of our increasing rapport occurred at another meeting of priests and observers. We decided to close the meeting by praying together what Catholics call the "Our Father," which is identical with our "Lord's Prayer," save that our version includes a conclusion that Catholics used to omit. When we got to the severance point for Catholics (". . . but deliver us from evil"), all the Protestants stopped at the Catholic ending, while all the Catholics continued to recite the Protestant ending ("For thine is the kingdom and the power and the glory forever"). This led to more than muffled laughter and appreciation that in a fit of unplanned ecumenical courtesy, we had prayed their version, and they had prayed ours. No one who is unimpressed by this event will ever truly understand the ecumenical movement.

The ecumenical bridge had been building from the Protestant side as well. After four hundred years of baleful sniping at one another, Protestants and Catholics had begun to eye one another covertly early in the twentieth century. By the time of the second assembly in 1954 of the World Council of Churches (comprising most Protestant and Orthodox churches), the WCC leadership felt that it was appropriate to invite the Vatican to send Catholic observers. But Rome declined. The time was not ripe. Even so, there was good Catholic coverage, because by a conservative estimate, 50 percent of the people labeled "press" were actually Catholic priests who wanted to know what was going on.

At the third world assembly of the WCC in Delhi in 1961, four official observers from Rome were permitted to accept the invitation. By this time the skids had been greased, and the plans for the Catholic Church to hold its first council since 1870 included an invitation to the major world bodies of Protestant and Orthodox Christians to send official observers. The world bodies responded positively. The Presbyterians, for example, were invited to send three observers via the World Alliance of Reformed and Presbyterian Churches: Herbert Roux from France, J. K. S. Reid from Scotland, and me from the United States. By the time of Vatican II, there were usually twenty-five or thirty non-Catholics at all sessions in St. Peter's, sitting in the "best seats in the house," way up in front, in the Tribune of St. Longines.

Our task was simply to observe, and to send periodic reports to our headquarters all over the world. This meant officially attending all the sessions—from which the rest of the world was banned. The morning sessions went from nine until perhaps 12:30 each weekday. All the proceedings were conducted in Latin. One of the nicest gestures of the Secretariat was to provide priests for us who could do simultaneous translation. Gus Weigel, my old ecumenical comrade from back home, was one of these, and as we all got to know one another better, he would offer pungent comments about the various speakers. Thanks to our translators, we had more comprehension of what was happening on the council floor than perhaps 98 percent of the participants. All the bishops knew some Latin of course, but for the vast majority it was (as in my case) pretty well confined to the vocabulary of the Mass. Many of them claimed to be befuddled by the torrents of Latin bombarding their earphones and counted on their *periti* (theological experts) to fill them in at lunchtime.

Each afternoon there was a press conference, when all the best reporters and all the best council theologians met for at least an hour of exchange, often with brilliant ripostes. Attendance at this event soared as word got out that it was the best show in town if you wanted to get the whole story on the morning's speeches. I never missed. At the last press conference in December, the reporters, acknowledging how handsomely they had been treated, gave a gift

to the chairman, Fr. John Sheerin of the Paulists, in appreciation of his openness, adroitness, and good humor. It was a gold-plated ping-pong paddle.

The rest of the afternoon usually went into getting my own accounts of the
events of the morning down on paper. I tried the expedient of doing this in the
form of "letters to Sydney," which was not a very smart idea, since her idea of
a letter from her husband, and an outline of episcopal speeches, were worlds
apart. In partial atonement for this continued intrusion of the council into our
domestic life, when I decided to transform the letters into a book about the
council (published the following spring as *Observer in Rome: A Protestant Report
on the Vatican Council*), it seemed only appropriate to dedicate it to her—in
Latin. I got a priest friend, Frank Norris, SS, who was himself at the fourth
session, to render my sentiments in conciliar language. "To Sydney," it went,

> UXORI CARISSIMAE, qui domi flammas amoris domestici splen-
> dide ardentes curabat dum ego Romae flammas dissentionis ecclesias-
> ticae paulatim extingui spectabam.

Its elegance in Latin is remarkable, for Fr. Norris included two Latin puns in
his text. He assures me that what he wrote was an accurate rendition of my
text:

> To Sydney, dearest wife, who kept the flames of family love burning
> brightly at home, while I observed the flames of ecclesiastical misun-
> derstanding being extinguished bit by bit at Rome.

The best place to track down rumors was at one of the coffee bars in St.
Peter's, which opened every day at 10:30 a.m., just when people were beginning to get restless or the speeches were beginning to get repetitious. The coffee bar nearest the observers had already gotten the nickname of "Bar-Jonah,"
this being the way Jesus referred to Peter (i.e., "Peter, son of Jonah"). There
was a similar bar near where the cardinals sat, and with equal promptness it
became "Barabbas," a robber in the Gospel account. We observers felt that
this would be a good way to keep the cardinals humble. When women, mainly
Roman Catholic sisters, were finally admitted as "auditors," it was proposed
by some that a new bar be created for them, to be called "Bar Nun," which
was, with typical Vatican ambiguity, either an invitation to all, or a warning to
many. Finally, when the document on the Jews reached the assembly floor, it
was likewise proposed that there be a fourth bar, "Bar Mitzvah." I cite these
apparent trivialities because they indicate the flavor of the proceedings, which
had moments of levity as well as moments of high drama and tension.

Each day, the first forty to sixty minutes were devoted to the celebration of
the Mass, save that the rite according to St. John Chrysostom always went over

an hour. Actually, the daily celebration of the Mass was a learning experience for the bishops, as well as for those of us in the Tribune of St. Longinus. This was especially true for those who are often called "Baedeker Catholics," who think (quite wrongly) that wherever you go in the Catholic world the Mass will be the same. As we soon discovered, however, the Mass is celebrated in many different geographical and theological forms, with very different music, and even language. On many days in St. Peter's, a lector would stand in the pulpit to explain to the bishops what was going on before their eyes.

It was simply not the case that things were always done in the same way by everyone everywhere, and I believe it was the puncturing of this myth that really opened up the council. It very soon became apparent that the conservatives in Rome, who called all the precouncil shots, did not represent anything like a majority point of view. They were in fact a tiny numerical minority, whose inability to muster up the votes was soon apparent. This meant that conservative proposals submitted for discussion could be sternly attacked, and almost every one was radically reworked in a more progressive direction. The advances were based on the discovery that isolated bishops all over the world had been led to think that proposals for change were unacceptable, whereas an accent on change actually represented the vast majority of the bishops, and they were able to register their newly discovered freedom almost every time a vote was taken.

It wasn't easy. It took the council four years (meeting each fall) to pass sixteen documents. It took that long partly because the conservatives were masters at "Vatican diplomacy" and delaying tactics. But in terms of what came forth, I would entertain any odds that no one in the entire basilica, or even in the entire world, expected half as much as what the council fathers lavishly provided.

There were unexpected breakthroughs in *the inner life of the church*: the decision to reform the liturgy and celebrate the Mass in the vernacular; rethinking the nature of the church as no longer a hierarchy but the entire church as "the people of God," that is, the laity, from among whom, as need arises, individuals are ordained and appointed ("set apart") as deacons, priests, and bishops; a new understanding of religious orders as representing a different, but not necessarily better, pattern for living the Christian life; a new view of the relationship of papacy to episcopacy that is collegial (a key word at the council) rather than hierarchical; a rethinking of the relationship of Scripture and tradition that guards against theological novelties that have no clear basis in Catholic tradition.

There were also changes in *the relationship of the church to the world outside*. These were of special interest to the observers, and we found ourselves existentially involved in their outcome. It was not our task to tell the Roman Catholic Church how to run its internal affairs, strong though the impulse frequently was. But if it was not our official task to instruct Rome about the world outside, it was at least important to be a sounding board for proposals popping up all over the council floor in which we had something substantial at stake.

The document most "observed" by non-Catholics was the proposed text on religious liberty. We had a pretty firm line: The integrity of the council would be lost if a new position on religious liberty was not forthcoming that explicitly guaranteed full religious freedom not only to Catholics but to everyone else as well. The church's record had been baleful and went: "Error does not have the same rights as truth, and since all branches of the Christian church are in error except the Catholic Church, the rights it claims must be given to it exclusively and denied to all other churches. . . . The Catholic Church alone is entitled to preach, teach and evangelize, so the Catholic Church can even call on the arm of the state to protect its right to full freedom and to deny full freedom to everybody else."

This was scarcely a popular view when examined through Protestant eyes. Its one-sidedness, its implicit threat of invoking the civil authorities, its demeaning of the genuineness of Protestant faith, were familiar stands within the living memory of all of us. So this was an issue on which the observers had to close ranks. It was *our* issue. Like some other observers, I pulled together a speech on this issue that I gave under a number of Catholic auspices perhaps half a dozen times. (I was in the midst of presenting this material to the Canadian bishops and *periti* at the council when we got word that President Kennedy had been shot. We did not have the psychic strength to continue the discussion, but we did become as one in the praying of the "Our Father.")

The document on religious liberty was shunted all over the council; the conservatives wanted no part of it. It finally wound up as, and was overwhelmingly approved during the fourth session as, a separate "declaration," one of the sixteen council documents finally promulgated. It met all our concerns, and today its role as part of official Catholic belief is uncontested.

Postscript: Every once in a while, the church comes through handsomely. Consider the case of John Courtney Murray, SJ, an American Jesuit who was writing about the issue of religious liberty long before the council convened. His ideas were rejected by Rome as too avante-garde, and for years he was forbidden to speak or write on the topic. He somehow got to Rome and became the resource person on religious liberty for the entire council. Not only was Fr. Murray the author of most of the final text, but on the last day of the council, when the pope chose a number of the *periti* to concelebrate mass with him, Fr. Murray was one of those chosen. Not everybody experiences total rehabilitation in his lifetime, and all of us who were Americans and had worked behind the scenes with him had special reason to celebrate.

The schema *De Oecumenismo* (*On Ecumenism*) represented another major landmark in the Catholic Church's understanding of its relationship to non-Catholic religious bodies. There was rousing debate on this document; issues were raised where sticking places will come for a long time still (e.g., Eucharist, ordination). There were many attempts to scuttle the text. But there was enough discussion at the end of session two so that when the council reconvened, a series of creative documents was passed, which included material on other world religions, along with the prickly matter of relations with Jews, where the church's historical track record has been a scandal.

Rereading these documents today, I find them rather flat and overly cautious. This, however, is a backhanded tribute to their timeliness, reflecting the situation in 1963 when they indicated the essential "next steps" on the road between then and now that make it possible for people to work together, far short of the ultimate deliverance. The term "separated brethren," for example, used to describe Protestants, is a clear advance over an earlier draft that defined us as "schismatics and heretics," though we now need the further revision of a gender-free term. We had to work hard to make the point that to refer to the Orthodox as members of "*ecclesial* communities" (in which something of the "church" still resides) and to describe Protestants as members of "*religious* communities" (with the implication that nothing of the "church" resides in us) would fail to help the dialogue progress. It was finally stated in the document that the church "subsists" (in however broken a form) in *all* non-Catholic churches. It might be hard for an outsider to understand this distinction, but such are the careful ways out of which cumulative breakthroughs finally occur.

I pursued this matter of interpreting council documents one evening with a small group of Protestants and Catholic bishops. I said, a little brazenly, that I regretted that in documents coming to the council there were always laborious efforts to catalog the insights of "Pope So-and-so of blessed memory," to make clear that whatever the new document was proposing, it was not proposing "change." One of the bishops responded with a comment that has come to my aid many times since. "Look," he said, "when you read a new text, don't worry so much about the statements of Rome's past grandeur. That is what we call *romanitá.* Look for the sentence or paragraph in which an arguably new idea is being introduced. We can live with the fact that the document will be 95 percent *romanitá,* for the sake of the 5 percent of a new idea we can get ratified. Then we can build a theology of the future that gives prominence to the 5 percent. That's how we incorporate continuity and change."

I've decided on reflection that that is a pretty good rule-of-thumb for Protestants as well. Don't expect to get everything at first; don't even expect to get much at first. You can edge up toward the issue. The little steps are the ones that are more likely to survive, because they don't risk some kind of excommunication. The fuller truth will emerge later. When the conservatives begin to back it, you're probably on the edge of a small breakthrough.

The other council document that relates particularly to the church and the modern world was not even submitted to the council for deliberation until session four. Entitled *Gaudium et Spes* and dealing with the theme of "The Church and the World Today," it is a teaching document I have frequently used in classes. It is long, not to mention a bit rambling, but it sets out a multiplicity of areas in which Catholics and non-Catholics can work together—such as the prevention of war, the rights of labor, issues of social justice, race, atheism, conscience, and nuclear weapons. Furthermore, it is addressed not just to "the faithful" (the familiar salutation from the pope to Catholics) but to "all persons of good will," an explicit invitation to ecumenical collaboration. A single example can illustrate its forthright style and prophetic thrust: "Any act of war aimed indiscriminately at the destruction of entire cities, or of extensive areas along with their populations, is a crime against God and humanity. It merits unequivocal and unhesitating condemnation" (para. 20).

When a small group of us went to Europe in December of 1972 after Nixon's carpet bombing of North Vietnam, we used this paragraph as an example of precisely what the United States government was doing in Vietnam and urged, without much success, that all those with whom we spoke should engage in the "unequivocal and unhesitating condemnation" the document calls for.

Unfortunately, the world has not yet caught up with the council.

It is not an exaggeration to point to Vatican II as one of the truly significant events of Christian history. The Catholic Church had seemed to outsiders, especially since the declaration of papal infallibility in 1870, to be retreating further and further away from the contemporary world, exhibiting a kind of "fortress mentality." Old positions, rather than being rethought, were merely being reiterated, and dogmas such as the bodily assumption of the Virgin into heaven, promulgated in 1950, seemed to make ecumenical exchange increasingly problematic and unlikely.

But (to put it theologically), the Holy Spirit seemed to have had other plans: a genial old man, considered "safe" and unthreatening to the ultraconservative power structure in Rome, was elected as a "caretaker pope," and then as John XXIII he took more "care" of the church in less than five years than his predecessors had done in over four hundred years. By the end of the council, what he initiated was already bearing fruit under his successor, Pope Paul VI, and about 2,300 other bishops who experienced an unexpected sense of liberation.

There were a few glorious years, in which pioneering and innovative projects began to spring up all over the Catholic world. Paul VI, elected during the break between the first and second sessions in the summer of 1965, began his pontificate by making John XXIII's agenda his own in many specific and symbolic acts, especially during the second session. But by the end of the third session, the opposition within the council was becoming stronger, and Paul seems to have been persuaded that what he was presiding over could end up as an irreversible step toward the dissolution of the Catholic Church. The pressures on him were beyond human endurance. I remember writing very negative assessments of what was going on between the third and fourth sessions. Fortunately, Paul's refocusing did not initially stifle the work of the council, though it became clear after the council adjourned that the pace of significant reform was decelerating. An early event that stands out particularly was Pope Paul's encyclical in 1968, *Humanae Vitae*, which uncompromisingly reiterated the traditional position of the church that artificial means of contraception were forbidden to Catholics—this despite the clear recommendation of three papally appointed commissions that the church revise its teaching. This event, probably more than any other, eroded much lay support for Catholic teaching authority.

At the same time, it must be noted, Paul VI was issuing creative encyclicals on economics and politics and concern for the poor, but the movement was already swinging in a conservative direction, which Paul's successor, John Paul II, has abetted with enthusiasm. (John Paul I, Paul's immediate successor, died after just thirty-four days in office.) It is now clear that the latter's legacy will be an increasingly conservative, if not reactionary, episcopate, and a spate of encyclicals from the pen of John Paul II make doctrinal mobility a thing of the past. More and more of the final adjudications of the faith, whether large or small, are now in the hands of the pope and his Roman Curia advisers. From my own perspective, almost all of the really creative thinkers on the contemporary Catholic scene have, in one way or another, been warned to hold their insights in check, and retreat from espousing positions about which there might be even a breath of novelty.

As a Protestant who has had many dealings with Catholics over a span of forty years, my response to these developments is one of deep personal disappointment and grief that a magnificent opportunity for the future of *all* Christians, working together in new ways, has been put dramatically on hold. That being said, I also believe that if the church does not self-destruct in the process, much good can still come from this time of travail. There will be more attacks from without and within, but it is still possible, under the mercy of God, that what the book of Malachi describes as "a purifying fire" can ignite, and that at rock bottom there is an assurance, claiming high authority, that when it comes to the church, "the gates of hell shall not prevail against it."

At the conclusion of the second session of Vatican II, in December 1963, Pope Paul announced what had been a well-guarded secret even in Rome: He would shortly make a pilgrimage to the Holy Land. This was a sensation in St. Peter's. There have been many spinoffs from this precedent-setting agenda of international papal travel. The adjective "peripatetic" has been irreversibly attached to the noun "papacy." Papal travel has not been just a series of hops, skips, and jumps. There have been permanent results, one of the most notable of which is surely the establishment of a center for ecumenical study, research, and prayer at Tantur, a village between Jerusalem and Bethlehem.

The manifest possibilities and fragilities of such an undertaking were clear from the start, and initial steps to implement the pope's decision were taken with both caution and hope. Representatives of the three participating communions—Catholic, Protestant, and Orthodox—met initially at a conference center at Bellagio, on Lake Como, while the council was in session, to formulate initial steps for Tantur. Meetings on Friday night and all day Saturday were held in drenching fog that entirely obscured the physical surroundings. Only by mid-morning on Sunday, the first Sunday in Advent, did the fog retreat, to display a panorama of breathtaking beauty and clarity—the Alps, the lakes, and the nearby fields combining to create a scene of spectacular harmony.

This unexpected unveiling has always seemed to me to be a visual parable of the beginnings of an ecumenical dream. There was initial uncertainty on our parts, groping in a foggy intellectual atmosphere without much initial sense of our mandate or direction. And then, as an unexpected gift, the beginnings of clarity came in a vision in which elements as diverse as earth, air, and water commingled in ways that persuaded us that elements as diverse as Catholicism, Protestantism, and Orthodoxy could also relate to one another. By the end of the meeting we had emerged from our initial confusion and were discovering, in good time, a sense of direction. There were subsequent meetings of the board, one in particular in Venice where exciting architectural plans were first discussed, and we had a brief audience with the patriarch of Venice, who later became Pope John Paul I.

There were moments along the way when that fog rolled in again and the way to proceed seemed treacherous. But we had all shared that initial vision, on that first Sunday morning, and it always got us back on track. The chief difficulties to be overcome were both financial and theological, and on this occasion the financial issues were initially harder to deal with than the theological ones, which are still being worked out. But thanks to some initial financial help from the Ford Foundation and the German church, augmented even more by the indefatigable fund-raising energy of Fr. Theodore Hesburgh, president of the University of Notre Dame, the result was a marvelous complex of buildings, already debt-free by the time the center was completed.

The center is located just off the main road between Jerusalem and Bethlehem, at Tantur, and is equipped to house a significant number of scholars from all over the world for study and reflection together. In addition to all the amenities of living, there is a rapidly growing library, a refectory, chapels, classrooms, and carrels. Any scholar would feel privileged to work in such an atmosphere.

The surroundings of the center reflect all the hopes and fears inherent in a Middle East location. Early on, even before the buildings were erected, the land set apart for the center changed hands between Jews and Arabs, and delicate negotiations were needed. It is no secret that relations between the Orthodox and the other branches of Christendom are sometimes strained, and issues involving Tantur have been no exception. A chapel on the grounds is not fully available for ecumenical worship. Members of the staff include both Arabs and Eastern Orthodox Christians, always a source of potential difficulty. Airfares to Tantur from outlying regions are prohibitively high for many third-world scholars who could benefit from a year of study in Jerusalem.

Such a list of problems could tempt less hardy folk to give up the dream. But the very difficulties of the setting and the conflicting viewpoints housed within it actually stand as a stimulus rather than a depressant. After several years of experimentation, a splendid chemistry developed between those at the center and the new rector, Thomas Stransky, CSP, whose ecumenical credentials had been forged during Vatican II, when he served on the Secretariat for Christian Unity. His strong and sensitive ecumenical work during those years prepared him to take on a task of formidable dimensions. And his selfless dedication to making Tantur a living example of ecumenical commitment and activity ensured that this experiment would not languish but would mature and deepen, just as, at our very first meeting at Bellagio, the last word was not dismay but commitment to a vision sure to be realized.

One way our respective institutions expressed these breakthroughs in ecumenical goodwill was by bestowing honorary doctorates across the lines of division—Protestants to Catholics, Catholics to Protestants. This was a breakthrough of significant proportions and always a heartwarming experience. Since I had been at the council and had written about it in positive terms, I was one among many symbols who could be publicly acknowledged not for who we were, but for what we represented.

Of course, there was a little awkwardness at first. Just what *kind* of a degree could a Catholic university appropriately give to a Protestant? A doctorate in theology was out of the question. It would have suggested that a Catholic institution was giving a public stamp of approval to theological convictions held, in the official language of the times, by "schismatics and heretics."

When the matter first came up, and the University of San Francisco, another Jesuit institution, offered me an honorary doctorate, I was even queried in advance about what kind of doctorate I would prefer. I could feel my friends in the Society of Jesus, each one sporting an "SJ" after his name, wondering how to deal with a potentially prickly situation.

Realizing that the choice was theirs, I replied that I really liked the new Catholic way of describing Protestants as "*separated* brethren," rather than as "schismatics and heretics," and that since my role in the ecumenical dialogue had been largely that of a journalist, it would be descriptively appropriate to combine these titles into a new category, "separated journalists," which would allow me for the rest of my life to identify myself as "Robert McAfee Brown, SJ."

Needless to say, that didn't get close to the upper rungs of the Jesuit hierarchy. But I thought they did pretty well when they gave me a LittD degree, "doctor of literature," surely the highest definition of his trade any "journalist" could covet, whether "separated" or not.

There is a postscript: My most recent Catholic degree came in 1992, thirty years after the council had opened, and it was from Santa Clara University, another Jesuit school, and one of my favorite institutions, within which I had had many contacts over the decades, even including a stint on the faculty. By 1992 the clock had spun around enough times so that many of the early cares and worries had been put to rest, and it was possible for Santa Clara to flat out give the degree STD, "doctor of sacred theology," to a spiritual son of John Calvin. We have come a long way.

We always need to be reminded that Christianity, along with Judaism from which it springs, cannot be conceived in individualistic terms. "Solitary Christian" is an oxymoron. For better or for worse, we are stuck with one another. If we leave the church, whether in apathy, in anger, or from an imagined better past, we do not move into individualistic piety; we simply become part of another institutional reality—political, sociological, or whatever—that in the long run will usually turn out to be a weak cup of tea with no staying power. Jesus, it is appropriate to remember, did not live alone. The first thing he did on the public scene was to gather a community. It was among other things a cantankerous community, a consoling reminder when it comes to community building. Christians had at least as tough going back then as the rest of us have had ever since.

The great temptation of the church is to claim more for itself than it can legitimate. At its best, it remains a vehicle *through which* we get such glimpses of divine reality as are available to us. Things get out of line when we equate *the church itself* with the subject of the vision—a sin to which Lutherans and Calvinists succumb just as easily as Catholics and Orthodox.

I believe that the future will not be mapped out so much at the center (Rome) as from the periphery (third-world lay Christians), with advocates of a liberation theology that disavows power grabs. Those in the third world will re-create a church not too dissimilar from that described in the Acts of the Apostles. Stripping it of much of the veneer and structural detail that was thought to protect it, they will bring it clean and shining into a world proposing to welcome those who are not only *servus servorum Dei* (servants of the servant of God) but a world in which the ancient papal title (whether the words are used or not) will describe not a single leader but every single member.

Indeed, if we can just begin to get our separate acts together, we might be able to discern together the fresh vitality of the Spirit.

THE HOLOCAUST COMMISSION

I can locate with precision the time and place I realized I could no longer postpone a serious confrontation with Judaism. The time was the afternoon of New Year's Eve in 1970. During a family outing in Sausalito I faded away from the group as we passed a bookstore (a maneuver I have developed with considerable skill). I checked out the paperback fiction section, and there, in a row, were Elie Wiesel's *Night, Dawn, The Accident, The Town beyond the Wall,* and *The Gates of the Forest.* For several years I had half-consciously avoided coming to terms with both Judaism and Wiesel. I felt distinctly uncomfortable confronting this one, for I knew that the Christian track record over two thousand years was abominable—an unparalleled posture of negation and persecution, culminating in the Holocaust, when Christians were complicit in the death of six million Jews. How much longer could I morally avoid this reality? I decided that the bookstore display was an invitation to begin. I read the books in the order of their composition, and was, as I had feared, devastated by what I encountered. But I was also sustained by the fact that Elie Wiesel could emerge from that inferno of hate not only not hating, but once again able to affirm, however agonizingly. He has been my "rebbe" ever since.

Wiesel has said that save for the autobiographical *Night* he has never written about the Holocaust. This apparently exaggerated claim can be allowed, if supplemented by a second claim that he has never written about anything *but* the Holocaust. Both statements survive scrutiny so long as they are not separated from one another. Although *sui generis*, the Holocaust is also the reality, writ large, that no human being can ignore, but we cannot begin to understand the Holocaust itself without putting it in the framework of the historical forces that created it. But even then we never fully understand. This has been, among other things, an important message for theologians, who usually look upon their task as one of answering questions. For Wiesel, this is an unproductive and even misguided venture. "I don't have any answers," he claims, "but I have some very good questions."

Wiesel reports that a judge at the Eichmann trial was asked, after Eichmann had been found guilty, whether the court's decision made it easier for him to understand the Holocaust. "Understand the Holocaust?" he repeated. "I hope I never 'understand' the Holocaust. To understand it would be worse than not to understand it." By which he meant that if there were a scheme of things into which, somehow, the Holocaust could be made to "fit," such a scheme would be evil, and its creator a moral monster.

One of the traditional tasks of Christian theologians has been the creation of theodicies, attempts "to justify the ways of God to man." Wiesel's stricture annihilates any such possibility. There exist both God and Auschwitz. We can to some degree "make sense" out of either one, so long as we explicitly exclude the other. No problem. The problem arises when we try to reflect on the two of them together. That is where we can formulate good questions, but had better not peddle answers that will soon be perceived as cheap.

I am already running the danger of suggesting that Wiesel is a theologian, a vocation he strongly disavows. He defines his role as a storyteller, and we must grant him that role, continuing to be challenged by his literary skill. But I must propose that storytelling may be one way to redeem the discipline of theology. Wiesel is actually a case in point. He tells contemporary stories, he tells Hasidic stories, he lifts stories out of the *Talmud*, and he finally gets back to the biblical stories, making very clear that the Bible is not a compendium of formal theological assertions, but a book with stories about a people, stories about a God, and stories about how a people and a God establish connections. This is surely several cuts above such traditional theological exercises as attempting to itemize the four attributes of God or derive a proof of God's existence from the sorry condition of the world.

Only recently has the discussion begun to move over into Christian territory. I think there are some legitimate things Jews and Christians can do here, so long as the ground rule is that to seek the "conversion" of the other party is out of bounds. "I had rather enter the gates of Auschwitz," Abraham Heschel once remarked, "than be a candidate for conversion." After a series of close encounters and experiences with Heschel when we were both protesting the Vietnam War, I asked myself, "What do I have to tell this man about God that he does not already know?" The answer was simple: nothing.

We can even begin to have dialogue about Jesus of Nazareth—the occasion of the chasm between us. The great Jewish question is, "The world is so evil—why does the Messiah not come?" This sometimes prompts superficial Christian enthusiasts to respond, "He has come, so rejoice with us." We need to be reminded that the great Christian question is simply the reverse of the Jewish one. Christians, if they are honest, must ask, "The Messiah has come—why is the world so evil?"

Ours are both messianic faiths, Martin Buber has reminded us. One group waits for a second coming of a Messiah they already know, while the other waits for a Messiah whose initial coming has not yet taken place. It is in that situation, Buber counsels us, that we can work and wait together. All that separates us is a timetable.

Franz Rosenzweig, Martin Buber's collaborator in a German translation of the Hebrew Scriptures, deals with the issue of conversion in a way that has been very helpful to me. Rosenzweig posits a "double covenant." God made a covenant with the Jews, and they became forever God's people. *One is born a Jew*, and by the very fact of birth is in a covenant relationship with God. Jesus of Nazareth is a Jew who acts as the missionary arm of Judaism, taking the message of the Jewish God to non-Jews, so that they too can become children of the covenant, and worship the God whom Jews proclaim. One is born a Jew, Rosenzweig distinguishes, *but one becomes a Christian*. There is no occasion to try to convert Jews to the God of Jesus Christ. That is a status they already occupy as part of the covenant people.

Wiesel does not deal directly with most of these themes, and I have highlighted them partly to position myself as one for whom these questions remain important and difficult. But Wiesel's novels are about loss of faith, rebellion from God, moments of redemption, anguished outcries—in other words, all the stuff of the human story, which is also the Jewish story, or more accurately, all the stuff of the Jewish story, which is also the Christian story. We can approach him either way, and be instructed and even transformed.

I learned this myself in writing a book about Wiesel. I planned to call it *Elie Wiesel: Messenger to Jews and Christians*, to indicate how much we Christians owe him. But the subtitle simply came unglued; it could only be *Messenger to All Humanity*. To illustrate this I am tempted to offer a few synopses and plotlines, but I have already done that elsewhere, and his books are available. It is much better to read him than to read about him. But let potential readers adhere to the requirement I put on students in my classroom: Read at least the first five books in chronological order—*Night, Dawn, The Accident, The Town beyond the Wall*, and *The Gates of the Forest*. One will not emerge unchanged.

Only once have I picked up the telephone and heard the words, "This is the White House calling." The operator asked if I was willing to cooperate in a "personal security check" as a condition of serving on a commission President Carter was creating. When the operator explained that this was for a commission to be headed by Elie Wiesel, I assured the operator of my full cooperation.

President Carter had been persuaded to create a memorial to Holocaust victims, and was appointing a commission to make recommendations. I was elated not only that such a step was being contemplated, but even more elated when I survived the security check. The commission was composed of a number of Jews, many of them "survivors," representatives of other groups who had been in the death camps, and a few non-Jews like myself.

While I indicate some of the issues and conflicts the group faced, I want to do so in the context of an event that truly bonded us across previously existing boundaries and created an ethos of mutuality and trust. This was a trip in the summer of 1979 to various Holocaust memorials in Europe, undertaken to stimulate our own approaches to creating an appropriate memorial in the United States. Here are some vignettes of that trip, which was a powerful, unsettling, but ultimately creative experience.

Sunday, July 29: I had set myself the task of reading Raul Hilberg's *The Destruction of the European Jews* during our trip, and began to read this sordid story shortly after takeoff. I was interrupted when Deanna Gottschalk, sitting next to me on the plane, pointed out the window. No sordidness out there, only sunset clouds and rainbows in a silent symphony of color. This would be the nature of the trip, I reflected: beauty and ugliness constantly jousting for attention. Noah got a rainbow at the conclusion of his trip, and we were getting one at the beginning. Or maybe Noah had one at the beginning too, but had no Deanna Gottschalk to point it out to him.

Monday, July 30: Our first stop was Warsaw, Poland. From the moment of our arrival, every single minute was scheduled. We went from the airport directly to a monument commemorating the Jewish uprising in the Warsaw Ghetto, with figures more than life size. Wiesel had insisted that we go first to this Jewish monument, "where we could pray as well as speak." Some of our number had been here forty years ago. Others had been here and were never able to leave. Grown men were openly weeping, as grown men ought to be able to do more easily when confronting tragedy. The rush of memories for some, the recognition that this was the very site of the most important act of Jewish defiance in World War II, the utter loneliness of the fact that there are so few survivors, the tendency of the world to forget—these are the poignant and tragic realities that came to focus here.

Tuesday, July 31: The next day we arrived at Treblinka, the death camp outside of Warsaw, efficient enough to cremate twenty thousand Jews a day. Total time from one's arrival by cattle car to one's departure through the chimney: two hours.

There are no buildings left at Treblinka; the Nazis tried to destroy all traces of the camp when word began to get out about what was happening there. But long trails through the woods were punctuated by concrete blocks. To me these initially suggested a virtually unending line of coffins. But no, these were not coffins. Who needs coffins when there is a crematorium? The concrete slabs were simulations of railroad ties, the true symbol of death in Warsaw-Treblinka, for the moment you were on a railroad car your doom was sealed. To be told to report to the *Umschlagplatz* in Warsaw was to board a train where the ticket was free but only one way. Beside other monuments is a large stone. Carved on it, in six languages, are the only words I saw in the entire memorial. They are the words "Never again." They are the point. The whole point.

We were at Treblinka for two hours—just the time it took to dispose forever of a human body. During those two hours I was torn by a desire to be alone (how can one speak to another about such things?) and a necessity to be with others (how can one deal with all this with only the solitary sources of one's individual psyche?). Walking at one point alongside Marion Wiesel I could summon no words, only a silent embrace. She summoned some words, some good words, a small affirmation in the face of such massive negation: "Bob, can you smell the lavender?" And that contrast—between the beauty of nature and the ugliness of human nature—is overpowering at Treblinka. If God ever decides to give up on the human venture, a lovely world will still remain. But God will not give up on the human venture, so a lovely world must be created. Treblinka is a monument to human depravity, but it is also a monument to human courage, to an indomitable will that still cries out, in the face of destruction, "Never again."

Wednesday, August 1: There were plenty of buildings left at *Auschwitz-Birkenau*—brick buildings as well as gradually rotting barracks. The entrance had the ironic motto, "Arbeit Macht Frei" (Work Makes Freedom). As we went into various buildings, the "tour" became chaotic. Some went up a stairwell, others went down, and we became divided. I tried to move from one group to the other and see where we should be. In a moment I was separated from both groups, lost in Auschwitz. I experienced genuine panic. How would I find my way out? Where would I ever find our group again? What minuscule fear, compared to the fears of those living during the Holocaust, when any inmate realized, (a) "I cannot get out except through the chimney of the crematorium," and (b) "There is no group to which I belong," or rather, "The group to which I belong is absolutely powerless."

The nearby location of Birkenau could have been called the Plain of Desolation. The railroad track goes into it and right up to the end of the camp. It still has some of the quality of the war years——towers for the guards to stand in and from which to shoot, high fences, barbed wire, many acres of destroyed barracks. But no guards. No dogs. No selection. And most of all, no smoke.

We gathered at the large monument beyond the end of the railroad track for a service. Various portions of the monument are dedicated to different groups who died at Birkenau. We stood before the Jewish plaque. Elie spoke.

Although I could not hear all of his words distinctly, he said, in effect, "Do not listen for human voices here. They have been stilled. Listen to the wind and the stones, for they alone cry out. Do not believe the sun shines here. This is the Kingdom of Night." He had reason to know. He had been here before.

This was a moment of profound desolation for me. As at Treblinka, I needed to be alone and I could not bear to be alone. I saw Marion Craig, a staff member of the commission, nearby. She was trembling. So I stood with her and she with me, and the desolation was at least a shared desolation. Solitude is easier to endure if it is not endured alone.

We moved on and stood on the destroyed crematorium. (Again the Germans had tried to destroy the evidence.) If Golgotha revealed the sense of the godforsakenness of one Jew, Birkenau multiplied that anguish at least three and one half million times. And God was silent. Human silence seemed the only appropriate response, and it was deafening. And then, quietly at first, human lips moved and formed human words, the great affirmation of the more than human, "Shema Yisroel, Adonai Elohenu, Adonai Echod" ("Hear, O Israel, the Lord our God, the Lord is one.")

At the place where the name of God could have been agonizingly denied, the name of God was agonizingly affirmed—affirmed by those with the most right to deny. Never again, because of this, can I deny God deeply out of some disappointment or even (I trust) personal tragedy. But never again, because of this, can I affirm God lightly out of some grand experience or even (I trust) personal fulfillment. Problems of belief were heightened, strained, and also in a mysterious way helped, by seeing and feeling and really sharing in the act of belief of Jews in that desolate spot. My impulse was almost to deny. Theirs was to affirm. I affirmed, but *with them, not alone.*

Thursday, August 2: In the morning we took a tour of the Warsaw Ghetto. The fact that there could be virtually no tour was the poignant reality. Not only was the ghetto razed by the Nazis, but after the war it was replaced with new streets, new buildings, new shops—none of them Jewish.

We visited the Umschlagplatz we had heard described the day before—the place of departure, the place where the angel of death kept all appointments, a holy shrine to martyrs. Warsaw Jews all knew what it meant when lists were posted each day of those who were to report to the Umschlagplatz. "He has gone to the Umschlagplatz" meant simply, "He has been taken from us forever." And the Umschlagplatz today? A filling station with a small plaque—an affront to memory.

Friday, August 3: Babi Yar, in Kiev, Ukraine, was another affront to memory. Wiesel had been there in 1965, when the location of the place was almost an official secret, a place where 85,000 Jews were shot between Rosh Hashanah and Yom Kippur. We were among the first to visit a massive, newly dedicated monument. There was not a single mention anywhere that Russian *Jews* had been the victims. They were only entitled to be remembered as Russians. It is not sufficient.

After this sobering experience our lunch hour was a time of gaiety and dancing. Such a sudden transformation! I could not understand it at first. And then I gradually realized that this was one of the secrets of Jewish survival: If you can't laugh your heart will break; you *are* laughing and your heart is still breaking; but as between laughing and crying, sometimes laughing is preferable.

Later that day, after an easy domestic flight, we were in Moscow. A group of us self-styled writers had an evening meal with Russian counterparts. One of the writers, a woman and a Jew, had written a trilogy about the Holocaust, entitled *I Must Speak*. Commenting on how hard it had been for her to relive all the horror again and again and again, she gave her rationale for doing so: "Better that one heart should continually break, if it means that a thousand other hearts need not be broken." The place whereon we sat was holy ground.

Saturday, August 4: Shabbat. We went to the synagogue about which Elie wrote in *The Jews of Silence*, and which provided the inspiration for *Zalem, or The Madness of God*. The warmth of greeting was powerful, and the stir and buzz and excitement over our presence were manifest throughout the service. There was much going to and fro, and it was explained that this was a religious but also a social event—the one time and place Jews can get together with a minimum of fear of detection or being informed on.

Monday, August 6: Our departure from Moscow was sober. Many of our company had feared that even today acts against the Jews might be perpetrated and were genuinely apprehensive about our safety. Once the plane was in the air, however, with Copenhagen the ultimate destination, there was applause and cheering. In Copenhagen, after all, Jews had been saved (95 percent of them) by non-Jews. There was an impromptu concert during a stop in Stockholm, created by Bayard Rustin, a non-Jew and a non-white, who led us in "Go Down, Moses," and "Joshua Fit the Battle of Jericho," to which a young Jew commented, "Hey, I like these new Jewish songs." Victory songs, from whatever struggle, inspire hope.

Tuesday, August 7: In Copenhagen, everybody has a story, especially those who lived through the Nazi occupation. Many of those who had saved Jews by getting them across to neutral Sweden in their fishing boats (called "resisters") were at a reception held at the palace of the prime minister, where they received our scroll of gratitude to the Danish people. Elie Wiesel made the presentation, pointing out that we had come from a week *in* the Kingdom of Night—Treblinka, Auschwitz-Birkenau, Babi Yar—and were now, for the first time on our journey, in the Kingdom of Light, where non-Jews had rescued Jews at great risk to themselves.

Denmark is designated a "Lutheran nation" even today, and since I was the closest thing we had to a Lutheran, I was asked to speak on behalf of the Christians in our group. What I said went something like this:

> Mr. Prime Minister, our commission is composed of both Jews and non-Jews. As a Christian, I have a special word of gratitude to speak to you. Christians and Jews have a common problem in relation to the Holocaust, and it is the problem posed for *belief*: How can one believe in God in a world in which a Holocaust can take place? But Christians have an additional problem, and it is the problem of *guilt*: Why were we so silent in the face of such blatant evil? There were a few isolated individual voices who spoke up, but they were too little and too late. In the face of that complicity we Christians therefore feel a special debt of gratitude to the Danish people, who not only spoke but acted. In a world in which we need to be on guard against repetitions of such evil, the solidarity of the Danish people in opposition to that evil is an example that helps in a slight way to redeem an evil Christian past, and in a large way to prepare us all for a different future.

At a reception following this event, many stories were told. There was the doctor who gave injections to children to quiet them before they hid below deck in the fishing boats, so that their cries would not give away their location. A member of our group and a survivor, Yaffa Eliach, told the doctor that she has used a film about him in her classes for many years. And then her story and his story came together, for Yaffa continued, "I have always wished there had been someone like you in the place we were hiding, for my one-year-old brother had to be strangled to death when his crying threatened to give the group away."

To the often repeated query about why the Danes helped Jews when almost no one else did, the most any Danish citizen would concede was, "Wouldn't you have helped to save your neighbors if they had been in trouble?" Everybody has a story, and most of the stories can be accounted for by the pervasiveness of this question.

But I am left with some unanswered questions. Why, among all the peoples of Europe, were the Danes the only ones to act corporately on behalf of the Jews? I am sure there are some historical, cultural, and sociological reasons for this. But I am now confronted not only with the mystery of the massive reality of evil in human life but also with the perplexing reality of good—a worthy confrontation.

Wednesday, August 8: Lod Airport. Tel Aviv. Israel. Jerusalem. Home. For many Jews, even those who have never been there, that is the way the sequence goes.

There was too great a contrast between the King David Hotel in Jerusalem (which on a scale of 1 to 10 would rate a 14) and the places we had seen, where people had been forced to live subhuman lives. After the emotional ups and downs of the past two days, I needed whatever this city could give me, and its appearance, at least, of serenity, was one of its gifts.

Yad Vashem, the Place of Remembrance of the Holocaust, was another gift, especially to me. For here, in the most graphic reminder of that horror, is a remarkable reality that points in a different direction: the Avenue of the Righteous Gentiles. Every time another case is authenticated of a non-Jew saving a Jew, another tree is planted with a memorial plaque. One day, a member of the staff told us, the Avenue of the Righteous Gentiles will enfold the whole of Yad Vashem, embracing it in an ongoing act of remembrance, that there were those who put help of the neighbor above personal security and even life itself.

Thursday, August 9: Before meeting with the staff of Yad Vashem, our group had an hour of evaluation of the trip as a whole. I record what I said on that occasion, as a public act of personal gratitude:

> During these last ten days I have had to relive the terrible history of the thirties and forties from a different perspective than most of you— the perspective of a Christian whose community of faith was silent when it should have spoken, and was complicit in events it should have opposed.
>
> In the light of that constant reminder of our history, it would have been appropriate if you had been suspicious of those of us who are not Jews, if you had hated us, or if (worst of all) you had ignored us. But you did none of those things. Instead, almost unbelievably, you embraced us. You told us your stories, you opened your wounds to us, you accepted us. I cannot begin to tell you what that has meant, and I hope that for the rest of my life I can return your embraces with the warmth and fervor you have extended to me. For that gift I am very grateful.
>
> I must also share two things this trip has taught me about the nature of the memorial we must propose. One thing is reinforced and another is new. The reinforcement is, of course, that after the trip, the opaqueness of the darkness is thicker than ever. I knew that with my mind. I now know it in my heart. We must portray the baseness of the executioners.
>
> But—and this is what is new for me—we must also portray the dignity of the victims. I saw those of you at Auschwitz who were survivors—Elie, Hadassah, Sigmund, Yaffa, Chris—all of you. You are survivors, but you are also victims who have been scarred. Then and now, you carry your scars with dignity. You embody the faint rays of light in the midst of the darkness, and you display a dignity that could not be destroyed by the most massive indignity human history has ever known. And in the light of that, I say that our memorial must be not only a record of despair but also a pointer to hope. I could not have said that ten days ago. I say it now: Our memorial will need to record light, however faint, in the midst of darkness, however strong.

To give a full account here of the trip through Yad Vashem is impossible, at least for me. So rich are the images, so heart-wrenching the exhibits, so full of a mixture of despair and hope, that any words I can summon will only trivialize the realities to which they are pointing. Instead, I will describe only the conclusion of the visit to the museum, wishing that everyone could spend days of self-surrender to its awesome message.

A trip through the museum leaves one devastated; the photographs, the artifacts, the sheer inundation of horror, write an invisible NO above the whole human enterprise. And then, having traversed a simulation of the Warsaw Ghetto sewers, one climbs the final stairs and enters the light, confronting a magnificent vista of the land of Israel. *The ending is hope*, not despair, creative beginnings rather than destructive endings—a breathtaking conclusion, but not one that forgets the past. For in a moment one sees that in the foreground of the wide sweep of the vista of the new land is a huge sculpture of human beings impaled on barbed wire. Israel today can be seen only through the barbed wire and the victims. And that, mysteriously, becomes a sign of hope.

Words of the Baal Shem Tov, founder of Hasidism, are carved by the exit, a final message to the visitors: "Forgetfulness leads to exile, while remembrance is the act of redemption." Amen, so be it.

My notes from the rest of the trip are spotty, reflecting how in the last couple of days our group began to fall apart. This had nothing to do with animosity but simply with the fact that the human frame can accept only so much reality at once. We had an extraordinary fortnight with magnificent highs but many dark lows as well. They took their toll.

A visit to the Western Wall, with the help of Yitz Greenberg, was a source of new energy, especially when we remembered the countless millions who have stood there, across many centuries, who have prayed, wept, and left their written prayers in the cracks of the wall. The wall somehow symbolizes the unquenchable power and commitment of Jews throughout time. Elie Wiesel has a scene in *A Beggar in Jerusalem* in which, reported in a kind of mystical vision, Jews through all times past gather at the wall and rally to affirm a future.

A remnant of us made the trip north to the first kibbutz established in Israel, appropriately enough by the survivors of the Warsaw Ghetto uprising. Beit Lochami Hagatteat provided a symbolic conclusion to our trip, since we began with a memorial in Warsaw itself. It was an experience of the holy to find that the kibbutz now has over four hundred members, building a new future that neither Hitler nor anyone else could finally destroy.

As a kind of coda, we stopped on the way back to Jerusalem at the Christian kibbutz of Nes Amin, created by Dutch Christians after the war, who decided to live in Israel as a commitment to a future so nearly denied to Jews in Europe. No attempts at conversion are made. That is not the point. The point is simply to create a living presence of solidarity with Jews. The kibbutz raised tulips to support itself, and lest the whole venture sound too ethereal, any profits beyond those needed for the survival of the kibbutz were given to the Israeli government. The simple directness of these people was very moving, perhaps most of all to the Jewish members of our group, who had not known about the creative existence of Nes Amin.

The final words in my journal were:

> I write at the end of Shabbat, on our last day in Israel, sitting on my balcony in the King David Hotel, overlooking the Old City, as shadows lengthen, the colors in the stone begin their magical transformation from white to pink, the lines get softer, the sounds more muted, the traffic patterns less frenetic. The heat recedes and peace descends like a benediction over this troubled city, which despite the contention and strife within its walls, still has the power to create a holy atmosphere, which, as Abraham Heschel has remarked, is a slight hinderer of hindrances to believing in God. Shabbat shalom.

Meanwhile, back in Washington, the presidential commission, soon to be renamed the Holocaust Memorial Council, began to create tangible proposals for beams and girders out of our inchoate dreams. Several times a year we met in Washington. The meetings were hardly legislative and usually consisted of an opportunity for each member to voice his or her concerns, hopes, expectations, and fears. Wiesel chaired these meetings and was graciousness itself, allowing and indeed encouraging a great variety of viewpoints, of which there were many. Even though this encouraged tedious repetition from meeting to meeting, it was a wise, indeed an essential, procedure, for when issues near the bone surfaced, there was already enough trust for us to hear each other out. (I make this assessment as one far from the inner precincts of power. It is clear that with many contradictory concerns under scrutiny, staff members did a magnificent job of finding ways to make them fit together.)

There were a couple of divisive issues that fortunately did not derail the council, although they certainly could have. The most chronic of these (which resurfaced at every meeting I attended over a period of several years) was the question of precisely *who* was being memorialized. For most of the actual survivors (Jews who had been in the death camps themselves), the matter was clear: Honor was to be paid to the six million Jews who did not survive. But there were also members (wisely included in the council from the beginning) who were not themselves Jewish but had seen their families and villages destroyed by the Nazis, as well as being rounded up themselves and sent to death camps. Many of them were Poles, but there were tens of thousands of other victims as well, notably gypsies and homosexuals. The Poles on the commission had invincible reasons for wanting to make sure that their kinfolk were not forgotten, while the Jews wanted to make sure that their unprecedented destruction—simply because they were Jews—was not diluted into merely another instance of human evil.

Fortunately, Wiesel was always able to say once again "for the record," that the memorial would honor *all* victims—a pledge that was surely redeemed in the completed building. Wiesel had a characteristically felicitous aphorism to make his case: While all Jews were victims, not all victims were Jews. The aphorism is more than felicitous, for it reminds us firmly of two things: (1) All Jews were victims, for simply by virtue of being born, all Jews became candidates for the gas chamber. Their "crime" was not espionage or murder or treason; their "crime" was being Jewish. Having the wrong grandparents made one a criminal. (2) Not all victims were Jews, which meant that many besides Jews died at the hands of the Nazi juggernaut for a variety of offenses—economic, political, religious—and they too must be remembered.

The issue took on a public coloration on one of the "Days of Remembrance" in Washington, which members of the council attended. Meeting in the Capitol, we had a service that featured a number of speakers, music, and the lighting of candles. There were speeches by members of the council, but also an eleventh-hour influx of members of Congress who obviously had decided that there was political capital to be reaped by participation in such a service. After the speeches, there was the lighting of the candles—six candles representing the six million dead, and then, since this was the anniversary of the slaughter of a million Armenians earlier in the century, the lighting of a seventh candle to honor their memory. I thought this was a splendid symbolic way of acknowledging not only that all Jews were victims but also that not all victims were Jews. Alas, the symbol that was unifying to me was divisive to others—either for giving too much attention to Jewish deaths, or too little attention to non-Jewish deaths, or too little attention to Jewish deaths and too much attention to non-Jewish deaths. Every critic had a vantage point from which it was in principle possible to lodge an objection. So go the fortunes of the Holocaust Memorial Council.

The single most critical test of the council's durability and even survivability concerned a specific event. This was a decision by President Reagan (against the counsel of almost all who had access to him) to visit the military cemetery in Bitburg, Germany, to honor the German dead of World War II. This was a gesture meant to heal, but it was not as simple as that, for in the military cemetery were buried members of the notorious SS squads, who symbolized and embodied the very worst of Nazism's evil. Reagan was adamant that he would not change his plans, even though he would be giving honor to the worst of the Nazis.

What should the council do, in light of the president's lack of sensitivity to our concern that we continue to condemn rather than condone the extremities of evil? For him to make the trip was to deny the integrity of all we were hoping to accomplish in our memorial. An emergency meeting was called. A small group felt that the only honorable action was for the entire Holocaust Memorial Council to resign in protest, and make the issue such a public one that the proposed visit would have to be canceled.

Early in the discussion I supported this position, but it was soon clear that the majority felt that such a gesture would not only be futile but might also be destructive for two reasons: First, a mass resignation might jeopardize the entire memorial project, since it had been established by one president and could be dealt a mortal blow by his successor. As a number of survivors argued, saving the council to witness to posterity was more important than creating a political flap, however unfortunate the president's decision might have been. Second, if all the members resigned, the president could not only accept the resignations but could appoint successors with a totally different view of the importance of a Holocaust memorial, and disregard all that had thus far been accomplished. The long-range importance of securing the memorial clearly prevailed over the notion of using it as a bargaining chip with an already alienated White House. One can hardly fault the decision of the council to hang in.

This was not quite the end of the matter. When Elie was awarded the Congressional Medal of Honor, he spoke directly to the issue that had so disturbed us, urging the president, before millions of TV watchers, to cancel the Bitburg visit. In prophetic fashion he "spoke truth to power." And in characteristic fashion, power declined to listen.

I had my own struggles during this period, which were not entirely atypical. I was becoming more and more disenchanted with everything President Reagan stood for, and I realized that a time might well come when I would have to protest more aggressively, perhaps in civil disobedience in Washington. I recognized that it would not help the council's future dealings with the White House to have members of its committee acting judgmentally in ways that could weaken the council's political leverage. I was, of course, a tiny fish in the pond, and had no reason to assume that my actions would be noticed by those in power. But they might be, so strong was the Reagan administration's dislike for dissent.

After reflection, I gave Elie an undated letter of resignation from the council, so that if at any point I became a hindrance rather than a help, the letter could be used. It was a somewhat uncomfortable position to be in. On the one hand, I did not want any of my activities to jeopardize in the slightest way the projects in which I so deeply believed. But I also had to be loyal to other commitments: I had to work for economic justice, the abolition of racism, greater concern for the poor, and other agenda items getting short shrift in the Reagan White House. The letter was never used.

A term of membership on the Holocaust Memorial Council was three years, after which individuals would either be renominated or replaced. Those of us in the original group, appointed by President Carter, were not renominated by President Reagan, with the exception of Elie himself. Elie resigned shortly afterward. The project became, in other words, something of a political football.

But anyone who has visited the now completed Holocaust Memorial Museum will surely agree that it is a magnificent achievement, and will keep alive and well within our own nation the solemn promise, "Never again."

10

World Travels:
Deepening My Connection
to Liberation Theology

Peter: My dad loved life. But still, he put himself in a number of pretty dicey places over his eighty-one years. Protest after protest on Vietnam, all the trips to jail, many dangerous accompaniment visits to Latin America, trips to South Africa, Cuba, and the Philippines in times of political turmoil. All these times worried me—and every time he returned, the family seemed complete again and the world was whole.

He put his body on the line—and he did it with eloquence. He talked a good game, he wrote an even better one, and he was there—hot, sweaty, and committed when it counted.

There was a change going on, and it had something to do with place names. Rather than familiar places like New York, Washington, and St. Paul, we began to encounter names brought to the foreground by World Council of Churches events: Uppsala, Nairobi, Bangalore, and, later, the Philippines. Another cluster of countries emerged out of my discovery of "liberation theology" and its impact—an impact that necessitated many trips to get some of the flavor firsthand. An initial trip with Sydney to Peru, Chile, Argentina, and Costa Rica later led to two trips each to El Salvador and Cuba, and to Nicaragua, where I went for nourishment on five separate occasions. Leading up to these occasions were trips with a basically European orientation. They included sabbatical time in Scotland and France, previously mentioned, and later a trip to South Africa.

I do not intend that this chapter should degenerate into a travel diary. To me the closest parallel to what I experienced is that of a pilgrimage—a journey to a (usually) far-off place, encountering strange customs or geography or modes of speech, presented both as challenges (scary) and opportunities (open-ended) from which I continue to learn. My indebtedness to those I met on the way will, I hope, be communicated in the text that follows.

I am very nervous when someone calls me a "liberation theologian." I reflect on the people I admire who fully live out what such a title represents, and the difference I notice between them and me is the lack of significant risk in my case. People may not like some of the things I say, or even sometimes the things I do, but they are not likely to destroy me, and that's a pretty significant difference. This does not mean that I should now go out and try to get myself destroyed. Indeed, it may actually mean that I am freed up to say and do certain things that the others should not say or do in their situations of jeopardy; the world needs them alive far more than it needs me dead.

I have reflected on this disturbing enigma since my discovery of Gustavo Gutierrez in the summer of 1971, and only recently have I found it stated in a way that begins to be helpful. Jon Sobrino, SJ, in exile for a while at Santa Clara University, was interviewed by Alfred Hennelly, SJ, on the problem of being a liberation theologian in North America. The interview completed, Jon was not satisfied. There was something more that needed to be said, the most important thing of all:

> If the dominant classes in your country applaud your work and shower you with awards, degrees, prestigious chairs, etc., beware—you can be sure you are on the wrong track. A hermeneutic of suspicion should be put into practice, since you may very well have become a tool, a weapon of the dominators.

That is the problem; that is the danger; that is the seduction. We are not liable to be destroyed or even greatly inconvenienced, and the costs to us will remain minimal. We will be fooling ourselves if we are content to write or speak (very movingly to be sure) about how other people have been destroyed, greatly inconvenienced, and called upon to pay tremendous costs—when our reporting costs us nothing at all.

One example of this contradiction pops into consciousness immediately. Some years ago I was invited by Princeton Seminary to teach a two-week course on liberation theology during the summer session. I saw this as an exciting pedagogical opportunity, since this particular seminary was not widely noted for its commitment to issues of social justice, not to mention a "preferential option for the poor." The course had an enrollment of a dozen or fifteen students. Things went swimmingly until the middle of the second week when I made a passing comment about how exciting it was to be sharing this particular material on the campus of this particular seminary.

One of the international students raised his hand and stated, slowly and deliberately, "Professor, there is something you don't seem to understand about this seminary. Its faculty, its administration, and particularly its board of trustees, would fight to the death against everything you are saying and teaching." I started to make a pitch for "academic freedom," but he interrupted, a little less patiently than before. "Listen to me," he said. "They've co-opted you by asking you to teach this course. And they've co-opted every one of us who enrolled in this course. They don't want liberation theology to make any inroads in our thinking and being here. So naturally they don't offer a regular full-semester course. Instead they offer a course in the last week of July and the first week of August, when none of the regular students are on the scene.

"They are having it both ways. To one group they can say, 'Of course we teach liberation theology, and we invite our students to subject themselves to its challenge.' And to the other group they can say, 'Don't worry. It's only offered in the summer when almost no regular students can take it.'"

Even allowing for some seasoned academic cynicism, the point is not easily dismissed.

THE WORLD COUNCIL OF CHURCHES: UPPSALA, 1968; NAIROBI, 1975

The earliest Christians were a cantankerous bunch, as any perusal of Paul's correspondence will demonstrate. Noisy, divisive, bigoted, they frequently found it too difficult to practice the gospel they preached, especially the part that admonishes us to love one another.

In 1054 there was a great rupture in the church, creating a division that still persists between the East and the West. In the sixteenth century, tremendous numbers of Christians—disavowing an ecclesiastical organization defined by allegiance to the bishop of Rome and calling themselves Protestants (from *protestare*, "to testify on behalf of something")—created scores of new denominations and sects all over the ecclesiastical landscape. Serious efforts to rebuild out of such destructiveness did not begin until the latter part of the nineteenth century. Such efforts persisted in the twentieth century, showering contemporary Christians with hope for the future.

That is almost sufficient background to position any discussion of the divided Christian family today. The "ecumenical movement," as it is called, seeks to reestablish the initial unity of the church throughout the whole *oikoumene*—Greek for "the inhabited world." Our century contains many attempts to regain a lost fellowship, and I will concentrate on two of them: the

World Council of Churches and the Roman Catholic Church that emerged out of the Second Vatican Council.

I don't know what would have happened to my involvement in the church had it not been for the World Council of Churches (WCC). I remember reading about its creation in the summer of 1948 in Amsterdam, just as I was returning to Columbia University and Union Seminary to pursue a PhD. I recall one Columbia professor early that fall engaging in a put-down of the Amsterdam assembly of the WCC on the grounds that it had produced no *mana*, or "wonderful power." My own estimate was that it had taken an incredible amount of *mana* even to get the divided churches back into conversation with one another. To anyone acquainted with the history of the four preceding baleful centuries, that was *mana* in spades.

As I continued graduate work, various representatives of the WCC were in and out of Union, and when I went to Oxford to write my dissertation, I knew that, being that close to the Continent, I wanted very much to visit Geneva, home of the fledgling WCC. To Geneva Sydney, Peter, and I went in June, staying for a full week with Paul and Audrey Abrecht. Paul and I, along with Roger Shinn, had shared an office at Union while pursuing our doctorates, and Paul took a tempting if temporary one-year internship with the WCC in the field of social ethics. He went to Geneva and never came back. The match was perfect, and before he finally retired, Paul had logged more years of continual service than anyone else on the staff, from Willem A. Visser't Hooft on down.

What the WCC provided many of us with was a vision of what the church could be and yet seldom is—an international body cutting across race, class, and privilege, and avoiding the dreary parochialism of so many long-established churches.

As I got into teaching, I depended increasingly on WCC publications. The reports of the world assemblies themselves—Amsterdam, 1948; Evanston, 1954; New Delhi, 1961; along with Uppsala in 1968 and Nairobi in 1975, both of which I attended—were often required reading. I found increasing wisdom in the council's emphases, and even occasional linguistic gems.

The statement at New Delhi that Christians are those "glad to dwell in the tent of perpetual adaptation" seems to me as beautiful and compelling a description of the pilgrim people of God as anything within the whole corpus of Christian literature. Ecumenical prose is not precisely the gift for which the WCC is known. If quizzed about this, one might get a phrase like "keeping the larder well stocked." An accurate accounting no doubt, but it fails to sing. How much more helpful is the phrase from New Delhi. To be responsible, we must keep the larder amply stocked and enough ahead of schedule to meet the immediate needs of the hungry. But the needs of the spirit must be met as well.

The WCC tries to minister to both. Every once in a while the spirit seems to break through and promises something new, and at least for a time comes through on the promise. Such a moment was realized in 1961 in the capturing of the phrase cited above.

As long as the topic is top-drawer productions, there is also the report of a 1966 conference planned by Paul Abrecht and held in Geneva on "The Church in the Social and Technical Revolutions of Our Time," a document so far ahead of its time that I used it for many years as a challenging text for undergraduates who perpetually wonder "why the church isn't doing anything."

The WCC represented for me a stout beacon of hope: Christians *could* get together and learn from one another; the WCC arms were capacious enough to enfold groups as diverse as the Russian Orthodox Church and the Chilean Pentecostal Church, who were received together into membership in 1961. Those within the WCC could help all Christians traverse liturgical and theological barricades; both the WCC and the Roman Catholic Church could begin to reach out to one another, discovering small breakthroughs particularly after the Second Vatican Council.

The WCC has taken on sticky assignments no smaller group could have handled, most notably its engagement with the white as well as the black churches of South Africa, and its refusal to accept apartheid as Christian. It is true that the WCC is not as vibrant as it was in those years, but it is the nature of the WCC that when it is making haste slowly today, it is helping to open new doors tomorrow.

There is solace in the story told by Lesslie Newbigin of the Church of South India toward the conclusion of the assembly at Uppsala. A train traveler was in a hurry to reach his destination. The train proceeded at a slower and slower pace until it finally stopped altogether. The passenger made his way to the front of the train and exploded to the engineer, "Can't you go any faster than this?" To which the engineer replied, "Of course I can. But I have to ride with the engine." The leaders of the WCC today are those who decided to "ride with the engine" and get it back in running order.

Alongside all my book learning about the WCC were the experiences of attending the 1968 World Assembly at Uppsala as a delegate, and the 1975 World Assembly in Nairobi as a "consultant" whose primary responsibility was to deliver the opening keynote address. Martin Luther King Jr. had been scheduled to give the keynote address in Uppsala in 1968, and his murder only six months before lifted the issue of racism to the top of the assembly's agenda. This led to the formation of an ongoing "Programme to Combat Racism," one of the most controversial and important actions ever taken by the WCC, which provided funds to groups committed to escaping racist policies in their own lands. In addition, the Vietnam War was at its height, and protest against it was escalating everywhere.

After a few days of plenary meetings in Uppsala, we were assigned to working groups. Mine was to assist in the creation of a statement on racism and economics, with inestimable help from Maynard Catchings, a black American who knew more individually about racism and economics than the rest of us would ever know cumulatively.

In addition, I undertook a personal crusade: to secure a statement from the assembly on the right of "selective conscientious objection" to war. This was no idle concern. Most churches were on record supporting conscientious objection to war, and a member of such a church could frequently receive exemption from military service. But it had to be conscientious objection to *all* wars. It was not enough to say, "I *might* have fought against Hitler, but I cannot under any circumstances kill Vietnamese peasants."

This presented an unendurable tension for young men of draft age, who were not confronting war in general, but the Vietnam War in particular. Their requests for exemption were almost routinely turned down, and they either had to (a) accept the draft board's decision and enter military service, (b) flee to Canada with no assurance that they could ever return legally, or (c) risk up to five years in jail. What they needed was a supportive statement from church bodies upholding the moral legitimacy of refusing, for reasons of conscience, to serve in the Vietnam War. It seemed to increasing numbers of us that such a clear statement from the WCC affirming the moral legitimacy of selective conscientious objection was vital.

Richard Fernandez, the head of Clergy and Laity Concerned about Vietnam, was in Uppsala for the assembly, and helped create a statement to propose from the floor. There was also help from William Thompson, a layman with legal training, who was the Stated Clerk of the General Assembly of the Presbyterian Church, a good definition of ecclesiastical clout. We used mealtimes, tea breaks, recreation, and a long weekend to lobby in support for inclusion of such a statement. On two occasions I was able to address the plenary in support of such a statement, which was ultimately adopted without significant objection. The relevant passage went:

> Protection of conscience demands that the churches should give spiritual care and support not only to those serving in armed forces but also those who, especially in the light of the nature of modern warfare, object to participation in particular wars they feel bound in conscience to oppose, or who find themselves unable to bear arms or to enter the military service of their nations for reasons of conscience. Such support should include pressure to have the law changed where this is required, and be extended to all in moral perplexity about scientific work on weapons of mass destruction.

There are at least two reasons why we succeeded in passing this modest contribution to ecumenical thought. First, the fact that I was speaking from the podium *as a delegate from the United States*, attacking the policies of my own nation, was seen as honoring the gospel rather than crusading in defense of my country—the latter being a position frequently exhibited by U.S. delegates at earlier WCC meetings. Second, not only was the Vietnam War an unpopular war at home, it was even more unpopular abroad. A majority of the delegates opposed it and the uncritical American imperialism that lay behind it. To be able to strike a blow against its legitimization was an action many delegates were willing to support.

One other event was the most Spirit-filled moment of the entire nineteen days. One task of the assembly is to elect new members to the Central Committee, which governs the WCC between assemblies. Those elected wield significant power, and the seats are widely sought after both by individuals and the churches they represent. The list of candidates had clearly been created *before* the assembly convened and took no account of the need for more black leadership. (The delegate next to me, a black North American, skimmed his list of nominees in approximately fifteen seconds, found almost no black nominees, and commented, not without bitterness, "They haven't heard a word we've been saying.")

So it was a proud moment for the assembly when David Colwell, a white nominee of the United Church of Christ and pastor from Seattle, Washington, arose and requested that his name be withdrawn from consideration and replaced by a black candidate. He was followed immediately by two other highly placed delegates who made identical requests in the interest of better balance within the Central Committee. All three were overwhelmingly elected. Black writer James Baldwin, who had spoken earlier at the assembly, was correct: "For my own survival," he had told us, "I must pay no attention to what you say, but must watch very carefully all that you do."

I was invited to give the keynote address at the next assembly in Nairobi in 1975. I was asked to speak on the assembly theme, "Jesus Christ Frees and Unites," which in a recent article I had argued needed to be expanded to read, "Jesus Christ Frees, *Divides*, and Unites," if the assembly were to take seriously the variety of responses that Christians had given to their leaders. To whatever degree the keynote address was memorable, it is probably not for its substantive content but because I gave it in Spanish. There were some important reasons why I did so, unexpected as the action was.

During the summer preceding the assembly, I had attended the first gathering of "Theology in the Americas" in Detroit, a bringing together of theologians from North America (liberal to left-wing) and Latin America (left-wing to far left-wing). The Latin American delegation included almost all the liberation theologians we had been reading in translation for the past five years, thanks to Philip Scharper's creation of a new publishing house, Orbis Books. It was a heady experience to spend a week with Gustavo Gutierrez, Hugo Assman, Leonardo Boff, Juan Luis Segundo, Beatriz Melano, Sergio Torres, Jose Miguez Bonino, Enrique Dussell, Gonzalo Arroyo, and Jose Miranda—to name only a few. The sessions were not merely polite; they were intense and critical. As the week progressed, various "caucuses" developed: a Native American caucus, a white women's caucus, a black caucus, and so on. Soon the only people left without a caucus were those who were seen by the rest as the *real* causes of misery in the world—the white, North American males.

It was unpleasant to be the object of such a widely shared attack, but there was enough truth in the indictment that we white males could not simply sulk, and it was a moment of tremendous liberation when we could announce the formation of a white male caucus, and we entered the fray aggressively as well as defensively. Yet after each evening session, when beer flowed fast and free, it was persons, rather than caucus members, who argued and joked and sang and laughed and even cried sometimes. That relaxed time, which went on until the wee hours, was when the most important exchanges took place.

However, the thing by which I was most struck was the fact that most of the North Americans knew almost no Spanish, while most of the Latin Americans knew a lot of English, which of necessity had become the lingua franca for exchange. Our lack of linguistic skill made it necessary for them always to discuss in a language other than their own. This problem was apparent in all WCC meetings as well, where the "official" languages were English, French, and German, with nary a bow to the third world. Realistically, delegates who wished to be understood by others had to speak English. And I was about to reinforce this imbalance in a few months before four thousand people with the keynote address in Nairobi, which I would, of course, deliver in English.

Or would I? Somewhere on the plane ride back from Detroit to Hartford-Springfield, I made a firm decision: that for once the gringos would meet the Latinos more than halfway. I would give the address in Spanish. It was a foolhardy decision, given my low level of comprehension of Spanish, and my even lower level of ability to utter complete sentences in this strange and foreign tongue. But I justified persisting in it for at least four reasons: (1) In a world of political, economic, and military imperialism, we would at least strike a blow against linguistic imperialism; (2) it would be a message to other delegates that not all those present intended to remain in the English-French-German linguistic pattern until the end of time; (3) the degree of my uptightness would indicate that we knew a little about how uneasy one feels trying to communicate in a language not one's own; and (4) it would be a modest reminder to all the English-speaking delegates that it was a nuisance to have to reset the headphones to a different channel and not have the linguistically correct text in one's hands.

Although the plan was not a secret, I did not go out of my way to signal it ahead of time. I got to the dais in Nairobi about fifteen minutes before Visser't Hooft arrived—the grand old man who had practically created the WCC *ex nihilo* by his acumen and forceful personality. Discovering what was about to transpire, he was furious, so much so that during one frightened minute I almost called the translators' booth to cancel the whole thing and speak in English. But I was not impressed with Visser't Hooft's argument that if we went through with the plan, "the Russians would want to speak Russian, the Japanese would want to speak Japanese," and so on. That seemed to me exactly to describe a level of communication (aided by simultaneous translation) that we should embrace rather than shun. I held my ground.

How had I, linguistically inept Bob Brown, who had barely passed his PhD German exam, prepared for what was to begin momentarily? Once I had written a text in English, I gave it to a graduate student at Stanford, a political refugee from Pinochet's Chile, and theologically (a very nice ecumenical touch) a Roman Catholic, who provided me not only with a typewritten Spanish text but also with a transcription on tape as well. We were very fortunate at that time also to have Sarah Mann, a high-school friend of Alison's, living with us. As well as being a warm and loving presence in the family, she had just returned from a year in Argentina and was fully fluent in Spanish. Sarah kindly spent many hours with me, helping me with Spanish pronunciation and getting me as comfortable as possible with delivering this speech in a language I barely knew. No one will ever know how many times I went through that text, with Sarah, and with and without the tape, with my recurrent anxiety levels resolved only by another run-through, but it must have come close to triple digits.

A few people agreed with *Christianity Today* that it was a cheap stunt in bad taste, and a few more took exception to its substance. One evangelical, after I tried to show him that yes, I *had* affirmed the resurrection, responded, "Yes, but Bultmann could have said that," a rebuttal no response can dislodge. William F. Buckley, the right-wing Roman Catholic columnist, proposed in a column that since I appeared to dislike my country so much, it might be a wise step for my country to deport me. I considered such criticism to be a badge of honor.

The thanks and *abrazos* I got from the Latin American Spanish-speaking delegates more than compensated for any lingering fears that I might have overplayed my hand. And when all the dust had settled after the assembly, it was announced that Spanish and Russian had been added to the list of "official" WCC languages.

I will limit further comments about the assembly to one episode in 1974 that epitomizes why, if there were not a WCC, it would be necessary to invent one. I have a friend from one of the Eastern bloc countries with whom I try to get caught up at any WCC functions where we are both present. We exchange information about our families and compare how our respective churches are dealing with problems of pastoral care and social justice. At Nairobi we got together early on for a noon meal, starting out in an isolated part of the dining room. As the table around us filled up, my friend's voice got lower and lower. Before he spoke he would look around to see who sat down nearby, who was passing the table, and who was simply lingering in the neighborhood. I realized that my friend was keeping a close eye out for an informer, someone who might hear something questionable and report it back home. He had been conditioned not to trust.

Yes, there are occasional informers who infiltrate the web of the churches affiliated with the WCC, so on that level there must be a low level of trust. But the overwhelming majority of the members are *not* informers, and one can soon pick out who might be, and who surely are not, so that on that level there can be a high level of trust. Such trust is never total, never naive, but is the difference between having a lifeline to which to hold and living utterly alone in a raging sea.

Shortly after Philip Potter's retirement as general secretary of the WCC, plans were quietly made to have a party for him, inviting people who had worked with him over the years. Although I felt a bit like an interloper, I was fortunate enough to make the guest list. The "party" went on for two days and nights at a retreat center near Geneva. There were sessions of reminiscence, wonderful meals, square dancing, more music, even some Bible study of revolutionary themes. I had never before been at a WCC gathering in which tenseness was not omnipresent.

I finally asked a WCC veteran how to account for the unprecedented atmosphere. I got a clear answer: "Look," I was told, "these are all staff people or ex-staff people, and this is the first time *any* of them have *ever* attended a meeting together without realizing that somebody was going to have to write an official report."

SOUTH AFRICA, 1972

The invitation was a gracious one: Would I deliver an address each morning at the General Assembly of the Presbyterian Church of Southern Africa in the summer of 1972? The church would be happy to provide round-trip transportation for Sydney as well. Those who made the offer knew where I stood on such matters as apartheid and racism and rampant capitalism, and it was clear that I could not only say what I pleased but should feel encouraged to do so, since I could probably say certain things that an insider could not say without inordinate personal risk.

Still, I was uneasy. By what right could I go to a deeply conflicted country, as a total outsider, and presume to tell South Africans how to solve their problems? The line between "inspired propheticism" and "human arrogance" is indeed a fine one. I expressed these concerns in my reply. Their reply to my reply was to acknowledge the validity of the concerns and make a counterproposal: Why didn't both of us come a month early and participate in a four-week trip they would arrange, in which we could talk to people from every perspective and form our own conclusions about what would be important to say at the General Assembly? As a result, we had an extraordinary month, visiting almost all geographic areas, and meeting (both on and off the record) with representatives of almost every position on and off the political and theological spectrum.

At the General Assembly itself, there were small-group discussions after each of my talks (the substance of which are contained in *Frontiers for the Church Today*). This was 1972, and Black Theology, and more particularly black power, were just emerging on the U.S. scene. This provided an ideal way to talk about *both* situations together, since, as I pointed out, both South Africans and North Americans were going to have to come to terms with these new phenomena. It was a useful device; when I described a situation in my homeland, it was not hard for my listeners to discern parallel situations in their homeland. I don't think the Special Branch of the Police, who were present taking notes, ever had a clue that they were reporting a critique of their culture as well as mine.

During one of the small-group sessions, I was asked to comment on the single deepest impression I had of South Africa after a month in residence. It did not take me long to decide that it was the pervasive sense of fear of what lay ahead, and the sure explosion of the time bomb called apartheid, with the inevitable and widespread violence that would precede and accompany it. A white pastor acknowledged this and, turning to the black pastor on his left, said directly to him, "I'm afraid too. I'm afraid that when *you* get control, you will treat us the way we have treated you."

Two things were notable to me about this comment: its utter honesty and its utter realism. The white pastor did not say to the black pastor ". . . *if* you get power"; he said ". . . *when* you get power." Nobody in the room doubted that a shift would come. The most whites could hope for was that it would not come for a generation or two.

One afternoon we had a chance to talk to a young South African black leader named Steve Biko, before he became so famous a figure that the South African government murdered him. He was initially very cool and almost uncivil. "Some more white liberals," we could almost hear him thinking, "who want material for their speech back home about what blacks are thinking." He was, of course, not far off the mark, and it was a comment of Sydney's that saved the occasion. "I think I know what you mean," she told him. "When men get up to tell people what women really want I feel pretty outraged. We can speak for ourselves." Sydney had divined where he was coming from, and Steve Biko smiled. It was a very warm, understanding, and accepting smile, and he and Sydney were suddenly on the same wavelength with each other.

When we had gone into the building in which Steve Biko's office was located, we had noticed a police car containing two white officers who took photographs of everyone who entered or left the building. Sydney commented to him on what an oppressive situation this must be to live with, day after day. "Yes," he responded, "it *is* oppressive. But we know, and the police know that we know, that if a day comes when I am no longer here, another person will be here to take my place, and if necessary, another person will take my replacement's place, and so on, and that we will finally win."

Through the good offices of some friends, we had most of a morning with Alan Paton, whom I had particularly wanted to meet, since I used *Cry, the Beloved Country* in my teaching. He was a fighter. He chose his own weapon— a pen rather than a sword—and as a pamphleteer, reporter, biographer, essayist, and (most successfully) novelist, he touched the consciences of the whites and the adrenaline of the blacks and became one of the most important men of his time—respected and feared, depending on who made the assessment. *Cry, the Beloved Country* and *Too Late the Phalarope* are still classics—tales whose depth has not diminished, tales set in one time and place that remain true of all times and places. Even as the situation in South Africa has changed drastically, the books have not lost their power.

We talked of many things, both his writing and his politicking, and of the many things he said, one in particular has always stayed with me. "You Americans are lucky, you know," he said wistfully. "You have a Bill of Rights in your constitution to which you can always appeal when justice is threatened, while we," he continued sadly, "have no Bill of Rights within our constitution, and it is hard to foresee how we will ever get one." Time has happily rendered his remark too pessimistic. But even then it was a word of good counsel to us, who are often complacent about the built-in rights that we take too easily for granted.

I used *Cry, the Beloved Country* many times at Stanford in a course called Theology and Contemporary Literature that mixed both Christian and non-Christian (as well as anti-Christian) writers together. One year when introducing the novel I decided to include a little local color, so I shared Paton's account of how Mr. and Mrs. Aubrey Burns, a couple living in Fairfax, California, not far north of Stanford, had befriended him when he was alone and forlorn at Christmas time in California, trying to finish the book. He allowed them to read some portions of it. They were so moved that they insisted on reading the finished draft, which Paton completed a few days later. They then arranged to get it typed in multiple copies and sent to various publishers, so that before he returned to South Africa a few weeks hence, Paton had a promise from Scribner's to publish the novel. These deeds of kindness from the Burnses were ones that Paton cherished for the rest of his life.

When the class was over, one of the students introduced me to his mother, who happened to be visiting the campus that day and had gone to class with him. "I'm Mrs. Aubrey Burns," she said, and whether it was coincidence or Providence, this was a lovely moment.

I want to record one other exchange about Paton because it has been of great help to me in understanding him. I wrote him after *Ah, But Your Land Is Beautiful* was published, and commented on how wonderful it seemed to me that given all the ugliness in his country, he could still find so many good people with whom to populate his novels, remarking particularly on the sheer beauty of Prem Bodasingh, who seemed almost to have been without sin. He picked up on this theme in his reply:

> A not unfriendly critic in Cape Town said that the book has too many "unquestioned saints." At the luncheon given by the publisher to launch the book, I mentioned this criticism, which is something I almost never do. I simply said that I must confess that I am much more attracted by goodness than by evil, and that I find good people more exciting. I suppose one would be more accurate by saying that it is goodness in the midst of evil that is exciting. [Trevor] Huddleston once said that the spectacle of goodness in Sophiatown [a black African township in Johannesburg] moved him to his depths. It is that that really makes the world so exciting.

One of the white ministers at the assembly told us how on the day he graduated from seminary, he was arrested by the Special Branch on charges of treason. Since he had not had an active political profile during his seminary years, confiding his outrage only to his roommate, he could not understand how the police had built a case against him until it emerged in court that his roommate and presumed best friend had been informing on him to the police throughout all his seminary years.

At a meeting of black seminarians after the assembly we discovered that the Special Branch did not practice racial discrimination; any skin color was appropriate for their spying. One of the black seminarians recounted to us how during the week before he entered seminary, he had been approached by a member of the Special Branch, who offered to finance his tuition, board, and room if he would pass along any information he overheard that was critical of the government. He said that he had turned down the offer. But one could sense a shift in the atmosphere: Supposing he had been approached and *had* accepted the offer, and even now was acting as a mole for the government.

These are the kinds of pressures that the South African government created with impunity for decades. They were not unusual measures. They were standard operating procedures.

We had an evening in Cape Town with white and black friends of Theo and Helen Kotze of the Christian Institute, one of the few structures in South African society that consistently called for and took risks for change. Our discussion was interrupted shortly after dark by a phone call from the police, reporting that they had received a warning that Theo would be shot that night. The police said they would provide a watch through the night at the Kotzes' nearby residence. The unspoken question in the heart of every person in that living room was: "But who will watch the watchers?" Three black guests departed early to begin surveillance of those who were supposed to be providing surveillance.

Fear we had quickly noted in our time in South Africa. But there was also unspeakable courage: the extraordinary courage on the part of black leaders who kept risking, kept risking, kept risking, even as they knew they could never expect a fair trial in a white court; the courage in the lives and actions of women, both white and black, trying desperately to raise their children in such a way that prevailing social mores would not permanently scar their outlooks or their psyches; and as well, the courage of whites to which we will return.

At the end of the General Assembly there was a Communion service. It was celebrated in a large white church in Durban, with many blacks present. Black pastors, white pastors, and I distributed bread and wine to the deacons, who partook before serving the congregation. They lined up before the Lord's Table—black, white, black, black, white, white, black, black, white—a random selection. The bread was passed from hand to hand, and whether black or white, each broke off a piece to give to his or her neighbor—no problem.

And then the common cup—a single chalice—was passed down the line, lifted first to black lips, then to white lips, then to black lips—no problem.

I, a visitor to that land, would not have believed it possible. The "spiritual" act of sharing the body and blood of Christ became an occasion of liberation for all those people—liberation for a moment from bondage to the "fierce laws" (Alan Paton's phrase) that on all other occasions forbade the sharing of food and drink by black and white together. One day the fierce laws would change, and the exception, enacted in that service in Durban, would be the rule. More blood—Christ's blood in Christ's children both black and white— would be shed before that was so, and it was a great tragedy. But it did come, in part because the distance between Christ's table and all other tables could no longer be tolerated. That is a great hope.

We must return to the issue of the courage of the whites, for whites every-where need role models for survival in an increasingly nonwhite world. There is a role model par excellence in South Africa. Beyers Naude was pastor of a large Afrikaans Reformed Church and a member of the Broederbund—a secret, exclusive group of about a dozen white African males who really ran the country. Naude went through a conversion and preached a famous sermon in which he denounced *apartheid* as un-Christian. There was no mercy. He was fired from his pulpit, expelled from the Broederbund and, in due time, "banned," that is, sentenced to house arrest for five years, during which he was never to be with more than one other person at a time. He never wavered.

Just before the banning, Naude was in the United States to receive the Reinhold Niebuhr Award for 1974 in token of his uncompromising stand. I was privileged to read the citation and make the presentation. Never have I shaken a stronger or warmer hand. The citation read:

> To Beyers Naude:
> Churchman, Pastor, Prophet, and therefore Risk-Taker on Behalf of Others;
> Affirmer of the Lordship of Christ and therefore Denier of the Lordship
>   of Caesar;
> Believer in God's Love and therefore Practitioner of Human Justice;
> Provider of Space for Total Sharing, and therefore Troubler of the Status
>   Quo;
> Exemplar of a Courage that Challenges Others to Risk More Because He
>   continually Risks All.

The speech Naude gave in response to this award was the immediate cause of his banning when he returned to his homeland.

As I write these concluding words decades later, I am witness to a brand-new script: Change *has* come to South Africa, change for the better, and it has come without the extreme bloodshed everybody, including myself, predicted and feared.

Watching the days of voting on television, the first democratic election in 430 years, was a time of almost unbelievable joy for everyone. There has never been, and probably never will be again, a story as unlikely as the South African story. We will continue to ask how it was possible for power to pass from one group to another in such relative peace. How did it happen?

On one level, it was a miracle, however one defines the word. On another level, it was the goodwill between the leaders, Nelson Mandela, who spent twenty-seven years in prison, and F. W. de Klerk, head of the government that kept Mandela in prison. De Klerk (for whatever reason and however induced) had a change of heart and became, and survived becoming, "a traitor to his class." On yet another level, it was the impatient pushing, prodding, and shoving by many generations of "good people": Chief Lutuli, Beyers Naude, Alan Paton, Desmond Tutu, Allan Boesak, and tens of thousands of nameless ones who never allowed the cry for freedom to be stifled. The economic sanctions against South Africa for years finally paid off, as apartheid became far too expensive even for uncompromising white zealots. Also it was the recognition that the need for new beginnings must not be built on hatred or vengeance or destructiveness, but on such long-buried qualities as compassion, forgiveness, and reconciliation. In the words of the psalmist, "Justice and mercy [finally] kissed each other." Compassion and justice ruled and must coexist. We never before believed deeply enough that it could be so, and where one would have least expected it, it was so. From now on, we dare not fail to believe that it can be so elsewhere as well.

A miracle, indeed.

BANGALORE, INDIA, 1978

At the Nairobi Assembly I was elected to the Faith and Order Commission of the WCC, which among other things was to contribute to a report for the 1978 Faith and Order meeting in Bangalore, India, on "Sharing in One Hope." My task was to prepare a report on signs of hope in the United States. It occasioned considerable controversy. The report was an analysis of eight documentary "signs of hope," drawn from a variety of groups and backgrounds: evangelicals, mainline Protestants, blacks, Roman Catholics, and residents of Appalachia. Reports from other areas of the globe were similarly presented, first for discussion in small groups and then as items for reflection by the commission as a whole.

The bulk of what I wrote was reportorial and descriptive, but at its conclusion I added a few reflections of my own. I expressed a fear that our own hope would be domesticated into "church talk," equating hope with the "up" side of the status quo. Those of us who are comfortably situated, I went on, have a special obligation to listen to Latinos, Asian Americans, blacks, and other oppressed groups in order to be reminded that our inordinate wealth is purchased by the exploitation of much of the rest of the human family. Our reliance on political, economic, and military power becomes our real source of hope, and must be repudiated. Improving on the apostle Paul, I asserted that we are "so afraid of being perplexed unto despair that we refuse to be perplexed at all." The beginnings of a modest hope can be nurtured, however, if we will learn to see ourselves as part of an interdependent world community rather than a nationalistic, introverted community. I continued:

> I do not know whether we have it within us as a nation to embody [such a] global perspective, beginning to see the world through the eyes of the dispossessed, beginning to realize that whereas others face the problem of having too little power, we face the problem of having too much. Indeed, I do not know whether we have it within our *church* to do these things. But I do know that if we do not, hope is indeed far from us.

That seemed to me a sober enough statement to be taken seriously. I would add, however, that I did not say explicitly what would have been clear enough at the meeting in Bangalore, namely, that when I was talking about our being part of a global community, I was referring chiefly to the WCC, and how dependent we North Americans were for direction signals from the third world.

The report that emerged from our discussion group was considerably more freewheeling, but to me totally defensible, since it represented an honest appraisal of the U.S. church and the United States itself, mainly seen through the eyes of third-world people. It was formulated to be sent on to the Faith and Order Commission of the National Council of Churches in the U.S.A. It laid a number of prophetic challenges on its U.S. counterpart. We were enjoined to reevangelize ourselves as well as the nation, to take "clear and vigorous stands on behalf of swift justice for oppressed minorities," to become more aware of how our national power and affluence stand in the way of hope for many, and the need "to develop keener political sensitivity."

All of this came before the notorious "paragraph 15," as it was called, to which explicit exception was taken and that read as follows:

> We hope your church [in the U.S.A.] will act together toward the withdrawal of U.S. military and economic support from oppressive and dictatorial regimes in Africa, Asia and Latin America. Our impression is that your churches still assume that the U.S. is seen as a sign of hope for oppressed peoples and a symbol of freedom and democracy.

> The reality today is often otherwise; U.S. policies are interpreted as bolstering regimes which exploit the poor and deny human rights; the Vietnam War is perceived in our countries as having been pursued for the sake of political and economic influence. Such realities must continually be confronted and addressed in the name of the Gospel.

The report did not sit well with some of the North American delegates, but their wrath was nothing compared to the ire of certain European delegates, led by Wolfhart Pannenberg, an extremely influential German theologian. Without once confronting those of us who had produced the report, they placed heavy demands on the WCC staff that the report must be rejected, and that if it were not there would be unspecified reprisals. Fortunately, Lukas Vischer and others on the staff were able to work out a viable solution. The statement would be printed and included within the overall report of the commission, for to have done otherwise would have been an intolerable infringement of the right of WCC delegates to speak the truth as they saw it. But an explanatory statement would precede it, a portion of which read, "It should be clearly understood . . . that the statement does not reflect the opinion of the Faith and Order Commission as a whole, but reflects a debate in one group." It was not hard to accept this, since it merely reflected the truth of the context. And it went on, I was delighted to see, to acknowledge that "the views expressed both in the statement and the reaction here are in fact *widely shared* [italics added] and must be faced in a study which seeks to facilitate the encounter of differing hopes." It was not possible, in other words, to pillory the report as simply the fumings of "a dissident minority." It voiced widely held opinions that would surely have been lodged against the other large powers in the world, had occasion demanded it.

CUBA

Only once have I interviewed a head of state. His name is Fidel Castro, and the interview took place in 1977. He surprised me. For one thing, in newspaper photographs he often looks scruffy—beard askew, uniform messy. But in real life he is tidy and trim. The adjectives "tidy" and "trim" also characterized his answers. There is a reason for this: In an interview with Castro, every question is first asked in English and then translated into Spanish, while every answer comes in Spanish and is then translated into English. Why the rigmarole when Castro's command of English is excellent? For a simple and legitimate reason: Under this arrangement he gets to hear each question twice and each answer twice, for a total of four renditions. There are plenty of chances to prevent misunderstandings—no cheating, just canny.

The interview came unexpectedly. It was on the last day of a seven-day trip to Cuba, and we were packing for the final time when the word came to the head of our group: "If you can be ready in five minutes, Fidel would like to meet you." Could we be ready in five minutes? We could be ready in five minutes. I do not know why the prearranged schedule was rearranged. But our discussion lasted two and a half hours, and pretty much covered the waterfront. I do not intend to cover the waterfront a second time. Instead, I shall mention only a few aspects of the Cuban scene that are important to our understanding.

In the years since "the triumph of the revolution" in 1959 there has always been Castro, and an outsider's attitude toward Castro is a litmus test of right-wing political orthodoxy. As I have discovered and rediscovered, to say a good word for Cuba, or the Cuban government, or the Cuban church, or any individual Cuban from Fidel Castro down, is to locate oneself completely off the political spectrum, exhibiting both the sins of naiveté and danger. If one is not a certifiable communist, one is at least an "unwitting tool" of the communists, unknowingly doing their work for them—hence the "naiveté." And to be less than the implacable foe of all things "communistic" was to hand Castro an inevitable victory, starting only ninety miles off the coast of Florida—hence the "danger."

If the above lines sound terribly familiar, it is a ubiquitous formula adaptable to any historical or cultural situation in which one wants to stamp out the possibility of change. Consider its manifestations: The church is preaching social justice? The church has been infiltrated by communists. Politicians are proposing new ways to count the ballots? Such politicians are secretly members of the Communist Party. Workers want to organize? It is well known that the workers want to bring down the government, a favorite communist trick.

So in Cuba, once Castro had come to power (replacing Juan Batista, a politician clearly in the hands of the army) it was necessary to get rid of him. He exists; therefore, he must be liquidated.

Perhaps the most annoying thing about Castro has been that, unlike other "communists" on the scene, he refused to disappear from the scene, as right-wing analysis had promised he would do. He has survived at least seven attempts on his life by the CIA; has outlived (and probably outperformed) nine U.S. presidents; has remarkably not been unsettled by domestic upheavals and, despite the lowering of human expectations about the revolution's promises, seems destined to remain in power as long as he desires.

It is important to realize that when Cubans talk about the "revolution," they mean "the triumph of the revolution." This is not a reference only to the military event of 1959 when Batista was defeated, but to an ongoing process ever since. It is still a challenge to create a new society, which was only initiated in

1959. The revolution per se is not an event solely attended by violence, but by education, political involvement, visions, and dreams. It belongs to the *present*, initiated but not completed in the past.

Like other guests in Cuba, we were given the official "guided tour," showing us what the revolution has achieved and what is still to be done. Like all "guided tours," its purpose was to register a positive impact on outsiders. No matter what the country, one must guard against being swept along too easily by the enthusiasm of the guides. In the case of Cuba, however, there is enough that is positive so that apart from the need for propagandistic manipulation, we ended with more trust in our guides than suspicions.

And yet, let's face it. Even showpiece Havana is drab. There is little in the way of shops, at least for Cubans. Food is neither plentiful nor exciting. Most ordinary commodities are hard to get. One must wait interminably for a replacement for a broken light fixture or a plumbing connection. But the revolution is infinitely more than such mundane pointers, and must not be trivialized.

If the human dream that Castro and the party have preached for three decades has really lost its luster, the blame can be laid only partly at Cuba's door. For the United States (and originally many other nations) has engaged in an economic blockade against Cuba for decades without having been able to destroy the regime in power. When critics claim that Cuba was almost totally dependent on the Soviet Union for its economic survival during the Cold War, the claim is in great part mitigated by the fact that during those decades there was no place else for Cuba to turn for economic help. Given the embargo, its sheer survival is something of a miracle. (U.S. business interests continue to press for a relaxation of the embargo, so that they can capitalize on new markets. Ill-conceived as the embargo was initially, the notion that the United States has anything to fear economically from tiny Cuba is ludicrous.)

That the economic strangulation has failed to achieve its initial intent says something not only about the shallowness of U.S. foreign policy; it also says something about the power of an idea in the hearts of the Cubans, in the face of tremendous odds. Early on, there was even a U.S.-sponsored military invasion—the so-called Bay of Pigs invasion—a disaster for the recently elected Kennedy administration, but a glorious victory for the poorly equipped Cuban military forces.

During another trip to Cuba several years later, we were driven to the site of the Bay of Pigs encounter by one of the most ardent members of the Cuban Reformed Church, and her manifest glee in recounting a number of clashes spoke volumes about the bracing effect on national pride that has continued ever since, keeping certain elements of the revolution alive and well.

In addition to Cuba, there have been a number of recent attempts to create nations based on "leftist principles," but also imbued with a deep nationalistic spirit—Nicaragua and Chile being two examples near at hand. That not one of them has "succeeded" is once again due not so much to their own failures as to the strong determination of nearby powers determined to thwart "the spread of communism" at whatever cost. After all, such nations have reasoned, if "communism" could succeed in a single small nation, would that not empower its neighbors, suffering under the worst of capitalist exploitation, to take their stand as well with the anti-imperialists? Henry Kissinger put this mind-set succinctly. Commenting on the "Chilean experiment" under Allende, which the United States helped to destroy, he asked rhetorically, "Why should we let Chile go communist simply because the Chileans don't know any better?"

Throughout our conversation, Castro was willing to listen as well as emote, and emoting is what he does best. No one who can address a political audience on a national holiday for three and a half uninterrupted hours, and hold their attention, is innocent of the art of persuasion.

During our conversation, Sydney, who had an agenda of her own, managed to get in a question Castro appeared to have ignored but did in fact respond to when the official gathering was over. She had said to him, "We've been driving along your coast and other places that are always open to wind and sun. Why don't you try to develop solar and wind power, which would not only be highly efficient in your country but would treat the environment with more care?" As we were leaving, Castro singled her out and said in English, "That's a very good suggestion about the development of solar energy and wind power along the coast. I'm going to have to think about that. Maybe we could, as you people say, 'Kill two birds with one stone,' increase electrical power and avoid environmental destruction. *Muchas gracias.*" I haven't yet read much about the Sydney Thomson Brown Officia del Poder Electrica, but somewhere, I am sure, the research is proceeding.

There was an exchange one afternoon at the Evangelical Seminary at Matanzas, between the rector, Sergio Arce, and one of our number, Methodist bishop James Armstrong. Jim asked whether there could be "really prophetic preaching" in a society that would be increasingly regulated (as he felt the Cuban society would become), when it would need prophetic preaching more than ever? Arce, a Presbyterian minister, had an interesting answer, and it went something like this: "I appreciate and share your view of the importance of prophetic preaching. But I think that in just a few years our situation has become quite different from yours, and demands a different answer. When we see manifest injustice, say, in our own *barrio*, we don't necessarily have to respond by 'preaching a prophetic sermon.' Instead, we gather those folk who share our concern, and we all go to the next meeting of the *barrio* block committee, and we talk about what is bothering us. Everyone has a chance to talk, and if we have a good case we send a statement through the block committee about what is going on to those who can deal with it. This way, we get something done, and it is an action that has the backing of a whole group of concerned people, and not just a solitary angry preacher."

What does Cuba have going for it that has attracted support from a significant number of North American Christians since 1959?

First, Cuba is a tiny nation seeking its own autonomy in the face of a long history of exploitation. Anyone concerned with justice and injustice, whether Christian or not, would be initially attracted and supportive.

Second, the revolution took human need seriously, and saw it as the responsibility of the body politic to provide decent living conditions for all its citizens. These included such things as an extensive education program, providing schooling for everyone and (for those so qualified) university training and graduate work in such fields as medicine and law and the cultural arts, along with health care made available to all, at no cost to the individual.

Third, Cuba included programs for job creation, the construction of extensive housing, social models inviting the sharing of political power at the lowest as well as the highest levels, and the underwriting of opportunities for the creation of literature, music, and the arts.

Fourth, while there was no encouragement given to the role of the church in Cuban society, there was no attempt to create martyrs. The dominant church, Roman Catholic, followed a long track record of hostility to communism, socialism, and other generally leftist points of view, and Christians (until recently) were not permitted to join the Communist Party and thus participate directly in nation building. I was pleased to discover that the small Protestant groups (chiefly Reformed, Lutheran, and Baptist) had members who took a creative attitude toward the new regime from the start, and were determined to work within the structures. It is true that when Castro first came to power, many Protestant pastors fled, fearful that the new regime would destroy them. But the true relationship of faith to the new society was exemplified by a clergy couple studying in the United States, Sergio Arce and Dora Martinez, who responded to the call of the revolution not by fleeing to the presumed safety of the United States, but by returning immediately to Cuba to help the church participate in the new regime, dedicated to establishing an atmosphere of justice rather than tyranny.

Exposure to Cuba, which contains inklings of what a humane realm might represent, makes me yearn wistfully for the creation somewhere and somehow of a socialist state that could be allowed to walk its own path, free of the need to be overly reactive to brutal pressures from those on the "outside" who genuinely fear the power of any socialist program and refuse to give it a chance to develop in its own way.

EL SALVADOR AND SANCTUARY CHURCHES

Shortly before Christmas 1984, a delegation appeared at the pastor's study in a Baptist church in Seattle, a church that had given sanctuary to an entire Salvadoran family. The visitors introduced themselves as part of a sanctuary church in Arizona that had originally befriended the family and made arrangements for them to relocate to a safer environment away from the Mexican border. They had Christmas presents to deliver, so that the children who had suffered so much upheaval might have a merry Christmas. There was just one thing: Since the family had moved out of the church building and into the community, could the pastor give the delegation the new address? The pastor did so, confessing later that it had been an act of naiveté. After expressing warm thanks and good wishes for the holiday season, the visitors left to call on the family—only they did not go to deliver Christmas presents. Instead, they reported the entire family to the police, and all of them, children included, spent Christmas in jail. The visitors were members of the FBI, and they supervised the family's deportation back to El Salvador, where their lives were once again in jeopardy. There is no record that Christmas presents were ever delivered.

This event took place in the United States. I was tempted to excise such tell-tale locaters as "Seattle," "Arizona," or "FBI," but I resisted. When things like this happen in other countries we must at least deplore them. When they happen in the United States we must stop them.

It is difficult to recreate the atmosphere into which many of us found ourselves thrust and propelled into what came to be called "the sanctuary movement." The movement was a simple demand that justice be done to all people, that laws be enforced evenhandedly, that persons be treated as having infinite worth, and that Christians and Jews make common cause on the side of decency in the midst of brutality.

But such an analysis distorts, for the sanctuary movement was not a matter of establishing abstract principles so much as supporting specific persons. Here is one such person, whose story I heard many times on different lips.

Maria, a young Salvadoran woman, has been in the midst of a battle zone ever since she was a small girl. Death squads roam the streets and infiltrate the countryside, killing any who stand in their way or who are the least bit critical of harshly repressive governments. In El Salvador, the governments come and go; the repression goes on.

Maria's "crime" is running a soup kitchen for children in her village. Its very existence is an implicit rebuke of the government, and that means, of course, that she is a "communist," and fair game for anybody who has a rifle.

Her husband has had his throat slit, and Alicia, a close friend, was gang-raped before being shot. Maria discovers that she is on a "hit list," and finally, at the urging of friends, she flees—walking north every night, hiding every day, until she arrives at the U.S. border. She has been told to apply for admission under the 1980 Refugee Act, which guarantees admission to refugees who have a "well-founded fear of persecution" because of their religious or political convictions. Our government, quite routinely, denies admission. The officials explain that she is obviously coming to the United States to better herself financially. This same decision is handed down, equally routinely, in 97 out of 100 such applications. For Maria, to go back home would mean death, so, desperate, she crosses the border "illegally."

Fortunately for her, there are a few individuals on the scene in addition to hard-nosed governmental authorities. There are churches on both sides of the border that call themselves "sanctuary churches," that take in people like Maria and hide them so that they will not be picked up in a periodic "sweep" by the Immigration and Naturalization Service. They offer "sanctuary," that is, places of protection from arrest and deportation, and stand unequivocally with the Salvadoran victims. To them, this is no more than a response to the biblical mandate "to welcome the stranger," as the book of Leviticus enjoins, and to feed the hungry, care for the sick, clothe the naked, and visit those in prison, as Jesus summarizes in a set of basic ethical commandments.

From these initial localized situations, the net of protection is gradually widened. Not only in Phoenix or Tucson or other cities near the border, but in the far reaches—San Francisco, Chicago, New York, and Seattle—churches begin to declare themselves "sanctuary churches," offering legal assistance to immigrants who wish to remain in the United States without risk of deportation.

This movement caught up with us in due time at First Presbyterian Church in Palo Alto. We had a study group, called *Comunidad*, that struggled for almost two years with the issue of our becoming a sanctuary church, so that wherever we came out after the internal debate would be a place where a significant measure of agreement would be found. One working analogy was the treatment of Jews in Europe under Hitler. In those days, when somebody came to the door and said, "The Gestapo are after me and they will kill me if they capture me," what was the appropriate response? It was easy to say from such a distance, "Come in. We'll hide you." And by that point we had sprung the trap on ourselves. For we realized that the concern for the refugee Jew back then was the same concern being expressed by the refugee Salvadoran right now.

We achieved virtual consensus by the church's governing body, the session (eleven ayes and one abstention) and declared ourselves publicly a sanctuary

church. So great was the magisterial efficiency of the Rev. John Fife, a Presbyterian pastor in Tucson, that within twenty-four hours we had four Salvadoran young men living in our church lounge.

Many people, church members and others, participated in our experience
with Alvaro, Jose, Oscar, and Salvador. The most immediately and initially
helpful, of course, were those members who could speak Spanish and had volunteered to have someone on the spot at all times. We also had a highly efficient kitchen crew of women and a few men, who presided over the cooking
and disbursement of three meals a day for the four sojourners, and who as a
consequence learned a new cultural fact: Salsa is an absolute necessity at every
meal. Some of our professorial types worked with the four on the rudiments
of English as a second language. At least one person slept with them every
night on the floor of the lounge, for we were initially wary of what the government might do to retaliate. Would they raid the lounge under cover of
darkness? Would they march the refugees off to jail? Would they confiscate
their belongings? Worst of all, would they seize them and put them on a plane
for El Salvador, brushing aside our helpless interventions?

It soon became clear that the government was going to initiate no sensa-
tional encounter on the corner of Kingsley and Cowper. The initial precau-
tions were gradually relaxed. The four Salvadorans felt freer to walk around
Palo Alto. One night one of them drank something of approximately the consistency of oil, and had to be taken to the hospital by ambulance to have his
stomach pumped. This was scary, not only for his physical well-being but for
his legal status. Would the hospital refuse to discharge him and instead turn
him over to the authorities?

Fortunately, he was back before daylight, but the episode, as can be imagined, engendered a crash course in political survival, with our best linguists on
hand, making absolutely clear that any repetition of such an escapade would
mean the termination of our (unsigned) contract.

One should not expect four young men between the ages of 19 and 23 to
sit demurely on a sofa in a church lounge, and as various people realized this,
members invited them over to their homes for meals and frequently hired
them to do manual labor, all of which helped while we were completing their
applications for temporary political asylum.

A certain fatigue began to be apparent on the part of those members who
were most deeply committed to the project. A voice was sometimes heard:
"Why couldn't they have sent us a nice Christian family without problems?"

But in the ensuing weeks, an almost chemical change was taking place that,
I am convinced, transformed the situation and the relationships, so the Anglos
didn't suffer burnout and the Salvadorans didn't expire of frustrated boredom.
There was a shift in our Anglo perceptions. What we got initially were four

"refugees," a group of abstractions that were even interchangeable in our minds for a while. There was no reciprocity, no genuine sharing. The almost chemical change that began to take place was that the impersonality and abstractness began to disappear, replaced by real live flesh-and-blood persons, each unique and different from the others, possessing a particular name and different experiences. It was no longer "four refugees who have had a hard time"; it was Salvador, whose college friends had been shot; Alvaro, who had been photographed by the Salvadoran police and was on a list; Oscar, who had joined the guerilla forces and whose wife and baby had been shot; and Jose, who had been arrested for being at a labor union meeting and had been tortured before being released. They were no longer abstractions, but *persons* who were hungry, who needed support, who needed protection, who needed a place to take a shower, and who showed us all courage of a sort we had never imagined.

When all this began to happen, the scene gradually changed. We realized, among other things, that while *refugees* could survive in Palo Alto, *persons* of Latino background would do a lot better in San Jose, with its large Spanish-speaking population and a variety of shared customs that we could not provide. So the four men left, gradually, as they found jobs. And we, instead of remembering "refugees," remembered Salvador and Alvaro and Oscar and Jose, who were both like and unlike us, but whose presence, simply as themselves, enriched all of our lives.

If that is the bare bones of the inner story, more needs to be said about the outer story—how all this meshed, or failed to mesh—with the policies of our nation.

During the decade when the repression was at its worst in El Salvador, over 70,000 Salvadoran civilians were tortured and murdered by military and paramilitary death squads. During that entire period our government was furnishing one million dollars a day to a corrupt army and a corrupt government. Despite our vaunted presence as a democratic model, not a single person was ever brought to trial during those years. One of the hardest things to acknowledge, and try to stop, was that our government was an unabashed proponent and supporter of the political and military savagery in El Salvador, and would not acknowledge that we were doing anything but supporting a fledgling democracy.

The utter callousness of the leaders of our nation during the Reagan-Bush years, the ignoring of evidence, the falsehoods that our leaders used to justify American policy, will probably not be fully known until there is more distance on the events and facts, and truth can be sifted out of the political cant of those who were in authority and, not incidentally, had access to and control of the media.

It was not even the case, those in the sanctuary movement argued, that we were "breaking the law." *It was the government that was breaking the law*, by passing a law allowing for the entrance of people whose very lives were in jeopardy, and then being unwilling to enforce its provisions. Perhaps the most pernicious act of our government during this period was to bribe Hispanics to infiltrate church groups in the sanctuary movement, tape the conversations that went on, and turn the material over to the government. The most well-known instance was a bribed spy with the ironic name of Jesus Cruz, who pretended sympathy with a Lutheran congregation and went to services and Bible study classes with a tape recorder hidden on his person, not to worship, not to pray, but to live out a total lie that our government rewarded him for enacting.

When enough such evidence had been gathered, seven of the most prominent members of the sanctuary movement were indicted and subjected to a trial that lasted seven months, in which they were found guilty of various crimes and misdemeanors. Much of our outrage was focused on the narrow amount of evidence the defense was permitted to introduce: no reference to the 1980 Refugee Act, no examples of torture, no itemizing of actual conditions in Central America. One of the jurors, questioned after the trial, provided its epitaph: "Yes," he replied, "the law was upheld, but justice was not done."

The basic moral principle that emerged through the sanctuary movement when it was not always clear whether we were breaking the law or trying to get the government to enforce the law, was this: *To save a human life is sufficient reason to break a law.*

I keep returning to the pastor's study in Seattle: the utterly crude, calculating dishonesty on the part of our governmental officials; a certain naiveté on the part of an otherwise astute pastor, motivated out of respect for the victims and an assumption that our governmental officials speak the truth; the utter disillusionment of the family seeing the forces of goodness ("presents for children") so devastatingly corrupted; and the trust of little children so manipulated and degraded. I would like to believe that, given the distance that now exists between these events and the present, some of those government officials feel malaise and even shame at what they did—which, rather than upholding justice, prostituted it.

On June 20, 1986, I had a chance to address the Commonwealth Club of San Francisco on "The Case for Sanctuary," following one week after another speaker had presented "The Case against Sanctuary." I tried to lay out something of the moral issues involved, and made my own profession at the end:

"Let me conclude on a personal note. While my own biases have not been exactly hidden in the previous comments, I feel obligated to state unequivocally where I stand, since I know that in so doing I speak for thousands of others.

"I fully support the sanctuary movement. I am part of a sanctuary church.

I have worked with, transported, and directly aided refugees from El Salvador whose personal safety depends on their not being apprehended by the immigration authorities. I will continue to do so, along with many others. We pledge to the refugees and to God that no attempt at governmental intimidation will deter us from this course. Those convicted at Tucson [the trial referred to earlier] have been convicted for what hundreds of others have also done, and will, let there be no mistake about it, continue doing. As three hundred sanctuary workers declared at a recent church service in Tucson in support of those convicted, 'If they are guilty, so are we.'

"And just as they continue to put the refugees first, so will we."

El Salvador was more than the issue of "sanctuary." It is a land of unbelievable heroism and courage, as well as dastardly evil, and one has not begun to do justice to it without taking account of that fact. One event in particular made a deep impact on me.

I was invited to Guatemala to be part of a delegation to "accompany" Medardo Gomez, the Salvadoran Lutheran bishop in exile, to San Salvador so he could be with his people for the Feast of the Epiphany, arguably the biggest day in the life of Central American churches. Our presence was based on the consoling assumption that however much the Salvadoran authorities may hate gringos, and especially clerical gringos, they realize that it is bad PR to shoot them or those in their company.

The van driver who transported us from the airport to Guatemala City, so that we might meet Gomez, was affable, stocky, and informative. After helping us hoist our gear on top of the van, he drove efficiently through the evening traffic, pointing out items of interest. When we arrived at our destination, he helped us get the luggage off the van and into the conference room. Eileen Purcell, our bilingual leader, asked us to introduce ourselves to the Central Americans hosting us. After this was accomplished, I asked, in a fit of democratic zeal, if we might know the name of the van driver. With a smile, he replied, "My name is Medardo Gomez."

As a Presbyterian, my experience with bishops has been limited. I had always supposed that other people drove bishops to meetings, rather than, as in this case, the reverse. If that is what bishops are really like, I will have to revise my ecclesiology.

The reason Bishop Gomez was in Guatemala instead of his native El Salvador was that in El Salvador he had been imprisoned, tortured, and subjected to death threats too numerous to itemize. After his church was bombed, his office raided and ransacked, and his family forced to leave the country because of death threats, Catholic and Protestant friends persuaded Bishop Gomez to leave the country.

I will not deny that being the constant physical companion of a man threatened with violent death creates a certain ambivalence within one. But there was an event at the San Salvador airport the next day that changed all that for me. When we entered the lobby after clearing customs, a huge crowd of Salvadorans awaited their bishop. I had not realized there were that many Lutherans in all Central America. Beautiful reunions ensued, as Medardo (nobody calls him "bishop") embraced children and was embraced by old men, young men, old women, young women—embraces that included us as well. As I walked alongside Medardo, having been very conscious of worst-case scenarios, I suddenly realized—quite consciously—"I'm not afraid anymore." It was true. And then I realized—just as consciously—that the sudden departure of fear was not because I had suddenly become "brave," but simply because the courage and love of those committed folk had rubbed off on me, contagious beyond anything I could have imagined. We were sharing a great burden and a great joy together, which is what the communion of saints is all about.

By the end of our visit I had learned two further things. First, I had learned why a Lutheran bishop is a threat to the government of El Salvador. The "sins" of Bishop Gomez are the sins of a host of others as well: He believes that the church's mission includes political involvement, that the gospel has a special concern for the poor that must be translated into the actions and policies of a nation, that a negotiated peace is preferable to an ongoing war, and that bishops often have to speak out and act in ways that are critical of the government. Such actions, whether by bishops or not, are actions punishable by death, and there are seventy-five thousand dead Salvadorans to attest to the accuracy of that proposition.

Second, I also learned why Bishop Gomez is so loved. Once he was back with his people, he realized that he could not truly be their bishop from the safety of another country, but must be in their midst, working, suffering, threatened, just like everybody else. And so Bishop Gomez returned to El Salvador, not just for this visit on a feast day, but for the long haul.

Several times in my life I know that I have stood on holy ground. Once was when I stood on the site of the murder of six Jesuits, their housekeeper, and her daughter, only two weeks after the murders themselves. I have been to shrines and sites of martyrdom before, but never at a place where the results of human destruction were so palpably present: shattered glass all over the floors, walls pockmarked with hundreds of bullets, the roof buckled from heavy military bombardment, bloodstains still visible on the walls and floor.

Three days earlier I had spent an evening in the United States with Jon Sobrino, the only one of the Jesuits residing there who was *not* murdered, simply because he happened to be out of the country when the killings took place.

Because of that connection, I found I had a very strong need to enter his room, to experience where he would have been had he been home that fateful night. I was told that the body of one of the Jesuits who was killed outside had been brought back into Jon's room. As the killers were moving the body, they dislodged one of the books from the bookcase, which fell to the floor and was saturated with the martyr's blood. In the morning it was discovered that the book was Jürgen Moltmann's *The Crucified God*.

The symbolism still overpowers me. Yes, in Jesus of Nazareth, God too was crucified, living out the fullness of human reality right up to the very nail prints. That we know by observation. But we also know, by faith, that the crucified God is also the resurrected God, which says at least that just as the crucified God was with the Jesuits in their death, so the Jesuits are with the resurrected God in their rising from the dead. That is the light of faith that sustains in time of darkness, when faith is tested to the uttermost.

Part of that "resurrection" is already visible, for the actions of the military, designed to scare off friends of the murdered Jesuits, failed to work. There was a ghastly appropriateness about the fact that all the priests were shot in the head, for the priests were thinkers, professors, researchers. They wrote. They spoke. And part of their message was that El Salvador need not remain a fear-ridden totalitarian state. And that constituted criticism of a government that would brook no criticism. But within days of the murders, hundreds of Jesuits from all over the world were volunteering to take the places of the six martyrs. That is the beginning of a resurrection.

The response to the killings was supposed to be, "They've killed the Jesuits for speaking out; therefore, we'd better not speak out or we will be killed also." Instead, the actual response to the killings was, "They've killed the Jesuits for speaking out, and therefore we must speak out for them."

But these are my thoughts. The most important response came at a memorial service for the slain, only a few hundred yards from the site of the killings, and it was spoken by a young Salvadoran woman, who quite possibly did not know how to read or write, but who certainly knew how to love.

"Do not mourn their deaths," she counseled us. "Imitate their lives."

THE PHILIPPINES, 1988

In the fall of 1988, when the National Council of Churches in the United States was on the verge of self-destruction due to internal staff tensions, Sydney and I were invited to the Philippines to participate in the 25th anniversary of the National Council of Churches in the Philippines (NCCP). Ten denominations were involved with this ecumenical experiment and have succeeded, not by playing it safe, but by being ever on the front line of social issues during the Marcos and the Aquino years, and simultaneously keeping themselves well grounded in the mysteries of the faith they all share.

Their dynamic leader, Feliciano Carino, helped them chart this course, and Sydney's and my experience was that rather than having come with stirring insights to share with them, we were the constant beneficiaries of their wisdom and commitment.

I was granted a symbolic answer to the reasons for all this at the first liturgical gathering we attended, held in the Anglican cathedral in downtown Manila. We were exhausted from our flight which, due to engine trouble, involved two sleepless nights en route, and the entire liturgy was in Tagalog, the most widely used of over one hundred Filipino dialects. Unable to follow the proceedings, I searched the printed order of worship to see if I could find any cognates. The closest I could come was a discovery that the Tagalog word for "holy" was *banal*. The discovery failed to enchant me; surely, the word for "holy" should be an exalted rather than a demeaning one. But as our visit went on, it became clearer and clearer that the vitality of the NCCP was due precisely to the fact that for them the "holy" was not located in some far-off place, but in the very midst of the banal, the ordinary, the apparently unexciting—the places we North American folk would not be likely to notice. Even the coming of the Messiah into the world was an example of banality: Jesus was a nobody from the boondocks. I count this interpretive key one of the major theological discoveries of my life.

The NCCP spelled out part of the way these things come together in its twenty-fifth anniversary message:

> We will fight forces that dehumanize, tendencies that deceive and distort truth, practices that perpetuate injustice. We will help build those conditions that make for peace. We will always be sensitive to the "cries of the people" and to their needs, to the sufferings and the aspirations of the neediest and the most deprived. We will do all this as part of our Christian confession and ecumenical obedience.

Yet there was more. Within the new edition of the Revised Standard Version of the Scriptures that was issued for the occasion is a collection of corporate statements on such subjects as evangelism, responsible parenthood, martial law, protest against U.S. intervention policy, ecumenical relations, peacemaking, economic development, and healing ministries. How banal.

One of the big issues while we were there was an escalating demand for the United States to pull out of its military bases. A visit to the huge naval base at Subic Bay certainly underlined the importance of this pressure. Olongapo had been a fishing village of a thousand souls or so. As Subic Bay, it had become a honky-tonk site of 192,000 persons, with over 16,000 *registered* prostitutes, along with three or four thousand young girls who acted formally as waitresses, relieved of such duties whenever a U.S. serviceman so desired. Furthermore, the bases were all under total U.S. control, and their importance in U.S. foreign policy was articulated by the statement of George Shultz, our secretary of state, that "the U.S. would have no qualms about destabilizing the present [Marcos's] government if it perceived that U.S. interests were being jeopardized." The long relationship with Marcos was dramatized when Vice President George Bush toasted Marcos at a public gathering with the words, "We love your adherence to democratic principles and to the democratic process." That any American official, let alone a vice president, could say such words to one of the most despicable of modern tyrants is unbelievable, and yet the words were spoken. Happily, the bases have since been vacated due to increasing pressure from the Filipino government and the timely intervention of a volcanic eruption that rendered Clark Air Force Base inoperable.

I was to give two major addresses during our stay, one in Manila and the other in the south, at Iloilo City. The first one seemed to me to be well-received, but by asking a few questions of my hosts, I gradually discovered that I might have done the cause of Filipino ecumenism no good and even possible harm. Members of a somewhat conservative denomination were considering joining the NCCP, but were apparently visibly shaken by one of my concluding suggestions that the role for a Christian in a society always flirting with the imposition of totalitarian control was to act as a "subversive," seeking to overthrow structures of injustice "from below," from the grass roots, rather than to give ultimate allegiance to any form of unjust state. This was not a new theme for me, but I felt that on this occasion I had not properly laid the groundwork, nor had I taken account of how totally the Marcos and Aquino regimes had co-opted the word "subversive" and given it a completely negative and sinister connotation for their own purposes.

Since I had a few days before the second presentation, I decided not to use the same speech in Iloilo City but to make a considerable number of changes, not to mute the concern, but to try to state my case in words to which my audience could be more receptive, so that the next quarter century of ecumenical expansion would not be hopelessly undermined. So I concocted an "ecumenical recipe," comprising ingredients I felt should characterize the church (and the council) in the future. The outline was distributed ahead of time, and I spoke briefly about each item. It was a better-crafted speech than its ill-fated predecessor, and even without the S- word I think it had more meat. At least I hope so, for I would not like to have sinned twice against such wonderful people. Here is the outline:

Take one world:

> a globeful of people, most of whom are victims;
>
> a handful of people passionately committed to justice;
>
> a God overseeing and supervising without usurping total control;
>
> an exemplary human life, in which the globeful of people
>   and the handful of people and the overseeing God are united,
>
> so that the particular human life is uniquely transparent to the divine;
>
> a healthy respect for the past and a healthy skepticism
>   about institutions that have an unhealthy respect for the past;
>
> human hearts in which anger and love are two sides of the same coin;
>
> a willingness to risk judgments that might be wrong;
>
> and an ultimate optimism combined with a provisional pessimism.

Mix well, and see what happens.

11

Avocations

It may be stretching things to call this a chapter on avocations, but not very much. The most rewarding part of my "professional" life has been that the line between vocation (my "regular work") and avocation (what I have done for pleasure) is almost nonexistent.

I cannot honestly say that writing is simply what the dictionary calls my "regular work." I also write because it gives me "pleasure." Often I write seriously, as at least a few books will testify, but I also write for relaxation and sheer fun, as the existence of St. Hereticus (more on him later in this chapter) bears testimony. Similarly, preaching is hard work, but I derive immense pleasure out of working on sermons and sometimes (by grace) having things gradually fall into place. Playing the cello is hard work, but on some occasions it has been sheer joy.

Conclusion: the dichotomy between "regular work" and "pleasure" is seldom sustainable. Thank goodness.

"THE APOSTOLATE OF THE PEN"

Shortly after my fifth birthday, I announced one morning that I wanted to be "a writer." My mother, to whom this wish was addressed, cooperated with my endeavor by constructing a desk out of an orange crate, supplying me with paper, pencil, pencil sharpener, and eraser, and removing herself from the scene so the muse could work unhindered. I sat down, sharpened the pencil five or six times, resharpened the pencil five or six more times, and after about ten minutes of really hard thinking repaired to the kitchen to announce, "I can't think of anything to write about."

My friends point out that such experiences have not inhibited my productivity over the last half century; indeed, there is quantity, if not always quality, to support their contention.

Theologians are particularly prone to opaque utterances. This is not entirely our fault. We have chosen the most arcane of all disciplines, for which "mystery" is the only appropriate boundary term. Any breakthroughs to clarity are undeserved gifts to be received with wonder, cherished with thanksgiving, and appropriated with humility. The sin we must avoid is the sin of equating the product of our descriptive powers with the One we are trying to describe. And even when all that is said, there remains the pedestrian task of translating our beliefs into words and images that clarify rather than distort.

On reflection, however, this is too pessimistic an appraisal. As Karl Barth frequently remarked, theological writing is also the most joyful and beautiful of all enterprises, an unashamed report of good news that cries out for utterance. According to Barth, the gospel is not "impenetrable darkness" but "indescribable light"—a distinction worth a lifetime of reflection.

This difficulty is not just a barrier for theologians. It is the basic problem in *all* communication. There is a gap we can never fully bridge: between what we are observing and our attempt to describe accurately what we are observing. At best we have only inadequate approximations, and an intellectual modesty at this point will save us from too much reliance on our own words. No descriptive skill will finally unite a description and the thing described, whether we are dealing with "angels" or "Auschwitz."

The term by which I try to cope with this built-in liability is the term "apostolate of the pen," the carrying out of an assignment by means of an instrument for sharing information.

In fifth grade I wrote a novel called *Sir Richard's Adventures*, a quest story set in medieval times, though I had no idea then what a "quest story" was. It was serialized in *The Brayton Bugle* and transformed into a play for a grammar school assembly. In the final scene, Sir Richard (guess who played Sir Richard) won the hand of Lady Elinor, played by Jean White, who was all I could have hoped for on stage or in real life, someone who was destined to be, as my deathless medieval prose put it, "the fairest bride in all of merrie England." If words could have become reality. . . .

The discovery that words nevertheless have the capacity to help us change things, coupled with strong affirmation by my senior high school English teacher, Miss Herrmann, convinced me that whatever I was going to do with my life would have words as a prominent component. My PhD dissertation, over two decades later, ran close to 600 pages, which in order to be even remotely publishable had to be cut to 170 pages. And I had to acknowledge, very quietly and privately, that the second version was better than the first.

The second version did get published, but the adjective "remaindered" (meaning roughly "casting the book to the wind") entered my life for the first and not the last time. Westminster Press offered to sell me the plates from which my book was printed, an offer I was able to refuse, though I did request the plate for the title page, which has been on my desk ever since, both as a paperweight and as an ongoing reminder of the mortality of my own prose.

In the great scheme of things, the contact with Westminster Press was also a contact with Paul Meacham, who had a decisive impact on all my future writing. The Presbyterians were experimenting with a new teaching tool called "The Christian Faith and Life Curriculum," which involved giving each student a clothbound book to be read at home and brought to church. There was a three-year cycle: the Bible, Jesus Christ, and the church. I was invited to write the senior-high book on the Bible. When I sent four initial chapters for appraisal, I received word that two of them "worked" but two did not.

This was a moment of truth. I mustered every device I could think of to keep high school students reading: different-sized type, slang, internal dialogues, much wordplay, wild analogies—an exercise that could only be called "creative irreverence." It worked, and *The Bible Speaks to You* was well received.

Something else happened that I had never anticipated: The book got wide usage among adults as well, and was even a source of sermon illustrations for many clergy. My earth-shaking discovery was "Brown's Law for Communicating Theological Insight": *If you write with teenagers in mind, some of the adults will understand.*

Forty years later I keep getting two kinds of comments on the book. The first goes: "You've never done anything as good as *The Bible Speaks to You*." I try to persuade myself that this is a compliment, but its message always suggests that as far as my writing goes, it's been downhill after the first flash in the pan. The other comment goes: "You must write very easily," the assumption being that clarity is attained with minimal effort. I promise that the clearer it is, the longer it took to get it that way. If a paragraph makes sense, it means that the paragraph went through five or six revisions.

The best advice I ever got about writing was the comment of my English professor at Amherst, George Frisbie Whicher, who encouraged us not to be immobilized because we couldn't dash off a brilliant initial paragraph. "Simply start writing," he said briskly, and then, luminously, "get the damn thing down on paper." We might have to throw away most of it, but we would have greased the skids for a subsequent overflow of acceptable prose—a gift from the gods.

A final point: Whatever my writing may or may not do for others, it does something important for me. I am frequently asked, "What do you think about *x*?" And I have to reply, "How can I tell what I think about *x* until I write it down?" "Writing it down" is my means of ongoing self-education.

THE DAY I GOT THREE REJECTION SLIPS FROM *THE CHRISTIAN CENTURY* . . . AND FOUND GOD

Affixed to the wall of my study is a profound truth by Elie Wiesel: "Words can sometimes in moments of Grace attain the quality of deeds." They communicate both empowerment and challenge. Words can make a difference, and hence are empowering. We had better craft our words well, so that they do make a difference, and hence are challenging.

When I get a rejection slip I can usually handle it and gain control by sending the piece in question to another magazine or journal. Sometimes I even agree with the stern editor that the piece I once thought so important has no merit.

But three rejection slips in one mailing? That is a mighty convincing message that a little less arrogance and a lot more humility is called for. Surely I'm not that far off the mark. But apparently I am.

How do I "find God" in all this? Most clearly, I think, in the realization that I shouldn't take myself quite so seriously—which I feel can be a very direct form of divine admonition—and that all this attention wrongly centered on my life and hard times should be directed back toward the divine Giver of life itself, and a different estimate arrived at about what's important. The notion that the world cannot survive without my wisdom on somebody else's printed page strikes me as an arrogant, if not ludicrous, attempt to evade a timely warning about not thinking of myself more highly than I ought to think.

And if that method of communication doesn't get through, there is a backup plan, clearly engineered from on high. I go back to the file drawer to cheer myself up by rereading, let us say, a "prophetic piece" I did in some journal a decade ago. And what I find is always the same: The paper on which it is printed is already crumbling to pieces in my hands, before it is even out of the drawer.

Sic transit gloria mundi: "That ought to show you how perishable your words are."

Mark: My earliest memory of my father's writing machine is of his stripped-down portable Underwood typewriter. He had somehow removed all of the letters of the alphabet and all of the numbers and punctuation marks from the keyboard. They were all perfectly blank circles. I think this was to prevent his classmates from borrowing his typewriter and depriving him of the means of recording his thoughts. He was the fastest typist I have ever known, as well as the quickest thinker. Because of this intimidating blank cipher of a typewriter, I didn't learn to type well until I had a primitive computer, which was long after I had graduated from college.

Tom: *Remembering my father, I think of him reading C. S. Lewis and Tolkien to Alison and me in his study in California, of falling asleep to the sound of his typewriter drumming out ways and means of ending apartheid, lifting South American oppression through liberation theology, stopping wars, quelling violence, and creating hope for a better world.*

Peter: *Of course, he made his own books. Book after book after book. When he quite literally was on his deathbed, a week before he drifted off, and still somewhat rational, I asked him how he was doing—I asked him what sounded good. I really wanted to know if he felt okay about dying. I thought he would say something to the effect that all was well, that he was unafraid, that life had been good, and that he was ready to move on to meet God, Bonhoeffer, Jackie Robinson, and all the others. Instead, he looked at me with great determination and said, "Publish that book." This book, the one you hold in your hands. And I'm glad we did.*

And he was glad to have published his one novel, Dark the Night, Wild the Sea, *though he thought the title a little romantic. His title had been* The Pipes of Erinsay, *but the editors had not been sure that people would know what the pipes were about (pipes to smoke? oil pipes?) and so he capitulated, to his initial regret, though later he would announce the new title with breathy mystery, a cock of his head, and just the hint of a brogue. He loved that book and the response that it got. I think he always wanted to write a novel, to write without initial purpose other than to tell a story—to let it unfold—and he loved the place. It was modeled on Colonsay, the island the McAfees once inefficiently ruled, so much so that they were eventually driven out, with the last one, Malcolm McPhee, shot through with an arrow and hung from a rock. Life on Colonsay was hard for the McPhees. When my dad went to Colonsay for the second time in the late sixties, someone noted that he was a McAfee, and he was asked if he were related to John McPhee, who had recently written a book on the island called* The Crofter and the Laird, *a book that apparently told a few too many island secrets. After assuring the man that there was no direct relation, my dad asked how the book had been received. "If McPhee comes back," went the reply, "he'll never make it off the pier."*

Still it's a beautiful and magical place, and all that magic is in his book. I think it was his favorite, though in the same way that an entire year in Heath would have left him restive with guilt, an entire life as a novelist would have gnawed at him. He needed to get directly at the world and its injustice, and he went at it with a tenacity, a vigor, and with deeply grounded courage—all the more remarkable in such a basically shy and unassuming man.

ST. HERETICUS

Shortly after our return from Oxford, the *New Yorker* accepted several pieces in which I poked fun at my theological brethren. My occasional attempts at satire were both for kicks and for dollars. (The first check paid the rent for four months.)

After this short-lived entrance into the big time, I joined the editorial board of *Christianity and Crisis*, a "left-liberal" biweekly that served as a platform for Reinhold Niebuhr in combating isolationism during World War II. It survived as "a journal of Christian opinion" for a full half century before financial considerations led to its exceedingly regrettable demise.

Fellow board member Dr. Van Dusen, overly impressed I am sure with my few successes in the *New Yorker*, picked up on a proposal by Douglas Horlin that I do an occasional humorous column for the journal. This had to be taken seriously since "humor" was not exactly Dr. Van Dusen's middle name. I had done an essay for *Religion and Life* in the Stephen Potter mode, entitled "Theological Gamesmanship, or How to Win a Theological Argument without Actually Cheating." But C. S. Lewis had already preempted the theological field with *The Screwtape Letters*, in which he presented Christian thought in "reverse English," that is, how to seduce a believer into unbelief. Despite these formidable precedents, the notion of a heretic commenting on things holy began to take shape, and one day the name "St. Hereticus" dropped out of heaven and we were off and running. Thus began a side of my life that continued for over twenty years, and frequently afforded enjoyment to others than just myself.

The original plan was to keep St. Hereticus's actual identity a secret, but this didn't work for long, even though the fiction was formally maintained that I had never been anything but his editor. Hereticus finally expired along with the journal.

It is tempting to cite some of the articles, such as "Six Elegant Proofs for the Existence of Santa Claus," which also linguistically demonstrated that "Santa" is a woman. But two volumes of St. Hereticus's "collected works" are still occasionally available in select secondhand bookstores, and I would rather comment on the employment of humor on the theological scene generally.

It is my firm belief, bolstered by masses of empirical evidence, that theologians take themselves far too seriously, and fail to see how laughable it is that mortal beings should imagine themselves equipped to comment accurately on immortal realities. What pretentiousness! How appropriate that they be cut down to size! How deliciously appropriate if the one doing the cutting down should himself be a theologian and thereby hoisted on his own petard. Why not make outrageous statements about God that reveal massive misinformation instead of precious insights?

Given the nature not only of human finitude (reading the evidence incorrectly) but of human sin as well (reading the evidence with self-serving intent), all those proposing to enter the field of theological endeavor ought to be exceedingly modest about the degree to which they dare to speak of things sacred. Yet modesty is infrequently ascribed to theological speech. As his sometime editor, I can risk suggesting that it was the deepest desire of St. Hereticus to restore the words "modest" and "theology" to their proper propinquity. If he did not quite succeed in that task, at least he gave it a good try, before the springs of living water ran dry.

The demise of *Christianity and Crisis*, which also brought about the demise of St. Hereticus, was a tragedy to all of us who worked on it over the years, and a tragedy as well to the faithful core of readers across the land who relied on it as a lens for viewing the world that was more left-liberal than *Time* and *Newsweek*. Those sharing such a perspective do not usually have an abundance of the world's goods to share, and the journal expired on a dismal day in 1993, because there was insufficient financial support to keep it going.

There is need of a long essay, or even a book, to document the impact of what Niebuhr always called "our modest little journal." The wise money would have banked on its demise after the retirement of Niebuhr, and later of John Bennett. But to the surprise only of those who did not know them, managing editors Wayne Cowan, and later Leon Howell, would drag it into solvency.

To paraphrase Voltaire, "If there were no *Christianity and Crisis* it would be necessary to invent one," and a time will surely come when, either under its old name or a new one, *Christianity and Crisis* will be resurrected.

Speed the day.

TRANSLATING

I keep asking myself why I translated three books from French into English, when my desk was always piled high with other tasks. I had plenty of my own writing to do, and my linguistic skills were far from evident.

1. The most hidden and least explored reason: my feeling that I had to do some specifically "scholarly" things in my professional life to gain acceptance within the guild.

2. The less hidden and better explored reason: my feeling that I could use the assignments to get more deeply grounded in another language and culture by constant engagement with it, so that I could use it as a tool in later reading and research.

3. The most expressed and, I hope, most deeply felt reason: my feeling that each of the books had a "message" that North Americans needed to hear,

myself included, and that it would be a good use of my professional time to make the messages more readily available.

In the case of Suzanne de Dietrich's *Le Dessin de Dieu*, a much deeper understanding of the details of the biblical story, coupled with a clearer overview of the Bible, was bound to result from intensive work on her text. In the case of Georges Casalis's *Karl Barth*, the book provided a drawing together of many of the disparate threads in Barth's thought. John Bennett and I had already taught courses at Union on portions of Barth's theology, and I needed an overview of the whole. I was also able to add a thirty-page introduction of my own to Barth's thought, which included ways in which it could be related to the North American scene. In the case of Andre Dumas's *Une théologie de la réalité: Dietrich Bonhoeffer*, many things came together, in particular a detailed refresher course on Bonhoeffer, who at that time (the early seventies) was immensely important to me and provided a model for theological and existential engagement for me on the issue of Vietnam, which related to the German "church struggle" against Hitler.

Would I take on these tasks again? On one level, no; the amount of time it took me to translate a single page was inordinate, and my references to French-English dictionaries unremitting. I was forced to neglect many other tasks, and I harbored deep insecurities about whether I was doing justice to both author and translator. But on another level, yes, I would do it again. I was forced into a better "feel" for French, of use in later reading and research, though most of it has now left me. But I did learn much more from a slow reading of the texts than would have been possible at an ordinary pace.

Suzanne de Dietrich's explanation of the Bible has remained foundational in my own living; Karl Barth has remained an inescapable presence, even though my interests have gradually moved from Barth to Gutierrez and liberation theology; Dietrich Bonhoeffer continues to nourish me when the temptation to idolatry of my country becomes insidious, and he continues to be one who always speaks the hard word I need to hear.

I need them all.

In my later years, I have increasingly wished I had learned Spanish. During the late seventies at Union, Sydney and I enrolled in a Spanish language course. It flourished for a few months, but there was an insufficient number of students with the monetary or existential resources for it to continue. As my own institutional responsibilities multiplied, I began to slight the Spanish class materials. After a high point of commitment and modest initial performance achieved after perhaps three or four months, I began to lose the minimal familiarity I was gaining, and gradually I became involved elsewhere.

This I now regard as a major error. There was no real way to build up a program at Union centering on Central and South America by persons who did not even know at least the rudiments of the language. "Mi casa es su casa," one of the most beautiful phrases of welcome any culture has ever created, will always deserve more than a blank stare in response.

PREACHING

Save for a year in the Navy Chaplains Corps, two years at Amherst divided between town and gown, and two academic quarters as acting dean of the chapel at Stanford, my professional life has been lived in the classroom more than in the sanctuary. I have more frequently spoken from a podium than from a pulpit. I have lectured many more times than I have preached, and my "liturgies," such as they are, have run the gamut from receiving draft cards from those who refused to fight, to blocking draft board entrances so that others would not have to volunteer to fight. The accumulation of my lecture notes over a lifetime would make a pile perhaps ten to twelve feet high, alongside a squat collection of old sermons.

So when I was asked, shortly into retirement, to preach half-time at our church until a pastoral replacement had been found, I didn't have an automatic answer ready. When I did say yes, I made two commitments to myself: (1) I would use no old sermons, and (2) I would use the lectionary.

The first demand was not hard to honor. Once perused, the old sermons were quickly discarded as unworthy of resurrection. The second demand, use of the lectionary, was wiser in retrospect than I could have foreseen in prospect. My informal poll of the congregation revealed that about 12 percent thought I should always preach from the lectionary, 23 percent thought it should be optional, and 65 percent asked, "What's the lectionary?" That readers may already have formed a version of the latter question prompts me to explain that the lectionary is a three-year cycle of selected biblical passages drawn from the Hebrew Scriptures, the Psalter, the Gospels, and the Epistles.

The rules of the game are simple: In preparation for each Sunday, you pick a text from one of the four selections and preach on it. The beauty (as well as the challenge) of this arrangement is that you can no longer recycle your favorite sermon topics; you have to explore topics that would otherwise be ignored, if the choice were strictly yours. Case in point: I don't think I had looked at the book of Malachi since graduating from seminary fifty years ago, and yet it popped up in the lectionary just when I needed material for a sermon on the fiftieth anniversary of the bombing of Pearl Harbor.

There was a surprisingly consistent pattern. Sunday looms, an event is plaguing us out in the world, panic ensues, and then the lectionary supplies a framework and some substantive material with which to connect it all. If it is a stern message, the congregation has to take seriously that the preacher did not create the text, but is simply trying to transmit it. The hallmark of a sermon, in other words, in contrast to a lecture, is that the sermon seeks a connection between the biblical situation and our own, whereas a lecture owes no such double fealty.

Diana Gibson: When I arrived at First Presbyterian Church, Palo Alto, as a young assistant pastor, people often talked about someone named Bob Brown. They would remark, "Bob said this . . . ," or recall, "When Bob Brown did that . . ." I was mildly interested, because what "Bob" said and did sounded pretty good, but I assumed he was simply one of the many fascinating members of this unique congregation whom I would soon meet. A few weeks later as I was being examined before presbytery (a requirement before beginning any new position), one person on the committee commented, "I don't mean to scare you, but the last person we examined was Robert McAfee Brown." I figured this was a joke. It was several days later, when yet another person from the church said, "Well, Bob Brown always says . . ." that I began to put things together: "Bob . . . Robert . . . Bob Brown . . . Robert Brown . . . Robert McAfee Brown . . . Was 'Bob Brown' Robert McAfee Brown?"

For the first few Sundays, when I'd get up in the pulpit to speak, I'd look out in terror for that shock of white hair, praying that Bob was out of town that week. But I soon discovered there was nothing to be nervous about with Bob, unless of course one truly did not want his or her own comfortable faith ever challenged by the example of another. Bob's gentle and humble spirit never sought to intimidate, never aimed to impress, and never demeaned the efforts of another. The only thing "scary" about Bob was that he lived with such courage and integrity. It made being a lazy Christian, or even just a comfortable Christian, well, uncomfortable.

I served First Presbyterian in Palo Alto for sixteen years, the final ten years as senior pastor. During those sixteen years Bob was our parish associate, meaning he took on a variety of teaching and preaching tasks when requested by the other pastors. (His book, Reclaiming the Bible, *is a collection of sermons from a three-year stint of preaching half-time for our congregation.) Throughout those sixteen years, I grew to know Bob as mentor, colleague, and friend. I came to continue to look out from the pulpit for his white hair, but it was always in the hope that Bob was there, for I knew then there was at least one person who would listen intently and respond thoughtfully.*

THE CELLO

To me, the cello is a symbol of creativity. In appropriate hands it adds something beautiful to whatever we already have. The means for creating that beauty are very humble: a casing made of wood, strings made of metal, and a bow made of horsehair. A cellist does not first destroy and then create; a cellist uses what is already created and dips and soars to recreate and make implicit beauty more explicit.

My love affair with the cello began during freshman year at Amherst, when Professor Vincent Morgan of the Music Department arranged for the Budapest String Quartet to give a concert on campus. As a sometime violinist, I had more than perfunctory interest in hearing them play, but I was not ready for the impact that the cellist, Mischa Schneider, made on me that evening. There is a figure of speech (at the time unknown to me) sometimes applied to cellists, which Schneider embodied: The instrument was simply an extension of himself. All his movements—of bow, fingers, and physique—bore out the truth of that description, and it was wonderful to behold.

I cannot state that at that moment I determined to study the cello. That didn't happen for forty years. But in the interval, string quartets became my favorite music, with ongoing gratitude to Beethoven, who left us sixteen of them.

I had occasional nostalgic desires to play the cello, one of which Alison heard as a genuine yearning—so much so that she created a sixtieth birthday "Robert Brown Cello Fund," to which she invited all my friends and relations to contribute, thereby amassing sufficient capital for the purchase of an instrument. The woman with whom I took lessons, Dorothy Barber, helped me pick a cello, which we discovered later had been made in the People's Republic of China, thus introducing politics into the transaction as well.

And there the matter rested for some time between Dorothy and me. We had a good arrangement: Every so often I would make an appointment and say in effect, "Check me out. What am I doing right and what am I doing wrong?" And then I would go back to work.

I had one ambition: Before I died I wanted to play "live" the Andante Cantabile of Beethoven's *Archduke Trio*, op. 97, which over the years had established itself in my mind and heart as Beethoven's greatest single utterance. It is a series of variations on a rich and glorious theme. (Fifteen years later I still have trouble with variation two, but the rest is, at least in some rudimentary sense, "within reach.")

A couple of years down the road I got up my courage and asked two friends, Phyllis Campbell, a pianist, and David Abernethy, a violinist, if they would play that piece with me. They agreed, we did, and I was fulfilled. This would have been the end of the story, save that Phyllis, after we finished, asked, not idly, "I wonder if we could do the first movement?" I scoffed at the idea, but the question was real. We were soon embarked on a lengthy journey together.

Thus did "the ABC Trio" come into being, our last names furnishing materials for an unforgettable acronym. About once a year we give a concert for *very* close friends and family who will continue to love us anyhow. We do portions of Haydn, Mozart, and Beethoven, with an occasional foray into Mendelssohn or Debussy. I am a very slow learner, and I struggle with sight reading. Their tolerance has held us together.

Our yearly concert also challenges us to create a printed program, complete with fictitious historical notes: "Robert Brown studied cello with Casals, Rostropovich, and Dorothy Barber, winning the Prix de Rome in 1937 for his rendering of an unaccompanied cello suite by the Spanish composer Juan Sebastiano B. His recent study has centered on learning how to correlate bowing and fingering." "The ABC Trio was formed in Rome, New York, in 1937, during the common sojourn there of its three members to receive recognition for excellence in their respective fields (left, center, and right). They are credited with having reintroduced tempo rubato (having certain notes lengthened while others are correspondingly shortened, or vice versa) as the central characteristic of their group musicianship."

The programs also include reviews and tributes from composers: "Never before has my music been played like this.—Wolfgang Amadeus Mozart," or "In the presence of such playing, my deafness constitutes a blessing.—Ludwig von Beethoven." Occasionally, the critics weigh in as well: ". . . breathtaking in their nuanced musicianship.—Arnold Schwarzenegger," or "Last night the ABC Trio played Beethoven; Beethoven lost.—unattributed sportscaster."

As a cellist, I will never be very good, and I increasingly begrudge the forty years I spent in the nonpracticing wilderness. I live for the occasional moments when a phrase, or even a single note, emerges sounding something like what the composer must have intended. When that happens, past mistakes are forgotten, and new beginnings are possible—a parable.

But if only I had started forty years earlier . . .

Mark: My father was always a musician and encouraged all of us to play instruments. I would often go to sleep listening to him play the music of Bach or Beethoven on the piano or cello, and would wake up to the atonal, staccato, machine-gun-burst beat of his manual typewriter—his fingers trying to keep up with the speed of his mind as he wrote one of his twenty-eight books.

Peter: My dad was a great maker of things. His relaxation for many years (as a creative workaholic) was to make things with his hands. He found it difficult not to produce at least something—so at Heath particularly, he would build: first the house, and when the house was close to done (but never finished), tree houses, forts, baseball backstops, furniture. This slowed a bit, but only a bit, when we got him a cello for his sixtieth birthday. Some of the energy went into this portable vehicle for music. We didn't have a piano at Heath (the instrument he used in California)—and with this cello, which he loved, but struggled with, he kind of built music at first. Within a couple of years, however, he was making it. And it sounded good.

Most of the time he was not confident enough to entertain others with this music (apart from the ABC Trio). He was embarrassed by his beginner status (although he had taken up the instrument at an outrageous age), and the thought of somehow bollixing up another's aural space was a sin not to have on his conscience—even though we loved to hear him play. So he often went out into the apple orchard, which was nice to see and hear: the music, the view to the mountains, the clouds, the waving grass, an obviously happy man. (I think he may have seen a photograph of Pablo Casals playing in a hayfield once.) He really played for himself, though, and he would sing along with the cello, sort of like Glenn Gould on the piano, humming contentedly. A lot of it was hard for him, but when he hit a phrase that pleased him, he was very, very happy.

If there was music, it was almost impossible for him to keep his mouth shut. He would always *harmonize, which of course could be embarrassing for those around him—he was good, but not always* all *that good. And sometimes he would do it in falsetto, in public, which as a teenager seemed completely beyond the pale—the Beach Boys could pull it off, or the Four Seasons (even that was a little embarrassing)—but they weren't singing hymns or classical music. I would try to act as though he were not related to me. When he did this in church I would sometimes nudge him a little bit.*

Granddaughter Caitlin (at age eleven): *In third grade I started to play the cello because of Bop, and I still play it today because I saw how great he had become in just a few years and knew that I could too. I am in the choir with Ms. Booker, one of the best teachers in the world, because of him. I loved hearing him sing and harmonize with any song, and I wanted to be just like that. Though his years with me came to an end much too quickly, the time I had with him was extraordinary. I loved and still love him very, very much.*

Grandson Aki (at age seventeen): *My grandfather and I shared the same two interests: music and social change. I wish he were still around. There are so many things I still want to talk to him about. I wish I could talk to him more deeply about his thoughts about social change and hear more about the things he did, like the Freedom Rides and antiwar activism. I wish we could have more years together to share our love of music and activism. He was a great man and a wonderful grandfather, and I will miss him.*

12

Marriage: Fifty Reasons

Peter: One thing that this book does not quite do well enough is describe my parents' marriage. They had a phenomenal marriage—happy, loving, mutually supportive, and intellectually engaged. Plus they were very funny. My father planned a chapter in his book on my mother, but did not live to finish it. Here, to try to fill in that gap, are a few reasons for the success of their marriage. I read this on the afternoon of my parents' fiftieth wedding anniversary party, a huge gathering in Foothills Park in Palo Alto in 1995.

FIFTY REASONS MY PARENTS
HAVE STAYED HAPPILY MARRIED FOR FIFTY YEARS

1. After an afternoon and evening-long conversation with one of my cousins, who was trying to decide whether or not to marry a man considerably older than herself, my mother woke up at three in the morning and gently elbowed my father awake. "Why do you think we've stayed married so long?" she asked him. "The reason we've stayed married so long," he said groggily but clearly, "is that you never ask me questions like that."
2. My father was persistent. He asked my mother to marry him three times and got three yesses and two broken engagements, but he kept at it, very much as though (it occurs to me now) he was going through drafts of a book—just trying to get it right.
3. They actually do love each other as much as their friends suspect that they do. This is the real thing.
4. They were more than lucky, and God was even kinder than normal.

5. They have four wonderful and modest children—Mark, Alison, Tom, and me—and they have five inspirational grandchildren: Colin, Aki, Jordan, Caitlin, and Mackenzie (and now Riley.)

6. They have four wise women and one wise man in the immediate family—Alison, Karen, Jill, Deb, and Paul—each of whom on a daily basis deals professionally with overstressed, confused, and emotionally overwrought people. Any of them can be called on in a pinch.

7. They both enjoy the occasional Scotch.

8. Heath, Heath, Heath, Heath, and Heath.

9. They have a huge network of friends.

10. The First Presbyterian Church of Palo Alto, which from a distance seems to keep them both in the thick of things and also appropriately humble.

11. My mother cooks, my father washes the dishes, and this does not change.

12. They are political soul mates.

13. They are religious soul mates.

14. Even so, they grapple tenaciously with all political and religious issues on which they disagree.

15. My mother buys the clothes. My father wears them.

16. They can leave each other for fairly lengthy periods of time without either seeming to feel too neglected.

17. They kiss and hug whenever they get back together again, and it's not just for show.

18. My mother has cut my father's hair for at least fifty years, instilling in him a momentary meekness that must in some way serve a purpose.

19. My father did not try to teach my mother how to drive.

20. Coffee.

21. More coffee.

22. They do not let their problems lie dormant for more than a few hours—although this is almost all my mother's doing.

23. My mother does not insist on watching baseball games.

24. My father does not insist on going into antique shops.

25. They both love to travel.

26. They watched *Dallas* religiously for years. My mother, a soap opera junkie from way back, has to be pried away from the set with promises of Mexican food and pitchers of beer. (That's not true—it's really not.) But they did watch *Dallas* and *Murder She Wrote, thirtysomething, Murphy Brown,* and now they watch *Seinfeld* with unabashed American pride.

27. They like Mexican food. And they continue to eat well despite my father's difficulty in distinguishing between various tastes and smells. He basically likes crunchy cold stuff or crunchy hot stuff, with the cold, I think, holding a slight preference at this point. My mother, who is a wizard in the

kitchen, continues to cook creatively and healthfully for both of them—
and often for all of us as well.

28. They have been extremely supportive of their children and helpful in the various trials and tribulations that we have experienced in our journeys through life. They leave us alone when we need to be left alone, and they are always there for us when we need them to be close. We all love to be with them.

29. This is not something that Presbyterians normally talk about—but there is a great and easy physical intimacy between the two of them.

30. My father can express most of his anger by making a huffing noise, sort of cocking his head to the side and doing something strange with his left eye and eyebrow while snapping a newspaper. This seems, at least momentarily, to take care of whatever is bothering him. My mother, on the other hand, slowly builds up pressure until steam begins to escape from her ears and her eyes begin to flash and zip around like a pinball machine about to tilt. Then words, at first clipped and hopping but then increasingly coherent, begin to tumble out until the point is eloquently and conclusively made. This combination, with fine tuning from my father and emphatic gesturing from my mother, seems to work perfectly for the two of them.

31. Despite these "talents" they both are remarkably happy, positive people. The norm is having fun, discussing events and ideas, being put out at something in the news, laughing together, sharing, and enjoying each other on a daily basis. Basically, after fifty years, they not only love each other—they still are in love.

32. They like other people. They are curious about them and they want to have them around—people stayed with us all the time. At one time they invited a young Dutch exchange student by the name of Leendert Colijn to live with us for a year. Interestingly enough, he straightened them both out politically, and they have not been the same since, nor for that matter have any of the rest of us. They also, I've been told by each of them—particularly recently—simply enjoy each other's uninterrupted company. They like being alone together.

33. They are able to do their work surrounded by chaos—or at least a lot of noisy kids. The dual sounds of my childhood were slamming screen doors and shouting hungry kids who had lost something and needed something to do and were either singing or telling loud stories or lies and needed to be taken to Little League or fishing or wanted to know where the bicycle was or where the peaches were or could I have some ice cream now. . . . All that accompanied by the sound of a typewriter just moving through the late afternoon like a lazy rumbling train.

And just as I wrote this, my daughter Caitlin came in wanting some oatmeal and for me to read her a book. These are her four unprompted reasons for why my parents have stayed together for fifty years:

1. Because they love each other very much.
2. Because they didn't want their granddaughter to come to one house and then have to go to the other.
3. Because they care about us.
4. Because they have fun together and they live in California and they live close to the beach.

Back to mine. I had missed that last one about the beach and so:

34. They have almost always lived in beautiful or interesting places—Amherst, Massachusetts; the mountains of North Carolina; Oxford, England; New York City; St. Paul, Minnesota; Heath, Massachusetts; St. Andrews, Scotland; Palo Alto, California; Tours, France; Geneva, Switzerland. But by and large, the physical places, the geographies they have chosen, have been as supportive of them as they have been of each other.

35. They both are very smart and very determined, and they are not intellectually intimidated, either by each other or by anyone else. Nor are they intellectually intimidating to others—although my father has needed a little help on this one over the years. It was hard initially for him to keep his firepower in check when confronted by his comparatively inarticulate rebelling postadolescent son, but he got it under control and learned to listen, and I got it under control and stopped shouting—at least most of the time anyway.

The bottom line is that my mother and father are intellectually nice people, as smart as all the pundits but unimpressed by academic jargon and thought for thought's sake. They are real and deal well with those who deal in the real, but for those protective and protected privileged people who deal in a cavalier fashion with the lives of others who are not so protected—watch out. You are fair game, and Bob and Sydney Brown are not people you want opposing you. As kind and as Christian as they are, they will put your lights out. And they will do it in such a way that you will probably end up thanking them. Justice will prevail.

36. They both love light and color. They are inspired by them and use them in wonderful ways in the places they live, the art they live with, and the clothes they choose to wear.

37. They can sing together in the car, and they still do—with my father sometimes contributing a strange but weirdly effective falsetto.

38. They like music, from Celtic tunes and hammer dulcimer to anything with a cello in it and Beethoven.

39. They share a mutual distrust of anything establishment—of corporate America, of the corporate church, of people with a little too much money.
40. They also share a mutual distrust of people who have had a bit too much therapy, with people with a bit too much spiritualism, with people who are a little too nice. Nuns, apart from Mother Teresa, whom my mother finds particularly galling, seem to be excepted, ex-nuns particularly.
41. They like to walk in the hills together.
42. They accept each other's differences. They can go to the beach and my father will sit on a bluff and look out to sea for an hour while my mother putters around, looking for carnelians and shells and treasure in the sand, and each will be happy.
43. They like to point things out to each other, and they appreciate what the other person has seen.
44. They share a mutual and perfectly honed sense of the absurd—and although most things do not seem absurd most of the time, they know when to call an idiot an idiot, when to let it all go and just laugh at the ridiculousness of so much that passes for normal.
45. At Heath, my father takes care of the fields and the blueberries and my mother takes care of the flowers and the vegetables. (A personal aside: In a major transgenerational cross-sexual move, I put in my second vegetable garden this spring, the first since I was six years old, and my radishes and carrots were coldly ignored by the sexist judges at the Heath Fair.) But when I was six, they seemed to be telling me in no uncertain terms that vegetables were no job for a man, or so it seemed to me given my family of origin's plant-life preferences: blueberries, okay; vegetables, no, no, no. But this spring I proved them wrong: Men can grow vegetables—and succeed.

    This is a very long way around to give you not a very good example of the kind of convoluted self-involved thinking that drives my father nuts—although he is of course a thoroughly confirmed killer of undifferentiated plant life, a speciesist of the highest order.
46. Neither of them will get near a computer, despite every reason to buy two of them. They are confirmed in their archaic but astonishingly effective working methods, and neither messes with the other's way of getting things done. In fifty years of marriage my father has moved papers of my mother's maybe twice—maybe only once. (More recently, with the new millennium, my mother has moved into the era of e-mail with aplomb.)
47. They are both very funny people, and they laugh a lot. Humor is right up there with political content. You often hear them in some other room of the house, either in Heath or in Palo Alto, chortling away. Upstairs together in bed at Heath they carry on like a couple of goofy teenagers. Laughter is a constant.

48. They never let the fact that each one of their children seems to believe that he or she is by far the most favored child interfere with the raising of the other three, slightly less important, ones.
49. They also love Paul, Karen, Jill, and Deb in the same ways that they love Mark, Alison, Tom, and me.
50. In their marriage they have achieved such a surplus of love that there is always more than enough for everyone—family, friends, and strangers.

Fifty years ago, my parents were in the right place at the right time. My father recognized this immediately, and after a tumultuous courtship he convinced my mother that he was, in fact, the perfect match for her. Once my mother recognized this important bit of news (she was, after all, only twenty-one, and she had half the Eastern Seaboard after her), they were married, with family and friends singing hosannas, and they turned to each other and they said, "Praise the Lord!" or words to that effect. "Holy Smokes! Look at us! Look at me! Look at you! Look what this means: We can do anything we want." And they did. They moved off into one of the greatest continuing love stories of the twentieth century.

These last few years have been by no means dwindling ones. My parents are still chugging along, perhaps more so now than ever. And I can't see them slowing down too much in the future.

My parents were graced by God, and in turn they have graced each other. They have made the most of a marriage with incredible potential, and through their love and their work they have literally changed our world—on personal, local, national, and global levels. And that is simply the remarkable truth.

These are two lives well lived by two people who have helped each other learn to live in loving and responsible ways. And then they've gone out and done it. Again and again they have brought us together. All who have been lucky enough to spend time with them have benefited immeasurably from Sydney, from Bob, from their love, and from their wonderful marriage.

We all love you very much, and we thank you.

13

Heath

Our grandson Aki, having heard about "Heath" for months but not knowing what it was or where it was, commented from the Heath sandbox where he was, for the moment, blissfully happy: "Heath is in just the right place."

Our granddaughter Caitlin, after having been asked by a friend, "Who owns Heath?" replied, "*Nobody* owns Heath. *Everybody* owns Heath. And *I* own it, too."

The last time I wrote a full-length autobiography (which was in seventh grade), it was customary to include a chapter entitled "How I Spend My Summer Vacations." For those who resonate with such an assignment, the present chapter may hold some interest. For those who want to know the full story, Heath has shaped me more than I could ever shape it.

In the summer of 1948, when Peter was only two months old, Bill and Eleanor Wolf came by to see us at Jaffrey, New Hampshire, where we were living rent-free in my grandparents' summer place. I was trying to learn German.

"We have about fifty acres at Heath we'd like to sell," Bill began. "It's just been logged, so it wouldn't be expensive." We decided not to talk price, our existential situation making it unrealistic to do so. But we did agree that just for a lark we'd drive over to Heath and see it.

Sydney recognized what we came to call "The Land" as a place to which she had hiked with Christopher and Elisabeth Niebuhr some years earlier. The unwooded area was next to an apple orchard, just beyond a stone wall.

There is a forest in the middle distance, and on the horizon the clear outline of Vermont's Mt. Haystack and Massachusetts's Mt. Greylock.

We decided to talk price.

Bill said they needed to get about six hundred dollars out of it, a sum unattainable at the time. But when Bill proposed our paying a hundred dollars a year for six years, we could not refuse. (Just to illustrate the kind of friends the Wolfs were, two years later they reported getting a small windfall, and that a third payment of a hundred dollars would wipe out our indebtedness.)

In the meantime we moved to Minnesota, and our only tangible relationship to Heath was the tax bill for "unimproved property," for which we were assessed eighteen dollars per year. When we moved back to New York in 1953, however, dormant Heath showed signs of life. Maybe, like the Niebuhrs, we could spend the summers in Heath and give our children an asphalt-free environment. Once established at Union, we made several trips north and discovered that Heath was a five-hour drive. (New freeways and thruways gradually reduced the time to a little over four hours, though Bill Webber once made it in three hours and fifty-seven minutes.)

We needed professional help to build on the land. An Amherst classmate, Al Rugg, lived in Greenfield, twenty miles away, and ran a lumberyard. He connected us to Harvey Hatheway, an architect, and to Wes Phillips, a contractor. All three agreed to give us assistance along the way, while letting us do as much of the work ourselves as we could.

We wanted to design our own house and to build as much of it as possible with our own hands. We sketched what we hoped to have, and Harvey Hatheway took out the glitches, redrew the windows to proper size, got the roof pitch aesthetically and structurally in sync, and then persuaded us to rotate the finished plan. The proposed exterior of red siding and white trim left us dreamy eyed.

During the winter before construction began, Herb Stetson, a resident who owned a sawmill and whose daughter had been in our church in Amherst, cut enough trees to provide us with many two-by-fours and rough boarding, so that a good portion of the house came from Heath and would always remain there. Wes Phillips started us on construction, coming on Saturdays with a couple of carpenters, and leaving us with assignments during the week. We learned how to use a Skilsaw, cement cinder blocks together, nail nothing down without checking with the level, pick up the stray nails we dropped, keep a space clear for piles of lumber from Al Rugg's lumberyard, and fold a flexible rule back up every time.

In an extraordinary act of kindness, the Dyer family, colleagues from Union Seminary, hearing we were planning to live on the site in two tents with two children, insisted that we stay with them. I do not know how we would have survived without this wonderful base of operations, which included not only caring people but amenities such as running water, telephone, refrigeration, and bathrooms.

In addition to constructing a home, I was acting as general editor for a twelve-volume series of books entitled *The Layman's Theological Library*, and I gave this a couple of hours each day. It was the small retainer from Westminster Press that enabled us to start building, even though completion of the house was light years away. At one point I thought we should call our construction "Layman's Lodge," or at least affirm one rock on which the foundation rested as "Layman's Ledge."

With a lot of extra help, we achieved what we needed to achieve before winter—a tarpaper shack sealed from the winds and snow. The colors at that stage were strange, but the lines were lovely. To be sure, there was no water, no heat, no chimney, no flooring but subflooring, no bathroom, no kitchen, and no interior walls except a forest of two-by-fours, sixteen inches on center. But we could camp inside relatively protected from the weather, and were content.

We began building in Heath in 1954, and the job is not yet done, nor will it ever be. Our one rule along the way was a decision not to go into debt. Whatever we had put aside by June each year comprised our assets for that summer. We got running water by laying a plastic pipe on the ground all the way to a very temperamental spring several hundred yards below us. The cows kept stepping on the plastic pipe and puncturing it, while the porcupines gnawed at the plastic system when we weren't around. Activating the water system each spring usually took a full day of laborious activity, and we had to go through the same routine every time the pipe broke. Never in those early days did I turn on a faucet without a silent prayer that water would come out rather than a hiss of cool air. Years later, emboldened by Bill Wolf's example, we drilled a well—a terrifying gamble, for people have been known to drill seven hundred feet and hit nothing. The gods were with us; we hit an ample supply at eighty-three feet.

We gradually got sheetrock up and differentiated the rooms. A couple of summers later I took up wallpapering, and the rooms began to have distinctive character, though in the long run we painted over most of the paper to get more light. I made doors for the interior: vee-notch pine with knotholes, held in place by wrought iron hinges.

For years there was a huge hole between the kitchen and living room, and about the fifth or sixth summer we had a local mason fill up the hole with a fireplace and chimney. There is a long story about our traumas in getting the fireplace built, but the final product was so efficient that I have consigned the steps in getting there to oblivion.

Not even a superefficient fireplace can heat an entire house, however. We discovered this one winter when we went to Heath during Christmas vacation. When we arrived, the temperature in the house was zero degrees. We had to store our food in the refrigerator to keep it from freezing. The first night we all slept in the living room, with as many blankets, comforters, and sleeping bags as we could discover, as close to the old Franklin stove as we could get. By 9 a.m. the next day the temperature had risen up to four degrees and was clearly incapable of going higher.

It did not take much effort to persuade me that we must buy a Scandinavian wood-burning stove that very day. We installed it with a makeshift flue up the chimney and gradually moved from the illusion to the sensation of warmth. From that time on, the stove has been a fixture in the living room— a piece of furniture in the summer, holding freshly picked flowers, and a furnace in the fall, set on the brick hearth in front of the fireplace. It is magic. Here is a black box on legs, which isn't too hot even when you are standing close to it. It has no moving parts, and yet you *know* that if you enter the house on a brisk fall afternoon, it will be warm and cozy.

During these years, with their demands and crises, Sydney was the glue that kept us all together. That is hardly an edifying image, but it is descriptively accurate. Much of this was unglamorous work: washing clothes and washing dishes, preparing meals and cleaning up after four children and one husband, who now realizes that his single-minded dedication to getting a roof on before the snow fell made him a less than adequate companion and sharer in domestic duties. Sydney also did her share of the hammering and painting and decorating, and supervised the cultivation of summer gardens of various sizes and shapes, usually festooned with a few mammoth sunflowers for good measure. Her tasks involved more and more time with her parents (also addicted to Heath) as they grew older, and through all times, crowded or lean, she had an ever filled coffee pot and ever expanding meals.

We always had visitors wherever we were, part-time residents or quasi-family members, whether on Ledges Road, 837 Cedro Way, 711 McGiffert Hall, 2E Knox Hall, 2090 Columbia, or even our overseas domiciles. In Sydney's eyes, there was always room for another plate at the dinner table, and she would take the initiative of inviting anyone in the house after, say, 5 p.m., to stay for dinner. She got many takers. I am not as good at this as she was—and is—and her outgoingness meant that we met, and broke bread with, all sorts of people whose presence enriched our lives.

By mid-August the grass, weeds, and shrubs would be waist high. I made it my job, with a self-propelled mower, to mow all the open areas before that time, so that we would have clear, freshly cut fields all around us.

Mowing is very satisfying work. It requires a lot of exercise to keep up with a self-propelled mower, which must be turned at every corner as well as around obstacles, and the driver must pull it away from unforeseen entanglements, not to mention pushing it back to the house when it breaks down. (Mowers never break down near the house.) My mood on any given day can be measured by whether or not the mower is in working order.

Each summer, I'd go along with Peter and Mark and get a fishing license that legitimated the boys, but I preferred monkeying around with the oars or the rented outboard motor or taking pictures of their catches rather than catching fish myself.

Fortunately, I *did* like baseball, and we did a lot of batting and throwing in front of the backstop in the pear orchard. I had had such a hard time as a kid acquiring any knack for baseball that I wanted to be sure we didn't have a rerun of the humiliations I had endured. Peter had a lot of natural athletic ability, and it carried him to Little League stardom. Mark and I were more relaxed about baseball proficiency, but for several summers he was Charlemont's shortstop and once made an unassisted double play.

Tom opted for other preadolescent interests. Reptiles and amphibians topped his list. Alison spent hours playing in a little house that I built for her made of two-by-fours and pine slab. Through Sunday school and vacation Bible school, she made many friends from the many farms around Heath. She also found friends among the "summer kids," and spent many hours exploring in fields and forest with her brothers. Tom's herpetological interests continued, with a wider area to draw upon than Manhattan Island. He collected frogs, snakes, and salamanders. His rapid entrances into the kitchen, hands cupped, were always followed by "Gimme a jar!" His snake collections, in terrariums we made together, won numerous prizes in the local agricultural fair at the end of each summer.

The Brown boys and the Wolf boys explored the woods, all one hundred acres of it, in exquisite detail. They sometimes took bows and arrows with them, but since no trophies of war were ever brought back, we assumed that the animal population of Heath remained unharmed.

There was one secret excitement held by the boys. By the time we began driving across the country, it would transpire that when we went through a state where the purchase of fireworks was legal, we would buy some and smuggle them into Massachusetts where such transactions were illegal. At about dusk on the Fourth of July, the cache of sparklers, Roman candles, firecrackers, and bottle rockets would mysteriously appear. One main worry, alongside the little matter of law breaking, was that sparks from a Roman candle might ignite the uncut grass in the apple orchard and that the Heath Volunteer Fire Department would have to come and do its thing.

A major event in 1968 brings Sydney back to center stage and explains how a new body of water came to be christened "Pond Sydney" by Kathleen Roberts. When the kids were little, the Wolfs provided a small asphalt-lined circular pool on the edge of the hay field, which was wonderful for rudimentary swimming. We had some years after this swimming at Rowe, the next town, which had a lake big enough for everybody in the entire county. But the inhabitants of Rowe grew tired of the daily Heath invasion, and enacted an ordinance that only those who had an appropriate sticker could use the beach and lake. This sounded reasonable until we discovered that you could only get an appropriate sticker if you owned land in Rowe. This did little to enhance good relations between the two towns.

Ten years before, the boys had discovered a marshy area in an old pasture below the Wolfs' property. Could this be a possible source of water, Sydney wondered, if the area around it were bulldozed and springs discovered? She called a county agent who looked the site over and expressed optimism—not only were there a lot of springs, but the slope of the runoff was perfect. More phone calls to other agents followed, and then one day Wayne Hillman and his son drove up with two bulldozers and the project commenced.

With consummate skill the Hillmans created a pond, ten feet deep in the middle, excavated to form an earthen dam at the lower end, complete with a spillway and a large overflow pipe. Soon there were trickles of water coming up through the dirt, and when, months later, the winter snows had melted, Bill phoned us to report that the pond was full. Shortly after, the pond was populated not only by people but by fish. The kids could have a ball while their parents had a social gathering place par excellence.

The magical power of Pond Sydney reached out as far as California. Our local herpetologist had new areas to conquer, and was chastised by his teacher for not paying attention in class. She reported his lassitude to his parents, and Sydney asked him what was going on. "Oh," he replied, "when we have a reading period I read ahead so I know what's in the story, and then I sit back and think about what's on the bottom of the pond at Heath."

There is another and very different reason why Heath has been so important to me. It has enabled me, for selected periods of my life, to do some very different things with my time. In California, I sit at a desk. I read. I write a few letters or a book review. There is usually nothing concrete to "show" for it in the short run. So "What did you do today?" is a hard question to answer, particularly if the interrogator wants an itemized reply, particularly if I didn't understand what I was reading, or the letters have been perfunctory, or the book review has failed to jell.

But at Heath . . . I finished mowing the pear orchard, I got that chair scraped and painted, we all went swimming together, I finally figured out where in the roof that leak over the dining room table is coming from, the boys and I finished building a new backstop for Pickerel Field. These are not world-shaking achievements measured by other standards of achievement, but they are tangible. There is a wall where there was no wall, and it will be there, seven feet nine inches high, for a long time.

None of the above captures the magic of Heath, for which "magic" is the only approximation that really works. How we had enough nerve to make that original six-hundred-dollar investment I'll never know, but it has repaid us many, many imes over. All of us have our memories: seeing the first deer down in the apple orchard; building a baseball backstop with chicken wire; building a boat from a Sears Roebuck kit; exploring the woods with the Wolf boys; camping out under the stars when the meteors were active; making a door and hanging it for the first time; welcoming friends who were as dazzled by it all as we were; singing with the Porters; planting new flowers side-by-side with the perennials; winning the pennant in Little League; being unhappy together when the first "back to school" ads began to appear in the Greenfield *Recorder*; going on rain walks looking for salamanders; visiting Granny's and Pawpaw's graves in the Center Cemetery and realizing (with calmness and not with fear) that we would join them someday; making entry after entry for the Heath Fair and sampling the Fire Department's homemade root beer; coming around the corner on the first visit each summer and discovering that, yes, the house had survived the winter and that the whole thing was not a mirage but real.

Mark: *Summers in Heath were always my favorite time with my father. He had much more time for us, and life revolved around family more than the national or international crisis of the day. When we were children he built us tree houses large enough to sleep in, a stockade in the woods named Fort McFie, where we had imaginary battles with the enemies of our Scottish ancestors, and a sturdy playhouse, which still is used by his grandchildren today.*

When I was four or five he bought me a new blue hatchet at Avery's general store. Soon afterward my mom helped me buy a twenty-five-cent heirloom poker at an antique shop in New England that we still use today. With these two essential items, he taught me how to build a fire and how to keep it burning. He showed me how to split kindling, demonstrated the use of paper as a starter, showed me how to stack logs atop it all with space for air to circulate, how to strike a match and use a bellows. On the many backpacking trips I have taken in the Sierras, the Appalachians, and the Alps, his lessons of fire have often warmed my body and heart. Every time I light a fire I think of him.

He taught me how to swing a hammer, cut wood with a Skilsaw, and how to build, paint, and maintain a home. He was a fine craftsman and carpenter who paid attention to detail. He taught me to first think about the task at hand, do the best possible job you could, finish the job, clean up, and put your tools away—advice that has helped me in all parts of my life since then. Most of this he taught by example. Although he was a minister, he never preached to me. His passion for his work, whatever it was, set a contagious standard for everyone, and expanded people's natural abilities.

When I was ten, my brother Peter and I needed a boat to get us out into the deeper waters of local New England lakes, where in theory there were bigger fish to catch. My father rose to the task, and together the three of us built a mahogany rowboat over two summers that we named "The Alison" for my baby sister and that we painted blue, which still is my mother's favorite color. And we caught more fish and bigger fish. He taught me to respect and care for the earth. He was the master gardener of our acre of blueberries below our house in Heath. He was a keeper of giant white birches and a steward of the land.

He was also a huge baseball fan. It was his favorite sport to play or to watch. When I was in Little League in the summer, playing shortstop for the Charlemont Firemen, he would throw grounders to me to ratchet up my fielding skills. When I was in a hitting slump, he pitched to me and was my batting coach. He helped me early and often throughout my life, whenever I was perplexed or had a problem, whatever it was.

Tom: *The closest I think I ever heard to my father actually yelling, the closest to a true display of anger or rage, had to be when his mower would hit a rock. I was never quite sure what he was yelling far off across the fields, with his ear protection on. I was just glad that he saved it for the opposition of the moment, a mower and a rock.*

Alison: *It seemed in our family like the rhythm was to work really hard for ten months of the year for social justice, the elimination of racism and anti-Semitism, and to right the wrongs of global injustice. This needed to be done by personal example, by activism, daily in school, in demonstrations, whatever was the right thing to do in the moment. To me as a young person who took things quite seriously and literally, it meant not wanting too many things, trying to be unselfish, because it seemed like any time we had anything extra, that might mean someone else might not have enough. Jesus could appear at any moment in the guise of a stranger (or even someone right in your community), so you had to be pretty vigilant and careful to be unselfish and giving and do the right thing. That was the way things felt for most of the year.*

And then, for two months, we went to Heath—magical, wonderful, sunshine and breezes Heath. A place where time had a different quality and the pace of family life slowed down. Papa never stopped working for a better world, and took time in Heath to work on his books, but he also cleared the woods, swam with us, and had time to play board games and hang out, have picnics at Harriman Reservoir, and enjoy blueberry pie.

In Heath, there were no night meetings, no constant ringing of the phone, and most of the time nobody was in jail. In Heath, Mama made bread and blueberry muffins, and we wandered the woods looking for antique bottles in old abandoned dumps. In

Heath, you could read a book for hours. At the Heath Church Sunday school, it seemed that the only requirement was that you treat others well and be good on a small scale. You could just be "good" and that was enough. In Heath, our daddy would go into the swimming pool at the Wolfs' house and play with us, throwing us up in the air so that we would fall into the cold water. Everyone hung out in the living room around the fire at night and talked, sang, played Scrabble.

I remember the ongoing joke when the phone would ring at dinnertime. Mama would joke with Papa, "Bob, it's Janetta Sagan [of Amnesty International] on the phone, and she wants you to immolate yourself on the White House steps to protest the war." The rest of the year, it might not have been funny, but in Heath it felt like there was some magical protection, that it was unlikely there that such a request would come in or be heeded. War and injustice seemed farther away. There was penny candy at the general store, agricultural fairs, trees to climb, and the amazing forts and tree houses and playhouse that my daddy built for us out of free scrap lumber.

Granddaughter Caitlin (at age eleven): *All I could see of Bop was a shock of white hair moving slowly down in the pear orchard pushing a bright orange mower. I sat up on my newly built swing waiting for him to finish mowing because we were going to start* Dr. Dolittle *by Hugh Lofting. We had just finished reading* Mary Poppins, *and I was looking forward to a new book that was about animals. About ten minutes later he started making his way up to the house, and I ran barefoot to beg him to hurry because the book might run away. This sped him up.*

A few minutes later we were settled in the big blue chair by the fire and he began, "Once upon a time, many years ago—when our grandfathers were little children— there was a doctor and his name was Dolittle—John Dolittle M.D. 'M.D.' means that he was a proper doctor who knew a whole lot." About forty-five minutes later he closed the book with a snap and said, "Well that's all for now." I pleaded and begged for him to read just a few more pages, and of course he did. The only thing that stopped him from reading most of the book was that it was lunchtime.

Bop was not only my grandfather; he was my teacher and mentor. He was the one (along with my parents) who set a fire beneath me to learn to read and to love books. He is the reason that I was able to say that I knew the plot and all the characters in Jacob Have I Loved *by Katherine Paterson, when I was in second grade.*

Peter: *My dad always made things, such as little goblets with aluminum foil. Give him a Hershey bar and three minutes later, after the chocolate was wolfed down, there would be a row of small silver goblets. He almost never used a pencil sharpener; instead, he whittled his pencils into points. After the Freedom Ride he built a stone wall in front of the Heath house because this was the only thing he could do. He cre-ated a landscape in front of the house—a labyrinth of paths through the blueberries, nooks in the ledges under the hemlock tree by the stone wall, a birch grove he tended at the bottom of the field, and a conifer forest to the south that he trimmed to look like* *something out of a fairy tale. He always had a project going, and he always had the energy to do it. His energy was phenomenal! At the age of seventy-five, just before the Lewy Body Syndrome started, he still gave me a run for my money in the fields. His physical energy was as powerful as his intellect. They undoubtedly were connected in important ways, but it seemed odd that he would do next to nothing throughout the academic year beyond biking to work at Stanford, or walking Hugo in New York, and then, for the next three months, he would work like a convict on a chain gang—half a day, every day, tremendous physical labor, with the first part of that at the type-writer, which he pounded away on with a ferocity that must have lost him consider-able poundage over the years.*

We all love Heath. We always have and always will. Who wouldn't? It's simply one of the most beautiful places in the world, and as such, we are more than lucky to be a part of it. Our house is set on the top of a hill, sheltered by maple, pine, poplar, and hemlock, but with wide views to the west and northwest—mountain range after mountain range. In front of the house is a carefully tended blueberry field, which is separated from a sloping old apple orchard by an even more ancient stone wall. Birches line the dirt road leading to the house, and our good friends the Wolfs live down the hill. Sunsets are spectacular; storms approach and we watch them. A pond is at the foot of a series of hay fields, and we fish and swim there, and friends abound. If my father ever felt guilt about owning such a home in such a place, as far as I know, thank God, he didn't show it.

Part of this political/spiritual contentment came, I think, from the fact that Heath really is quite removed. It's a poor town up in the hills above the Deerfield River. And as beautiful as it is, it's not the Berkshires, which are to the south and more moneyed. People sometimes remark about how wonderful it must be to be so close to Tanglewood, and we look embarrassed and say we almost never get there because we don't want to leave Heath. And it's not ski country, like the Green Mountains to the north—with its bands of tourists, lodges, and tasteful shops. So there are no conventional bragging rights to the place—which was fine for my dad. My parents got it cheap, and it has stayed cheap until recently, when taxes have jumped.

The other part of this lack of guilt (a question that interests me because it was a state that so often attached itself to my dad in relationship to physical things—and he did own *Heath) is the fact that the place has always been shared. This was not always my father's primary desire—he really wanted to be left alone. He never wanted a sign by the road pointing out where we lived, and if people showed up, initially anyway, he always groaned.*

The sharing was more my mother's idea, and indeed way of life, but my dad went along with the program, and once whoever had arrived had been established in a room, or had been fed lunch and at least a provisional time of departure had been established, my dad seemed to relax and give in to the inevitable. And then he became a wonder-

ful host—funny, expansive, and open to conversation. In a way, he was rescued from a potential quagmire of guilt by geography and the hospitality of my mom. And the grace of God.

Two peripheral points are not made often enough: First, without my mom I think my dad would have been much more of a conventional scholar, although not fully happy with the academic life. I'm sure he would have made written forays into the world of religion and politics, but nothing like the host of issues that he pushed himself into with the support and urging of my mother (and of course his students and geographically spread colleagues.) Second, although he was a naturally funny, charismatic, and brilliant guy, without my mom and her openness to all, he would have been much less a social animal.

For my dad, I think Heath finally was an unconscious effort to create an ideal life, one that included family and more than a hint of monasticism: physical labor, mental effort, spiritual delight in the outdoor world, and the creative mix of a community of like-minded souls. And he truly did it. We are a close-knit group at Heath, and the delight of the place has always been the place plus the people.

Tom: *Just after his death, I drove up Ledges Road, seeing in a different light what he has left to us: the house that Bop built, and not just a house but a place we all think about and dream of all year; an idea; a light—a place that lives, breathes, and exudes all that he is.*

Epilogue

PAPA'S FINAL DAYS

Alison Ehara-Brown

Papa broke his hip in the summer of 2001, and that was the beginning of the slow dying process. Mama, Jill, Peter, and Caitlin were with him the day he fell and when he was operated on, and it was clear from the start that it was going to be a hard time for him. A week after he fell, Jill and Caitlin returned to Texas for school, but Peter, Tom, Mama, and so many friends stopped by daily to sit with him, talk, sing, and lend a loving presence. Although he was sedated and moved in and out of consciousness, most of the time he was remarkably loving in his pain, sweet, and clearly happy to be with his family and friends. By late August, he was at the nearby Poet's Seat Nursing Home. I remember one day the nurse wheeled him out onto the porch to be with us— Carlos Rojas, Chilean refuge and part of our extended family, my father's sister Betty and her partner Audrey, Mama, my brothers Tom and Peter, and me.

I was struck both by how thin Papa had become and how handsome he was, his Celtic bone structure showing strongly. His muscles had weakened, and it was hard for him to sit up. We took turns stroking him and holding his hand. I recall the warmth of his hands and how firmly he'd grip my hand during certain songs. We spent the day with him on the porch, singing. We sang every hymn we could remember that he loved, every folk song, and we also sang, over and over, his favorite Scottish song, the "Eriskay Love Lilt," which had inspired his novel:

When I'm lonely, gentle heart
Dark the night, and wild the sea
By love's light my foot finds,
The old pathway to thee

Vair me o, o ro van o,
Vair me o, o ro van ee,
Vair me o, o ru o ho
Sad am I without thee

Thou'rt the music of my heart,
Harp of joy, o Cruit mo cridh
Moon of guidance by night
Strength and light, thou art to me

We all cried at the "Sad am I without thee," so we changed it to "We are here beside thee," and took turns singing so that some could cry while others sang.

The next day, when we arrived Carlos was already there, holding Papa's hand and playing classical music. Papa was in some pain, and it took time to get him stabilized. But once again we joined together on the porch. I remember especially vividly that when Carlos and I sang "Las Mananitas"—a special song to wake you up in the morning, that is sung in Mexico and Latin America on a person's birthday or a saint's day—he got so excited. He squeezed my hand, clearly trying to talk to us, wanting to communicate something, but unable to get out the words. He went in and out of consciousness that day, but in moments like this, we had a strong sense that he was present with us, being reached by us and reaching for us. It was hard to leave that night, but as we drove away Ned Wolf and Diana Roberts, whose ties to our family go back to my father's days in seminary and at Union with their parents, were arriving for an evening visit.

Carlos had his farewell with Papa the next morning, knowing this was the last time he'd see this wonderful man, who had been a father to him. That day, my father's usually warm hands were cool. His skin felt different; his body was changing. He went in and out of contact more frequently. We continued to tell him how much we loved him, and we continued to sing the "Eriskay Love Lilt."

That night, at ten o'clock, the nurse called to tell us that his breathing had changed and that we should come down. The night was clear, full of stars, with a huge bright moon. Mama, Peter, and I drove down the hills to Poet's Seat. Once again, we all sat with him. Tom and I held and stroked his feet, Peter held one hand and Mama held the other, stroking his hair. As I rubbed his legs and feet, I could feel his bones and was reminded again how very thin he had become. The warmth was leaving him, and his skin felt different.

Around midnight, his breathing stabilized. It seemed like he'd be with us a while longer, and Peter told him we would be back in the morning. We each whispered things to him before we left. I remember singing softly, "Sleep my papa, peace attend thee, all through the night. Guardian angels God will send thee all through the night. Soft the drowsy hours are creeping, hill and vale in slumber sleeping, I my loving vigil keeping, all through the night." We all told him we loved him, that he was just perfect, and that we wanted him with us as long as we could have him. We told him that Mark, who was arriving the next day, would love to see him, but that if he needed to move on before that, we would all be with him in spirit, all of us, whether we were there with him physically or not. I remember the moon, the shadows of the bright night, coming up on the view of Burnt Hill in the moonlight, and singing to him softly, "I my loving vigil keeping, all through the night."

Around five in the morning the phone rang again. It was the nurse, saying he was dying, and to come quickly. He died just moments before we arrived. We went into his room and sat with him again, talked to him, and cried. His hand was warm; his skin felt normal again; his body was relaxed, at peace. Sunlight streamed in the window, and he was incredibly handsome in the morning light. He felt so present as we sat with him and told him we loved him and said goodbye.

A nurse from the night shift told us that she had been with him, that she'd held his hand and told him that she knew he was a very special man, loved by many, many people. She told him that we were coming, but that we were already there with him in spirit, and that if he didn't stay through our arrival, he could know that we were present. She told us that he died peacefully, holding her hand, and we were grateful that she had been with him and had shared that with us.

We rode back up into the hills, mostly quietly, this time singing the actual words to the "Eriskay Love Lilt," "Sad am I without thee." At Heath, the sun was shining on the orchard and Papa's birch grove, and the mist was rising, and I could see the children dancing that Papa had often seen. Peter, Mama, and I sat in the living room in tears, talking. It was cold, and Peter went out to the woodshed to get some wood for a fire. I sat at my mama's feet, both of us crying, when suddenly a lovely big dog came bounding into the house, licked our tears and romped upstairs into Papa's study. It felt like Papa was visiting us in the form of the dog. The sun was sparkling, and Rob Riggan, our neighbor and friend, arrived with a huge bouquet of flowers. He'd been awakened with a strong message to bring flowers to Sydney, so he'd gone out into his garden, picked the flowers, and driven over, having no idea that Papa had just died. Later Mark arrived, and the day became filled with people, tears, memories, a sad and magical time together.

Since then, I often feel his presence in the early morning. I see a single pelican flying beside me, or a heron, or I hear a piece of music suddenly, and I softly say, "Hello Papa, I know you are there." It's subtle, just a soft, strong sense of his love still present here with us. Or I'll be driving to work and turn on the radio and "Jesu, Joy of Man's Desiring" will begin playing, and I will feel him. One morning about six months after he'd died, I was driving to work early, worried about many things. It was a gray, cloudy day, but all of a sudden, the sky turned bright pink and purple, incredibly beautiful. Miraculous. After about five minutes, the sky returned to gray. But I felt a strong message of assurance that all was well, that he was with me, that it was all going to be okay.

HEATH, SUMMER 2002

Sydney Brown

We missed Bob more than we can say. We felt his presence and wept for his absence as we sang "The Beauteous Day Now Closeth" as we sat down to supper. We looked for him down the hill, expecting him to be weeding our blueberry field or cutting back the hardhack. We listened for him upstairs, we listened for his flying typewriter fingers, for his harmonizing as we sang on long car trips. Our hearts ached; we longed for him and loved him; we loved each other.

We all came together on August 3, 2002, for the service to bury his ashes at the Heath cemetery in the plot we had chosen long ago, surrounded that day by too many friends who have since died, close to the graves of Bill Wolf and John Porter, old friends from seminary who instigated our moving to Heath so many years ago. Howard Thompson, the farmer down the road, asked me long ago where I wanted to be buried—by Bill Wolf or Angus Dunn? I replied, "Bob likes the shade and I like the sun," so that is what we have— sun and shade in that beautiful spot.

When I'd just begun to think about planning Bob's burial service, Meg Marnell, Bob's therapist and our dear friend, told me of burial services, either Catholic or Buddhist, in which loved ones put symbols of the person's life into the box containing the ashes. We liked the idea and, in fact, had a great time thinking of all the items that spoke of Bob. Peter proposed baseball and mitt; Mark proposed axe and matches for fire builder Bob; Tom proposed a power mower. We quickly moved to miniature replicas.

So at the service, into the beautiful Celtic wooden chest went Bob's ashes, in a simple round Shaker box. And into the chest went more symbols than we could at first have imagined—blueberries, chocolate, licorice, a cello, a piano, a typewriter, a power mower's pull start handle, a star of David, a Celtic cross, a Salvadoran cross, a piece of faded and worn blue denim, a piece of chocolate brown flecked tweed, a Bible, a bilingual dictionary, a memento of the Freedom Rides, a pencil (knife sharpened), some music, a stone from Iona—items that spoke of his life, love, commitment, passion, and enjoyment. Already I remember more—a tiny bottle of Scotch, a dish towel, work gloves (one of his, one of Peter's), a valentine—many, many bits and pieces that spoke of his full life. Family and friends spoke as they put the items in.

Bill and Randy Coffin came down from Vermont. Bill spoke movingly and amusingly about death being our final friend: how impossible and interminable life without death would be; how overpopulated the earth would become; how long and boring our days would be without our knowledge that we're here but for a brief time. It was wonderful having Bill in leadership, an old guy who had plotted and planned actions for peace and justice along with other brave and gutsy leaders of another era. His presence was a good reminder of our need to keep up our protests today and that action for justice comes from ordinary people acting together.

Pam Porter helped lead us too, by reading from Isaiah. Alison read from Matthew 25 and Micah 6, grounding the readings in her experience in Chile during and after the coup, when, if a stranger came to your door and said, simply, "Matthew 25" or "Micah 6," you knew that the stranger was a friend and could be welcomed. All of the readings tied into Bob's connection to Latin America, liberation theology, and basic courage.

The service was simple and moving. Jamie Roberts, age fourteen, began with Bach on the tenor saxophone and ended with "Joyful, Joyful, We Adore Thee." Pam led us in a South African song at the end. We sang the Scottish melody for "The King of Love My Shepherd Is" and wept, nearly unable to sing the "Eriskay Love Lilt." Our granddaughter Caitlin, age twelve, sang in Gaelic, "Gealis, Gealis," which means "faithful." It was simple and moving, and Bob would have loved it. And we think he did!

Back at our house, Mark and Peter tossed some remaining ashes into the air, out over Bob's blueberry field, and they rose up, high, high, blowing up over the orchard—mysterious and beautiful. We miss him, love him, and long for him. And we are glad that he is free at last.

SUMMER 2003, COLONSAY

Sydney Brown

A different and special summer. In July all fifteen of us traveled to Scotland, to Colonsay, with the rest of Bob's ashes. How Bob would have loved it. And, maybe, how he did love it. Who knows?

Colonsay: island of light, shadow, mystery, wonder, sea, islands, bays, shells, rocks, birds, scallops, mussels, sheep, sheep, sheep, and friendly people.

We walked from Colonsay to Oronsay when the tide was low, from one island to the other, good walkers all, including five-year-old Riley, a sturdy walker. We walked across the strand, up the long road to the priory remains—the old buildings, the chapel, and the gravestones from the 1500s, including the carving of Donald McDuffie, abbot, who looked strikingly like Alison!

We gathered on the grass outside the chapel. We scattered Bob's ashes outside of the chapel; we scattered them inside the chapel; we scattered them through the windows of the chapel—even as Bob had given his energy outside the church, inside the church, and through the windows, connecting the two. It was right.

We scattered his ashes also at Kiloran Bay, one of his favorite places—incredibly beautiful, blue, green, turquoise, rocks, kelp, beach—and then also at the bottom of our croft's garden, by the old, old stone wall, facing sheep nearby, and in the distance the seawater and Paps of Jura, mountains on the island across the water. Each of us tossed some ashes and said what we wanted to about Bob. Riley finished: "When we get back to Heath, let's take some of the magical fairy dust and sprinkle it on Bop's Dead Stone." He really summed it up: Bob's ashes had truly become a magical fairy dust of connection.

We blessed Bob, loved him, cherished him. And how we miss him.

Our grandson Colin Masashi Ehara, hip-hop spoken word artist, shared the following poem to hip-hop beats at his grandfather's memorial service. It communicates his grandfather's gifts to the next generations—his students, children, and grandchildren.

Colin: To the Emancipator of My Hopes and Dreams

> To the emancipator of my hopes and dreams
> I thank you for your
> generosity, prosperity, and curiosity
> For the fact that you took society's hypocrisies
> and showed them your philosophy
>
> Righteous men dream dreams
> that cannot always be fulfilled
> yet . . .
>
> You found a way each and every day
> to emancipate my hopes and dreams
>
> You obliterate depression by abolishing oppression
> taking small pieces of peace and piecing them together
> to create a masterpiece

A Celtic warrior who fought by not fighting
who violated by being non-violent
and who loved by being his being

To the emancipator of my hopes and dreams
I thank you for your generosity, prosperity, and curiosity
For the fact that you took society's hypocrisies
and showed them your philosophy

It's a wonder
I never dreamed you would live forever
inside of my heart and soul
without a measure

a musical storyteller
who liberated theology
and was aware of the psychology
of a stratified society

You and I possess a mutual understanding
we understand
that the only thing in this world worth hating
is hate
and that no one is free
as long as others are oppressed

So, I thank you from the bottom of my heart
for helping me realize
that a rich man is simply someone
with knowledge, happiness, and
love in his heart

You are one of the richest men I have ever known

enemy of:
racism, sexism, anti-Semitism,
and every "ism" you can schism
except for activism . . .

You battled homophobia in hopes of a utopia
righting the wrong through civil rights.

And so,
to the emancipator of my hopes and dreams
I thank you for your
generosity, prosperity, and curiosity
for the fact that you took society's hypocrisies
and showed them your philosophy.